El Teatro Campesino

The UFW struggles to ban child labor. Photo shows a young girl bagging onions she has picked, California, c. 1970. Courtesy of the Archives of Labor and Urban Affairs, Wayne State University.

El Teatro Campesino

Theater in the Chicano Movement

by Yolanda Broyles-González

University of Texas Press
Austin

Copyright © 1994 by the University of Texas Press
All rights reserved
Printed in the United States of America
First edition, 1994

Requests for permission to reproduce material from this work should be sent to
     Permissions, University of Texas Press, Box 7819, Austin, TX 78713-7819.

∞ The paper used in this publication meets the minimum requirements of American
     National Standard for Information Sciences—Permanence of Paper for Printed
     Library Materials, ANSI Z39.48-1984.

Library of Congress Cataloging-in-Publication Data
Broyles-González, Yolanda, date.
     El Teatro Campesino : theater in the Chicano movement /
     by Yolanda Broyles-González. — 1st ed.
          p.   cm.
     Includes bibliographical references and index.
     ISBN 0-292-72082-3 (alk. paper). — ISBN 0-292-70801-7 (pbk. : alk. paper)
     1. Teatro Campesino (Organization)—History. 2. Workers' theater—California—History.
3. Mexican American theater—California—History. I. Title.
PN3307.U6B76 1994
792'.022—dc20   94-935

Permission granted by the following persons to quote from oral material is gratefully acknowledged:
César Chávez, Olivia Chumacero, Linda Cantu Cubillo, José Delgado, Roberta Delgado, Augustín Lira,
and Diane Rodriguez.
     The following publishers have generously given permission to use quotations from copyrighted
works. From Bertolt Brecht, "Questions from a Worker Who Reads." Reprinted from *Bertolt Brecht Poems
1913–1956*, Willet, John and Manheim, Ralph, eds., (1976), by permission of publisher, Routledge,
New York.
     From "ROSE OF THE RANCHO" by David Belasco and Richard Walton Tully. Copyright © 1915 by David
Belasco. Copyright © 1936 by David Belasco Literary Trust. Reprinted by permission of Samuel French,
Inc. CAUTION: Professionals and amateurs are hereby warned that "ROSE OF THE RANCHO," being fully
protected under the copyright laws of the United States of America, the British Commonwealth
countries, including Canada, and the other countries of the Copyright Union, is subject to a royalty. All
rights, including professional, amateur, motion picture, recitation, public reading, radio, television,
and cable broadcasting, and the rights of translation into foreign languages, are strictly reserved.

Contents

Acknowledgments

The work of one is always the work of many. This book would have been unthinkable without the strong support of various intersecting communities. I am most grateful to those whose intense participation in the dailiness of my life sustained me through this project: Francisco González, Leopolda Rodríguez (for the power of her daily blessing), Julia V. de Arana, Roberto Perales, Gregoria Elías (gracias, Goyita!), and Lily Beltrán. I gratefully acknowledge Dr. Antonia Castañeda: the remarkable convergence of word and deed—of theory and practice—observable in her life has always been a strong inspiration to so many of us. That convergence is the very essence of *tener palabra*. Very special thanks to Olivia Chumacero, whose life I consider the best living example of the Theater of the Sphere. My *querida comadre* Dr. Sabine Gross acted as midwife to the bibliographic apparatus in this book as well as to me during delivery of both my children. Dr. Ursula Mahlendorf always generously provided valuable advice and friendship. Very special thanks to César Chávez and the United Farm Workers of America for facilitating my search for photos and granting access to their own photo archives. My deep appreciation goes also to Jim Vieth for putting the entire manuscript on the computer and always with such good cheer.

This book grew out of living contact with people and theatrical production. I am grateful to the original members of the Teatro Campesino ensemble, who welcomed me into their homes and lives, who shared their stories with me over a period of many years, who made manuscripts available to me, along with newspaper clippings and work diaries from their personal Teatro Campesino archives. I would particularly like to acknowledge the generosity of those Teatro Campesino performers who provided encouragement for this project: Felipe Cantú (en paz descanse), Agustín Lira, Olivia Chumacero, Francisco González, Yolanda Parra, Roberta Delgado, Rogelio "Smiley" Rojas, as well as Itzpapalotl, Ehecatl, and Yaxkin. Diane Rodríguez, Phil Esparza, and José Delgado provided valuable insights. Luis Valdez provided a healthy opposition. For a period of over eighteen months I was allowed valuable access to the Teatro Campesino archives in San Juan Bautista and participant observer status within the company.

Several individuals deserve credit for their roles in the emergence of the book or its various chapters. Dr. Margaret Wilkerson provided invaluable and lasting encouragement when I initially contemplated writing the book. With regard to chapter 1 I am grateful to my mother, Julia V. de Arana, whose life as a laborer and whose detailed reminiscences of the popular performance arts in Mexico and Los Angeles of the 1930s and the 1940s, awakened my love for this field. To her also I am grateful for the experience of weekly attendance at the Mexican performance spectacles of the Million Dollar Theater in Los Angeles during my childhood. To Professor Tomás Ybarra-Frausto I owe the inspiration that has come of his research and writing on the Mexican/Chicana *carpa* (itinerant tent show) and *tandas de variedad* (variety shows). Marc De Witt read sections of chapter 2 and offered interesting comments. For the book in its entirety, but most especially for chapter 3, special acknowledgment goes to the women of El Teatro Campesino for their encouragement and collaboration.

I am grateful to those not directly involved with the book but always present across geographical distances: Dr. Wolfgang Schmieder; Francisco Gil Arana; Altagracia González and *familia*; Dr. Siegfried Bartels; Janice Wezelman; Dr. Beverly Harris-Schenz; Hannelore Teutsch; Comadre María Hernández; my *ahijada*, Ruby Cenobia Hernández; Dr. Juan Flores; Raquel Rubio-Goldsmith; Fernando Broyles Arana; my *tía* Nely Aguilar and Tío Arturo; Marlise and Peter Schorn and family; Dr. Bernd Münk; and Dr. Diana Manning.

I want to thank those involved in the book's production, especially Theresa J. May, executive editor of the University of Texas Press, who combined graciousness with superb editorial professionalism. Thanks to Mary Rojas Muñoz, who steadfastly combed through the final manuscript.

Very special thanks to the American public, whose tax and other dollars came to me through various agencies, foundations, and universities. Principal funding for this book came in the form of a Ford Foundation Postdoctoral Fellowship. A National Endowment for the Humanities Summer Stipend provided support at a critical time, as did the University of California, Santa Barbara (Academic Senate and FCDA grants). I acknowledge as well the benefit to my research that came from a UC MEXUS grant as well as from a resident fellowship at the University of California Humanities Research Institute.

This book was written in the face of many obstacles, most of which I was able to turn to my advantage. For that I am indebted to the Chicano/Mexicano communities in which I grew up, and to the United Farm Workers of America for teaching me struggle as a way of life. Finally, I thank my beloved children, who make my spirit invincible: Guillermo Francisco Broyles González and Esmeralda Guadalupe Broyles González, as well as the three *angelitos*.

To César Chávez and Helen Chávez and to all who live that legacy of struggle.

Farm laborers suffering abysmal living conditions (such as this family living in an old crate) joined to create the first agricultural union in labor history: the UFW. Courtesy of United Farm Workers of America.

Introduction

The numerous social and political struggles of the 1960s and the 1970s—such as the civil rights movement, the United Farm Workers movement, the antiwar movement, and the women's liberation movement—were intimately bound to a multifaceted cultural renaissance. Perhaps the single most inspirational struggle for Chicanas/os was the David and Goliath standoff between the United Farm Workers Union and the agribusiness giants in California and other states.

That first successful farm labor union in United States history began in 1962, when, against all odds, César Chávez, Helen Chávez, and Dolores Huerta began to organize farm laborers. That struggle—which continues into the present—created a national and international support coalition in an effort to end the multiple abuses of farm laborers and consumers. For farm labor, those abuses included exploitation by growers, crew leaders, and parasitic labor contractors; the widespread use of child labor; pesticide and herbicide poisoning; substandard housing; generally inhumane working and living conditions; and no health or other benefits (McWilliams 1939, 1973; Daniel 1981). For consumers, the struggle is against contaminated food and water supplies.

The injustices against farm labor manifested themselves in a life expectancy of 54 years, an hourly wage of 85 cents, annual income well below the poverty level, as well as through the indignity of racial and sexual harassment. The 1965 grape strike and boycott, along with the UFW's 1966 landmark 280-mile pilgrimage for justice (from Delano to Sacramento) highlighted the political determination and moral strength of the nation's poorest. The United Farm Workers' strikes were to become the longest and most dramatic in U.S. labor history (Nelson 1966; Dunne 1967, revised 1971; Matthiessen 1969; Day 1971; Levy 1975; Ross 1989; Leggett 1991). These events inspired and directly influenced all sectors of Chicana/o artistic and political activism, such as opposition to the war in Vietnam; efforts to secure equality before the law; and demands to end discriminatory practices in the schools, universities, and labor market.

One manifestation of that spirit of activism was the Chicana/o theater movement, which spread across the Southwest, the Northwest, and the Midwest in the 1960s and the 1970s. In virtually all centers of Chicana/o population as well as on campuses everywhere, theater groups sprang up dedicated to portraying the life, heritage, and problems of Chicanas/os in this country.

Under the wing of the United Farm Workers Union based in Delano, California, El Teatro Campesino (The Farm Workers' Theater) emerged in 1965, conceived as a union tool for organizing, fund-raising, and politicizing. In its beginnings El Teatro Campesino performed numerous highly improvisational skits (called *actos*), which expressed the exploitative living and working conditions of farmworkers in boldly satirical words and actions. All of the early skits also underscored the need to unionize against the abuses of agribusiness. In addition to regular performance—often on the backs of flatbed trucks—before farmworkers, the group also played college campuses and toured Europe repeatedly. A group viewed and appreciated by farmworkers simply as an effective organizational tool, became, curiously, idolized in intellectual circles and was converted into a Chicano icon for the academy. Euro-American scholarship and the press followed suit. Today the name Teatro Campesino enjoys almost mythical status, even though the ensemble that established that reputation no longer exists. (El Teatro Campesino, Inc., exists only as a production company.)

This book tells the story of the Teatro Campesino collective *ensemble*, which is not the same as the story of Luis Valdez, nor the story of the post-1980 production company. I distinguish between the 15-year period of the collective ensemble and what came afterward. The ensemble years extend from the group's beginnings in 1965 to approximately 1980. In retrospect it is fair to state that the ensemble years were the most dynamic, inspirational, and creative years of El Teatro Campesino.

Much has been written concerning the Teatro Campesino, mainly in the press and in scholarly articles. Only a few sustained analyses exist, consisting for the most part of unpublished dissertations. Published materials on the Teatro share three characteristics: they are chronological, text-centered, and male-centered. The text-centered approach is closely related to the chronological approach. El Teatro Campesino's work and development are examined only in terms of textuality and of how texts changed over time. These treatments usually include a discussion of how Chicana/o social issues are reflected in Teatro Campesino texts as "content." In other words, the discussion of Teatro Campesino productions or plays has wholly obscured the living relations of production which enabled those texts and are encoded in them. A third dominant strain in the writings on El Teatro Campesino is an absolute male-centeredness. The history of the company has been constructed as the history of the life and times of Luis Valdez. As such, El Teatro Campesino history has been shaped into a male-dominated hierarchical structure that replicates oppressive dominant tendencies within society.

That historical construct un-self-consciously replicates patriarchal structures and correspondingly eclipses any oppositional dynamics as well as broader historical contexts and the collective accomplishments of the Teatro Campesino ensemble.

The great-man/text-centered/chronological-linear approach, a construct predominant in Eurocentric history and print culture, in fact obscures more than it reveals. In contradistinction I position El Teatro Campesino within the Mexican working-class tradition of orality and oral culture. Within oral culture, performed words make sense only as communal creations and as part of a larger historical performance context. In the absence of that greater communal performance context, only the great man—and not the community—becomes identified with the written text. The communally created text is thus reduced to an act of individual authorship or individual genius; a community's cultural practices become the intellectual private property of one man. Within this great-man/text-centered/chronological-linear approach to history many dimensions of the company's history recede into oblivion: the reality of collective creation; the contributions of women (and other men); the entire Mexican working-class experience and popular tradition of performance, which nurtured the collective work mode and the irreverently humorous Rasquachi Aesthetic; and the material social process of production. These are among the elements I seek to bring back into the company's history.

A great deal has been said about the writing of history, be it theater history, political history, literary history, or any other. That discussion extends to include all forms of representation. In the tow of the Chicano movement of the 1960s, an emergent Chicana/o scholarship sought to overturn existing models of thought and writing—models considered at odds with Chicana/o community interests. Ethnocentrism (usually Eurocentrism) and elitism in scholarship were both questioned and challenged. Yet the reality of Chicanas/os breaking into print and the dynamics of Chicano (mostly male) institutionalization bred new forms of academic tunnel vision. Among the most glaring of Chicano scholarship's omissions has been the dismissal of

Striking United Farm Workers demanding labor
contracts, Coachella Valley, California, 1965.
Courtesy of the Archives of Labor and Urban Affairs,
Wayne State University.

the work and experience of women, and an inability to perceive and valorize age-old popular forms of discourse and self-representation—most notably the working-class culture of orality.

The present study is born of a different time and spirit than that which informed much of Chicana/o theater historiography of the 1960s, the 1970s and the 1980s. Earliest Chicana/o theater historiography (discussed at various points in this book) displays both the strengths and the weaknesses of pioneering work in the field. It manifests a strong descriptive tendency, a tendency to present basic facts to Chicana/o readers. Yet the approach to "facts" was in most cases naïve, that is, without benefit of theoretical perspectives. Facts were (as is always the case) gathered, arranged, and presented along particular lines reflective of the author's unconscious yet very real politics, be it of gender, of class, of race, or of culture. Most early writings share a strong sense of advocacy for Chicanas/os and Chicana/o creativity. Yet at the same time they variously reveal deep-rooted and subtle elements of gender discrimination, Eurocentrism, or even classism. Positioned as it is within dominant academic institutions, we cannot be surprised that so much of Chicano research has internalized elements of the oppression it seeks to contest.

In departing from and challenging the established and accepted male-centered history of El Teatro Campesino I experienced a gender dynamics similar to that which this chapter describes and analyzes. My decision, for example, to publish the chapter on the women of El Teatro Campesino prior to the publication of the book met with considerable resistance and resentment (from male colleagues) at what was perceived as iconoclastic treatment of Luis Valdez. The 1982 Renato Rosaldo Lecture Series monograph editors who commissioned my essay on the Women of El Teatro Campesino subsequently stopped its publication, while also eliminating *any reference* to my Renato Rosaldo lecture from both the 1985 introduction to that lecture series as well as from its published list of lectures. Ironically, this lecture series was ostensibly seeking to stimulate "interest in the story of *las mujeres de Aztlán.*" The earlier version of this chapter on the women of the Teatro Campesino, ready for publication in 1982, thus went unpublished until its inclusion in the 1986 anthology *Chicana Voices* and its further circulation in the 1989 book *Making a Spectacle: Feminist Essays on Contemporary Women's Theatre,* published by the University of Michigan. These attempts at censorship were based on certain gender based forms of ideological blindness. What was not understood is that a more inclusive and nonlinear treatment of El Teatro Campesino serves to empower the collective while in no way diminishing the important contributions of Luis Valdez or any other individual.

Finally, during my research residency with El Teatro Campesino I was presented with a contract requiring me to submit my work "for review and approval by Luis Valdez before handing it over to any publisher." This requirement, insofar as it assumes the ability to edit or censor the findings of a study, is not acceptable in the academic world; naturally I never signed the contract. In the end, Luis Valdez denied his permission to quote from any Teatro play as well as from the oral histories with him, after I refused to submit the final study to him for his approval. El Teatro had also contacted the University of Texas Press in an effort to obtain a copy of this study and inspect it prior to publication. The gendered politics of citation and publication can be understood as efforts to control the direction of scholarship, particularly the feminist scholarship of Chicanas. While the omission of certain material does not detract from my analysis, such controlling efforts to direct scholarship raise very serious questions about established principles of academic freedom and First Amendment rights. These are only minor examples of the overriding conditions for the production and circulation of knowledge that affect the scholarly work of Chicanas in the academy.

My own writing emerged in dialogue with what came before. Each chapter reveals facets of that dialogue. Yet beyond that I seek qualitatively to broaden our understanding of *teatro Chicana/o* by analytically probing four key (and neglected) areas in depth. They represent a departure from the bulk of

Chicano theater research. In my research and writing I have been guided more by a concern with the dynamics of the Teatro Campesino's creative *production process* than with a harvesting of seemingly discrete "facts" or the formal properties of individual works. I am more concerned with examining crucial ruptures and contradictions than with constructing a homogeneous chronological and linear continuum; more concerned with group and collective movement than with individual achievement (or the myopia of approaching history solely through the study of individuals); more concerned with a broader performance history than with a reductionist textual history; more concerned with unveiling various realms that dominant male-centered perspectives have obscured than with affirming the "official" academic story of the Teatro Campesino. Issues of class, gender, and ethnicity are the key guideposts.

I have correspondingly departed from the beaten path of Chicano theater history and from conventional politics and practices of citation and credibility snowballing: the first researcher is quoted by the second researcher; the third bases her or his work on that of the first two; the fourth uses the first three as sources but adds quotes by Luis Valdez; and so forth. Existing research was of little benefit in providing data for my own research. Asking new questions has required the designing of a new informational politics. Scholars whose research involves gender, class, or race can attest to the lack of sources and the barriers to obtaining basic information. The parameters of what is considered information or information worth collecting are among the first limiting factors in Chicana/o studies research. Creating new sources remains the laborious task of any Chicana/o studies research that wants to chart new pathways.

In the first twenty years of Teatro Campesino research only one person, Luis Valdez, was quoted or interviewed. The implications of that are far-reaching. In an effort to expand the limits of information available on the Teatro Campesino I began to collect oral histories of the ensemble members. Although I initially imagined this process as one that would take a few months, the richness of ensemble members' narratives led me to continue the oral history and transcription process over a ten-year period. None of the persons interviewed had ever been approached for an oral history. The classism and sexism that informs the production of knowledge made it unnecessary to approach those ensemble members for an oral history. Long-standing members of the ensemble had never been viewed as legitimate or necessary interpreters or experts of their own work and life experience.

In addition to collecting oral histories I spent one and a half years as a participant-observer with the Teatro Campesino. During that research residency, I not only closely observed the company's functioning (onstage, back-stage, and offstage) but also had access to all Teatro Campesino theater arti-facts: scripts or scenarios, production notes, diaries, publicity materials, letters, archival material from the press, and so on. Very helpful were the work diaries that various ensemble members shared with me. This book could not have been written without the treasure house of oral histories and extensive documentary material, and without the benefit of an extended research residency with the Teatro Campesino.

The exploration of new sources enabled me to write a qualitatively dif-ferent history. The four chapters of this book avoid the distortional linearity of "chronological" history, of male-centered history, of text-centered ap-proaches. Instead, each chapter treats a particular stratum of roughly the same temporal experience or period of the Teatro Campesino's history. I seek to expose various layers of the material social process, of the living circum-stances and concrete human work that informed all ensemble productions. Without an understanding of that material social process our understand-ing of the Teatro Campesino ensemble and its performance pieces must re-main a truncated understanding.

In the first chapter I examine the elements of continuity (and difference) between the working-class Mexican oral performance tradition and the col-lective performance practices of the Teatro Campesino. More specifically, I situate El Teatro Campesino historically within the comedic performance tra-dition of the Mexican *carpa* (itinerant tent shows) and discuss the Rasquachi Aesthetic common to both. *Rasquachismo*, or the Rasquachi Aesthetic (all spell-ings are acceptable), encompasses a shared memory system of performance elements grounded in a working-class, underdog perspective. The second chapter discusses the Teatro Campesino's Theater of the Sphere project, a theory and practice of communicative action based in Native American (Mayan and Aztec) knowledge. Theater of the Sphere is a method of perfor-mance and life training developed by the ensemble after 1970. I describe the Theater of the Sphere as an alternative pedagogy or new Chicana/o human-ism that sought to explore and foster not an abstract human potentiality but a Chicana/o human potentiality rooted in the Americas. In the third chapter I explore the gender politics operative within the Teatro Campesino. The ensemble's most enduring contradictions are revealed in the company's gen-der relations. Yet the chapter tells not only a story of oppression but also one of resistance and of the women's contributions to the company. I illustrate how women creatively challenged and circumvented patriarchy in an effort to establish their dignity within a context of confinement. This third chapter dates back to a 1982 Renato Rosaldo lecture (University of Arizona), reworked for the 1984 National Association for Chicano Studies conference (Broyles-González 1986). This is the only chapter published previously, and I include the original here with only minor changes. In the final chapter I analyze the dynamics of the mainstreaming project: of *Zoot Suit* in Hollywood, on Broadway, and on film. That analysis serves to illustrate how changes in theatrical relations of production (i.e., "mainstreaming") have an impact on theatrical work. On the one hand, I examine the many transformations (i.e., rewrites) of *Zoot Suit* as it moved to ever bigger houses or production contexts. On the other hand, I demonstrate the long-term effects of that mainstreaming on the Teatro Campesino ensemble: the ensemble's process of disbanding beginning in 1979 and the transformation of "El Teatro Campesino" into a production company patterned after Euro-American corporate proscenium theater.

Readers will note that the Chicana/o construction is used throughout. Standard Spanish language subsumes women within masculine adjective endings. That practice has been part of the process by which women have historically been blurred, erased or negatively represented. I depart from standard usage in order to overtly reference Chicanas and foreground gender. Chicano is left unchanged when it references something male or male-centered: hence Chicano Movement.

Among the most difficult challenges I faced in writing this book was the desire to balance two competing urgencies: (1) the need to reference and elaborate on theoretical and critical perspectives and (2) the need to tell a good story. Early in life I learned, principally under the auspices of my maternal grandmother and my father, the importance of telling a good story. Yet popular forms of communication and academic ones are indeed at odds. That tension is reflected in this manuscript, which seeks to tell a good story while also adhering to certain standards of academic research. In an effort to write in a manner comprehensible to as broad a readership as possible I have cultivated a style of writing that deemphasizes scholarly jargon and emphasizes clarity. Theoretical perspectives inform the text from beginning to end. Yet for the sake of readability I give sources in the text and confine virtually all theoretical discussion, crediting, and "academicized" discourse to the notes.

I view my own work on El Teatro Campesino as an invitation to other writers and researchers. Each chapter treats an area of the ensemble's work activity never before explored in depth. Each chapter seeks to open a door to a new realm of Chicana/o performance history in need of both critical examination and recognition.

El Teatro Campesino

The 1966 farm worker march from Delano to Sacramento (280 miles) featured the slogan: Peregrinación/Penitencia/Revolución [pilgrimage, penitence, revolution]. Here the marchers arrive in Fresno. Copyright 1978 George Ballis/Take Stock.

The legendary Mexican comedian Mario Moreno's "Cantinflas" began as a pelado figure in the carpa tradition. Here he is featured in the underdog role of bellboy dressed in characteristic disheveled attire, pants tied below waist with rope. Yolanda Broyles-González Collection.

1. El Teatro Campesino and the Mexican Popular Performance Tradition

The year 1965 marked the beginning of a widespread Chicana/o theater renaissance. In that year the celebrated Teatro Campesino came suddenly into existence, seemingly from out of nowhere. What is more, an entire Chicana/o theater movement exploded onto the cultural scene in a matter of months. Dozens of Chicana/o theater groups made their appearance across the Southwest and the Midwest during the 1960s and 1970s, performing, for the most part, within Chicana/o communities. Generated by the anger and hope of the progressive social movements of the time—such as the civil rights movement, the antiwar movement, the United Farm Workers movement, the Chicano movement, and the women's movement—a widespread theatrical mobilization sought to affirm an alternative social vision that relied on a distinctly Chicana/o aesthetic. Despite existing differences among Chicano theatrical groups they nonetheless manifested an astounding degree of similarity or common ground. Those commonalities were rooted not only in a shared working-class social experience but in a shared cultural heritage of performance forms. Kanellos (1978:58), for example, at the time elaborated on how "all these groups incorporate folkloric material." He furthermore pointed out that "these theaters not only represent the world view of their *pueblo*, but often carry on traditional forms of acting, singing, and performing."

Notwithstanding occasional references to "traditional forms of acting," the body of research on the Chicana/o theater renaissance and especially on El Teatro Campesino has focused almost entirely on aspects of its textuality, its topical themes, and the political conditions of its founding and evolution. El Teatro Campesino is characteristically viewed in and of itself, and not as a phenomenon that, like the mythical phoenix, arose from the ashes of its own past. Wherever antecedents or a past are briefly named we invariably find Eurocentric references to the Italian commedia dell'arte, to the German playwright Brecht, or to Russian *agitprop*. By way of illustration I quote two very notable historians of Chicana/o theater. Both find precursors of the Teatro

Campesino *acto* (short sketch) in all manner of places *except* the Mexican performance tradition. One historian tells us: "The *acto* is not a new form in the annals of world theater. Earlier examples of didactic theater include Bertolt Brecht's *lehrstucke* [sic], or learning pieces, and the agit-prop theater of revolutionary Russia, which influenced political theater in this country in the 1930s. In the 1960s other political groups employed street theater techniques similar to *the acto form that Valdez evolved*" [emphasis mine] (Huerta 1982:15). Another prominent writer on Chicana/o theater similarly indicates: "The *acto* which is highly indebted to agitprop theater and to commedia dell'arte, was *introduced by Luis Valdez to the farmworkers* [emphasis mine], who subsequently made it their own" (Kanellos 1978:60).

In seeking to establish the origins of the Chicana/o theater movement as a whole, many researchers point to the Teatro Campesino ensemble. It is widely regarded as the theatrical fountainhead from which all inspiration and technique trickled down to other Chicana/o theaters. Critics' conceptualization of creativity usually narrows even further, crediting one individual and ignoring groups of people. Luis Valdez is seen, as in the foregoing quotes, as the omnipotent agent who variously "brought," "introduced," who "wrote" for, who "directed" the anonymous others (see chap. 3). This top-down view of creation—related to the great-man ideological construction of history—is symptomatic within dominant Western print culture, which a priori conceptualizes theatrical (and other) production as the work of an *individual* male "creative genius." An alternative construction or model might well invert relations and reveal to us, for example, that the farmworkers introduced the *acto* form *to Luis Valdez*, who subsequently made it his own.

A more far-reaching model for constructing our understanding of El Teatro Campesino and of the Chicana/o theater movement is one that seeks out a commonality of origin within the Mexican popular performance tradition. Only these common older roots can account for the notable homogeneity of a Chicana/o theater movement that exploded onto the American scene from the *physical memory* of a dormant tradition. In what follows, I seek to reconfigure the genealogy of El Teatro Campesino by establishing its lineage from the largely overlooked Mexican popular performance tradition, both secular and religious. Elements from that tradition abound within the performance activity of all groups within the Chicano theater renaissance and most certainly within El Teatro Campesino during the ensemble years: 1965–1980.[1] I establish the vital linkages between El Teatro Campesino and expressive cultural practices from the Mexican popular performance tradition not in the manner of an inventory or grouping of disparate or discrete elements.

Instead, I seek to conceptualize those cultural practices as constituent parts of a larger unified field of interlocking cultural practices, which I call Mexican oral culture or the popular performance tradition. What I posit here, in other words, is that the Mexican culture of orality (used here interchangeably with "popular performance tradition") constitutes the conceptual bedrock from which a coherent understanding of seemingly disparate or unconsolidated surface manifestations of Chicana/o theater becomes possible. In placing the concept of orality at the center of my analysis I consciously depart from the bulk of Teatro Campesino research, which has constructed the work of that ensemble as a written textual practice and which has sought to credit individuals or European culture for work generated within a working-class collective Mexican cultural tradition. It is my contention that the inordinate strength of El Teatro Campesino was not so much a function of innovation as of its reliance on tradition: its grounding in Mexican oral culture.

The presence and strength of oral culture and performance within the Chicana/o lifeworld is among those realities least understood and recognized within academic circles, which have traditionally privileged the inert objects of print culture. In another place I have signaled the very difficulty of approaching even written Chicana/o fictional texts without situating these in relationship to orality (Broyles 1984). Yet the entire field of Mexican oral culture—as a unified field of cultural practices—is very much in need of critical elaboration. The present situating of El Teatro Campesino within the popular oral performance tradition will, I hope, serve to enhance our understanding of both the ensemble and the larger field of interlocking Chicana/o cultural practices. Although there is no lack of writing on Chicana/o "folklore," virtually all publications focus on one oral performance form or practice and not on the body of oral performing practices as an organic system of interrelated practices. A recent step toward a more holistic conceptualization is Charles Briggs's landmark study of performance forms in Córdova, New Mexico (1988). Teatro performances are ideal for illustrating how seemingly discrete oral expressive forms in fact function as a unified cultural field.

What is oral culture and specifically the oral performance mode? A brief answer is impossible. At one level the very concept of "oral" or "orality" is misleading and distortional for it was formulated by scholars in order to subsume the "other" of the written word. ("If it isn't written it must be spoken or oral.") In reality oral culture is typically not just spoken words but words defined by their lifeworld context, hence inseparable from that context and from the body and voice that utters them. Various researchers have compellingly shown how oral performance functions in the social life of dominated communities (Limón 1977, 1982, 1983; Paredes 1958, 1966, 1970, 1978, 1982; Peña 1980, 1985; Reyna 1980). More recently, Briggs (1988) has painstakingly shown, through an impressive analysis of actual live performance, how traditional oral performance forms cannot be understood without understanding the performer's momentary positioning relative to the community and its extended history. In other words, so-called oral culture is by definition situational and not abstract or reducible to a question of *spoken* words as opposed to *disembodied* written ones. Furthermore, much of what is referred to as oral culture or oral tradition involves not only *words* ("the oral"), but the entire body engaged in the "dailiness" of life. And it involves words usually in conjunction with other forms of cultural expression, such as music, dance, or ritual, or no words at all. Given these facts, cultural phenomena designated as oral culture, orality, or oral tradition are, perhaps, more accurately encompassed by a term such as "popular performance." Yet that term is problematic in that it often connotes mass industrial performance forms not necessarily "traditional" or oral. Perhaps what is called for is a new hybrid term such as "traditional popular performance" or "oral popular performance."

I choose here to retain the concept of "orality" because much of what has been theorized by researchers as "oral culture"—although in need of transposition—is of relevance to Chicana/o culture.[2] In attempting to represent the parameters of oral culture and specifically of the Mexican popular performance tradition (which I postulate as belonging to that culture of orality) I rely heavily on the key concepts of human memory, the body, and community. These are interlocking concepts that both circumscribe that performance tradition and distinguish it from performance forms produced through reliance on dramatic literature (i.e., written scripts).

The primacy and function of human memory, the body and community experience constitute essential links between El Teatro Campesino and its antecedent Mexican popular performance tradition, which extends back to time immemorial. Although some affinity may be sought and found between El Teatro Campesino and European models, be they German (the Brechtian), Italian (commedia dell'arte), Russian (agitprop), or Spanish (Golden Age drama), it seems spatially and temporally more compelling to investigate the question of origins in our own backyard first, especially when the Mexican lineage is more than evident.

Oral Tradition: Human Memory, the Body, Community

In seeking to characterize El Teatro Campesino, Luis Valdez (1966:55) kiddingly described it as "somewhere between Brecht and Cantinflas." A statement issued more in an effort to orient a non-Chicana/o audience (in this case *Ramparts* readers) was promptly taken at face value by many critics.[3] Critics avidly seized the European reference to Brecht—an influence I consider less than negligible—while discounting the Mexican reference and tradition.[4] To this day, the strong linkages between El Teatro Campesino and the popular Mexican performance tradition remain unexplored. In this chapter I provide a first exploration into those linkages with the older Mexican tradition, encapsulated by the name of the great Mexican comic Cantinflas. In exploring that continuity, I look at both the secular Mexican performance tradition and the more spiritual (or sacroprofane) traditions, which are linked to religious celebrations. To some extent they overlap and both are strongly grounded in oral cultural practice.

The name Cantinflas is virtually synonymous with a Mexican popular tradition of comedy associated in the past two hundred years with the *carpa*, or tent show. It is impossible to define the Mexican *carpa* as one thing, for it encompassed a field of diverse cultural performance practices popular among the poorest segments of the Mexican populace. The *carpa's* central association with the blood, sweat, and tears of the disenfranchised masses of Mexicans certainly accounts for the obscurity of its origins and evolution: it has not been the object of sustained scholarly research activity or documentation. Mexican playwright Emilio Carballido (1988:2) places the origins of the *carpa* in the eighteenth century, if not earlier: "Un teatro carpero popular viene desde el siglo XVIII pero muy probablemente desde antes, y a veces ha dado algo de su vena vitriólica a nuestro teatro político culto" [There is a popular tent theater that comes down to us from the eighteenth century, but more than likely even before that; it has given something of its vitriolic quality even to our elite political theater]. (All translations are mine unless otherwise noted.)

The Mexican *carpa* and, more broadly speaking, the Mexican popular performance tradition have throughout history served as a counterhegemonic tool of the disenfranchised and oppressed. As will be shown, the *carpa's* periods of vigorous revival coincide with periods of social upheaval and popular distress. In twentieth-century Mexico the carpa experienced a major resurgence in connection with the Mexican Revolution and its aftermath. Among Chicanas/os in the United States its revival coincides with the global

popular liberation movements of the 1960s and the 1970s. The Mexican
artist Covarrubias (1938:596) describes the world of the carpa in the 1930s:

> collapsible, barn-like carpas, show tents that were drawn on trucks and even
> mule carts from suburb to suburb and from village to village, quickly set up
> in the main square or out in the middle of the street, a presage of a coming
> fair. The carpa, a development of post-revolutionary Mexico and now a
> permanent institution, consists of a canvas tent, often walled by detachable
> wooden panels, a gaudy small stage with bizarre painted drops, lit by a single
> naked glaring electric bulb. The music is provided by a melancholy orchestra.
> . . . The "house," simply rows of home-made hard benches, is generally
> packed with a most colorful crowd, an amazing variety of types: workers,
> Mexican Apaches, soldiers, Indians from the country, proletarian women with
> babies, in their blue rebosos, side by side with overdressed city girls and
> white collared men of the middle class. Barkers go in and out, leaving the
> entrance curtain partly open to entice the customers, describing the
> excellences of Lupe la Veracruzana, tropical torch singer, the ludicrous skits of
> the mad comedian "Chicote," or the Rabelaisian humor of "Conde Bobby."
> (1938:596)

This same observer speaks to the sociocultural importance of the rough, elemental and hilariously ribald world of the carpa: "However crude, vulgar and
tainted with bad taste they may be, they have created a style and a technique
of the disconcerting mixture of rough slapstick and fine, biting satire that is
characteristic of the Mexican humor. The very informality of these performances and the highly cultivated art of improvisation give an intensity and
a liveliness that is sadly lacking in other theatrical efforts" (p. 596).

Other related performance forms also emerged in the 1920s and the
1930s that temporarily captivated working-class audiences but did not enjoy the longevity of the carpa. Within Mexican working-class communities,
for example, the so-called teatro frívolo emerged from the carpa as a lighthearted
preburlesque performance form. Essentially escapist and strongly imitative
of foreign models, it rose to popularity briefly and then subsided and vanished. Spanish zarzuelas—operettas—as well as sainetes and entremeses also made
their appearance in Mexico beginning in the nineteenth century. From
France came the boldly uninhibited chorus lines and acts of the Bataclán,
which inspired some Mexican forms, most notably a Mexican parodistic
version called Rataplán (Morales 1987:86). U.S. entertainment forms also
made an inroad in the form of vaudeville and burlesque influences, which
had come to be felt as early as the 1920s in the tandas de variedad and the teatro

de revistas (vaudeville and musical revue).[5] The foreign influence was strongest in—and often limited to—the urban areas, particularly Mexico City where, for example, the entire Hollywood Revue took up residence in the 1940s. Much of what was featured in the way of fabulous expensive wardrobes and foreign song and dance numbers did not become part of the standard repertoire within the itinerant carpas of more modest means and grass-roots regionalist orientation. Although various foreign-bred forms might have intersected with the carpa at various junctures they were shed in time, leaving a basic eclectic structure of music and dance orbiting around and within the vitriolic comic sketch. Also discarded were the animal and acrobatic and other circus acts incorporated in earlier times. Carlos Monsiváis humorously elaborates on how the carpa was at once heir and traitor to the circus tradition:

> La carpa hereda y traiciona al circo, con el apoyo del talento real y el talento que aporta la buena voluntad de los espectadores. Allí la sensación de bienestar se inicia—humor y sustitución—con el desfile de "fenómenos": lo observado en la calle con indiferencia, si se anuncia de modo conveniente, provoca azoro en la carpa. Se imponen las novedades-que-nunca-lo-son: la soprano vestida de china poblana reemplaza casi literalmente a los trapecistas, las bailarinas de tap se habilitan como tales gracias a las corcholatas en las suelas, se excluye a los animales (excepción hecha de los que sepan tocar guitarra), y se incluye a Rabanito y Alfalfa, enharinados y felices ante la ausencia de niños que obliguen al "humor infantil."
>
> No hay enanos. Los últimos se fueron cansados de los malos tratos, y la Mujer Barbuda es una más del coro de viejas que se frotan las partes pudendas . . . [With the help of true talent and the talent contributed through the goodwill of the spectators, the carpa inherits and betrays the circus. A sense of well-being is initiated—a sense of humor and substitution—with the parade of "freaks": what is observed on the street with indifference, if cleverly advertised, will spark amazement under the carpa. Novelties-that-in-fact-never-were predominate: the soprano wearing a "china poblana" dress almost literally replaces the trapeze artists, the tap dancers are able to perform as such thanks to the bottle-caps on the soles of their shoes, animals are excluded (excepting those that can play the guitar), while Rabanito and Alfalfa are included, made up with flour and happy to perform in the absence of children who would require "an infantile sense of humor."
>
> There are no midgets. The last ones left, tired of being mistreated, and the Bearded Lady is just one more in a chorus of women who rub their private parts.] (1988:77–78)

The *carpa* continued with full force into the 1950s and the early 1960s, a resilience probably attributable to its native and working-class roots, as well as its ability to speak to the daily reality of Mexican workers in an entertaining manner. This is the world of working-class performance inherited by El Teatro Campesino.

On numerous occasions Luis Valdez and other members of the Teatro Campesino ensemble have affirmed and reaffirmed their strong roots in the *carpa* tradition and the *carpa* aesthetic, usually referred to as the Rasquachi Aesthetic within the Teatro Campesino. ("Rasquachi" is rich in connotations and can be used to express affection or disaffection while referring to something earthy, unpretentious, gaudy, resourceful, etc.) Valdez indicates: "We evolved—in our own earthiness—characters that emerged from Cantinflas and the whole comic Mexican tradition of the *carpa*, the tent" (Broyles 1983:38). It was particularly the performing family of El Circo Escalante that made a great impression on the young Valdez. The Escalantes were itinerant artists who at times lived from performance income and at other times from farm labor income. That was to become a model for the early Teatro Campesino.

Linguistic markers pointing to a relationship between El Teatro Campesino and the Mexican popular tradition also abound: the term "*carpa*" appears in the titles of Teatro Campesino performance pieces such as the classic *La gran carpa de los Rasquachis*; another piece, for example, was entitled *Carpa Cantinflesca*. Like most Teatro Campesino pieces the latter is based in the Mexican performance style embodied by the great *carpa* comedian Cantinflas, particularly popular from the 1930s through the 1950s and now legendary. Charlie Chaplin, in fact, referred to Cantinflas as "the world's greatest comedian" (Tobar 1993).

Cantinflas's mass appeal was due to many factors. Chief among them is the fact that his performance techniques and character were derived from the popular Mexican Rasquachi performance aesthetic and the plight of the underdog. His shabby attire was the standard poor-man attire of generations of comics. Cantinflas also enjoys the distinction of having brought the Mexican popular performance techniques of the *carpa* to the silver screen. Those techniques were not solely his, but based on the arsenal of popular performance techniques found (with variations) in all *carpas* and in all Mexican and Chicana/o communities into the late 1950s. In other words, Cantinflas was but one very prominent and gifted representative of a tradition much larger than himself. It is a popular performance tradition that has thrived in Mexicano working-class communities throughout Mexico and the U.S. Southwest. The performance techniques, forms, language, style, characters,

La gran carpa cantinflesca (UCLA, Ca. 1976) *featured all actors dressed Cantinflas style, as* peladas/os. *Top row left to right: José Delgado, Arturo "Negro" Gómez, Phil Esparza, Manuel Pickett. Middle row: Felix Alvarez, Olivia Chumacero. Bottom row: Frances Romero, Ernesto Valles, César Flores, two unidentified UCLA students. Courtesy of Olivia Chumacero Archive.*

audience relationship, performance sites, and social relations of production of El Teatro Campesino emerge from that Mexicana/o community context and history—and not from Europe or from one individual.

The *carpa*/Cantinflas performance tradition was absorbed into the Teatro Campesino at its beginnings and through the agency of all members of the collective. Although theater historians have singled out Luis Valdez, others contributed equally and vitally to that undertaking. What follows is an attempt to write a less hierarchical and more horizontal account of the Teatro Campesino, situating the Teatro within the larger Mexican oral performance tradition. A knowledge of the *carpa* aesthetic was very much a part of the farmworker sociocultural environment in whose midst El Teatro Campesino emerged. Prior to the establishment of the Teatro Campesino in 1965 César Chávez had been wanting to use a *carpa* as an organizing tool. As a child and young adult he had witnessed the power of *carpa* performances and was keenly aware of the value of humor as a vehicle of critique and mobilization. Chávez's strong reliance on Mexican cultural practices—the *carpa* and other more spiritual practices—to consolidate farmworkers politically was new in the annals of U.S. labor unions. Chávez perceived a need to organize by means of a specific cultural language shared by the overwhelming majority of farmworkers:

United Farm Workers founding President César
Chávez speaks at rally in front of a Teatro group,
c. 1967. Courtesy of the Archives of Labor and
Urban Affairs, Wayne State University.

I had the idea of using the *carpa* in the Farm Workers Union. I had seen *carpas* a lot in Mexicali, Tijuana, and Nogales. I wanted a *carpa* in the union for purposes of communication. With a *carpa* we could say difficult things to people without offending them. We could talk about people being cowards, for example. Instead of being offensive, it would be funny. Yet it could communicate union issues. When the Teatro Campesino was formed I gave the early characters their names: Don Sotaco, El Patroncito, El Coyote, etc. (Interview, 3/7/93)

The intimate relationship between the Mexican *carpa* tradition, César Chávez, and the Teatro Campesino was referenced recently by Luis Valdez, who indicated: "Without César, there would have been no Teatro Campesino" (Benavídez 1993).

One very important transmitter of the Mexican Rasquachi performance aesthetic of the *carpa* was the farmworker Felipe Cantú. Cantú worked with the earliest Teatro Campesino ensemble almost from its beginnings, until the Teatro separated from the Farm Workers Union in 1967. The eldest of the early Teatro formation (forty-four years old), Cantú came to be regarded as a maestro whose superb performance skills became legendary among all Teatro Campesino ensemble members. Ensemble member Olivia Chumacero (interview, 1/19/1983) later recalled: "He is the funniest man I have ever met in my entire life." In a *Ramparts* article (Valdez 1966:55), Valdez referred to him as "a comic genius" who "made his talents apparent on the picket line, where lively dialogues between pickets on the road and scabs in the field inspired his Mexican wit. . . . He speaks no English, but his wild, extravagant Cantinflas-like comic style needs no words." Teatro Campesino cofounder Agustín Lira referred to Felipe Cantú as "the heart or soul of the *actos*" and described how other characters orbited around Cantú's Cantinflas-like underdog character, Don Sotaco:

Para mi la persona más importante del Teatro Campesino era Felipe. No nomás en lo personal sino en su talento. De todos los caracteres cómicos que han salido y que he visto yo, sean cómicos mexicanos como Cantinflas, o cómicos de Europa o otras partes del mundo, no he visto yo todavía a una persona con un talento cómico como el de Felipe Cantú. [To me, the most important person of the Teatro Campesino was Felipe. Not just personally, but talentwise. Of all the comedians who have been around and whom I've seen, whether they're Mexican comedians like Cantinflas, or comedians from Europe or other parts of the world, I still haven't seen anyone with the comedic talent of Felipe Cantú.]

All he needed was the idea. He would take that idea and peel away everything it was NOT. Like making a statue. He took the rock and carved away everything that was not the character. We were left with the statue: a character. El tenía esa naturaleza de meterse en sus caracteres. Por eso el carácter de Don Sotaco formo el corazón—o el alma—de los actos en aquel tiempo. El era la víctima y nosotros nos movíamos alrededor de este carácter. [He had a natural talent for getting into his characters. That's why, back then, Don Sotaco's personality was the heart—or soul—of the actos. He was the victim and we moved around that character.] (Interview, 3/22/1983)

Even the *Wall Street Journal* took note of the "incisive comic shenanigans of Felipe Cantú" (O'Conner 7/24/1967).

What earned Felipe Cantú the title of maestro was that he transmitted a concrete working knowledge of community-validated performance skills to the Teatro Campesino. Luis Valdez (1989) describes Cantú's pivotal role within the Teatro: "Felipe became the prototype of El Teatro Campesino. He established a level of performance that influenced the whole CHICANO THEATRE movement. Many of the techniques the Teatro learned on the road were assimilated by osmosis from Felipe. A lot of people don't realize the impact of one campesino."

Although Cantú's impact as an individual was indeed great, we can understand that impact fully only if we situate him within the broader performance tradition of which he formed a part and from which he emerged. How then did Felipe Cantú serve as "prototype of El Teatro Campesino"? What were those "techniques the Teatro learned"? In my discussion of the Teatro Campesino I put forth the concepts of memory, the body, and community as chief guideposts. These are the vital performance elements that underlie both the Teatro and the oral culture of the Mexican *carpa* performance tradition.

Felipe Cantú, who worked his whole life as a migrant farmworker, was heir to a long working-class performance tradition. In vivid testimony concerning his formation as a performer, Cantú first of all spoke to what he learned in the "circo y las carpas" (circus and the tent shows). Of prime significance within this performance tradition is its reliance on *memory* (which he refers to as *grabar*, to record):

En primer lugar, allí llegaban muchos circos en Mexico. Bueno quizás le agarraba una que otra palabra a un payaso. Y mañana o pasado llegaba otro circo, y yo agarraba otra palabra. Tuve la dicha que se me grababa. Y así agarrábanos palabras del uno al otro y otro. Y en la calle también agarraba mucho. Cuando yo salía con mis amigos y ellos me contaban un chiste, pues ese chiste se me grababa . . . Se quedaba aquí en mi cabeza. Me decía yo: Quizá mañana o pasado lo pueda desempeñar. Y así fue desarrollándose el sentido que llevaba yo nomás. Y así toca que me vine a meter con estos bandidos [laughter], el Teatro Campesino . . .

A mí me gustaba mucho ir al circo y a las carpas. Cosas cómicas eran las que me gustaban a mí. Me gusta agarrar ideas de los grandes cómicos. Para mí el Chavo del Ocho es uno de ellos: y Cantinflas. Porque Cantinflas comenzó desde pequeño. [To begin with, when I was in Mexico many circuses would come through. Well, perhaps I would get one or two bits from a clown. And tomorrow or the next another circus would arrive, and I would get another bit. I was lucky that I could memorize them. And that's how bits would circulate from one person to another and then another. And I would also get ideas in the street. When I went out with my friends and they'd tell me a joke, I would memorize it . . . It would stay in my head. I would tell myself: Maybe tomorrow or the next day I can act it out. And that's how I was able to develop my sense of style. And that's how I happened to become involved with these crooks [laughter], the Teatro Campesino . . .

I used to love to go to the circus and the *carpas*. Funny things was what I liked. I like to get ideas from the great comedians. To me, one of those is Chavo del Ocho, and Cantinflas. Because Cantinflas started when he was a kid.] (Interview, 3/22/1983)

Memory is indeed the cultural storehouse. Together with the human body it constitutes the central vehicle of cultural transmission within Mexicano (or any other) oral culture. Both cultural identity and cultural survival within an oral culture depend on memory. Memory should not be understood here as a cerebral, individualistic, psychological process, but in its collective and *physical* manifestation: as remembrance and transmission of the community's knowledge through that community's performance forms (be they storytelling, *dichos* [proverbs], historical discourse, prayer, dance, jokes, skits, songs, etc.). What Felipe Cantú—as well as other Teatro members—remembered and transmitted was the Chicana/o working-class's sociohistorical and performance legacy. Far from attaching a privatistic or individual significance to memory and the creative process, Cantú constantly affirmed the shared communal nature of all performance material and techniques. He acknowledged the process of free and constant sharing. By playfully referring to this process as "stealing," he implicitly repudiates the dominant entertainment industry's private-property approach to performance and entertainment:

Yo también agarré muchas cosas de los otros muchachos. Me las robé. Ellos
no se dieron cuenta. Yo robaba otras inteligencias que tienen ellos, ¿verdad? Y
quizás ellos aprendieron algo de mí. Me lo robaron, porque en cosas de esas
hay que robarse el uno al otro. En esa forma trabajé yo desde México. Desde
México empecé a oír payasos, a oír otras personalidades, especialmente a mi
padre. [I also got a lot of ideas from the other guys. I stole them. They didn't
notice. I stole other clever stuff that they had, right? And perhaps they learned
something from me. They stole it, because when it comes to these things, we
have to steal from one another. That's how I worked from the time I was in
Mexico. From the time I was in Mexico, I started listening to clowns,
listening to other characters, especially my father.] (Interview, 3/22/1983)

In the course of Cantú's narrative we are made to understand how a knowledge of our collective identity and history was constituted in and by these
collective forms stored in physical memory.

Before embarking on a discussion of the communal forms that passed
from the carpa into the Teatro it is necessary to understand that all such forms
were transmitted from generation to generation principally from memory.
Indeed, the primacy of memory as repository of discourse and of its corresponding forms strongly links both the carpa and El Teatro Campesino to the
Native American cultures of the Americas—all of them oral cultures that do
not rely on writing.[6] Unlike the dramatic literature tradition of print culture,
the carpa and Teatro Campesino performance mode relied exclusively on
memory and not scripts. A contemporary of the great carpa comic Cantinflas
describes how Cantinflas's performances were generated by the power of
improvisation and never by "authored" (i.e., written) texts: "Llega
[Cantinflas] a la carpa a decir cosas que se ocurren graciosas. No habla por
boca de ganso, o sea, no dice lo que escribió un autor, dice lo que se le
ocurre, lo que improvisa y eso le hace gracia al público." [He doesn't speak
through someone else's mouth, that is, what an author wrote; he says whatever comes to mind, whatever he improvises, and that is what is so pleasing
to the public] (Granados 1984:96). El Teatro Campesino also did not work
from scripts or the written word. The collection Actos published in 1970 was
compiled as a transcription of a recorded performance, not as scripts used
by the Teatro at any time. And although Actos circulated widely within the
Chicano theater movement they did so, as Kanellos (1978:60) points out,
principally with reliance on memory: "But it must be emphasized that much
of teatro is learned and transmitted orally and visually without the use of
scripts or notes."

Evidently, when Felipe Cantú entered the Teatro Campesino, some tendency to use written notes was in the incipient stage: he indicated that prior to rehearsal he was once handed some paper with the lines he was supposed to learn. He rejected these outright, affirming his reliance on both memory and his own verbal and movement skills. Cantú's insistence on memory ("con papelitos no") was decisive, for it blocked the path to forms of dramatic production grounded in scripts:

> Me hicieron unos papelitos para que yo aprendiera lo que me tocaba decir. Pero yo les dije que no, que con papelitos no. Díganmelo en persona. La verdad es que yo estuve en la escuela por fuera. Yo me atengo mas a cuando las personas me hagan la plática; eso se me queda. Escrito lo puedo estudiar quince días y no se me queda nada. Por eso le dije a él: Dime lo que tengo que decir. Me dicen: Esto y esto otro; y Pas! Ahora sí. La presentación, déjamela a mí, les dije. Déjamela a mí la presentación. Esa sí déjamela a mí. Quedamos conformes. . . .
>
> Ellos me decían algunas palabras. Pero quizás las re-vestiría yo las palabras aquellas. [They prepared me some slips of paper so that I could learn what I had to say. But I said: no, not with slips of paper. Tell me face to face. Truth is, I only knew school from the outside. I rely more on people talking to me; that's what sticks. If it's written, I can study it for two weeks, and it won't stick. That's why I told him: "Tell me what I have to say." They said: "This and that"; and, wham! Now I got it! Leave the presentation to me, I told them. Leave the performance to me. Yeah, you can leave it to me. We agreed. . . .
>
> They would tell me a few things. But I would take those things and dress them up as I saw fit.] (Interview, 3/22/1983)

Yet even after the process of improvisation, discussion, and memorization, the performance flowed from an agreed-on general scenario and not from verbatim memorization of a fixed script. Dialogue was not rigidly finalized but subject to further change and improvisation during the course of a performance. The nature and direction of such improvisation could depend on numerous factors, most notably, however, on the composition of the audience and audience response and participation. With the oral performance tradition, performance skill depends to a large extent on a group's ability to carry off such an improvisational process. Essential to this process is each individual's split-second timing and capacity to think on one's feet. In other words, the entire human body is at all times fully involved in the production of meaning—often producing even more meaning than any words uttered, and many times to the exclusion of words. The Mexican popular performance mode calls for a capacity to anticipate physically and to react continually to the unexpected. Bodily fluidity and expressivity in improvisational performance requires from performers the ability instantly to read each other's bodies: gaze, voice (pitch, volume, speed), gestures, head and body movement, while also gauging and anticipating the rhythm and speed of all body movement: its musical beat. (A memorable dimension of virtually all Teatro Campesino productions was their pacing, rhythm, or beat—which in turn no doubt served as an aid to memory and recall.) Equally important is the complementary ability of performers to speak in a wild yet nuanced fashion with the body. In this regard also Felipe Cantú was a maestro whose *carpa* style of acting—involving a highly articulate body— stayed with the Teatro Campesino ensemble until its dissolution in 1980. Agustín Lira recalled Cantú's talent:

> Hay alguien que escribió que Felipe la hacía de Cantinflas o algo así. No. Cantinflas no le llegaba a Felipe. Nunca le ha llegado. Cantinflas es un pendejo en comparación. Yo he trabajado en muchos grupos y he visto gente talentosa de a madre. Pero nadie le llega a Felipe. Sin decir palabras, sin hablar, Felipe le daba a usted a entender lo que le estaba pasando a él. Usando el mime, sin hablar, le enseñaba todo al público. . . . Era su forma de moverse que la gente iba entendiendo. [Someone wrote that Felipe played the role of Cantinflas or something like that. No. Cantinflas didn't even come close to Felipe. Never even came close. Cantinflas is an idiot in comparison. I've worked in a lot of groups and I've seen people who are damned talented. But no one comes close to Felipe. Without using words, without talking, Felipe could communicate, you know, what was happening to him. Using mime, without speaking, he would show the audience everything. . . . It was the way he moved that made people understand.] (Interview, 3/22/1983)

Total body involvement was a performance "language" to which Chicana/o and Mexicana/o audiences were accustomed. To these audiences, understanding a performance meant a great deal more than a semantic decoding. It entailed an apprehension of tone, of silences, of body movement, of images, of sounds in all their variety. Unlike the bulk of Western proscenium theater, the *carpa* and Teatro Campesino performance aesthetic capitalized on mime. It was for the most part based on human body movement and expression and not on language. Words only refined the substantial meaning carried by physical action. It was, indeed, a *visual* art. Luis Valdez (1984d) has variously affirmed the primacy of bodies in motion: "It's not primarily language-based theater. Okay? It's theater of rhythms, beats, of ritu-

Farm worker and comic genius Felipe Cantú plays the guilt-ridden *pelado* scab in "La conciencia del Esquirol." Copyright 1978 George Ballis/Take Stock.

als, of visual imagery, you know, it's *something else*. It's theater of *action*. It's either social action or we're doing sacred theater, but it's *action*. Action."

It is interesting that much of the transmission of the Mexican popular performance tradition happened not from the top down, as is often assumed by critics, but from the bottom up. This is evident not only in the collective work mode, which relied on the collective talents of a *group*, but also in the fact that farmworker audiences often gave the Teatro performance guidance or feedback. It was the farmworker audience, for example, that demanded of the Teatro Campesino a performance aesthetic foregrounding action. Valdez ("The Talk of the Town," 1967) recalls how the Teatro grew in response to farmworker input: "When we started the Teatro, workers came up to us after performances and said, 'There's not enough action,' so we introduced more slapstick. We use even more slapstick when we perform for Mexican-American farmworkers than when we perform for a middle-class audience in New York."

Left to right: Felipe Cantú (floor), Danny Valdez, and Clarice Luna perform in the acto Quinta temporada (1967). Primavera (spring) brings new hope and urges worker to fight for his rights. Courtesy of the Archives of Labor and Urban Affairs, Wayne State University.

This parallels what Tomás Ybarra-Frausto tells us concerning the *carpa* and related *tandas de variedad*: "In the tanda sketch, action is foregrounded over text" (1983:47). Ybarra-Frausto's rich description of the acting style of the legendary San Antonio actress La Chata Noloesca is equally applicable to the *carpa* and El Teatro Campesino: "Drawing heavily from clowning and miming techniques, the core of her comedy routines was centered on the physicalization of ideas, so that psychological and emotional stages were made externally transparent through physical action. Few words in the routines were left without gestural accompaniment, either facially or bodily. Movement was constant, fast-paced and slapstick" (1983:46).

The human body, memory, and community are intertwined phenomena that came to bear on the *carpa* and Teatro Campesino oral culture of performance in yet other very significant ways. For one thing, memory extends far beyond the momentary absorption and retention of dramatic dialogue. In other words, memory here is associated not only with short-term memorization but with long-term historical memory and physical knowledge of life in the urban barrios and rural enclaves, of social relations of oppression and resistance. Within an orally based culture, memory and the body are the sites of a community's self-knowledge. Memory in this context signifies a remembrance of lived experience within a community, usually one's directly lived experience combined with the greater communal historical experience transmitted to youth by elders in oral historical discourse.

Memory, of course, is also the repository for performance forms themselves: forms such as historical discourse or comedic *carpa* forms. Historical memory—which always informs the present—not only flowed into the entire improvisational process of the *carpa* and the Teatro Campesino but also constituted the overriding impetus for all performance activity. Initially for the Teatro Campesino it was the physical memory of farmworker exploitation by agribusiness. The struggle against farmworker abuse was at the core of the Teatro Campesino's early performance pieces. Later the scope broadened to include a wider variety of issues facing Chicanas/os: racism in the schools, the war in Vietnam, urban problems, or questions of identity and colonialism. Felipe Cantú, for example, frequently emphasized that his reason for performing was a desire to express and share what he called his "sentimiento" or sentiment ("Yo todo lo que formaba en mi cabeza me nacia del puro sentimiento, era puro sentimiento que traiba."—Everything that I shaped in my mind was generated by sentiment; it was sentiment that I carried with me). Among the most memorable of my research experiences was the epic that unfolded when I asked Felipe Cantú to elaborate on his *sentimiento*. Felipe spoke for three days, narrating the living historical memory of Mexican peonage and slavery as lived and told by five generations of his family. The historical memory of Chicana/o slavery was very much alive in the California farmworker communities, which created the United Farm Workers of America, as well as the Teatro Campesino. When talking about his family, for example, César Chávez always described himself as a descendant of slaves; his grandfather escaped from slavery in Chihuahua in the 1880s. Felipe linked that collective historical memory (or *sentimiento*) of multigenerational oppression to his work in the Teatro Campesino. That was the guiding force in his performance:

> Una cosa de esas como El Teatro Campesino es una cosa muy grande; es una cosa muy grande porque lo guia a uno un sentimiento. Es un sentimiento que guarda uno desde que principiamos a trabajar en este mundo. Ese principio fue muy triste para mí. ¡Pues que sería pa' nuestros padres! ¡Pa nuestros abuelos! [Things such as the Teatro Campesino are very important; it's very important because you are guided by a particular sentiment. It's a sentiment that we carry from the moment we begin to work in this world. Those beginnings were very sad for me. Imagine what it was like for our parents! For our grandparents!] (Interview, 3/22–3/25/1983)

Within the oral performance mode of the Teatro Campesino, historical memory provided the very raw materials from which all production was generated. Performers relied directly on the memory of the Mexican working-class community's experience within the dominant society. The dynamism of memory provided the foundation for an understanding and critique of the present. A critical exploration of that social experience was at the heart of all Teatro Campesino performance work. Teatro Campesino ensemble member Olivia Chumacero (interview, 1/19/1983) commented on the intimate and direct relationship of continuity between the individual's performance work and life experience: "You had to draw from yourself, from where you were coming from. Things came out from you, from what you thought, from where you were coming from, from what you had experienced in life. It was wonderful. It was not a mechanical learning of lines, word for word. Words that someone had put in your mouth. It was your life."

The creation of pieces within the Teatro involved a collective process of discussion and improvisation, with the human memory as repository and foundation. The key within this collective process of creation is the body, or physical memory. Within the collective creation process creational faith is vested in the social wisdom of the body, a wisdom that emerges in the process of improvisation. Improvisation in the Mexican oral performance mode entails thinking something through with the body. Thoughts are never cerebral only. The generation of ideas and plays within El Teatro Campesino was achieved through the active work of the entire body. Improvisation is the bodily process of thinking. As an exploratory process, improvisation involved a trial-and-error system of rehearsal. Meaning was rehearsed through the body until a play took on a general form. In 1967 Luis Valdez described the process: "We take a real situation—often something that happens on the picket line—and we improvise around it. When we get an improvisation that we like, we're ready. An acto is never written down" ("The Talk of the Town," 1967).

All Teatro Campesino performance pieces went through various transformations and discussions before being committed to memory (not to written form). Yet that form was always subject to new improvisation, not least of all during performance. This approach to theatrical creation and performance was also championed by Enrique Buenaventura, who worked intensely with Chicana/o theater groups in addition to elaborating his own system of collective creation in Colombia. Buenaventura affirms (personal communication, 10/18/1990): "El cuerpo sabe más que la cabeza. Las ideas vienen del cuerpo a la cabeza. Es importante que el cuerpo guíe la cabeza y no al revés. La idea debe de nacer del trabajo corporal" (The body knows more than the head. Ideas come from the body to the head. It is important that the body guide the mind—and not the other way around. Ideas should be generated by bodily work").

Born of and for the working-class farmworker community, the Teatro Campesino's actos directly enacted the physical sociocultural memory of that

The 280-mile protest march from Delano to Sacramento in 1966 featured
evening performances by El Teatro. Shown here is a scene from acto Las tres
uvas performed on a flatbed truck, featuring improvisational master Felipe Cantú
(on right). Copyright 1978 George Ballis/Take Stock.

community's experience. Memory indeed was the prime conduit for all
performance work within El Teatro Campesino. And the power and instrumentality of memory, rooted in the community and in the body, made
possible the immediacy, authenticity, and vitality characteristic of the
ensemble's work.

The Political Economy of Chicana/o Comedy

In elaborating on the emergence of the Teatro Campesino from the *carpa* tradition it should be made clear that change and evolution were constants
within both the *carpa* tradition and the Teatro Campesino. At no point did
they exist in a static monolithic state. Even the term *"carpa"* refers to a number of different kinds of performance spectacles: some rural, some urban,
some even imitative of Eurocentric middle-class forms, most of them working-class motley assemblages. Similarly, El Teatro Campesino went through a
process of constant change, even as it remained constant. What I explore here
are the elements of constancy that traversed its changing trajectory, those
elements that constitute what I have called the bedrock of oral performance

culture. Understanding the elements of constancy necessarily involves moving beyond the particulars of memory, body, and community to a more concrete and comprehensive understanding of their function within the Mexicano and Chicana lifeworld. The concepts of memory, body, and community, central to our understanding of the Mexican popular performance tradition, necessarily converge around the question of the *carpa*'s and the Teatro Campesino's performance mission, its discursive logic, or what could also be called their political economy of performance. In other words, to what ends do memory, community history, and the human body merge within the social practice of performance?

In addressing the *carpa* and Teatro Campesino telos of performance, a closer look at specific characteristics of orally based cultural practices is essential. One very basic feature of orally based thought and expression is its closeness to the lifeworld. Oral cultural practices always are constituted directly within the lifeworld community context of *human action*. They never exist outside of an operational context. This contrasts with written forms, which—as Ong illustrates—"structure knowledge at a distance from lived experience" (1982:42). For the Teatro Campesino the operational context initially was the Mexican farmworker community and its intense struggle against the exploitative labor practices of agribusiness.

In conceptualizing the *carpa* and Teatro Campesino as oral cultural practices, I seek to illustrate how the direct and intimate existence of such practices in the lifeworld of a working-class culture strongly determined their performance telos. In no way should "cultural practices" here be construed as different from "social practices" but as one kind of constitutive social practice. Culture here is not viewed simply as a way of interpreting the world, but also as a way of living within the world, of creating one's world and altering reality.[7]

Oral performance forms are memory forms of and by the community. As a cultural complex they sustain Mexican working-class cultural identity and a knowledge of the world through an ongoing process of negotiation, of preservation and change, of being and becoming. That constant negotiation through performance forms is always a challenging social process, one of "verbal and intellectual combat" (Ong 1982:44)—an excellent metaphor for the performance work of the *carpas* and El Teatro Campesino. Ong (1982:43–44) argues that "writing fosters abstractions that disengage knowledge from the arena where human beings struggle with one another. It separates the knower from the known. By keeping knowledge embedded in the human lifeworld, orality situates knowledge within a context of struggle. Proverbs and riddles are not used simply to store knowledge but to engage others in verbal and intellectual combat."

One must not underestimate the importance of the "context of struggle" of verbal art forms within oppressed communities and of the very real *need* for "verbal and intellectual combat." Combat is usually joined for cultural and physical survival. As such it cannot surprise us that impartiality is out of the question. The Teatro Campesino's militance was a direct response to the needs of the United Farm Workers struggle from which it emerged. There was an urgent need to unionize in the struggle against the multiple abuses of agribusiness, which included large-scale pesticide poisoning of farm laborers, exploitative wages, substandard housing, child labor, and no benefits. At times of lesser political ferment the critical exploration of social experience could assume less explicit—if equally pungent—performance forms. The transmission of knowledge within oral performance forms never feigns neutrality, "objectivity," or detachment. A critique is usually implicit or explicit, lines are drawn, sides are taken, particular forms of social behavior are regarded positively, others viewed askance, solutions to problems are put forth or implied. Critiques within the Teatro Campesino were often embedded in performance forms involving verbal jousting, which calls into question norms of language and conduct as well as dominant and oppressive paradigms of "correct" speech and meaning. The Teatro Campesino described its work within this very combative style, a style that emanated directly from an intimate relationship to the urban and rural struggles of Chicana/o communities. The performance telos involved a grounding in the community experience of the working class, in a social vision and critique. In the company's own words:

> ACTOS: Inspire the audience to social action. Illuminate specific points about social problems. Satirize the opposition. Show or hint at a solution. Express what people are feeling.
>
> So what's new, right? Plays have been doing that for thousands of years. True, except that the major emphasis in the acto is the social vision, as opposed to the individual artist or playwright's vision. Actos are not written. They are created collectively. (Valdez 1971a:6)

The *carpa* was similarly combative, privileging humorous sketches that often enacted conflictive and satirical situations between persons of authority and underdogs. A satirical sting of the established order—usually with a comic figure at its center—was a hallmark of the *carpa* tradition. One veteran of that tradition points to the centrality of caustic critical humor embodied

The 280-mile march from Delano to Sacramento in 1966 by the National Farm Worker's Association (which became the United Farm Workers of America) brought national attention to the demands of farmworkers for justice. Copyright 1978 Matt Herron.

in the comic figure. That comic figure was the chief "magnet" in attracting the popular masses:

> El cómico se volvió el imán que atrajo al pueblo para oír, de labios de quien ayunaba como él, las bromas cáusticas con que burlaba y criticaba a la sociedad injusta. [The comedian—who went without eating just like his audiences—became the magnet that attracted the people to hear the caustic jokes that made fun of and criticized the unjust society.] (Ortega 1984:15)

The critical thrust of the *carpa* and the Teatro Campesino constitutes a prime characteristic that aligns both with the greater Mexican popular oral performance tradition. In his landmark study of Mexicano and Chicana performance forms, Charles Briggs (1988) highlights the inordinate critical capacity of traditional Mexicano performance forms such as historical discourse, *cuentos* (storytelling), *dichos*, legends, or jokes. These oral performance forms play a dynamic and vital role in the daily social life of dominated communities. Indeed, these performance forms are among the basic social practices that constitute Chicano community and identity. Individually and as a group, oral cultural practices provide an alternative interpretive system, which resists the dominant hegemony by critically exploring and shaping social experience from a specifically Mexicano working-class and ethnic perspective. As such, the dynamism of the oral performance tradition contributes continually to the creation of new ideologies and social formations. This is true of the *carpa* tradition, of the Teatro Campesino, and of the entire spectrum of discursive forms within the Mexican popular performance traditions.

In what follows I offer a more sustained examination of the memory system shared by the *carpa* and El Teatro Campesino. In addition to discussing the significance of humor within that memory system, I elaborate on the conventions active within the social practice of performance. Much of orally based thought and expression relies on performance conventions, formulas, standard thematic settings, and other memory devices. Ong (1982) points out that oral performance forms can be sustained only through reliance on memory systems. Retention, retrieval, and community reception (participants' expectations) call for a shared set of performance conventions and forms.

Prime among the performance conventions of the *carpa* and the Teatro Campesino was a strong reliance on comedic technique and forms (particularly the comic sketch), on musical performance and dancelike movement. Virtually all explorations into social phenomena were conveyed through the medium of humor, often accompanied by music. The overriding tone of social critique and reflection was raucous. Performance elements characteristically aimed to produce laughter. These elements included the wildly exaggerated and broadly mimetic acting style; the archetypal stock characters, such as the hilarious *peladito/peladita* (underdog); or the witty and irreverent attitude toward language and norms of propriety conveyed through a general spirit of *picardía* (ribald humor). Yet in essence this humor was dead serious. It provided the means of exploring and commenting on social oppression and life's day-to-day struggles. The relationship between laughter and human necessity, between slapstick and tragedy is expressed by Luis Valdez (1972b:360): "Our use of comedy originally stemmed from necessity—the necessity of lifting the strikers' morale. We found we could make social points not in spite of the comedy, but through it. Slapstick can bring us very close to the underlying tragedy—the fact that humans have been wasted for generations." Walter Benjamin similarly comments on the importance of laughter as a catalyst of serious reflection:

> Nur nebenbei sei angemerkt, daß es fürs Denken gar keinen besseren Start gibt als das Lachen. Und insbesondere bietet die Erschütterung des Zwerchfells dem Gedanken gewöhnlich bessere Chancen dar als die der Seele. [Incidentally, let me remark that there is no better trigger for thought than laughter. And in particular, as a rule you stand a better chance of reaching the brain through moving the diaphragm rather than the soul.] (1966:113)

The *carpa* as well as the Teatro Campesino were sustained principally by the comedic spirit. Before elaborating further on the various mutually reinforcing elements from the memory system shared by the *carpa* and the Teatro Campesino, the significance of laughter and humor within that memory system needs to be addressed. Humor, far from being incidental to the memory system, to meaning, far from being simply a frivolous dimension, in fact constitutes a fundamental positioning or bedrock within which *carpa* and Teatro Campesino performance could unfold. It has meaning in and of itself. The predominance of humor does not mean that pieces with a less-humorous orientation—such as *Soldado Razo*—were not included in the Teatro's or the *carpa*'s repertoire. Yet those occasional pieces that sought to sustain a serious tone were punctuated with humorous elements and belonged within a larger repertoire based primarily on the culture of laughter. At the center of most performance acts was the clown or a reincarnation of the underdog clown figure. We witness the drive to suspend the culture and ideology of official seriousness even in a later piece like *Zoot Suit* through the *pachuco* character. At the height of victim Henry Reyna's tribulations and lament the *pachuco* interjects a humorous distancing comment: "Hey, don't take the pinche play so serious!"

Laughter—triggered by satire, the grotesque, parody, jokes—represents a relationship to the social whole, indeed, to all of creation. Petrarch tells us, for example, that parody is an attitude toward history. It has also been postulated that parody is the form of the marginalized. Our understanding of the significance of laughter and humor within the social formation is enriched by the work of such well-known theorists as Mikhail Bakhtin or Sigmund Freud. Yet prior to their arrival and popularization in the Americas Mexican philosopher Jorge Portilla anticipated much of what Bakhtin elaborated concerning humor and laughter. Portilla's little-known *Fenomenología del relajo* (1966) is grounded in the Mexican popular context and the Mexican concept of *relajo*, a humorous practice perfected within the Mexican popular performance tradition. Portilla addresses the popular Mexican culture of laughter, its oppositional relationship to imposed values and to the seriousness of officialdom, and its affirmation of the possibility of freedom. The act of *relajo* (along with *burla* [mockery], *sarcasmo* [sarcasm], *choteo* [derision]), so pervasive in Mexican everyday life, is variously defined by Portilla as "una burla colectiva" [a collective mocking], as "un desvío de algo" [a derailing of something] (p. 20), or as "la suspensión de la seriedad frente a un valor propuesto a un grupo de personas" [the suspension of seriousness in the face of a value posited before a group of persons] (p. 25). In its essence, then, the spirit of *relajo*—a disruptive group cheekiness—constitutes a subjective positioning of dissent vis-à-vis the dominant values of the social whole. *Relajo* seeks to suspend or "aniquilar la adhesión del sujeto a un valor propuesto a su libertad" [annihilate the adhesion of the subject to a value placed vis-à-vis her or his liberty] (p. 18). More specifically, Portilla refers to how the collective laughter of *relajo* facilitates the collective "negación a la conducta requerida" [negation of required conduct] (p. 24) as well as of values or entire value systems. Insofar as the laughter of *relajo* follows on the overturning of values, of the expected, of what has been assumed valid, it constitutes a rehearsal of collective freedom.

It is interesting to note that, although Jorge Portilla's phenomenology of *relajo* is for the most part abstract, that is, without concrete reference to or discussion of cultural practices, he at one point does single out Mexican comedic figures such as Cantinflas to illustrate how *relajo* can be achieved corporally through sheer mime:

> La función expresiva del cuerpo, asumida en la intencionalidad activa del relajo, permite que la acción constituyente del mismo sea una pura mímica. El ejemplo más perfecto de esta función activa de la expresividad corpórea es la total supresión de la seriedad que se manifiesta en ciertas actitudes de Mario Moreno [Cantinflas]. No hay situación, por grave que sea, cuya seriedad no quede completamente disuelta por la demoledora expresividad del gran mimo. La acción constitutiva del relajo puede ser una serie de meras actitudes "cantinflescas", por decirlo así. [The expressive function of the body, assumed in the active intentionality of *relajo*, allows for its constitutive action to be pure mimicry. The most perfect example of this active function of corporal expression is the complete suppression of seriousness that is manifested in certain attitudes of Mario Moreno. There isn't a situation, no matter how solemn, whose seriousness isn't completely dissolved by the devastating expressiveness of the great mime. The constitutive action of *relajo* can be a series of "Cantinflesque" attitudes, so to speak.] (1966:27)

The Teatro Campesino was heir to the performance memory system of the *carpa*. From its earliest to its last collective performances that "demoledora expresividad" (devastating expressivity) was visible and audible: an intense, boisterous, and exuberant energy created by an exaggerated use of the body, as well as by a bare-bones staging of social relations facilitated by the humorous use of archetypal characters and situations. Within the early Teatro Campesino, whole plot lines characteristically unfolded in the direction of a social utopia brought about miraculously by union membership, a labor strike, or a deus ex machina apparition of our Lady of Guadalupe. It was the topsy-turvy spirit of *relajo* that could magically cut through or subvert the existing order, that could open up new vistas of freedom for the Chicana/o collective.

Portilla elaborates on the collective quality of *relajo*, on its frequently "noisy" ("ruidoso," "estrepitoso") nature, and on its insistence on a new order ("el relajo es una invitación al movimiento desordenado"/relajo is an invitation to disordered movement [p. 29]). Such disordered and raucous movement, hilarious disrespect before authority, such linguistic and situational comedic reversals were staples with both the *carpa* and the Teatro Campesino. The occasional use of miraculous intervention—through the apparition of an indigenous deity, for example—had a similar utopian quality. Although heavily criticized by Marxist critics at the time, the miraculous also served to question and challenge the established order. In its own way the miraculous could mock, pull a trick, or defy business-as-usual and overturn the seemingly immutable social order.[8] Such mockery or trickery is in essence a critique of power.

Of considerable relevance to the understanding of the Mexican popular culture of laughter is Mikhail Bakhtin's theory of the carnivalesque, of laughter, and of their relationship to oppression and freedom. Unlike that of Portilla, Bakhtin's theory is grounded in the concreteness of a class society. Although it is not Mexican society about which he writes, his theory parallels much of what is observable in the Mexican culture of laughter. Bakhtin conceptualizes laughter as a patently oppositional tool of the popular masses. He illustrates how the culture of laughter in its many forms and manifestations has traditionally opposed the authoritarianism and protective seriousness of the ruling class. Through the ages laughter has for the oppressed functioned as a rehearsal of freedom. Laughter challenges all that appears immutable, stable, and unchanging—most notably the existing social hierarchy and dominant authority. Bakhtin elaborates on the unbridled essence of laughter and its social importance to the oppressed in the defeat of social fear. As such, laughter constitutes a symbolic and tentative victory over all forms of social violence:

> The serious aspects of class culture are official and authoritarian; they are combined with violence, prohibitions, limitations and always contain an element of fear and of intimidation. . . . Laughter, on the contrary, overcomes fear, for it knows no inhibitions, no limitations. Its idiom is never used by violence and authority.
>
> It was the victory of laughter over fear. . . . It was not only a victory over the mystic terror of God, but also a victory over the awe inspired by the forces of nature, and most of all over the oppression and guilt related to all that was consecrated and forbidden ("mana" and "taboo"). It was the defeat of divine and human power, of authoritarian commandments and prohibitions, of

death and punishment after death, hell and all that is more terrifying than the earth itself. Through this victory laughter clarified man's consciousness and gave him a new outlook on life. This truth was ephemeral; it was followed by the fears and oppressions of everyday life, but from these brief moments another unofficial truth emerged, truth about the world and man. (1984:90–91)

The practice of turning social hierarchy and dominant authority into something laughable is evidenced in virtually all Teatro Campesino productions. One very striking example is the *acto La conquista de México* in which the devastation and terror of conquest is mitigated by and distanced through humor. Chief among these humorous devices is the fact of Aztec nobility speaking in twentieth-century Chicana/o street idiom.

It is important to underscore laughter's positive regenerative power as well as its power of negation, its relationship to a new life and to "another unofficial truth." The centrality of comic images and laughter within the representation of the people's alternative and unofficial truth concerning the world is everywhere evident within the *carpa* and the Teatro Campesino: symbols of power and violence are overturned, death and the devil (the omnipresent *calavera* [skeleton] and *diablo* [devil] characters) are hilarious and friendly helpers within the natural and social life cycle; above all, the primacy of the iconoclastic central comic figure constantly asserts a different order of things. That different order of things is literally affirmed in the *acto Las dos caras del patroncito*, in which we witness the hilarious reversal between the boss and the abused farmworker. Everything considered menacing is ultimately transformed into something funny. In the *acto Vietnam campesino*, the deadly and crippling reality of airplane cropdusting with toxic pesticides is humorously portrayed on stage by the boss's child, who drops "pesticides" on farmworkers in the form of talcum from a toy airplane.

Fundamental to the people's unofficial truth is also the consistent affirmation of the life and death cycle and of human bodily functions, which affirm the hope of regeneration. The perennially popular truths of birth, copulation, and death are manifest in a multiplicity of ways. Among them is what could be called biological humor: direct or indirect references to all facets of what Bakhtin calls "the material bodily lower stratum" (1984:86). Mexican writer Carlos Monsiváis (1988:82–83) provides us with a description of the *carpa* that testifies to its insistence on the unofficial and counterhegemonic truth of the lower stratum against middle-class decorum and norms of "good conduct":

En la carpa, no hay "mal gusto". Hay lujos de la intimidad, y la certeza de que cualquier forma de fracaso es regocijante: los defectos físicos, las apetencias malogradas, los traspiés de las funciones fisiológicas. Aquí imperan los movimientos soeces (impensables en las clases medias tradicionales, rígidamente maquilladas por el decoro o frenadas por un nacionalismo de buena conducta: "el mexicano decente no ronca ni utiliza poses indebidas mientras duerme"), y se extiende el "doble sentido", que en vuelta magistral extrae inocencia de la procacidad y procacidad de la inocencia. Para el Pueblo (la Gleba) el meollo de las frases sin sentido es el éxtasis ante el sexo, y los andares y los manoteos son confesiones, denuncias, peticiones. . . . Lo que no se puede decir, se insinúa y se expresa con las imágenes que forman los movimientos corporales. En el pueblo, lo escatológico (lo "obsceno") no es gozo secreto sino expresividad elemental. A la ira, a la charla paródica, al deseo y al regaño les hacen falta las "groserías" (una mala palabra *aquí* es un término insustituible *acá*), y al no estallar en la carpa las "palabrotas" se precipita el vértigo de risas y chiflidos que acompaña al eufemismo. [In the *carpa* there's no such thing as "bad taste." There are the luxuries of intimacy, and the certainty that any type of failure is joyous: physical defects, unsuccessful yearnings, the foibles of bodily functions. Indecent movements reign here (unthinkable among the traditional middle classes, rigidly painted over with decorum or restrained by a nationalism of good conduct: "a decent Mexican neither snores nor sleeps in improper positions"), and the "double entendre" dominates and in a perfect turnabout manages to extract innocence from insolence and insolence from innocence. For the masses (Plebes) the essence of phrases without meaning is the ecstatic dimension of sex, and movements and gestures are confessions, accusations, petitions. . . . What cannot be said is insinuated and expressed with images formed by body movements. Among the people, the scatological (the "obscene") is not a secret pleasure but rather a fundamental expressiveness. Anger, desire, and scolding all need profanities (what for some is a "bad" word becomes indispensable in another context), and when these "bad words" don't explode at the *carpa*, a frenzy of laughter and whistling is triggered by every euphemism.]

The lower stratum—primarily the reproductive organs, belly, even the feet—serve continually to bring one down to earth and away from the abstract ideals propagated by the dominant order.[9] What is more, the closeness of the lower stratum to the life cycle offers the perpetual promise of renewal. Bakhtin indicates: "The material bodily lower stratum and the entire [popular] system of degradation, turnovers, and travesties presented this essential [liberational] relation to time and to social and historical transformation" (1984:81). Within the performance economy of the *carpa* and the Teatro Campesino—frequently referred to as the "Rasquachi Aesthetic" by the latter—laughter is embedded in a memory system that privileges physicality, travesty, profanity, the ribald, parody, and other elements of *picardía* from popular culture. Together they fly in the face of official pretense and seriousness while affirming the life cycle's promise of change and renewal.

Although this is not the place to trace in depth the ancient roots and evolution of the *carpa* tradition, it must be stated that the culture of laughter and humorous performance forms involving buffoonery, acrobatics, clowning, and satire has been an important part of the Mexican social formation since before the arrival of Europeans. The Spanish Franciscan chronicler Bernal Díaz del Castillo as well as the Dominican chronicler Diego Durán document the existence of buffoonery and clowning in native performance genres of the sixteenth century, to which the *carpa* is heir. One pre-Hispanic American performance form described by Durán in fact bears a striking similarity to the Cantinflas-type *pelado*, or underdog figure, of the *carpa* and the Teatro Campesino: "A su modo, había un baile y canto de truhanes, en el cual introducían un bobo, que fingía entender al revés lo que su amo le mandaba, trastocando las palabras" [In their own style they had a song and dance of buffoons which featured a fool, who pretended to understand backwards what his master ordered, by mixing up words].[10]

The juxtaposition of "truhanes" and "amo," of lowly buffoons and master, of underdog—versed in the art of humorous verbal self-defense—and authority figure constitutes an ancient performance paradigm in the Americas. Similarly, the *Historia de Chimalpáin* informs us of various native pantomimic dances in which buffoons intervene. Miguel León-Portilla (1959:27) similarly tells us about the pre-Hispanic *bufón declamador*, or oratorical buffoon, who delights audiences with his juxtaposition of joking and serious reflection: "En lo que va declamando aparece ciertamente lo cómico y jocoso, pero tampoco está ausente la reflexión más honda que hace pensar. El pueblo contempla y se divierte" [Both the comical and the humorous certainly appear in his recitation, but it is also not lacking the kind of profound reflection that makes one think. The people are attentive and have fun]. León-Portilla, in fact, names "actuación cómica" (comedic performance) as one of the four major categories of pre-Hispanic Nahuatl theatrical activity.

The pre-Columbian culture of laughter is also partially documented in the *Historia natural y moral de las Indias* by P. José de Acosta, S.J. He describes the hilarity of a mock sacred adoration of Quetzalcoatl in Cholula "con que hacían reír grandemente al pueblo" [by which they made the people laugh wildly].[11] Chavero, in *Mexico a través de los siglos*, informs us of how the elements of music, dance and poetry were combined to produce comedic pieces:

> Como se ve, algunas danzas se convertían en representaciones dramáticas; pantomímicas en su principio, debieron combinarse después con el relato de un solo actor. . . . La combinación de la música, del baile y de la poesía, debió producir verdaderas obras cómicas. [As can be seen, some dances could turn into dramatic performances; pantomimic at the beginning, they were later combined with the narration of just one actor. . . . The combination of music, dance, and poetry produced genuinely comedic works.][12]

Whereas much scholarship has, in neocolonial fashion, sought to establish a European ancestry for the *carpa*, the deep and ancient Native American roots of Mexican farce and comedy remain relatively unexplored. León-Portilla's statement that research into the multiplicity of pre-Hispanic Nahuatl comedic performance is in its infancy is still as true as it was in 1959:

> Interminable sería pretender adentrarnos en el estudio de todas las formas de divertimiento y solaz más o menos cercanas a la prestidigitación o al sainete, que se fueron desarrollando en el mundo náhuatl prehispánico. Debe notarse al menos que es este tema tan rico y abundante que ya de por sí ofrece materia para una obra especializada. [It would be an interminable task to attempt to study in detail all the forms of diversion and recreation developed in the pre-Hispanic Nahuatl world that were roughly similar to sleight of hand or the one-act farce. It should be at least noted that this subject is so rich and abundant that it, in and of itself, offers enough material for a specialized study.] (1959:27)

Even in what is today's southwestern United States—far from the well-documented Aztec Empire—clowning and bawdy, irreverent humor remain a staple of native cultures. Although often in the form of ritual humor, other more profane forms of humorous performance are part of the ancient Mexican performance legacy. This legacy continues into subsequent centuries. One rare testimony from 1858 tells of such entertainment in Tucson, Arizona, enacted by local Indians: "The dance was a grotesque affair, like all other Indian dances. They had a clown, like a circus, to act the fool. He was not permitted to speak but acted pantomimes. He at the proper time would provoke the motley group to laughter."[13]

The ancient and contemporary native comedic, pantomimic, and acrobatic presence may well account for the ease with which some similar European spectacles—circus and one-act short burlesque farces such as *sainetes*—could find some acceptance in Mexico.[14] Other Spanish genres not

Burlap backdrop illustrative of the Rasquachi Aesthetic. José Delgado as Diablo in El Teatro Campesino's La carpa de los Rasquachi, European tour, 1978. Courtesy of Diane Rodríguez Collection. Photograph by Ferdinand Schuster.

assimilable into native performance forms and essentially foreign to popular taste flourished briefly and then vanished. Covarrubias comments on the vitality of the native working-class *carpa* tradition, which existed in contrast and in tacit opposition to those Spanish imports of the middle class: "the theater of the bourgeoisie—Spanish farces and operettas—was too remote, too foreign to their [the popular masses'] taste and spirit" (1938:596).

We can surmise that class relations and the growing inequalities of a class society in Mexico did their share to foster the proliferation of working-class comedic forms. Although the comedic—buffoonery, clowning, mockery—was an integral part of pre-Columbian cultural expression, existing alongside other performance forms, over time the culture of laughter gained strength and momentum. The ravages of Mexican history—the Conquest and colonial domination followed by industrialization, capitalist expansion, and exploitation—were no doubt factors that served to maximize the need for laughter, *picardía*, and *relajo* in all their forms.

Rasquachi Performance Aesthetic and Historical Memory

In what follows I offer a schematic inventory from the arsenal of generic and stylistic conventions from the Rasquachi Aesthetic common to both the *carpa* and the Teatro Campesino. Rasquachi Aesthetic refers to the creation of artistic beauty from the motley assemblage of elements momentarily seized. Performances within the *carpa* and in El Teatro Campesino manifest a shared memory system anchored in working-class history and its arsenal of performance practices. I want to elaborate particularly on those formulaic performance features shared by the *carpa* and the Teatro Campesino.

It was perhaps in response to the political economy of oral culture, which demands what is memorable and of social relevance, that such formulaic or conventional performance features emerged over time and became standard. The memory system shared by the *carpa* and the Teatro Campesino embraces elements of plot, acting style, language usage, characters, genres, and tone. Related conventions include the nature of the relationship between performers and audience, the question of performance sites, and the social relations of production. A correspondence exists between the interpretive discursive needs of working-class communities and traditional performance forms. It would appear that the need to address working-class reality and communally to share in the basic processes of the social formation favored the types of performance forms and styles—most notably those of the *carpa*—that facilitated that process. As will be shown, these conventions are for the most part anchored in the comedic spirit and in the logic of laughter; they are mutually reinforcing performance elements that conjoin into a counterhegemonic discourse, a working-class aesthetic and social practice.

Among the most striking of conventional elements common to the *carpa* and the Teatro Campesino is the gamut of stock characters, most important the comic underdog character—a direct descendant of the *payasa/o*, or "clown," who previously formed the nucleus of the *circo* (circus) from which the *carpa* was born. Within the *carpa*, a whole array of stock comic characters emerged whose chief trait was the element of uproarious *vulnerability* coupled with resourcefulness, in the context of a hostile or difficult environment. That vulnerability was manifest through an inherent weakness (of gender, age, class, or general social positioning), or through a disadvantage that the character usually managed to turn to her or his advantage. We can include under the heading of *peladita/peladito* such stock characters as the penniless trickster, the orphan, the down-and-out Indian, the recent immigrant, the infant, the naughty child, the indigent drunkard, the naïve country bumpkin (*ranchero*), or the altar boy, all of which populate the *carpa* tradition. The performance logic of these characters pivots around their maneuvers within the larger established social order and its system of power relations. That order is often represented by another set of stock characters, usually in the form of straight men or straight women off of whom the *pelado/pelada* plays. Famous pairings in the Mexican tradition include el Tartamudo y el Boby as the orphan and his tutor; Chicote and Bravo Sosa as priest and altar boy; Jesús Martínez ("Palillo") and Issa del Rey as the infant and his mother; and Cantinflas and Schilinsky as poor and rich man. None of these characters consisted of fleshed-out figures, nor did they seek to render the psychological workings of individuals. Instead each character stood for a broad social category. Their archetypal nature facilitated a skeletal portrait of the structure of social relations.

Each archetypal comic character—executed in the bold strokes of a caricature—was a composite of working-class mannerisms and behavior. The great comic Mario Moreno describes the genesis and working-class appearance of his character, Cantinflas:

> Y yo era un artista de última categoría. Trabajaba en las carpas a las que acudía la gente sin dinero para entrar a un teatro caro.
>
> Cantinflas había nacido y empezó a crecer.
>
> Poco a poco tomó forma la apariencia física de Cantinflas. Adoptó la vestimenta de la gente humilde, la necesidad escogió el atuendo. Camisa de algodón de largas mangas, que alguna vez fue blanca. Pantalones arrugados y no muy amplios, sostenidos no en la cintura sino en las caderas. Y zapatos que le quedarían mejor a un hipopótamo. Sobre esta vestimenta venía un pedazo de trapo conocido como "la gabardina". [And I was an artist of the very lowest class. I worked in the *carpas* frequented by people without the money to go to an expensive theater.
>
> Cantinflas had been born and began to develop.
>
> Slowly, the physical appearance of Cantinflas took shape. He adopted the clothes of the poor, necessity chose the costume. Long-sleeved cotton shirt, which at one time was white. Wrinkled pants, not very wide, held up not on the waist but on the hips. And shoes that would fit a hippopotamus far better. Over this attire hung a piece of cloth better known as "la gabardina" (the raincoat).][15]

As a group, the *pelada/o*, or underdog, characters were bawdy, bold, gutsy, hilarious, thoroughly unpretentious, usually irreverent, and determined to survive. This comic underdog figure is by no means restricted to the *carpa* tradition. Popular fascination with the underdog-trickster figure traverses Mexican popular performance genres. This generic character appears in numerous guises yet always bears an inordinate critical thrust couched in humor. It is the Pedro de Ordimalas figure, the Quevedo figure, or the Pepito figure prominent in the joke-telling tradition. It is the anthropomorphic rabbit, the poor *ranchero*, or the Indian peasant ("*indito*") figure familiar to us from legends and *cuentos* (storytelling).

From this rich tradition of comic underdog figures or buffoons were born the Teatro Campesino characters, most important the *pelado*—a character immediately recognizable by a shabby and grotesquely raggedy appearance. Within the early Teatro Campesino the comedic spirit was embodied primarily by Felipe Cantú, who most frequently played the underdog, or *pelado*, a combination of victim and hero, of weakness and strength, of comedy and tragedy, of the boldly funny and the fearfully timid. Olivia Chumacero recalls: "You will see in some of the pictures of the old *actos* that he is dressed that way [like a *pelado*] for some of the characters of the *actos*. Felipe Cantú was the one who inspired Luis to use that character. And, in fact, I would say that a lot of the comic relief that they used to have in the *actos* at that time came from this man's way of being, his expressions. He was a funny person. People remembered him" (interview, 1/19/1983).

As in the *carpa*, this comic *pelado/pelada* character was the axis around which other characters and the *acto's* logic rotated. Agustín Lira (interview, 3/22/1983) recounts: "Lo más importante en los actos era eso de tener la víctima y el héroe en un personaje. Con eso ya tenía lo más importante para componer cualquier cosa" [The most important thing within the *actos* was the business of having the victim and the hero be the same person. That provided us with the most important element on which to expand]. The *pelado's* naïveté, her or his desperate situational entanglements and survivalist instinct would keep audiences oscillating between laughter and tears. Lira recalls:

> Es una forma mexicana cuando algo es tan trágico que se vuelve cómico. Y al reverso también: cuando algo es tan cómico que se vuelve trágico. Felipe podía hacer a la gente sentir eso. Estando en algo trágico lo podía hacer a usted llorar, y tres o cuatro segundos después reírse a carcajadas. [It's a typically Mexican form: when something is so tragic that it turns comical. And the opposite is also true: when something is so comical that it turns tragic. Felipe could make people feel that. In the middle of enacting something tragic he could make you cry, and three or four seconds later you would be bursting with laughter.]

The inordinate attraction of the comic *pelado/pelada* figure stemmed, for one thing, from the ease with which audiences could identify with the character. Characters such as the Teatro Campesino's Don Sotaco rendered the experience of the working-class person on the street. Audience identification

The acto Quinta temporada *satirized the corrupt farm labor contractor, played by Agustín Lira (co-founder of Teatro Campesino) as Don Coyote, while Felipe Cantú plays the unsuspecting farm worker or pelado figure (Don Sotaco). Copyright 1978 George Ballis/Take Stock.*

was not of a *sentimental* nature, however. Audiences were in no way naturalistically lulled. Instead they were constantly jolted by the *pelado*'s grotesquely exaggerated physical antics and appearance. The exaggerated sting and self-conscious quality of Mexican comedy were built-in distancing devices, which constantly dispelled any sentimental illusion.

The presence of the *pelada/o* remained a constant within the Teatro Campesino from its earliest days to the very end of the ensemble's collective work. Even as the Teatro's plays evolved from short comic sketches to plays of greater complexity and length, the *pelado/a* remained the Teatro's performance nucleus, be it in the guise of the exploited farmworker, the recent immigrant (the character of Jesús Pelado Rasquachi in *La gran carpa de la familia Rasquachi*), or of the *vato loco* or street dude (the character of Mundo Mata in *Fin del mundo*). Like the *pelada/o* figure, all other characters were also stock or archetypal characters emblematic of the structures of social relations. Within the early Teatro they were characters such as El Coyote (the crooked labor contractor), El Patroncito (the powerful yet ridiculous boss), the *pelada/o* "Farmworker" or "Worker," or the strikebreaking "Scab" or "Esquirol."

The contrastive bipolar use of characters facilitated yet another convention shared by the *carpa* and the Teatro Campesino: a plot line frequently offering momentary or permanent reversals or inversions by which the underdog ends up on top or at least temporarily opens up that liberational possibility. The possibility of the underdog's outwitting the boss, indeed of momentarily being "on top of things"—evidenced in Teatro Campesino *actos* such as *Las dos caras del patroncito, Los vendidos, Quinta temporada*—offers a re-

Characteristic comedic role reversal between farm worker and scab (Esquirol: Danny Valdez) and boss (Patroncito: Luis Valdez) in Las dos caras del patroncito. Copyright 1978 Matt Herron.

hearsal of freedom, an overturning of established relations through comedic means. The exploited suddenly emerge as the ones who turn the tables on the power holders. In *Las dos caras del patroncito* the lowly farmworker manages to invert power relations by trading places with the agribusiness boss. In another *acto* the California governor suddenly turns into a Mexican farm laborer.[16] In *Quinta temporada* the coyote (labor contractor) is physically shown to have some power over the grower or boss (*patrón*), although this is not expressed verbally.

Only the magic of laughter could radically and credibly suspend the seriousness of the entire social system of oppression. Wit was the crucible; all manner of reversals, momentary or permanent, were facilitated by the wit and cunning of the underdog. The Teatro Campesino was clearly heir to the cunning and wit of generations of Mexican comics such as Cantinflas, Leopoldo Beristain, Lupe Rivas Cacho, or Delia Magaña. Luis Valdez commented on the social reversals enacted through the vehicle of witty double-talk, a prime performance weapon of the underdog struggling to survive against oppression: "[Cantinflas] was identifying with the low man on the totem pole, he was the victim of fate, and yet trying to survive in his own way, using his wits; outwitting the rich, outwitting the powerful, doing a double-talk that everybody knew was nonsense but it was imitative of education, it was imitative of being powerful. And so he became a very popular hero, and a magical hero to watch" (Broyles 1983:39).

Likewise within the *carpa* tradition, reversals were characteristically tied to a set of conventions and formulas. The vast freedom of imagination evidenced through improvisation during performance was, paradoxically, at the same time harnessed by means of various comedic verbal conventions such as puns, joke-telling, the verbal competition of *albures* (verbal jousting with sexual overtones or insinuations), *cábula* (banter or verbal dueling), double entendres (particularly of a sexual nature), misunderstandings, and other ad-libbed forms. Tomás Ybarra-Frausto provides a concise description of the verbal strategies evidenced within the Mexican comedic tradition to which the *carpa* or *tandas de variedad* are heir:

> Laughter stimulated by verbal virtuosity is a staple of Mexican comedy. Directly linked to the *picardía* of spoken language, especially among the urban working-classes, much humor stems from adroit manipulation of linguistic resources such as puns and double entendres. The *albur*, an aggressive chain of wisecracks predominantly of a sexual nature, is a common source of much proletarian Mexican humor.
>
> Marginalized sectors within the Mexican and Mexican-American subcultures weave pyrotechnical displays of language that often function as subversive strategies against imposed orders and hierarchies. Official political rhetoric, for example, when lampooned by exaggeration, can be rendered ineffectual as soon as its meaningless sloganeering base is exposed.
>
> *Tandas de variedad* employed many comedy routines involving a *peladito* usually ensnared by authority. As a defense mechanism, the *pelado* directs a torrent of verbiage against his oppressor. Spontaneously composed with verve and crackling wit, such clusters of meaningless banter are not only delightfully amusing, but by their very redundancy they expose the accomplice nature of language to authority. The theatrical example par excellence of such verbal strategies is the inimitable Cantinflas. (1983:46)

As Ybarra-Frausto points out, the *pelada/o* figure Cantinflas and other comics appropriated the subversive verbal strategies commonly found among the marginalized popular sectors or subcultures. Cantinflas's verbal acrobatics were based on various oral performance genres of the streets, ranging from the colorful vernacular to the *albur*, *choteo* (mockery), *cábula*, *chiste* (joke), *doble sentido* (double entendre), deliberate misunderstanding, eloquent use of profanity, and so on. These verbal combat forms characteristically played a major role within the comic sketch or political sketch. *Pelado* figures such as Cantinflas appropriated such genres from the popular art of speaking, radicalized them, and used them to the total exclusion of what could be called "normal" speech—whereby "normal" or "proper" speech constitutes norms created and upheld by upper-middle-class institutions. Taken as a group, these speech genres of the street are the basis for the cheeky spirit of *borlote* or *relajo*, so essential within the *carpa* and the Teatro Campesino.

The social significance of language manipulations rests in part in their taking on a whole system of logic imposed by upper-class authority. Michel de Certeau groups "the popular art of speaking" (1984:24) among that "mobile infinity of tactics" (1984:41) by which the weak go against the imposed structures of the established order or social system—be they economic, political, or linguistic. When Cantinflas became the champion of non-sense it was in the context of a class society in which the dominant caste sought to impose its definition of sense on the entire populace. In commenting on Cantinflas, Monsiváis describes the essential role of such non-sense among those living in conditions of oppression:

> En el rompe y rasga verbal de la barriada, el *Nonsense* dispone de un significado contundente: uno dice *nada* para comunicar *algo*, uno enreda vocablos para desentrañar movimientos, uno confunde gestos con tal de expresar virtudes. [In the verbal wear-and-tear of the barrio, Non-sense has a strong meaning: one says nothing to communicate something, one entangles words in order to lay bare movements, one confuses gestures so as to express virtues.] (1988:88)

Given the impossibility of discarding the received language (or the established order altogether), the humorous juggling and inversion of dominant grammatical linguistic practices at once assimilate and subvert the "proper" language of officialdom by deploying it against itself. De Certeau describes this popular everyday process of subverting imposed systems, what he calls "playing and foiling the other's game," a process rendered in heightened or exaggerated form within the *carpa*:

> More generally, *a way of using* imposed systems constitutes the resistance to the historical law of a state of affairs and its dogmatic legitimations. A practice of the order constructed by others redistributes its space; it creates at least a certain play in that order, a space for maneuvers of unequal forces and for utopian points of reference. That is where the opacity of a "popular" culture could be said to manifest itself—a dark rock that resists all assimilation. What is there called "wisdom" . . . may be defined as a stratagem . . . and as "trickery.". . . Innumerable ways of playing and foiling the other's game . . . that is, the space instituted by others, characterize the subtle, stubborn, resistant activity of groups which, since they lack their own space, have to get

along in a network of already established forces and representations. People have to make do with what they have. In these combatants' stratagems, there is a certain art of placing one's blows, a pleasure in getting around the rules of a constraining space. (1984:18)

The *carpa* repertory of verbal forms of combat found its way into the Teatro Campesino. These forms were employed within the *actos* in the course of any dialogue; or they flourished at times between *actos*. *Albureos*, for example, could even supplant an *acto*. Olivia Chumacero recalled one such occasion when the train of thought for the *acto* was lost and performers slipped into an *albur* session, which continued until the train of thought returned:

y luego nos quedamos tres días, tres días enteros—de día y de noche—tres días enteros trabajando en la obra [*La calavera de Tiburcio Vásquez*] para terminarla para la fecha de presentar. . . . Entonces al terminar el tercer día, pues ya ibanos a presentar ese día, . . . It wasn't in great shape, but we had finished. . . . then we went and did the show. You know las locuras about doing shows when you do something like this. Everything had changed so much that we had to put a piece of paper so we'd know who was going to go on next, verdad? Entonces estabanos todos fatigued to the bone, right? . . . And we were in the middle of the show. Luis was backstage giving us lines and giving us cues; era una locura because we had put the piece together and then changed things at the last minute. Even though it was written down as an outline. We didn't have scripts. We never used to have written scripts. . . . All of a sudden, nadie se acordaba que seguía. Y estabanos blank. We all blanked. [and then we spent three days, three entire days—day and night—three full days working on the play (*La calavera de Tiburcio Vásquez*) so that we could finish it by the date of the performance. . . . Then at the end of the third day, well we were gonna perform that day. . . . It wasn't in great shape, but we had finished . . . then we went and did the show. You know the madness about doing shows when you do something like this. Everything had changed so much that we had to put a piece of paper so we'd know who was going to go on next, right? Then we were all fatigued to the bone, right? . . . All of a sudden, nobody remembered what was next. And we went blank. . . .]

The audience probably didn't notice because we continued in the same style. The style allowed for us to blank and improvise. So that's why he had us go out and just do what we wanted. . . . So then Luis just pushed Negro and me out on the stage. . . . He and I used to do *albureos*. . . . Un conversational back and forth. We were using the Cantinflas style, so we got out and did this number. . . . I went out, and nobody knew I was a girl. So we were dressed like Cantinflas characters. We had all seen a lot of Cantinflas movies. . . . Anyway we went out there and did what is sometimes called "the stick" in the style of Cantinflas and Felipe Cantú. After we did it, of course we never remembered what it was we did, but we had the audience roaring. After it was over, one person from the audience who knew us came to us and asked "Were you guys high or something?" "You guys went up there and did your act and something happened." There were a lot of middle-aged Mexicanos at that performance, people who understood our language. It was mostly all in Spanish porque Negro no hablaba inglés. [because Negro didn't speak English.] I would do a little kick-back in English but it was mostly en español. We did this whole number where I fell down, all improvised. Probably we somehow remembered one of those numbers that Cantinflas did, and it just came to us. We did the whole thing without really thinking. (Interview, 1/19/1983)

The art of linguistic manipulation practiced within the *carpa* and the Teatro Campesino cannot be understood independently from the physical language of the body, which conjoined with words to create meaning. Olivia Chumacero points to how the exchange of *albures* centered on the physical act of falling ("We did this whole number where I fell down"). The Teatro's full-body, wild, burlesque, and heavily mimetic acting style provided the very foundation for verbal acrobatics. Body language and movement were as articulate as the storehouse of language manipulations deployed in any given performance. This interdependency of verbal meaning and physicality, not characteristically shared by the dramatic literature of print culture, was a hallmark of *carpa* performance as well. Carlos Monsiváis has commented on the interplay of "verbal incoherence and bodily coherence" exemplified by Cantinflas:

A Cantinflas no lo apuntalan sus guionistas sino su don para improvisar las cosas que no se le ocurren. A la falta de recursos, Cantinflas le opone la feliz combinación de incoherencia verbal y coherencia corporal. El libera a la palabra de sus ataduras lógicas, y ejemplifica la alianza precisa de frases que nada significan (ni pueden signifcar) con desplazamientos musculares que rectifican lo dicho por nadie. La lógica noquea al silogismo, la acumulación verbal es el arreglo (la simbiosis) entre un cuerpo en tensión boxística y un habla en busca de las tensiones que aclaren el sentido. [Cantinflas isn't prompted by scriptwriters, but by his talent for improvising what does *not* occur to him. Cantinflas compensates for that lack of resources through the

Fin del mundo (1977) stage set designed by Robert
Morales. Courtesy of Olivia Chumacero Archive.

happy combination of verbal incoherence and bodily coherence. He liberates
the word from its logical bonds and exemplifies the precise alliance of
phrases that don't signify anything (nor can they signify) with muscular
contortions that correct what wasn't said by anybody. Logic knocks out
syllogisms, verbal accumulation is the working arrangement between a body
flexed like a boxer's and a way of talking which searches for tensions that
yield meaning.] (1988:87–88)

The improvisational physicality of carpa and Teatro Campesino performances was, so to speak, enhanced by numerous verbal conventions. Yet
taken by themselves the words were "incoherent." For this very reason, much
of the performance material created within the oral performance tradition
of the carpa and the Teatro Campesino resisted the disembodied medium of
print and publication. Teatro Campesino ensemble member Diane Rodríguez
recalled: "When you take something like Fin del mundo and script it, it doesn't
make sense. Because the piece that we performed in 1980 was a visual piece,
and to explain that in a script and to have another theater company do it,
well they just couldn't" (interview, 12/28/1983). Luis Valdez (1984d) similarly affirmed the primacy of action and visual images over words and spoke
to the impossibility of "reading" most Teatro Campesino plays: "The plays
[of El Teatro Campesino] are easier to see, and I think more appreciated than
if they're just read. You know what I mean? I've never been particularly fond
of theater as literature. . . . So it's a little difficult to take something like 'Fin
del mundo,' you know, and just sell it as a script to people. They won't know
what it is."

The fact that comic figures grew out of community oral performance
contexts—that is, audiences comprising men, women, and children—no

doubt also had an impact on the *carpa* and Teatro Campesino performance aesthetic: all figures and their movement had to be immediately recognizable and allow for *visual* apprehension, thereby communicating and successfully competing for attention in the presence of families *with children*. As such the *pelada/o* figures—like all others—were caricatures. This contrasts markedly with performance practices in so-called legitimate theater, which bars children and any other human expression considered disturbing or disruptive. Comedic figures were themselves a disruption par excellence of the established order of authority, hierarchy, and imposed social norms. A closeness to audiences and extreme sensitivity to audience needs and audience response were fundamental and informed the *carpa* in essential ways.

Improvisational fluidity included the audience, whose members could give cues and alter the course of events. Direct audience intervention was the rule, not the exception. It is in this spirit that Luis Valdez (1971b:1) spoke to the nature of audience participation in Teatro Campesino performance: "Audience participation is no cute production trick with us; it is a pre-established, pre-assumed privilege. Que le suenen la campanita!" [Hey, sound the gong].

The tradition of intense audience involvement is characteristic of the Mexican popular performance mode. Performances are considered community events in which active communal involvement is the norm. This tradition can hardly surprise us given the fact that the forms, figures, and genres performed were communally validated and always subject to community approval or disapproval.

In the days before the Teatro Campesino, community involvement often took extremely physical forms ranging from conversational exchange (or risqué *albures*) between audience and actors, to the throwing of objects ranging from flowers to hats and bottles. In the nineteenth century, in fact, "audience participation" came to be regarded as a second spectacle running parallel to the chief spectacle. Actively participating audience groups came to be known as *cócoras* and their liveliness often succeeded in supplanting the stage attraction. One eyewitness of the 1860s tells us of the participation of *cócoras* at a picaresque puppet theater performance: "Their lively remarks, witty puns and suggestive cat-calls provoked improvised responses from the puppets . . . their off-the-cuff interjections and smart remarks . . . developed into a clearly defined social practice."[17] This social practice of intense audience participation within the working-class world of performance remained a constant into the twentieth century. Miguel Covarrubias (1938:593) tells us of *carpa* audiences of the 1930s: "The audience is unruly and informal and takes an even more direct participation in the performance than in the popu-

Among the performance elements which the Teatro Campesino drew from Mexican tradition were the títeres [hand puppets] shown here in La conquista de México. *Copyright 1978 George Ballis/Take Stock.*

lar theatres, exchanging wisecracks and calembours with the actors who wave nonchalantly at their acquaintances in the house and ask them for cigarettes. The public makes loud demands upon the actors and often hisses a bad singer off the stage."

The great comedian Cantinflas reflected on the very physical audience displays of approval or disapproval when he performed in the *carpas*:

> En la carpa, si uno gustaba se lo hacían saber de inmediato dando golpes en las bancas de madera o aplaudiendo. Y si no estaban con uno lo demonstraban a punta de chiflidos o, cuando llegan a la violencia, arrojando a la cabeza de uno —con gran puntería—botellas vacías de cerveza. [In the *carpa*, if the audience was pleased they would let you know immediately by banging on the wooden benches or clapping. And if they didn't like you they would show it by whistling or, when they became violent, they threw empty beer bottles—with remarkable aim—at your head.] (Monsiváis 1988:80)

The Teatro Campesino also worked off and with audience response. Spectacle and audiences were involved in performances together. Yet the nature of that involvement varied greatly depending on the constitution of the audience. Olivia Chumacero recalls:

In performances for raza (Mexicans), such as in community centers or labor
camps, the audiences had no qualms about expressing their emotions,
thoughts or opinions out loud. We had cat-calls, piropos, gritos, and running
commentaries. Negative characters would often be hissed or have profanities
yelled at them. You didn't ignore what people called out. You acknowledge it;
you pick it up and—if needed—threw it back. The audiences in labor camps
in particular no dejaban pasar nada [don't let anything pass].
(Interview, 10/17/1990)

Non-working-class audiences or European audiences were a different matter. Chumacero continues: "If the audience was upper-middle-class or Anglo,
they were far more restrained and quiet." Among the working-class Mexican audiences, by contrast, every performance was a tribunal where actions
were intensely examined and publicly judged.

The counterpoint, or freeplay, of verbal acrobatic genres, audience participation, and intense physical expression in the *carpa* and the Teatro was
enhanced by the free mixture or juxtaposition of various oral performance
genres in a myriad of styles. These could include various dance forms, the
use of marionettes (*títeres*), live musical performance in a range of styles,
prerecorded music, slapstick, agitprop, joking, chanting, acrobatics, and the
like. Although the aggressively hilarious sketch was the centerpiece or main-
stay of the *carpas*, they could also incorporate individually authored dramatic
pieces or a histrionic (and beloved) traditional recitation by a *declamador* (oral
poet). True to the spirit of improvisation—an art that flourishes in conditions of necessity—both the *carpa* and the Teatro Campesino exercised great
freedom in mixing styles (agitprop, show biz, the folkloric, etc.), performance genres, musical forms, or anything else. The contrastive eclecticism
of the Rasquachi Aesthetic in no way respected the classical illusions of uni-
formity and consistency of establishment middle-class theater. Instead it applied all means and elements at its disposal to convey the desired meanings
and effects.

The *carpa's* origins in the circus are evident in the multiplicity and variety
of acts it characteristically included: something for everybody. Monsiváis
(1988:82) describes the heterogeneous mixture of performance elements
available for ten cents: "Por diez centavos, una tanda de cuatro números: can-
tos y bailes, chistes, marionetas, ventrílocuos, cómicos. . . . A la entrada, al
lado de la cortina de franela, un gritón: 'Esta y la otra, por un solo boleto!'"
[For ten cents, a set of four numbers: songs and dances, jokes, puppets, ven-
triloquists, comedians. . . . At the entrance, to the side of the flannel curtain,
a barker: "This and that, for just one ticket!"]. Another eyewitness, Pedro

Granados, similarly describes the host of acts featured in the *carpa*, whose central axis, however, was the clown or *pelada/o*:

> En ellas hacen pantomimas, bailables, canciones, saltos, maromas, pero ante todo el "payaso", que siempre fue y ha sido el personaje central del espectáculo. . . . Al frente de las carpas, antes de comenzar la función, se ponían los músicos. Trompetas y timbales muy estridentes para llamar la atención del público y tres o cuatro gritones anunciaban. [Inside they do pantomimes, dances, songs, acrobatics, somersaults, but most important is the "clown," who always was and has been the central character of the spectacle. . . . The musicians would congregate in front of the *carpas* before the program started. Very loud trumpets and kettle-drums to grab the public's attention; and three or four barkers announced the performance.] (1984:53, 55)

The merger and collision of disparate performance elements within the Rasquachi Aesthetic of the *carpa* and the Teatro reflect the working-class scramble to make do, to survive by drawing on all of one's resources. Disparate performance elements are routinely mixed and matched depending on momentary needs. Tomás Ybarra-Frausto incisively describes multiple manifestations of the Chicana/o sensibility of *Rasquachismo*:

> Rasquachismo is brash and hybrid, sending shudders through the ranks of the elite, who seek solace in less exuberant, more muted and purer traditions. In an environment always on the edge of coming apart (the car, the job, the toilet), things are held together with spit, grit, and movidas. Movidas are the coping strategies you use to gain time, to make options, to retain hope. Rasquachismo is a compendium of all the movidas deployed in immediate, day-to-day living. Resilience and resourcefulness spring from making do with what is at hand (hacir rendir las cosas). This use of available resources engenders hybridization, juxtaposition, and integration. (1991a: 156, also in 1991b)

Monsiváis describes the momentary necessity at work within the survivalist freewheeling performance logic of the *carpa* (and equally applicable to El Teatro Campesino):

> Cada noche, en feroz competencia con charros cantores y títeres y tenores que no salen al escenario porque siguen borrachos, los movimientos ordenan el caos de los vocablos, y el cantinflismo es el doble idioma de lo que se quiere expresar y de lo qe no se tiene ganas de pensar. . . .
> Un cuerpo acelerado traduce temas urgentes: lo caro que está todo en el

mercado, la chusquería involuntaria de gringos y gachupines, las bribonerías de la política, la incomprensión del acusado ante el juez, la estafa que acecha en todo diálogo entre desconocidos. Con trazos coreográficos, el cuerpo rescata sustantivo y adjetivos en pleno naufragio. [Each night, in fierce competition with singing charros and puppets and tenors who don't come on stage because they're still drunk, movements bring order to the chaos of words, and "cantinflismo" is the double language consisting of what they're trying to express and what they don't want to think. . . .

A fast-paced body translates into urgent topics: how expensive everything is at the market, the involuntary slapstick of gringos (Anglos) and *gachupines* (Spaniards), the roguishness of politics, the bafflement of the accused before the judge, the element of potential betrayal that lurks in all dialogue among strangers. With choreographed steps, the body rescues nouns and adjectives from utter shipwreck.] (1988:87)

Ybarra-Frausto (1984:52–53) elaborates on another related key element of the Rasquachi Aesthetic, its spirit of defiance (discussed earlier as the spirit of *relajo*) rooted in the working-class perspective: "The 'funky' milieu of the *carpa* engendered its pervasive aesthetic, *rascuachismo*, a way of confronting the world from the perspective of the downtrodden, the rebel, the outsider. To be *rascuachi* is to possess an ebullient spirit of irreverence and insurgency, a carnivalesque topsy-turvy vision where authority and decorum serve as targets for subversion."

The Teatro Campesino continued in the performance tradition of the *carpa*, although it did to some extent economize by excluding the more overtly circuslike numbers. Prime among the generic and stylistic elements it inherited were mime, music, dance, song, dancelike movement and some acrobatic motion, *títeres* (marionettes), but, above all, the primacy of a stinging humor and the central underdog comic figure. These combined in the Chicana/o *acto* of the 1960s and the 1970s—a direct descendant of the comic sketch and political sketch genres of the *carpa*. As in the *carpa*, the Teatro Campesino featured the preshow *convite*, or group of musicians who played to attract audiences. That was among the duties of the Teatro Campesino's Banda Calavera. Musical performance was a featured part of *carpa* and Teatro Campesino performances. The *carpas* of the turn of the century and into the 1950s, in fact, toured with various musical performers in order to attract audiences. Many of the best-known Chicano musicians began their careers as performers in the *carpas*. Such is the case, for example, with Lydia Mendoza, Chelo Silva, and Valerio Longoria. Within the Teatro Campesino music was a prime element, especially in the pieces created after 1970. The *corrido*—a key genre from the oral tradition—formed the backbone for pieces such as *La gran carpa de la familia Rasquachi*, *Fin del mundo*, or *Corridos*.

The *carpa* and the Teatro Campesino must be understood as *performance conglomerates* that incorporated heterogeneous performance acts from the repository of Mexican popular culture: joke-telling, *corridos* and other musical forms, *declamadores*, comic sketches, marionettes, and so on. The Rasquachi Aesthetic, epitomized by the *carpa* and the Teatro Campesino, fused, severed, combined, invented, reinvented, and refurbished whatever was necessary to meet the changing entertainment needs of the Mexican popular masses. El Teatro Campesino drew most heavily from the comic sketch, musical performance—in particular the *corrido*—and the mythological/spiritual dimension. Although theater critics have constructed the Teatro Campesino's trajectory as a linear development from *actos* to *mitos* to corridos, in fact, these were never separate performance forms. Rather, they were usually fused within performances. Early *actos* usually were preceded or followed by the singing of *rancheras* or *corridos*—corridos being one of the oldest song genres from the Mexican oral tradition. Later, however, the *corrido* was dramatized, yet interspersed throughout with the traditional acting style of the *actos*. At given moments, mythical and spiritual elements could also be incorporated. Depending on the effect sought, one or more of these elements could become the prime focus, but never were they neatly separated, nor did they evolve in linear fashion.

With regard to the Teatro's reliance on Mexican popular culture, it should be noted that the dramatization of the *corrido* genre has a long tradition in Mexico. Theater historians tell us of the popularity of *corrido* dramatizations in Mexico City after the Mexican Revolution of 1910 and continuing into the late 1950s, perhaps as an expression of a new nationalism. These productions were in some cases elaborate enough that artists such as the young Diego Rivera participated in their scenic design and personally painted entire backdrops.

Although the *carpas* of various eras and the Teatro Campesino share a basic reliance on Mexican forms of popular expression and a freewheeling juxtaposition and fusion of forms, they also display a divergence corresponding to the needs of their time. Because each was *of its time*, the *carpa* and the Teatro Campesino each reveals its own particular historicity and differences with regard to the appropriation and mixture of elements from Mexican popular culture. In spite of overarching similarities and a kindred performance spirit and idiom, a certain divergence is also palpable, audible, visible. Far from being museumlike or static, each is imbedded in a different matrix of historical conditions. In spite of their commonality as expressive forms of the

oppressed, in spite of their shared manifestations drawn from the oral tradition of the people, in spite of their rootedness in the aggressive spirit of *relajo*
and *picardía*, the Teatro and the *carpas* from different eras were also nurtured
and shaped by the particulars of the historical context in which each
emerged. For example, the turn-of-the-century *carpa* in Mexico flourished
as a result of the Mexican Revolution, while the Teatro Campesino emerged
as part of the Chicano movement and the United Farm Workers Union
struggle. These different historical realities are inscribed in their respective
performance practices, just as each historical period is to some extent constituted by particular performance practices. Mexican *carpistas* (*carpa* performers) consistently attribute the *carpa*'s vitality in the twentieth century to the
turmoil of the Mexican Revolution in which it participated.[18] Such is the
view, for example, of Luis Ortega, who witnessed the resurgence of the *carpa*
in the 1920s. He describes how the *carpa* emerged and existed very much
outside the dominant sector's institutionalized proscenium theater. Ortega's
testimony also speaks to the importance of the *carpa* in the affirmation and
consolidation of the Mexican working class's self-identity:

> Doctos investigadores de nuestro acontecer socioeconómico derivan a
> LA CARPA del Mester de Juglaría medieval, otros, encuentran sus raíces en
> los Misterios que importaron los frailes hispanos misioneros. Nosotros
> aceptamos su autorizada opinión, pero preferimos creer que las raíces de
> LA CARPA están en la Revolución Mexicana.
>
> En apoyo a esta aseveración, queremos recordar al lector que hacia
> principios de este siglo el pueblo mexicano, sobre todo el provinciano, no
> tenía espectáculo propio. El teatro estaba dedicado a las clases sociales
> privilegiadas y la Opera, la Opereta, la Zarzuela, el Melodrama y la Comedia
> eran géneros sin arraigo popular, pues se presentaban en idiomas ajenos o
> planteaban problemas que nada tenían que ver con el sentir y el vivir
> populares.
>
> Y vino la Revolución. Los teatros cerraron sus puertas, los cines aún no
> existían y los circos nómadas perdieron a sus animales porque no tenían para
> darles de comer y tuvieron que ser utilizados como alimento.
>
> Pero "no sólo de pan vive el hombre", y el pueblo creó su espectáculo.
> [Wise researchers of our socioeconomic reality derive the *carpa* from the
> medieval minstrel verse; others find its roots in the Mysteries imported by the
> Hispanic missionary monks. We accept their authoritative opinion, but prefer
> to think that the beginnings of the *carpa* are in the Mexican Revolution.
>
> In support of this assertion, we would like to remind the reader that at the
> turn of this century the Mexican people, especially the rural population,

didn't have their own form of entertainment. The theater was dedicated to the privileged social classes; and the opera, operetta, zarzuela, melodrama, and comedy were genres that didn't have popular roots since they were performed in foreign languages, or dealt with problems that had nothing to do with the feelings and lives of the common people.

And then the Revolution came. The theaters closed their doors, the cinema didn't yet exist, and nomadic circuses lost their animals because they couldn't afford to feed them and in fact had to use them for food.

But "man doesn't live by bread alone," and the people created their own kind of spectacle.] (1984:14–15)

The widespread resurgence of *carpa* activity in Mexico City on the heels of the Mexican Revolution is also documented in a 1930s testimony by Miguel Covarrubias:

> Throughout critical years of intermittent revolutions and between military coups d'etat a new theatre has been making its appearance, born of the new nationalistic "proletarian" consciousness that grew out of the Revolution. However crude, improvised and disreputable, this theatre is vibrantly alive and, for the first time, here is entertainment aimed at the common people, speaking their language and reflecting their own peculiar brand of humor. Never before have there been actors on the Mexican stages that impersonated typical Mexican characters, sang Mexican songs, and spoke, not the studied Castilian of the stage, but the colorful slang of the lower classes.
>
> The history of the popular theatre runs parallel to, and has the turbulent and lurid characteristics of the military and political upheavals that shook the nation. Musical shows dealing with political satire were already ridiculing the new revolutionary government of Madero in 1911. (1938:587)

Popular performance has always been a constant and vital part of the social formation. In the *carpas*, as with El Teatro Campesino, realities of dominance and subordination have always been enacted from a working-class perspective. The humorous sketch has always been the site of critical inquiry into the nature of social relations. Covarrubias illustrates how for every corrupt politician and every period of popular distress and agitation a great comic rose to the occasion and achieved prominence, riding the crest of popular opinion and discontent. In his 1938 article (p. 595) he pairs leading politicians and their chief popular rivals within the *carpa*: "The development of the brand of humor of Cantinflas is a manifestation of the present Leftist labor politics as it was with the advent of Beristain in the bourgeois nationalistic time of Carranza, or with Roberto Soto in the Obregón-Calles period with the shady labor leadership of Morones. Thus a parallel seems evident between Carranza-Beristain, Soto-Morones, and today Cantinflas-Lombardo Toledano, the Mexican John L. Lewis."

Monsiváis, like the Mexican critic Salvador Novo, sees a correlation between the rise of Cantinflas, of Cantinflas's particular brand of humor, and the rise of political demogogy in Mexico. Monsiváis (1988:86) states: "la asociación con la política (con la demagogia) es impulso definitivo en el éxito de Cantinflas" [the association with politics (with demagogy) is a definite impulse in Cantinflas's success]. Salvador Novo describes this in greater detail:

> Amanecía una época verbalista, confusa, oratoria, prometedora sin compromiso, que los periódicos sesudos llamarían demagógica. La antena sensible que recogió la nueva vibración, que dio en el clavo del humorismo en que la nueva época descargara sus represiones, se llamaría Cantinflas, . . . Si la dislogia y la dislalia en que por la boca de Cantinflas disparata nuestra época, ha alcanzado éxitos y consagración, es porque ocurre y da la casualidad de que también fuera de México los hombres respiran desde hace algunos años el clima asfixiante de la verborrea, el confusionismo, las promesas sin compromiso, la oratoria, la palabrería ininteligible, malabarística y vana. . . . En condensarlo (a los líderes): en entregar a la saludable carcajada del pueblo la esencia demagógica de su vacuo confusionismo, estriba el mérito y se asegura la gloria de este hijo cazurro de la ciudad ladina y burlona de México, que es Cantinflas. [It was the dawn of a verbalistic era, confused, oratorical, promises without commitment, an era that sharp newspapers would refer to as demagogic. The sensitive antenna that picked up the new vibration, the person who hit upon the humor with which the new era could unload its repressions, was called Cantinflas, . . . If the dislogic—the nonsense of our epoch spoken by Cantinflas—has achieved success and consecration, it is because it just so happens that, for some years now, people outside of Mexico as well have been breathing the asphyxiating climate of verbiage, confusion, promises without commitment, oratory, that unintelligible wordiness, tricky and empty. . . . By condensing it (the talk of politicians): by delivering the demagogical essence of political leaders, empty mumbo-jumbo to the healthy laughter of the people, Cantinflas attains merit and glory—Cantinflas, the laconic son of the glib and mocking city of Mexico.] (Salvador Novo in Nueva grandeza mexicana [1948], quoted by Monsiváis [1988:86])

In summary, the carpas in Mexico are positioned within the postrevolutionary thrust toward nationalist consolidation and regionalist celebration; they became a popular voice that responded to the political demagogy of the 1930s and the 1940s; they played out the tensions of the growing schism between urbanization and rural impoverishment. In the southwestern United States the itinerant *carpas* from the turn of the century until after World War II grappled with basic issues of economic survival and discrimination, of acculturation and other questions of identity. Ybarra-Frausto describes the many important sociocultural functions of the U.S. *carpas* of the 1930s and the 1940s:

> Essentially a form of entertainment for the masses, *carpas* helped to define and sustain ethnic and class consciousness. Their robust ribaldry and rebellious instincts were wedges of resistance against conformity and prevailing norms of middle-class decency within Chicano communities. *Carpas* motivated and helped establish a new sense of self-identity for the Mexican American in the Southwest by a) valorization and vitalization of Chicano vernacular, especially incipient forms of code-switching; b) elaboration of a critical mode exemplified in the anti-establishment stance of the pelado; c) maintenance of oral tradition and humor in its various modalities as a cultural weapon applied symbolically to annihilate and vanquish oppressors; d) elaboration of a down-to-earth, direct aesthetic deeply imbedded in social tradition. (1984:53)

The Teatro Campesino, on the other hand, had a somewhat different historical trajectory. Born of the United Farm Workers struggle of the 1960s and nurtured by the Chicano movement of the 1970s, the Teatro Campesino displayed the militancy of its time and place. As such the Teatro enacted the struggles of Chicanas/os within the larger Euro-American and global classist and racist society; equally important, it became a spiritual, cultural, and ideological standard-bearer of the Chicano movement, offering an alternative interpretive system pertaining to Chicana/o identity and social struggle. In response to the confrontation with Euro-American colonization, for example, El Teatro Campesino responded with strong reliance on the traditional performance strategies of the Mexican *carpa* and the culture of orality.

Although much of the Mexican verbal humor and artistic mimicry that Cantinflas used—and that even predated him—carried over into El Teatro Campesino, the Teatro also developed a verbal humor of its time and place. While continuing in the rough, elemental, bawdy, and satirical tradition of the *carpa*, elements such as bilingualism, bilingual humor, or performance entirely in English, or in *pachuco caló* (the vernacular speech of working-class youth), as well as the Teatro Campesino's thematics situate the Teatro in a different era and place than the *carpa*.

Historical necessity in time motivated the adoption or evolution of yet other characteristics within the Teatro's Rasquachi Aesthetic. Most notably, the Chicano Movement's strong thrust to restore and reclaim the roots of Chicana/o identity in the struggle against cultural colonialism opened up new performance vistas. The widespread consciousness of and pride in the native ancestral heritage of Chicanas/os in the 1970s, for example, motivated El Teatro Campesino to introduce elements or components from Mexican oral culture suited to this historical need (structurally comparable to the earlier *carpas'* incorporation of folkloric scenes in the interest of Mexican nationhood). The newly infused elements from the repository of oral culture included *danza indígena* (indigenous ritual dance) as well as reliance on elements from indigenous mythology and spirituality. In time, the Teatro expanded the Rasquachi Aesthetic of the *carpa* into what came to be known as the Theater of the Sphere (treated in chap. 2).

Like all other *carpa* acts before it, the Theater of the Sphere was quintessentially a performance conglomerate. It facilitated the coming together of, for example, the *pelado* figure Jesús Pelado Rasquachi with the feathered serpent Quetzalcoatl and the earth mother Guadalupe (in *La gran carpa de la familia Rasquachi*). The emergent performance conglomerate named Theater of the Sphere was a Chicana/o holistic performance orientation based in Native American philosophy and grafted onto the oral performance practices of the *carpa*. The result was a uniquely Chicana/o performance aesthetic capable of reuniting the spiritual, ritualistic performance path with the secular performance world of the *carpa*. The Teatro Campesino, faced with a different set of concrete historical tasks than was the *carpa*, transformed and amplified some of the basic elements of the Rasquachi Aesthetic of its *carpa* precursors. Yet common to both the *carpa* and the entire Chicana/o theater movement of the 1960s and the 1970s is their contestatory relationship with the established order. As constitutive parts of the social formation, both affirmed alternative meanings, values, and social practices.

The reality of existing in an alternative and contestatory relationship with the dominant powers was not without considerable hardship. Economically speaking, the performance spectacles of the *carpa* and the Teatro Campesino were for the most part frugal undertakings and not particularly lucrative. Performers survived for the most part on a shoestring. In the case of El Teatro Campesino, the ensemble lived at bare subsistence level or below during the fifteen years of its existence. Each member was paid $10 per week and at times even less. Members were provided housing paid for by meager performance income. Beyond that, ensemble members either fended for themselves—for food and all other life necessities—or, in better times, received modest stipends. The creation and survival of El Teatro Campesino depended largely on the willingness of ensemble members to sacrifice all material comforts. Olivia Chumacero recalled aspects of that material reality of production:

En todos tiempos El Teatro Campesino necesitaba dinero. Mira, cuando llegamos a San Juan Bautista primeramente nadie nos quería rentar, porque decían que éramos comunistas, verdad? Entonces vivíamos en el escenario. Allí llegamos a vivir como veinte personas al mismo tiempo. Y luego poco a poco encontramos otro espacio que era igual que el de San Juan Bautista: un *storefront*. Era un espacio grande y allí vivíamos. Poco a poco encontramos dos casas en San Juan. En cuanto a la comida pues como nadie te estaba pagando pues a cada quien le tocaba diferente mes, a ver quien iba agarrar estampillas [laughter]. Y si no era posible, entonces le caíamos a la mamá de Félix, por ejemplo, porque tenía un restaurante. O si no, íbanos a traer comida del gobierno. Esos huevos horribles, ese Spam tan feo. Por eso yo jamás comeré Spam. [At all times El Teatro Campesino was in need of money. Look, when we arrived in San Juan Bautista first of all nobody wanted to rent to us because they said we were Communists, right? So we lived on the stage. Up to twenty persons ended up living on that stage. Then little by little we found another space, which was the same as the one in San Juan Bautista. With regard to food, since nobody was paying you, each one was in charge of a different month, to see who could hustle some food stamps. (laughter) And if that was not enough we would hit on Felix's mom, for example, because she had a restaurant. If not, then we would go and round up some government food. Those horrible eggs, that ugly Spam. That's why I'll never touch Spam again.]

At other times, necessity forced Teatro Campesino members occasionally to engage in some "Robin Hood" maneuvers. One ensemble member, who prefers to remain anonymous, gave the following account:

I used to steal. That's what I did. Yo me iba a las tiendas y me echaba ratios, y me echaba cosa y media. [I would go to the stores and take radios, I'd take any number of things.] Y luego [and then] I used to sell them. I used to get bikes. Te digo, nosotros hacíamos esto y otras cosas. Entonces así podíamos seguir comiendo. Porque la intención era nomás para comer. Era todo lo que yo necesitaba para poder seguir haciendo el trabajo que quería hacer. [I tell you, we did these and other things. That's the only way we could continue eating. That's all I needed in order to keep doing the work I wanted to do.]

Until 1980 the company consistently refused any government or foundation grants in order to avoid economic dependency and outside aesthetic or political control. Survival was possible only through the collective lifestyle, which usually meant shared living quarters and shared responsibility for securing food and additional income through agricultural field labor (when not on tour), food stamps, welfare, or donations from friends and family. At times the ensemble went hungry. Politically speaking, both the *carpas* and the Teatro Campesino were forced to withstand political persecution and at times even violence from political powerholders. One of the chief reasons behind the Teatro Campesino's move from Fresno to San Juan Bautista in 1970 was the threat of violence. During one performance in Fresno they were shot at repeatedly and narrowly escaped without harm in a van. Bomb threats were not unusual. At one time in San Juan Bautista, the local John Birch Society saw to it that none of the local landlords would rent to Teatro members. The entire ensemble ended up living in a storefront room in the nearby town of Gilroy.

Carpas in Mexico similarly suffered the fate of constant supervision and censorship by government officials and politicians who sought to repress the genre's grass-roots politics and style. Censorship has been a reality of Mexican theatrical life throughout the past four centuries. Theater historian Armando de María y Campos (1939:254–255) describes how the Apollo Theater was closed down and Victoriano Huerta, president of the republic in 1913–1914, had whole groups of theatrical performers arrested on account of their vitriolic humor and "bad taste." Mexican playwright Emilio Carballido (1988:2) comments on the great critical freedom exercised by the comedic figures of the *carpa* and the constant governmental efforts at repression: "La libertad de los cómicos, su crítica irrestricta, provocaron serias represiones desde los años 40: nuestros gobiernos casi lograron asesinarlo. . . . Pero resucita" [The freedom of the comedians, their unrestricted criticism, have provoked serious repressions since the 1940s: our governments almost succeeded in killing it. . . . But it has been resurrected]. Like virtually all genres from the oral performance tradition the *carpas* have gone through repeated cycles of ebb and flow, of decline and rebirth. The Chicana/o theater movement of the 1960s through the mid-1970s was a period of rebirth.

El Teatro Campesino and Mexican
Sacroprofane Performance Genres
The Teatro Campesino's rootedness in the performance forms of Mexican popular culture extends to areas beyond the secular world of the *carpa*. From its beginnings the Teatro Campesino affirmed the need for a theater "com-

Scene from the Teatro Campesino Pastorela (1976). Left to right: Greg Cruz, Andrés Gutiérrez, Julio González. Courtesy of Rogelio Rojas Collection.

posed of actos or agit-prop but [also] a teatro of ritual, of music, of beauty and spiritual sensitivity. A teatro of legends and myths. A teatro of religious strength" (Valdez 1971b:3). From the vast repository of Mexican spiritual performance practices the Teatro drew considerable artistic inspiration. These spiritual performance practices ranged from prayer, ritual dance, and other spiritual exercises to the reenactment of traditional miracle plays. Although I to some extent make a distinction between the secular and the sacred, in the popular Mexican traditions they do not represent two mutually exclusive poles or antithetical performance realms. Rather they represent two possible points of emphasis in a unified multilayered performance spectrum. Within the organizing work of the United Farm Workers, for example, there was no separation between the political (the profane) and the sacred. At all times, the spiritual and political dimensions of struggle were united, such as through the use of religious emblems and deities (our Lady of Guadalupe) on marches, or through the celebration of masses at rallies. During the early strikes, for example, the back of César Chávez's old station wagon often served as a portable shrine replete with holy images, flowers, and picket signs. Striking workers kept vigil there twenty-four hours a day; union meetings and daily mass were celebrated at the station wagon shrine parked next to vineyards. César Chávez, at once a political and a spiritual leader, used fasting, for example, as an act of personal purification as well as a call for noncooperation with an exploitative labor system. That sacroprofane fusion marks much of the work of El Teatro Campesino as well.

In the course of the Teatro Campesino's development—particularly after 1970—the ensemble increasingly fused or incorporated elements of spiritual performance practices into the larger *carpa* Rasquachi Aesthetic (see chap. 2 on Theater of the Sphere). Other spiritually focused practices were, however, also cultivated in and of themselves, yet always with a consciousness of the larger struggle in society. A sacroprofane fusion is evident even in the more spiritually oriented genres as well, however. As will be shown, the secular spirit of *picardía* and *relajo* is never fully absent even in religious celebration.

Among the popular traditional genres adopted by El Teatro Campesino were the seasonal sacred pageants performed in Chicana/o Mexican communities for hundreds of years. Most notable among these are the performances linked to religious holidays: the *Pastorela* (Shepherds' Play) and *Las cuatro apariciones de la Virgen de Guadalupe*. The *Pastorela* enacts the story of a journey to Bethlehem by a group of shepherds who encounter an army of devils and an army of angels. *Las cuatro apariciones de la Virgen de Tepeyac* (sometimes billed as *La Virgen de Tepeyac* for publicity purposes) reenacts the story of Mexico's most revered goddess, Guadalupe-Tonantzin. Although these dramatic pieces exist in written form, they nonetheless manifest numerous traits that link them to oral tradition and to the oral performance mode: improvisation, oral transmission from generation to generation through memorization, the use of a number of generic stock characters, the existence of numerous versions throughout the Mexican republic and the southwestern United States, their rootedness in a community (not in individual authorship) and in community celebration. It is in fact highly probable that pageants such as the *Pastorela* (also known as *Los Pastores*) and *Las cuatro apariciones* were originally orally composed and memorized and only later transcribed.

In typical oral tradition style, all scripts undergo constant transformation according to local circumstance as well as over time and according to actors' whims. One observer in San Antonio, Texas, in the 1950s graphically described how, for example, *Pastorelas* migrate and coalesce, and how they undergo transformation as they pass from person to person to paper:

> At least four other Mexicans here in San Antonio treasure, as he [Doroteo Domínguez] does, a manuscript. . . . Doroteo set down crudely parts of *Los Pastores* as it was presented in the towns and country districts of San Luis Potosí, and afterward he paid a man to copy them in a book. Sacramento Grimaldo, the able First Shepherd, learned the play in a village near San Antonio, and being a man of monumental memory he committed it to paper in great detail. But his sister helped him, and her husband wrote in some of

the songs as he had heard them in communities along the Rio Grande. When this group coalesced with that of Doroteo Domínguez, the shepherds adhered to Sacramento's text, while the devils followed Doroteo's "book." Thus we have a single company using two manuscripts written down by no less than six variously literate hands!

Santos Esparza . . . inscribed the play from memory when a cousin took the family manuscript away. Old Salvador . . . copied it when he was a boy of fourteen or so from the book of his particular director in the town of Irapuato—some of it he just remembered. A priest long interested in folklore has sponsored the translating and printing of a much reduced version of this manuscript, with language purified and details transposed in the cause of logic. And he has not only organized but aided a richly costumed group of players. Esperanza Arias has abbreviated her grandfather's "book" to meet the capacity of a charming company of young girls and children. (Waugh 1955:44–45)

As is evident from this passage, the *Pastorela* and *Las cuatro apariciones* have traditionally survived as community events and not as the work of theater companies or trained actors. For at least four centuries these genres have existed as cyclical community rituals that address and transmit communal beliefs, critiques, and values. Pageants such as these are characteristically followed by shared meals of tamales, buñuelos, atole, canela, the breaking of piñatas by children, and other all-night festivities.

The Teatro Campesino first resolved to perform the *Pastorela* with hand puppets in January 1976, then with actors in December of that same year. *Las cuatro apariciones* was first performed in 1972. Both these pieces underwent a process of appropriation and adaptation into theater spectacles. A qualitative transformation occurred. Yet the Teatro's more embellished performances would have been impossible without the example and volunteer work of local community members. The very scripts that the Teatro used were those performed locally for many years. In the case of the *Pastorela* the script was provided by Longina Moreno Montoya, who directed the pageant for many years in the nearby community of Hollister. Mrs. Montoya's script, which she brought with her when she migrated from San Luis Potosí, Mexico, was adapted from litany form to dialogue form by Teatro Campesino ensemble member Olivia Chumacero and then reworked by the Teatro Campesino collective. The script for *Las cuatro apariciones* came from a combination of sources. Teatro member José Delgado found a Lady of Guadalupe litany script, while the songs and novenas came from Elodia Contreras Carrillo, the mother of Arturo Gómez. This pageant was converted from a community event to a more public spectacle. In spite of these conversions and the increased commercialization of these pageants in the 1980s, the performance substance of these miracle plays—whether community-oriented or commercially oriented—is very similar.

Notwithstanding the great variety of *Pastorelas* and *Las cuatro apariciones* that have existed over the centuries and that exist today, they all share some very basic and characteristic elements. Common to both pageants is what I call a "sacroprofane fusion," although each accomplishes this fusion in a very different way. In *Las cuatro apariciones* the fusion of sacred and profane is accomplished through the grounding of miraculous events—the four apparitions of our Lady of Guadalupe—within the social context of colonialism. The *Pastorela*'s sacroprofane fusion is of an entirely different order. As will be elaborated, it is the central presence of *relajo* within the *Pastorela* that signals both its rootedness in Mexican indigenous tradition and its contestatory relationship vis-à-vis the dominant colonial order.

In anchoring both these sacred pageants within the profane I consciously depart from existing treatments or interpretations of these genres that construct the spiritual as a realm of otherworldliness separate from social reality and struggle. As will be shown, these pageants enact the spiritual dimension of social relations of domination and subordination. Although presented in spiritual terms—an overarching reverence for the sacred forces—both pageants enact the constant process of negotiation and critical exploration of spiritual practice *within the social formation*. Neither of these pageants presents a purely abstract transcendent spirituality. Instead, the spiritual is explicitly or implicitly positioned in a network of social relations.

In *Las cuatro apariciones* the positioning is explicit. The pageant reenacts the story of the four apparitions of the Mexican goddess Tonantzin/Guadalupe to the Indian Cuautlatoczin (whose Spanish name was Juan Diego) in 1531. In her apparitions, the goddess designates Juan Diego as her emissary to the Spanish Catholic church. She requests that the Spanish churchmen build a temple in her honor.

What might, on the surface of it, appear as a simple miracle tale in fact carries the entire blueprint of colonial and postcolonial Mexican history. What is played out are the social, cultural, and historical tensions of imperialist Spanish Catholicism and the indigenous struggle for self-determination and self-legitimation. The forces of Spanish colonialism and Catholicism are symbolized by the incredulous friars or church officials whereas indigenous resistance and self-determination are symbolized by the Indians' tenacious insistence on the adoration of the Holy Mother Tonantzin/Guadalupe.

Guadalupe is the indigenous deity whose apparitions are denied by the Spanish powerholders.

But few figures from Mexican popular culture have given rise to so many divergent interpretations as our Lady of Guadalupe, generally recognized nonetheless as the highest-ranking deity in Mexico. The Catholic church, for example, after failing in its intense campaign against Guadalupe, finally appropriated and recast her as one more manifestation of the Virgin Mary. In many intellectual circles Guadalupe is erroneously viewed as an instrument invented by the Spaniards and the Catholic church to lure the indias/os into the Catholic faith. Within the Aztec oral tradition, however, a vastly different interpretation prevails.[19]

For the Indians, Guadalupe represents a manifestation of the Indian deity Tonantzin. Guadalupe (or Coatlashaupe in the original Nahuatl) is viewed as the chief indigenous instrument in the active resistance against Roman Catholicism and colonial violence. In one of her apparitions (in which she spoke in Nahuatl) Guadalupe stated that she had come in order to save the Indians from annihilation. As a reincarnation of a native deity she found immediate acceptance among the indigenous population. Her veneration became a popular cause of such momentum that it ultimately broke down the resistance of the Catholic church. The Catholic church thus became a place where worship could at least in part happen on native terms. Thus, the widespread militant native resistance to Catholicism—and mass persecution of natives refusing the church—was mitigated. For these reasons, Guadalupe has come to be regarded (within the oral tradition) as a popular symbol of resistance, hope, and survival—the chief Mexican spiritual and political symbol of the oppressed Mexican masses.

Fully aware of Guadalupe's counterhegemonic potential, the Spanish scholar and monk Bernardino Sahagún (1499–1590) referred to Guadalupe as a "Satanic invention" who "cloaks idolatry" (1982:90). Sahagún was quick to understand that Guadalupe/Tonantzin was part of a subversive native strategy to continue traditional religious practices in camouflaged form. He found Guadalupe/Tonantzin "suspicious" and commented as well on how the native population avoided visiting the Roman Catholic "churches of Our Lady" while flocking to Guadalupe/Tonantzin: "It appears to be a Satanic invention to cloak idolatry under the confusion of this name, Tonantzin. And they now come to visit this Tonantzin from very far away, as far away as before, which is also suspicious, because everywhere there are many churches of Our Lady and they do not go to them. They come from distant lands to this Tonantzin as in olden times" (p. 90).

When the Indians finally pressured the Catholic church into building Guadalupe's temple at Tepeyac, the ancient site of worship for Tonantzin Xochipilli, the cornerstone was laid for the Indianization of the Mexican Catholic church. The Teatro Campesino enacted this interpretation of Guadalupe derived from the Aztec oral tradition. That interpretation was transmitted to the Teatro from the teachings of contemporary Aztec elders, particularly from the teachings of Andrés Segura.

Regardless of which interpretation is brought to bear on the script, however, a Mexican historical blueprint constitutes the play's basic structure: the conflictive interplay of antagonistic class forces (Indians and colonizers), their dispute over Guadalupe, and the Catholic church's unwilling but inevitable acceptance of the Indian deity.

In the Aztec oral tradition Guadalupe's entry into Catholicism is viewed as a great historical triumph for the indigenous population of the Americas. By contrast, most scholarly sources—in neocolonial fashion—view her incorporation as a tool of conversion (or defeat) of the indigenous population. Whatever the interpretation, the pageant of *Las cuatro apariciones* constitutes a sacroprofane fusion. It enacts the negotiation of spirituality within social relations of subordination and domination. A direct reflection of that sacroprofane fusion is the fact that the Teatro Campesino ensemble undertook this performance on a yearly basis as both a deeply devotional offering and a political statement.

In spite of heavy criticism from Marxist and other critics, the Teatro Campesino ensemble insisted on the inseparability of the spiritual and the political spheres. Not surprisingly, moments of miraculous intervention or illumination were not confined to the spiritual pageants but found a place in the more straightforwardly political performances of the Teatro Campesino as well. Such was the case in one version of *La gran carpa de la familia Rasquachi*, for example, when the main character, Jesús Pelado Rasquachi, encounters our Lady of Guadalupe at the peak of his agony within a system of social injustice. In *Carpa cantinflesca*, the intercession of Quetzalcoatl similarly precipitates a character's turnaround and sociocultural self-recognition.

The integration of the miraculous into the daily life struggle of characters was easily accepted and understood by popular audiences. Most theater critics, however, reacted disapprovingly and regarded the use of the miraculous as romantic and divorced from reality. Although many scholars are prone to assign stories of miracles to the realm of an abstract faith, to fantasy or make-believe, Michel de Certeau, the theorist of everyday life, offers a view of the miraculous that is more differentiated than that of most theater critics. Although not in reference to El Teatro Campesino, he highlights the op-

positional and counterhegemonic nature of the American indigenous tradition of popular miraculous narrative (to be distinguished from that of the
church). He conceptualizes miracles as an affirmation of a utopian space full
of possibilities, as a counterdiscourse and countermemory in the life of the
oppressed. This miraculous utopian space is a form of protest that coexists
with and stands in utopian contrast to "an experience deprived of illusions"
and to the official "analysis of socioeconomic relationships." De Certeau
elaborates:

> the religious scene . . . in the mode of supernatural events, . . . by means of
> celestial landmarks, creates a place for this protest. The unacceptability of an
> order which is nevertheless established, was articulated, appropriately
> enough, as a miracle. There, in a language necessarily foreign to the analysis
> of socioeconomic relationships, the hope could be *maintained* that the
> vanquished of history—the body on which the victories of the rich or their
> allies are continually inscribed—might, in the "person" of the humiliated
> "saint" . . . rise again. . . .
>
> Without diminishing in any way what one sees every day, the stories of
> miracles respond to it "from aside" with irrelevance and impertinence in a
> different discourse, . . .
>
> In spite of everything, they provide the possible with a site that is
> impregnable, because it is a nowhere, a utopia. They create another space,
> which coexists with that of an experience deprived of illusions. . . .
>
> The rural "believers" thus subvert the fatality of the established order. And
> they do it by using a frame of reference which also proceeds from an external
> power (the religion imposed by Christian missions). They re-employ a system
> that, far from being their own, has been constructed and spread by others,
> and they mark this re-employment by "superstitions," excrescences of this
> belief in miracles. (1984:16–17)

If any deity of the Americas has served to "subvert the fatality of the established order" it is certainly the miraculous Indian goddess Guadalupe.
Through her, the native peoples were able to turn the genocidal tide of religious persecution.

Although the Teatro Campesino performance of Las cuatro apariciones has
undergone many transformations since the initial performance in 1972, in
all its versions it underscores the agency of Cuautlatoczin (Juan Diego) and
Guadalupe in the Indianization of the Catholic church in Mexico. Guadalupe
is adored in her manifestation as nurturing and protective Earth Mother and
in her political role of protector of the native Mexican population. It should
not be overlooked that all Mexican colonial and postcolonial liberational

struggles were fought in the name of our Lady of Guadalupe. The United Farm Workers Union, with which the Teatro Campesino was affiliated for years, also marches behind the Guadalupe banner.

The *Pastorela*, like *Las cuatro apariciones*, is performed during the Christmas season in hundreds of Mexicano communities across the Southwest and Mexico. The Teatro Campesino ensemble typically performed one of these pageants yearly. On the surface of it the *Pastorela* incorporates more Christian icons than *Las cuatro apariciones*: there is an army of devils headed by Lucifer and commanded by Satanás (Satan); an army of angels headed by San Miguel; and a group of shepherds for whom the performance piece is named. In describing the play most scholars center it around the shepherds' journey to the Christ Child in Bethlehem, a reference to the European tradition of liturgical plays. Almost one hundred years of *Pastorela* research has positioned the *Pastorela* within the genealogy of European (Spanish) medieval culture: the *Pastorela* is typically constructed as a dramatic biblical story taught to Indians by proselytizing Spanish Catholic friars in the sixteenth century (see Rael 1965; Cantú 1982; María y Campos 1985). Although this is not the place for a sustained evaluation of *Pastorela* research, the bulk of such research minimizes the human agency of Mexico's and the southwestern United States' Indian communities. In what is usually an unspoken ideology of race relations, researchers construct Indian communities as passive receptacles of European culture. The work of Richard R. Flores (1989)is an impressive move toward recognizing the human agency of dominated communities. Although he too sees the *Pastorela* as derived from Spanish progenitors he cogently illustrates how the San Antonio version of *Los pastores* is marked by elements of ideological and social resistance to the dominant social order. My own analysis of the Teatro Campesino *Pastorela* also highlights its dimensions of social critique, yet in an entirely different configuration.

Although on the surface the *Pastorela* would appear to reproduce the hegemonic Christian order it is my contention that beneath its Christian camouflage it, more importantly, enacts relations of power and competing values and that in Christian guise it effectively fights or at least questions Christianity. We must recall that the appearance of the first Franciscans in 1523 followed on the heels of the military conquest of Tenochtitlán. It is by force that the native population was encouraged to act out biblical stories. The *Pastorela*, born of this violent assimilation of Catholicism, is not, and never was, a free space in which openly to enact a story of resistance to domination. As a hybrid form it instead illustrates the reality of living in the other's field, of living within an alien order established on the ancestral homeland. But it also exemplifies how in the midst of an established and imposed order of things, that order is destabilized. The imposed Christian system is clearly evident in the *Pastorela*, but it is a different order of things.

The *Pastorela* covertly manifests a spirit of resistance, chiefly through two means. On one level it is through the spirit of *relajo* (collective mockery/*burla collectiva*), which pervades the entire piece. It is significant, for example, that the entire *Pastorela* is dominated by a strong comic spirit. The overriding tendency is to sacrifice theology to humor. Occasional seriousness and solemnity are suspended throughout and displaced by a frivolous spirit, a spirit that seems to suggest a parody of the Christian theology espoused at intervals throughout the piece. Here we witness the sacroprofane fusion. The spirit of *relajo* is strongly embodied in each individual character. The Bartolo character, for example, is notoriously lazy, of strong appetite, and reluctant to go to Bethlehem. He stands in contradiction to the Hermitaño (Hermit), a hypocritical religious zealot who fasts and does penance. The Teatro Campesino's Hermitaño is played as a *pícaro* or dirty old man.

Although the *Pastorela* seems to privilege the colonial Christian order, that order is at another level subverted by the spirit of *relajo*, which invades the entire Christian order of things. Portilla (1966:18) makes the crucial connection between the practice of *relajo* and the possibility of freedom. "La significación o sentido del relajo es suspender la seriedad. Es decir, suspender o aniquilar la adhesión del sujeto a un valor propuesto a su libertad" [The significance or meaning of *relajo* is the suspension of seriousness. That is to say, the subject's suspension or annihilation of any adherence to a specific value placed before her or his discretion or liberty]. It is, hence, not surprising that *relajo* (embodied in hilarity, wit, comedy, parody, humor, joking, satire) is a form privileged by the marginalized, for it can serve to marginalize symbolically that which is submitted to the spirit of *relajo*.

The sacroprofane fusion of *relajo* and spiritual and philosophical discourse within the *Pastorela* is in itself an ancient practice visible in the Native American oral tradition. The presence of a clown or jokester figure that embodies the comedic spirit is observable in Native American ritual dances throughout the Americas. These include the Hopi Koshare Clown figure, the Navajo Tasavu, the Yaqui Pascola , or the *bufones* among the Conchero dancers, to name only a few. The presence of buffoonery and clowning even in solemn native rituals is documented by the Jesuit friar José de Acosta (1539–1600). He tells us, for example, of a presentation in honor of the god Quetzalcoatl in Cholula that included a feigned visit to the deity during which Quetzalcoatl was petitioned with "burlesque presentations" and "absurdities" that "excited the laughter of the listeners." Included in the theatrical presentation was the direct mockery of priests in the form of "ridiculing expressions" and "blowing bits of earth at the priests through pea-shooters." In Acosta's own words:

> In the atrium of the Temple of that god there was a little theatre thirty feet square, curiously whitewashed, which they adorned with branches and embellished with careful attention, decking it with arches of feathers and flowers, on which hung birds, rabbits and curious objects. There the people came together after eating, and the actors presented themselves, giving their burlesque presentations, pretending to be deaf, to have colds, to be lame, blind and mute, and asking the idol for health. The deaf replied with absurdities, those with colds coughed, the lame limped, and all related their ills and miseries, exciting the laughter of the listeners. Then appeared other actors in the roles of animals, some in the guise of beetles, others as toads, others as lizards, explaining their respective functions to each other, each exaggerating his own. They were much applauded, as they knew how to act their roles with great ingenuity. Then came some boys of the temple with wings of butterflies and birds of different colors, and climbing trees placed for the effect, they blew bits of earth at the priests through pea-shooters, adding ridiculing expressions in favor of some and against others. At the end there was a great dance of all the actors, and thus the function terminated. This was done on the most solemn feast-days. (From *Historia natural y moral de las Indias*, quoted by Sandi [1938:611–612])

Garibay (1971:93) similarly describes various pre-Columbian sacro-profane spectacles. The culture of laughter, mockery, and buffoonery played an important role in sacred celebration: "Vemos ya, en la misma celebración sagrada, meterse los elementos bufos" [We already see, in the midst of sacred celebration, the merging of comical elements]. Garibay refers to the many examples collected by the sixteenth-century chronicler Durán that illustrate this sacroprofane fusion: "A lo grave une el indio lo frívolo, en amoroso consorcio, como el de la vida misma" [With the solemn the Indian always unites the frivolous, in loving harmony, as in life itself] (p. 93). At other times buffoonery and comedy were performed outside of religious celebration. Durán gives us this example of "danzas y farsas y entremeses y cantares, de mucho contento":

> Otras veces hacían estos unos bailes, en los cuales se embijaban de negro; otras veces de blanco, otras veces de verde, emplumándose la cabeza y los pies; llevando entre medias algunas mujeres, fingiéndose ellos y ellas borrachos, llevando en las manos cantarillos y tazas, como que iban bebiendo. Todo fingido, para dar placer y solaz a las ciudades, regocijándoles

con mil géneros de juegos que . . . inventaban, de danzas y farsas y entremeses y cantares, de mucho contento. [At times they would do particular dances for which they would paint themselves black; other times white, other times green, covering their heads and feet with feathers; taking some women along, all pretending to be drunk, carrying in their hands pitchers and cups, as if they were drinking. Everything was feigned, in order to provide pleasure and entertainment in the cities, merrymaking by means of a thousand kinds of games that . . . they invented, and by means of dances and farces and interludes and songs, which were very joyous.] (Durán, *Historia azteca*, II, quoted by Garibay [1971:94])

The other major feature of the *Pastorela* that reveals an indigenous origin and a resistance to its own outwardly Christian colonial façade is the foregrounding of the struggle of opposites, of the struggles, tensions, and physical battles between devils and angels, between the positive and the negative—the interlocking of antagonistic forces. The core of the *Pastorela* story rests with the shepherds' involvement in the competition and battles between angels and devils. The Teatro Campesino *Pastorela* climaxes in a physical battle between San Miguel and Lucifer. This core, I might add, is precisely what is not a biblical story. The Christian names, the sighting of the star at the beginning of the performance, and the concluding adoration of the child serve only as the outward frame, or camouflage, for the core story. The Christian figures and Catholic thematics recede, in fact, into marginality. What is more, Catholic names such as Lucifer or San Miguel are at the service of a different set of principles than those assigned them in Catholic theology. Just as the Mexican masked dance of Moros y Cristianos does not literally represent or denote Moors and Christians, the Yaqui Fariseos and Matachines do not constitute a literal reference to the Pharisees or anyone else.

The *Pastorela* privileges the idea of struggle, of contradiction, which is at the core of Native American world vision. The idea of duality (as both polarity and complementarity) or what I here call native dialectics is the supreme concept within most Native American cultures. The symbolic representation of this concept within Aztec thought, for example, is the deity Ometeotl, the dual god, considered the origin of all generation and giver of all life in the cosmos. León-Portilla (1974:386) tells us: "En él se resumen todos los atributos de la divinidad, a tal grado que el mundo aparece como una omeyotización universal" [Ometeotl contains all the attributes of the divine, to the extent that the world can be viewed as a universal Omeyotization]. In Mayan terms this supreme concept is Hunabku, meaning "the giver of measure and movement." Both Ometeotl and Hunabku—to name only two ex-

amples—symbolize the supreme Native American universal law of the duality of all movement, of the unity of opposites, in other words, dialectics. I
propose that Lucifer and San Miguel—along with their respective armies of
angels and devils—find acceptance on this continent only as a Christian expression or camouflage of native concepts.

In its foregrounding of this struggle of opposites the *Pastorela* shows itself
to be much closer to the indigenous tradition of masked dance than to European mystery plays. This is not to deny the imposed colonial presence of
the European mystery plays in the Americas. Yet my own conceptualization
of that presence in the *Pastorela* focuses on how dominated native peoples have
always used imposed systems to "foil the other's game" (De Certeau
1984:19). If European genres like "mystery plays" found a degree of acceptance among native populations it was because they were easily assimilable
into existing native cultural practices. The idea of struggle or contradiction,
the complementarity of opposites, is foremost in dozens of Native American masked dances. All over the Mexican republic and in the southwestern
United States Native American ritual dance fervently reenacts and affirms the
centrality of contradiction, of the struggle of opposing forces fundamental
to all movement, to all life. Such is the case with the Mayan *Baile de los gigantes*
(which the Teatro Campesino also performed for many years), the Yaqui
Easter dances, numerous Conchero dances, Tarahumara dances, the Jaliciense
Danza de la Conquista, Moros y Cristianos, the dance of Los Negritos in
Veracruz, and on and on. In short, throughout the Republic of Mexico and
the southwestern United States community performances and rituals in syncretic guise allow for the expression of a community's ancient identity and
values so often denied and suppressed. The religious ritual is thus at one level
always political; the sacred and the profane become indistinguishable. Maestro Andrés Segura, a contemporary ritual leader within the Danza Azteca and
maestro to El Teatro Campesino for many years, conceptualizes—from a
native perspective—the subversive nature of the syncretism between Catholic and native philosophy and cultural practice. He emphasizes the post-Con-
quest practice of camouflaging ancient values and concepts with new
Christian names.

> Con este claro conocimiento de Dios, surge este sincretismo, entre la religión
> cristiana y la religión de nuestros antepasados. Ellos entendían y sabían, todo
> ese mecanismo de las leyes cósmicas; tan lo entendían, que es verdadera-
> mente satisfactorio y halagador demostrar con esto, que en cierta forma los
> conquistadores, como siempre sucede, fueron los conquistados. De una
> manera muy sutil, puesto que únicamente se tomó un nuevo nombre, el

concepto permaneció el mismo, porque había una comprensión y un conocimiento claro. [(Through our ancestors') clear knowledge of God, this syncretism emerges between the Christian religion and the religion of our ancestors. They understood and knew all about cosmic laws; they understood it so well that it is truly satisfying and flattering to demonstrate that in a certain way the conquerors, as always happens, ended up conquered. In a very subtle way: only a new name was adopted, while the concept remained the same because there was a clear understanding and awareness.] (1973:24)

With specific reference to the Spanish colonization of the Americas, de Certeau similarly theorizes how the Indians diverted colonization and Christianity "from its intended aims by the use made of it." He (1984:32) indicates: "They [the Indians] metaphorized the dominant order: they made it function in another register. They remained other within the system which they assimilated and which assimilated them externally. They diverted it without leaving it. Procedures of consumption maintained their difference in the very space that the occupier was organizing."

The reality of a politics of camouflage (as Segura says, "únicamente se tomó un nuevo nombre, el concepto permanecio el mismo") forces us to perceive the worldly-political dimension of any Chicana/o or Mexicana/o spiritual performance in a postcolonial popular context. Cast in these terms, the *Pastorela* emerges as a sacroprofane struggle of competing discourses embodied in cultural and symbolic form. It is illustrative of how an oppositional consciousness is invested in symbolic forms that, on the one hand, appear permissible—within the standards of hegemonic officialdom—yet that, on the other hand, allow for the transmission of seemingly suppressed cultural values and critiques although in shielded or camouflaged form. The common Eurocentric conceptualization of a one-way transatlantic transfer of medieval mystery plays to the Americas by Spanish friars is a neocolonial oversimplification, for it overlooks the dynamics of native resistance as well as the resilience and richness of native culture. One very notable scholar of religious theater in the Southwest expresses the top-down neocolonial views of many others when he states: "The conquering Spaniards had a dual mission to perform upon arriving on the shores of the new world: to conquer and to convert" (Campa 1934:7). The agency or "mission" of the native population is nowhere discussed. And so it is that Campa can conclude that "any similarity found between Christianity and the pagan religions was capitalized by the missionaries in accelerating the process of conversion" (p. 7). If we adopt a perspective that allows for the human agency of the native population, the inverse of what Campa claims can be asserted: Any similar-

Luis Oropeza as the Hermitaño (Hermit) in the 1976 Teatro Campesino Pastorela. Courtesy of Rogelio Rojas Collection.

ity found between Christianity and the native religions was capitalized on by the native population in decelerating (i.e., resisting) and even simulating the process of conversion.

We cannot overlook that the *Pastorela* flourished in spite of the church's vigorous efforts at suppression and censorship. It is interesting that the drama born to some extent within the Catholic church ultimately served to aggravate the relationship of enmity between the native population and the Roman Catholic Church. By 1574 the Spanish Inquisition attempted systematically to censor all such pageants. Censorship measures continued throughout the seventeenth and eighteenth centuries, yet without much success. The church could not eliminate what had already become an oppositional oral tradition disseminated throughout Mexico. It is not surprising that the *Pastorela* flourished for centuries in Indian communities, performed in Nahuatl and other native tongues, and passed down from generation to generation. *Pastorelas* in Spanish did not exist until the mid-eighteenth century when many were translated from native tongues (Horcasitas 1974).

In adopting the *Pastorela* the Teatro Campesino positioned itself within this long indigenous sacroprofane tradition. Chief informant for the *Pastorela* production within El Teatro Campesino was longtime ensemble member Olivia Chumacero. She remembered the *Pastorela* of her childhood among the Tarahumara Indians in the mountains of Chihuahua. At that time, it was performed in the native Tarahumara language. Chumacero (personal communication, 10/14/1990) indicates: "The first Pastorelas I remember being a part of were among the Tarahumara in the mountains of Chihuahua. Everything was performed in the Tarahumaran language. Only much later did they begin to perform it in the Spanish language." Chumacero also recalls how the *Pastorela* was transmitted in oral-tradition mode, by memory within families and communities: "You learn the lines from generation to generation from your *tíos* and *tías* [uncles and aunts]. They pass the lines on to you."

Although Olivia Chumacero's early migration north from Chihuahua to the United States in some ways severed her connection with the Tarahumaran *Pastorela*, her memory of that tradition led her to seek out the *Pastorela* from a local San Juan Bautista (California) elder, Longina Moreno Montoya, who had also migrated north to California. What remained in both women was a knowledge of the indigenous origins of the pageant. Efforts to reflect this reality are very much present in the Teatro Campesino's approach to the *Pastorela*. For one thing, the *pastores'*, or Shepherds', actions and attire symbolize the indigenous population. They are cast as Indians in order to illustrate that the *Pastorela* came from that sector of the population. Needless to say, the *Pastorela* is a fluid entity that undergoes changes across both time and space. To cite but one example: the *Pastorela* players of the Tarahumaran community in the highlands of Chihuahua wore animal masks, whereas most Chicana/o *Pastorelas* confine themselves to painted faces instead of masks. Also, the Teatro Campesino *Pastorela* incorporates a great deal of dialogue in the English language. Yet in spite of the inevitable changes, some very strong and fundamental elements of continuity manifest themselves: a strong spirit of *relajo* and a foregrounding of the complementarity of opposing forces as the basis of all life on the planet.

Although the *Pastorela* and *Las cuatro apariciones de la Virgen de Tepeyac* became the two major sacroprofane spectacles performed by the Teatro Campesino on a yearly or biannual basis, other spiritual performance forms from the oral tradition were practiced as well. Among them were the Chorti Mayan *Baile de los gigantes* (Dance of the Giants), a ritual dance performed on the day of the summer solstice; the *velación de ánimas*, or night vigil, on the Day of the Dead;

and also indigenous-based marriage and baptismal ceremonies. Although the *Baile de los gigantes* was occasionally performed publicly, the other forms were never practiced as public spectacles. Nonetheless they represent performance forms from the Mexican oral tradition that were cultivated by the Teatro Campesino ensemble. After the ensemble began to disband in 1979, the Teatro Campesino, Incorporated, continued the practice of the *Pastorela* and *Las cuatro apariciones* in alternate years. Many of the former Teatro Campesino ensemble members continued the practice of *danza* (ritual dance) under the leadership of maestro Andrés Segura, a ritual leader within the Aztec Conchero tradition.

Conclusion

The Chicana/o theater movement of the 1960s and the 1970s exploded onto the American scene from the physical memory of a dormant collective tradition: the Mexican popular performance tradition. The Mexican culture of orality constitutes the bedrock from which a coherent understanding of El Teatro Campesino and of many seemingly disparate manifestations of Chicana/o theater of the 1960s and the 1970s is possible. Memory, the body, and the community are pivotal concepts. Within an orally based culture, memory and the body are the sites of a community's self-knowledge. As is evident within the Teatro Campesino, the power and instrumentality of memory rooted in community history and in the body enabled the immediacy, authenticity, and vitality characteristic of the ensemble's work. In conceptualizing the *carpa* and the Teatro Campesino as oral cultural practices, I have sought to illustrate how the direct and intimate existence of this field of interlocking cultural practices emerged from the lifeworld of a working-class experience. The performance world of the *carpa* and the Teatro Campesino Rasquachi Aesthetic is a constitutive part of the social formation: not simply a way of interpreting the world, but also a way of living within the world, of altering reality, of being and becoming. Audiences are an integral part of this constitutive social practice. The memory system shared by the *carpa* and the Teatro Campesino—performance conventions, formulas, the culture of laughter, standard thematic settings, and other memory devices— is a body of mutually reinforcing performance elements deeply rooted in the Mexican popular performance tradition. This working-class memory system allowed for reliance on a common performance vocabulary based primarily on collective and improvisational creation.

The late 1970s, the Reaganomics of the 1980s, and the Bush years brought a sharp turn in the political tide, and a general worsening of economic and political conditions for the Chicano masses. Many *teatro* groups that had managed to survive with scarce resources were forced to disband. Survival on a shoestring became less and less feasible in the economically austere 1980s.

Related to the decline in theatrical activity is the decline of the Chicano movement and the general ebb of New Left and alternative cultural expression. Some of the most prominent Chicana/o theater workers of the 1960s and the 1970s saw an opportunity to make it in the arena of commercial mainstream theater and left behind the collective oral performance mode. (Although the world of mainstream theater is widely referred to as "professional" or "legitimate" theater, I deliberately avoid terminologies that ideologically imply a lack of professionalism or legitimacy in other theater traditions such as that of the *carpa* or the Teatro Campesino.)

The presence of Latinas/os in Western proscenium-type theater is of course not a new phenomenon.[20] What is new are recent efforts by Chicanas/os to carve a niche within the English-language, Euro-American theater establishment, efforts to play in traditionally white houses and the attendant imperative of appealing to audiences regardless of their ethnicity (see chap. 4). The novelty of this project and the inexperience of Chicanas/os within white mainstream proscenium theater has prompted some theaters (notably the Southcoast Repertory Theater, the now-defunct Los Angeles Theater Center, and the Old Globe) to set up adjunct Latina/o apprentice or tutorial programs—largely assimilationist in orientation—in order to facilitate the mainstreaming of Chicanas/os and the development of Chicana/o plays in English. Even in their naming, these so-called Hispanic Development Theater Projects are reminiscent of foreign aid to the "underdeveloped." Indeed it is a world apart from the bawdy Rasquachi Aesthetic of the Teatro Campesino. What separates the two theatrical worlds is not just budget, but a whole system of relations of production and of social orientation. In the upper middle-class world of commercial mainstream theater every move and every aspect of every production is assessed in dollars and cents before it can happen (see chap. 4). Economic profit was hardly a primary consideration in the artistic vision of so much of the work within the oral performance tradition.

The single greatest difference between commercial mainstream theater and the oral performance mode is that the former is based primarily on individualism and individual credit, individual authorship, and so on, whereas the Mexican popular performance tradition is grounded in collectivity, in the historical and cultural memory of the collective, and in the collectively improvised theater product. In the world of the *carpa* and the Teatro Campesino, the collective family unit constituted the core around which ensembles were formed. The mainstream commercial world of theater is, by contrast, the antithesis of collectivity: each person enters on an individual basis. When the Mark Taper Forum commissioned *Zoot Suit* in 1978, for example, it symptomatically commissioned Luis Valdez and excluded the Teatro Campesino ensemble, which had collectively improvised many of the core ideas for the play. The relations of production in mainstream American theater and institutions foster and recognize the work of individuals and not of collectives. That individualistic ideology, which converts intellectual endeavor to private property, is inherent in media and educational institutions as well.

It is hence not surprising that academic and journalistic writers credit Luis Valdez for the *collectively authored* work of El Teatro Campesino. The tendency to eclipse the reality of collective creation and credit solely one individual continues into the 1990s, in part through the agency of Valdez himself. Chief among his efforts to expropriate the collective works of El Teatro Campesino and to represent it as individually authored work is the 1990 publication entitled *Luis Valdez—Early Works: Actos, Bernabé and Pensamiento Serpentino*. Yet the *Actos* were not individually authored. Similarly, all *acto* performances that toured in the 1990s (there were virtually none in the 1980s) were billed with Valdez as author. Also, Valdez credits himself (and not the Teatro Campesino emsemble or the Mexican performance traditions) as "creator of a distinct theatrical tradition," quoting as well one writer who describes him as "the only living creator of a generic form of theater" (Valdez 1990:2).

In the process of moving into mainstream corporate theater houses Chicana/o actors and directors not only have relinquished the performance style and spirit of the oral performance mode, they also have lost the ability to respond quickly and inexpensively to the burning issues of the day. The very cumbersome and expensive nature of commercial productions has all but severed the direct connections between sociopolitical and theatrical mobilization, between popular causes and artistic performance. Also difficult to bridge is the distance between Chicana/o audiences and the remote theater districts and buildings where the Hispanic Development Theater Projects are housed. The Teatro Campesino and the *carpas*, for the most part, brought their performances to the people instead of making the people come to them.

The widespread renaissance of the Mexican popular performance tradition evidenced through the work of the Teatro Campesino ensemble and much of the Chicana/o theater movement of the 1960s and the 1970s has subsided in the 1990s. Most alternative theaters of the 1960s and the 1970s era have ceased to exist or—like the new Teatro Campesino, Incorporated, production company—perform only sporadically. The practice of Chicana/o theater as a collective oral tradition could be said to have entered a new cycle of dormancy, very similar to that immediately preceding the Chicana/o theater renaissance of the 1960s. Yet it is entirely possible that in the fullness of time it will again awaken into a new cycle of creativity.

*Ritual Mayan solstitial dance Baile de los gigantes
performed by Teatro Campesino at 1974 TENAZ Festival at
the pyramids of Teotihuacan (Mexico City). Courtesy of
Olivia Chumacero Archive.*

2. Theater of the Sphere: Toward the Formulation of a Native Performance Theory and Practice

On Formulating an Indigenous
Alternative Performance Aesthetic

The multifaceted achievements of the legendary Teatro Campesino ensemble have been examined and recognized in publications around the world. Common to these publications is their brevity—article or chapter length—and their reactive quality. Most of them were authored in direct response to new performances and developments within the ensemble. As such they are contemporaneous with the Teatro Campesino itself and take a piecemeal, linear approach: this play, then that play, then another. A handful of dissertations also take the text-centered and chronological approach.[1] From today's retrospective perspective—years after the dissolution of the famed ensemble—the nature of the company's contribution to Chicana/o theater and culture needs to be considered or reconsidered. The ensemble's legacy can hardly be assessed solely in terms of a body of plays—the vast majority of which were neither published nor publishable.

Nearly thirty years after the founding of the company, public knowledge of the ensemble's dramatic creativity has entered a state of oblivion or dormancy much like that of the production company that today bears the name El Teatro Campesino, Inc. Teatro Campesino plays were never written in dramatic literature fashion but composed in the oral performance mode: through the collective improvisation process.[2] Only a handful were subsequently scripted. A knowledge of these plays exists today in scattered and largely obscure sources: as constructs by critics who witnessed and critiqued them.

Anyone seeking to grasp or actually to appropriate the Teatro's legacy by means of existing critical writings will come away with an understanding of a very particular nature. Critical accounts invariably record the story of El Teatro Campesino's emergence as an organizing tool of the United Farm Workers Union during the great grape strike of 1965. Also well documented is the company's subsequent positioning on the cutting edge of the Chicano

Movement: its dramatization of the Chicana/o people's victimization and resistance in virtually all social arenas (education, labor, culture, history, politics). What we know of El Teatro Campesino from critics invariably has as its focus a particular performance, a particular play or plays.

Although I in no way wish to detract from the importance of the Teatro's performance spectacles and critics' analyses of them, my endeavor here is to penetrate beyond the public spectacle or play and examine El Teatro Campesino's broader project, consisting of the elaboration of a native Chicana/o performance theory and practice that was at the same time a philosophy of life: the Theater of the Sphere. Very broadly speaking, the Theater of the Sphere is a method of performance and life training developed by the Teatro Campesino ensemble between 1970 and 1980. It seeks to maximize and effectively to deploy a person's performance energies both on- and offstage. On one level Theater of the Sphere can be described as a theory and practice of communicative action based on Native American (Mayan and Aztec) wisdom and teachings. A deeply humanistic undertaking, the Theater of the Sphere constituted a sustained effort to explore, understand, and develop not an abstract human potentiality but a decolonized Chicana/o human potentiality or performance energy, one rooted in the Americas. Of course the oral culture performance complex of the Rasquachi Aesthetic or *carpa* aesthetic (see chap. 1) was the particular historical and cultural vessel or manifestation of that performance energy. Olivia Chumacero described the importance of cultivating a performance energy based in a non-European, *native* mythological reality:

> Theater of the Sphere at that time [the 1970s] was also part of the Chicana/o movement. It was making valid a reality that existed for us as a people as well as a reality that we could build upon. Anglo Saxons take Greek mythology as a reality which they can draw from, for example. For us we realized we have a mythological reality as well, and that's the one we drew from. And we made it valid, you know, made it something that was ours and that could expand and could be given to the world as a whole. . . . Consider my children. Where are my children going to find a space and time in which they can do something like this? Where? Something that is totally connected to your cultural way of being.

My intent here is to approach El Teatro Campesino using categories of analysis that allow us to examine the company from the inside out and on its own terms. Not one essay, article, or interview concerning the Theater of the Sphere has ever been published. Nor is the Theater of the Sphere even mentioned in the secondary literature. Critical approaches to El Teatro

Campesino have to date taken roughly the same direction: plays constitute the central object, and these are then grouped and discussed according to themes or genre. The trajectory of El Teatro Campesino is for the most part conceptualized in terms of a supposed linear development from an early dramatic genre (actos) to another dramatic genre (corridos) to another dramatic genre (mitos) or to combinations of the aforementioned. Within this centrist conception of the text, the Teatro Campesino ensemble's performance activity and creative process has been reduced to what Williams (1973) has called "art as object" (p. 15), as opposed to art as social practice. The art as object approach treats plays as fairly isolated artifacts. They are taken and "consumed" (i.e., understood and described) by means of various literary theories and their application without regard to the social conditions of artistic production. At best, dimensions of social reality are glossed as background components. A fixation on the work of art as object, as text and "textuality" has, correspondingly, obscured any preoccupation with and knowledge of the intimate connection between those "texts" and the actualities of human life, the nontextual domains of human activity that result in texts. Edward Said—in his call for a "secular criticism"—has criticized the proliferation of critical theories (theorists) and practices (practitioners) divorced from the realities of daily life entailed by and contained in texts. He comments:

> "Textuality" is the somewhat mystical and disinfected subject matter of literary theory. Textuality has therefore become the exact antithesis and displacement of what might be called history. Textuality is considered to take place, yes, but by the same token it does not take place anywhere or anytime in particular. It is produced, but by no one and at no time. . . . Literary theory has for the most part isolated textuality from the circumstances, the events, the physical senses that made it possible and render it intelligible as the result of human work. (1983:3–4)

What I seek to examine here is a central dimension of the Teatro Campesino's "human work," that is, the conditions of that artistic practice, including questions of authority and power. My focus is on the Teatro Campesino's recourse to the Native American ancestral heritage (mainly Mayan and Aztec) as it pertains to the ensemble's intense and sustained efforts to forge an alternative and native Chicana/o performance theory and practice. Existing writings concerning the Teatro Campesino's preoccupation with the Native American heritage for the most part ignore the nontextual domains of El Teatro Campesino's creative project and reduce that activity to "art as object" by isolating performance texts (i.e., plays) and converting them into a tidy genre (called a mito or myth).

Reliance on critical orthodoxies—such as that of genre—may well obscure more than it illuminates. What is obscured or discarded are "the circumstances, the events, the physical senses that made it possible and render it intelligible as the result of human work" (Said 1983:4). Indeed, the intense collective human and aesthetic exploration process undertaken by the Teatro Campesino ensemble over a period of more than ten years—named Theater of the Sphere—is in many ways as interesting and vital to Chicana/o performance history as the occasional outward "textual" manifestations of that process; that intense exploration deeply embedded in a system of social relations enabled those performance ("textual") manifestations. It was through that collective exploration that the ensemble elaborated a Chicana/o popular performance training program and pedagogy both oppositional and native. The in-house designation of this long-term project was Theater of the Sphere. In attempting to conceptualize the Theater of the Sphere we must keep in mind that it consisted and consists of far more than a text, isolated and reduced to a dramatic genre designated as mito or to a play or series of plays. Correspondingly, I focus here not on performed plays or "products" but on the exploration process itself.

The theory and practice of Theater of the Sphere is very much in need of critical elaboration, for it bears considerable historical and contemporary relevance. Its significance comes into focus when cast in terms of minority self-determination and counterhegemonic cultural negotiations vis-à-vis a dominant system. The Theater of the Sphere must be conceptualized in part as an oppositional or alternative social practice and long-term educational process intertwined with a larger system of social practices and power relations. That "larger system" is nothing less than a centuries-old system of colonial exploitation and deformation, which has been in progress since the first arrival of Europeans on American soil. The human labor involved in sustaining a counterculture, countermemory, and general spirit of resistance to the dominant society is embodied in Theater of the Sphere.

In attempting to lay bare the contours of Theater of the Sphere and assess its significance for Chicanas/os, it is necessary to understand its dual thrust: on the one hand, as a reactive cultural activity contesting hegemonic and dominant white social, cultural, and political practices (particularly those originating within the white culture industries); on the other hand, as an ethnic cultural activity that primarily seeks to come to terms with its own discrete self-identity, that seeks to perceive its own axis instead of cultivating only oppositional qualities in direct relationship to the Other. In approaching the Theater of the Sphere I primarily seek to describe it as an axis and not an as oppositional pole. In so doing I heed Teshome Gabriel's (1988) call for a theory and criticism of independent cultural movements which do not submit to a hierarchical model of dominant pole/oppositional pole. His reflections concerning black independent cinema and what he terms the "nomadic aesthetic" are very relevant to our consideration of "emergent tendencies" within Chicana/o culture:

> One of the limitations of mainstream theory and criticism has been its tendency to see the cinematic movement as tied to one of two poles: Dominant (Hollywood) and oppositional (reactive) cinema. Typically, Hollywood and similar practices are lumped into the former while Third World and independent movements are associated with the latter. . . . Thus, even in critical writings, Hollywood has been seen as a purveyor of colonial discourse and as a betrayer of others' cultural values. Understood merely as oppositional, black independent cinema could not be seen but as a reactive cinema. However, black independent cinema's search has gone far beyond this, for it is in fact a search for a newly born cinema, one with its own discrete identity, evolving on its own axis. It must be understood as more than a reactive pole—but rather as the development of new, emergent tendencies which are more difficult to categorize in established norms. . . .
>
> To try to define black independent cinema merely in terms of otherness is also to create merely another reactive role. Theorists of otherness fail to take into account that otherness speaks the same language of oppositional cinema. Culture and cinema are heterogeneous and multiple and need not and cannot be fitted to a hierarchical model. To succumb to the notion of the other is to be a part of the same, to be trapped within the confined and prescribed boundaries that limit it. The other is always that which Western culture excludes in order to exploit. (1988:72–73)

The present conceptualization of Theater of the Sphere primarily as axis instead of oppositional pole is undertaken in an effort to reconstruct what has in recent times been the most sustained effort to formulate a Chicana/o performance theory and training, one pertaining equally to the stage and to daily life. The Teatro Campesino's Theater of the Sphere is a process necessarily without closure and stands as a continual challenge to present and future generations of Chicanas/os.

A few words concerning the difficulty of reconstructing the Theater of the Sphere are in order. The work of a human collective spanning more than ten years of intense physical experimentation and self-education cannot be rendered adequately in the confines of one book chapter or perhaps even one book. The present encapsulation of that process cannot do justice to its complexity. My outline or skeletal rendering of what was a sustained exploration into Chicana/o creativity must be seen as an invitation to other researchers and theater workers.

The difficulty of the present research task is twofold: for one thing, virtually no documentation of the Theater of the Sphere process exists, for it was never codified on paper. My own understanding is based on oral histories, on participant observation, and on discontinuous notebook material provided me by various Teatro ensemble members. A second difficulty rests with rendering a physical, intellectual, emotional, and spiritual process of human transformation in words alone.

Fully aware of the impossibility of presenting the Theater of the Sphere as a written account of supposedly objective facts, I have sought to approach it for the most part with an attitude of sympathetic understanding. Much of what I present renders the process from the Teatro's perspective. The controversy or negative criticism generated by the Theater of the Sphere, however, is given consideration in the final section of this chapter.

Theater of the Sphere: Affirming the Chicana/o Axis

El Teatro Campesino's theory and practice of a Chicana/o performance training emerges from a preoccupation with Chicana/o social, political, and cultural reality. Although initially motivated by direct involvement with the United Farm Workers, El Teatro Campesino soon separated from direct involvement (in 1967) and embarked on a cultural mission rooted in the broader Chicana/o reality and Chicana/o notions of reality. It is of significance that the performance techniques employed by the Teatro were invariably drawn from the vast storehouse of Chicana/o oral performance tradition: the acto (a direct descendant of the Mexican "sketch cómico"), albures and cábula (virtuoso and transgressive deconstruction of "normal" speech), corridos (narrative ballads), and various other musical genres, the use of títeres (puppets), the use of stock characters, but above all, reliance on improvisation and memory instead of on writing. The Teatro's ties to orality and oral culture encompassed the vast realm of Native American culture as well. From the onset the Teatro Campesino sought to affirm the ancient native roots of Chicano philosophical and physical existence in the Americas, to better understand and cultivate nativeness in a time and place where the native had come to be regarded as alien or even immigrant.

Of course the cultural reclamation project designated as Theater of the Sphere was but one expression of a broader indigenist movement: the Chicano movement's (from roughly 1965 to 1980) deliberate recourse to the native ancestral culture, the celebration of roots. Along with the more

conventionally and narrowly defined political activism of the Chicano movement came the politics of self-definition and of the self-construction of
Chicana/o identity. Within the performing, visual, and literary arts we witness an intense, widespread resurgence of a cultural consciousness of the
indígena (Native American) that finds expression in a multiplicity of forms
across the southwestern United States.

The process of recovering the ancestral native culture at times took on
properties bordering on what to some seemed like the idealization of a supposedly remote past or a desire to return to what some considered "the past."
I maintain, however, that the Theater of the Sphere is eminently a thing of
the present, for as Stuart Hall (1988:30) has argued, there is no such thing
as leaving the present for the past: "There can be no simple 'return' or 'recovery' of the ancestral past which is not reexperienced through the categories of the present; no base for creative enunciation in a simple reproduction
of traditional forms which are not transformed by the technologies and the
identities of the present." Within the Teatro Campesino the process of recovery was based not only on abstractly intellectual considerations but equally
on the "identities of the present." It was generated from a living collective
memory and the presence of lo indio (that which is native) among ensemble
members, such as Felipe Cantú's awareness of his Indian grandparents and
his Indian family name, which (as a survival technique) was replaced by
"Cantú"; such as Luis Valdez's knowledge of his Yaqui origins; such as Olivia
Chumacero's awareness of her Tarahumara ancestry.

In the case of El Teatro Campesino, the various tribal ancestries merged
into a common process of recovery based on Mayan and Aztec knowledge
and mythology. Why Aztec and Mayan? The merger and choice of a common
ground was conceptually facilitated by the teachings of the Aztec Conchero
dancer Andrés Segura and Mayan specialist Domingo Martínez Paredez, who
provided—as a living Mayan maestro for the Teatro and as a scholar of Mayan
culture—a theoretical foundation postulating the essential cultural unity of
all American tribal peoples (in Un continente y una cultura). The recourse to Mayan
and Aztec knowledge was also in part dictated by historical convenience:
these are among the best documented of American tribal cultures. It also
appeared justified by the general recognition of the strong indígena presence
in Chicana/o barrios, regardless of tribal specificity and provenance. Although the focusing on the native ancestral culture was certainly the cultural
nationalist self-validation process of the Chicano movement, the Teatro
Campesino never posited "the native" as an essentialist notion of race, or as
a pure or unadulterated ideal state. To the contrary, "the native" is typically

discussed as a thoroughly historical and heterogeneous construct, indeed as a *necessarily* syncretic body of contemporary cultural practices. In the words of Luis Valdez:

> Man has been in the Americas for more than 38,000 years. White men have been around for less than five hundred. It is presumptuous, even dangerous, for anyone to pretend that the Chicano, the "Mexican-American," is only one more in the long line of hyphenated-immigrants to the New World. *We are the New World*. . . .
>
> During the three hundred years of Nueva España, only 300,000 gachupines [Spaniards] settled in the New World. And most of these were men. There were so few white people at first, that ten years after the Conquest in 1531, there were more black men in Mexico than white. . . .
>
> Miscegenation went joyously wild, creating the many shapes, sizes, and hues of La Raza. But the predominant strain of the mestizaje remained Indio. By the turn of the nineteenth century, most of the people in Mexico were mestizos with a great deal of Indian blood.
>
> The presence of the Indio in La Raza is as real as the barrio. Tortillas, tamales, chile, marijuana, la curandera, el empacho, el molcajete, atole, La Virgen de Guadalupe—these are hard-core realities for our people. These and thousands of other little human customs and traditions are interwoven into the fiber of our daily life. América Indígena is not ancient history. It exists today in the barrio, having survived even the subversive onslaught of the twentieth-century neon gabacho commercialism that passes for American culture. (1972a:xiv–xv)

It is clear that the recourse to the native heritage in no way signaled a denial of the colonial *mestizaje*, or cultural syncretism in Chicana/o life. Yet within that syncretic reality that embraces the confrontation, collision, and partial merger of antagonistic cultural, social, political, and economic forces, the *indígena* or *indio* (native) heritage is acknowledged as central, as the existential core of Chicana/o identity. The native heritage—target of 500 years of direct colonial attack, of denial and disdain, of annihilation—is described by Luis Valdez as the brown face beneath the white mask:

> Yet the barrio is a colony of the white man's world. Our life there is second hand, full of chingaderas imitating the way of the patrón. The used cars, rented houses, old radio and TV sets, stale grocery stores, plastic flowers—all the trash of the white man's world mixes with the bits and pieces of that other life, the Indio life, to create the barrio. Frijoles and tortillas remain, but the totality of the Indio's vision is gone. Curanderas make use of plants and

herbs as popular cures, without knowing that their knowledge is what remains of a great medical science. Devout Catholics pray to the Virgen de Guadalupe, without realizing that they were worshipping an Aztec goddess, Tonantzin. (1972a:xvi)

The Theater of the Sphere consists of a sustained attempt to restore "the totality of the Indio's vision," to affirm the submerged collective memory while making it the foundational training for a Chicana/o pedagogy and life performance.

A clarification of the terms "performance" and "acting" is in order. In the case of El Teatro Campesino those terms—as well as the term "aesthetic"—do not refer to an artistic practice in any way separate from life practices within society at large. The Teatro Campesino ensemble had always been keenly conscious of the continuity between life on and off the stage. The stage work was but one dimension of an overall cultivation of a performer's human potential. "Performance" for the Teatro Campesino was in no way aestheticized into an independent or separate artistic realm. Performance was viewed as part of the material social process of life; as such it always entailed consciousness of community and of one's sense of belonging to and participating in the life of a community.[3] (The company's persecution by John Birchers and other conservative elements in San Juan Bautista speaks to the external perception of the company's involvement in the community.) The Teatro Campesino's concept of actor and performer was wholly antithetical to the mainstream division of labor and specialization wherein actors work at pretending to be who they are not in reality, or enact a situation essentially foreign to them. Over the years, Theater of the Sphere evolved as a life philosophy and life practice extending into the stage work. The insistence on (or striving for) an essential unity of a person onstage and offstage motivated ensemble members collectively to formulate a self-education and training program aimed at sharpening individual and collective life performance skills. With this holistic approach, the Teatro's ultimate goal was defined as the formation of the Spherical Actor or complete human being.

Notwithstanding its utopian thrust, one very real dimension of this endeavor rests in its effort to counteract the human fragmentation and deformation inherent in capitalist society. As such it constitutes a socially and artistically significant struggle to reclaim a full human identity within a dehumanizing society. This process of developing full human potential was conceived by the Teatro Campesino as both political and deeply spiritual. This is expressed in statements concerning the use of theater as a means of training that awakens and cultivates human potential. From its inception the

Teatro called for a broad vision combining the "mass struggle in the fields and barrios" with "an internal struggle in the very corazón [heart] of our people. . . . And that again means teatro. Not a teatro composed of actors or agit-prop but a teatro of ritual, of music, of beauty and spiritual sensitivity. A teatro of legends and myths. A teatro of religious strength. This type of theater will require real dedication; it may, indeed, require a couple of generations of Chicanos devoted to the use of the theater as an instrument in the evolution of our people" (Valdez 1971b:3).

The process of experimentation, rooted in indigenous (primarily Mayan and Aztec) precepts and philosophy, sought to reconstitute performers with a sense of human wholeness. The Theater of the Sphere was a multidimensional pedagogy that included the intense program of the Veinte Pasos (Twenty Steps); participation in pláticas (teachings) by indigenous maestros; danza; interaction with different indigenous communities in the United States and Mexico; a program of readings and discussion; and the work of stage performance and community involvement.

The Theater of the Sphere is rooted in a particular understanding of the natural world (considered the most fundamental reality) and of the position of human beings within that larger order. Each human being is considered a model—on an abstract plane that is nevertheless experienced very physically—of the universe at large. Mythical stories are (as I shall elaborate) the encapsulation of that model.

In contrast to today's prevalent Western ethos, the Native American ethos positions humans within nature and not over and against nature. This micro- macrocosmic insight concerning human beings' relationship to the larger cosmic order became the basis of the Teatro Campesino's project of creating the Spherical Actor. At all times the Theater of the Sphere seeks to integrate the performer (as human being) within the natural world or cosmos, given that the same energies, relationships, and principles that shape the natural world are said to be operative in the human body. The process of integration or harmony and balance insures that the individual at once supports the natural order of the universe and is supported by it. The result of such integration is an extraordinary physical and spiritual presence and control of the performer's bioenergies (i.e., human energy resources) both on- and offstage.

Fundamental to our understanding or reconstruction of the Theater of the Sphere is some discussion of the concept of myth. At the heart of the Theater of the Sphere are various key myths, regarded as systems of relationships or blueprints concerning all life and being. Each people has its own mythology with which it seeks to illustrate a life wisdom or construct. The Teatro

Campesino turned to *indígena* mythology in the assumption that all visions, dreams, and human functioning are culturally conditioned and out of a conviction that Chicana/o cultural life is most deeply rooted in *indígena* knowledge (i.e., mythology). A consideration of the concept of myth is furthermore indispensable because the Teatro Campesino came to rely heavily on native mythological configurations within certain performance pieces. Although this is not new in the annals of Mexican theater, native Mexican mythology had perhaps not formerly been explored theatrically with the same rigor.

A word of caution is in order concerning the use of the terms "myth" and "mythology." These terms are essentially a construct of Western colonial discourse. The concept of "myth" is in fact nonexistent within the indigenous cultures and thought systems to which it has historically been attached. The conception of a "mythology" that exists as a body distinct and separate from history, politics, art, religion, or any other human endeavor or reality stems from a colonial grid of analysis whose fragmented categories are alien to the cultures they claim to interpret and understand. Maya scholar Raphael Girard (1979:13) hints at the highly integrated and encompassing system of knowledge to which the so-called myths give expression: "The essential truths expressed by the myths concern interrelated concepts. Cosmogony, theogony, ceremonies, calendar, mathematics, astronomy, economy, family, society, government, etc. are derived from the identical patterns or models. We are faced with a reciprocal grafting of all into a cosmic whole at each moment. No cultural element can be extricated from that whole to which it is solidly linked."

On the surface of it, and broadly speaking, myths come to us as stories. They are a central part of the oral tradition of storytelling. All myths are exemplary: the stories they tell dramatize or even personify culture-bound relationships reflecting fundamental concepts of humankind, god, and the universe. They constitute—to quote Teatro Campesino members—"blueprints of reality" or "patterns." Within this understanding, a myth is symbolic, a metaphor for the matrix of forces and dynamics at work within visible reality. Mythic blueprints become manifest through visible reality but they usually are not directly visible.

Most mythologies incorporate the idea of a god or gods in order to hint at the larger and unknowable force constituted by the confluence of forces; that force is considered present and at work in each animate and inanimate object. The Teatro Campesino's Theater of the Sphere also incorporates a strong sense of the divine. That divinity or "god" is, however, not bearded and anthropomorphic or of a personal sort but a symbol of what Joseph Campbell (1988:31) describes as "an undefinable, inconceivable mystery, thought of as a power, that is the source and end and supporting ground of all life and being."[4]

When El Teatro Campesino sought to ground the Theater of the Sphere in Mayan and Aztec mythology it did so with the conviction that those myths constituted an active force within Chicana/o reality. Ensemble members regarded those myths (and not Greek mythology) as the submerged "wisdom of life"—conscious or unconscious—for Chicanos. This conception of mythology as an active force, a harmonizing force, closely resembles Campbell's conception of mythology (1988:55): "Every mythology has to do with the wisdom of life as related to a specific culture at a specific time. It integrates the individual into his society and the society into the field of nature. It unites the field of nature with my nature. It's a harmonizing force." Myths are symbolic representations or stories whose reality is (ideally) manifest in this world. Mythologies can serve to guide and empower humans for they are lessons concerning the "powers that animate our life." In Campbell's words (pp. 22–23): "A god is a personification of a motivating power or value system that functions in human life and in the universe—the powers of your own body and of nature. The myths are metaphorical of spiritual potentiality in the human being, and the same powers that animate our life animate the life of the world."

In short, the Teatro Campesino's understanding of a "supporting ground of all life" or of "powers that animate our life" or of "motivating powers . . . that function in humans" was based on a native reality: that mythology "narrates" physical laws and forces symbolically as a system of relationships symbolized as divine powers. In other words, physical law is metaphorized into stories of deities, that is, myths. The materiality of myth is evident in Mayan culture, which bases all mythological discourse on scientific inquiry, most notably astronomy, mathematics, calendrics, or medicine—all inseparable from religious and mythological thought and human action.

The Formation of the Spherical Actor:
A New Chicana/o Humanism

Of central importance within the process of the Theater of the Sphere was a training consisting of "Twenty Steps," called the Veinte Pasos. These twenty steps or stages educated performers concerning the powers that animate human life, in order to maximize the harnessing of those powers to a humanly creative end. Before describing the Veinte Pasos, some discussion of key mythical concepts is essential. Perhaps the key myth (i.e., "personification of a motivating power or value system that functions in human life" [Campbell 1988:22]) within the Theater of the Sphere is that of the feathered serpent, or Quetzalcoatl, symbolic—among other things—of the unity of the spiritual (*Quetzal* = feathers) and the material (*Coatl* = serpent) inherent in the entire creation, in life.[5] Quetzalcoatl connotes the presence of energy (*K'inan* = spirit) in all matter and of energy and spirit as the mover of all things. As such Quetzalcoatl stands as a symbol of the creation, of the life process. Quetzalcoatl is said to have created humankind, in conjunction with Cihuacoatl. Quetzalcoatl furthermore is the generator of the arts, of science, and of the calendar. As protector of the Calmecac, Quetzalcoatl came to be regarded as the supreme symbol of knowledge as well as of the whole of Nahuatl wisdom. He represents the virtues of life: such as *respeto* or creating with the heart (*yolteotl*). In essence, Quetzalcoatl could be said to epitomize a manner of life and behavior, a humanistic philosophy.

Among the goals of the Theater of the Sphere is to foster what is called the "Living Quetzalcoatl," or "Feathered Serpent Blueprint," within the self. I offer here the Teatro's own articulation of that blueprint:

> Once you are secure and conscious of SELF you will no longer need to plan your doings. Because the plan is already in you. You watch yourself move and reveal the plan to yourself. You are a serpent composed of the evolving nature of your own unique being. And it is GOOD because it was designed and planned by the CREATOR. . . .
>
> The CREATOR: as always He is present within the DOER, and the sooner the doer allows himself to be "taken over" by the CREATOR he becomes capable of more actions and deeds. Such self-deliverance is the essence of all creation. (El Teatro Campesino Research Group, 1973)

Feathered Serpent is synonymous here with "the plan" or "the creator." The deity or divine power is considered present within each of us as a "plan" or a "blueprint" that we reveal to ourselves as we move through life. Although the language used would seem to hint at an anthropomorphic being (and male at that!), such terms are applied only to symbolically explicate how we are a model or blueprint of the universe at large. What is at work in the universe is considered at work in each of us as well. In this view, the Feathered Serpent constitutes a model of life and of behavior present as potentiality within each individual. The goal is to cultivate that potentiality. The story or myth of Quetzalcoatl serves as paradigm, model, or blueprint for a dimension of life wisdom. The idea is to see the myths within us and to learn to move like the myths. These are—above all—blueprints for motion and not for thought. Being "'taken over' by the CREATOR" or Feathered Serpent signifies arriving at an advanced stage or realization of that human potentiality. Campbell (1988:23) indicates: "The myths are metaphorical of spiritual potentiality in the *human being*" (emphasis mine). Each individual is a potential manifestation of the creator, Quetzalcoatl. Realizing that, potential means becoming harmoniously integrated within a whole system of relationships: becoming whole or spherical. Teatro Campesino ensemble member Olivia Chumacero affirms this understanding of divine presence or "god" as innate within humans:

> I don't believe in the symbol of god, of a god *out there*. That's like a contradiction. A Spherical human being is not going to have to identify anything with god. A Spherical being is going to BE—and you don't even have to use the word "god." A Spherical human being is going to be a complete human being. Not a complete human being in the purely material sense but Spherical in the wholeness of understanding your energy on the material plane, on a cosmic plane, or on a very concrete labor-related plane. You can be at any of these planes. There is no separation. That is the spherical human being. You are the creator. (Interview, 8/18/1989)

For the Teatro Campesino, all mythological entities such as "God," "the Creator," "Jesus Christ," and "Quetzalcoatl" are personifications of relational systems linking human life and the universe.[6]

The relational system called Quetzalcoatl (or the Quetzalcoatl narrative) has a multiplicity of meanings pertaining to the creation or to all creation. The plumed serpent is among the most complex of American symbols expressing creation: the plumed serpent expresses the reality of the universe, that is, how everything moves and changes within the creation. The serpent, on the one hand, symbolizes the law of transformation, which is said to govern all life. Just as the serpent crawls out of its skin, so are all earthly things and beings subject to constant transformation. Hence the serpent is associated with time, evolution, life and birth, and, on another level, with phenomena such as the dialectical movement of history, of thought, or of politics. As a symbol of the transformational process to which all things of this earth are subject, the serpent became associated with the earth and water, or materiality. Feathers and birds, on the other hand, symbolize the spirit (i.e., energy) of the sun and the air (the heavens). The four elements (fire, air, water, earth) are thus united in Quetzalcoatl whose spiritual and material duality symbolizes the essence of humanity. Luis Valdez describes the connection: "And we are feathered serpents. We human beings—it's another way to describe it. It's another symbol for us, because we're of the spirit, but also of the flesh. But the spirit is in the flesh" (Valdez 1984c). Quetzalcoatl, the feathered serpent, constitutes a symbolic form or paradigm—the *invisible* realm of culture that becomes manifest or *visible* within cultural expression.[7]

Within the Mayan cultural, scientific, and religious system, which establishes a close mathematically based relationship between heavens and humans, between the celestial order and the human order, the concept of the serpent ("*Coatl*" in Nahuatl; "*Can*" in Mayan) is central. It is assigned the number four (in turn, highly symbolic) and also symbolizes energy because of the undulant *serpentine* quality of energy flow. From Martínez Paredez we furthermore know that the

> serpent is also an important figure in chronology and astronomy, since it appears carrying planetary symbols on its back, with the Sun on its head. All of this indicates that the Mayan philosopher is referring to nothing less than the Solar System. The Solar System was conceptualized as an enormous serpent flying in the infinite, encompassing 4 aspects of great importance— Space, Time and transfer and rotation which are Movement and Limit respectively, with days, nights, months, and years—be it solstice and equinox and zenith movements of the sun. (1964:41)

Although the vast complexity of Mayan and Aztec philosophical, scientific, religious, and cultural systems cannot be elaborated here, it is important to point out that an intense study of those systems was conducted by Teatro Campesino members in connection with their application within the Theater of the Sphere. In describing this performance theory and practice I refer only to the chief guiding concepts underlying the Teatro Campesino's exploration and attempt to reconstruct them as the Teatro Campesino ensemble understood them. The Mayan and Aztec teachings were acquired by both oral and written means: through the oral teachings of Domingo Martínez Paredez and Andrés Segura (both from Mexico City) and through available scholarly writings, chiefly those of Domingo Martínez Paredez, whose experiential knowledge in having been raised as a Maya, speaking contemporary Mayan, allowed him to arrive at various unorthodox findings concerning the Maya, chiefly through the tools of linguistic and philosophical analysis. Among his most important works pertaining to Mayan thought sciences are *Un continente y una cultura* (1960), *Hunab Ku: síntesis del pensamiento filosófico maya* (1964), *Parasicología maya* (1977), and *El Popol Vuh tiene razón* (1976). It is from these works and from their author that El Teatro Campesino drew in constructing a philosophy for performance and life praxis.

Much of the philosophy so fervently elucidated by Martínez Paredez is restated by Luis Valdez in his long poem, *Pensamiento serpentino*, in which he explicitly refers to the mentorship of Martínez Paredez as well as to three of Martínez Paredez's works. The very title of the poem is directly influenced by Martínez Paredez, who variously illustrates how "human beings are viewed as serpentine" in Mayan and Aztec thought. Correspondingly, human thought is considered "*Pensamiento serpentino.*"[8] *Pensamiento serpentino* ("serpentine thought") is an extended poem/treatise that unites much of the Teatro Campesino's philosophical and worldly perspectives. The intellectual (i.e., nonphysical) dimensions of Theater of the Sphere were usually referred to as *Pensamiento serpentino* by the ensemble, although at times the two terms were used interchangeably.

In espousing a new Chicana/o-Mayan humanism, El Teatro Campesino adopted as well the concept of "*in lak'ech,*" one of the most important Mayan principles governing human action. *In lak'ech* is the term used by the Maya to designate the "other" person, commonly referred to in English as "you"; in the Mayan tongue it is rendered as "you are my other self." *Pensamiento serpentino* elaborates on the sphericality of human interaction ("whatever I do to you, I do to myself"), in ways both philosophical and political. It refers, for example, to the bombing of Hanoi by the United States as an act of self-violence. Along the same lines it indicates that hatred of others always comes back to the person who hates. This is deemed a law of nature. The philosophical precept of in lak'ech corresponds, for example, to Hindu concepts of karmic law or to Newton's Third Law.

Among the other fundamental concepts expressed in the poem/philosophy *Pensamiento serpentino* are, for example, that of the fundamental unity or fusion of all human action and performance, theatrical and other; of the fundamental unity of all living beings and of all races; the idea that faith in oneself— a manifestation of divinity—is a prerequisite for meaningful action and nonviolent struggle. *Pensamiento serpentino* also directly calls for the decolonization of Chicanas/os through recourse to the non-European wisdom of one's own people. It stresses the importance and need for a Chicana/o education and liberation grounded in a knowledge of native teachings.

Another very important concept adopted by El Teatro Campesino is the Aztec "*yolteotl,*" designating the supreme human ideal of "having deified one's heart." Closely related is the concept of "being in dialogue with one's own heart" (*moyolnonotzani*). A third concept—*tlayolteuiani*—is viewed as the outcome of *yolteotl*. The deification of one's heart (*yolteotl*) is prerequisite to the capacity to "deify things in life by virtue of having deified one's heart— tlayolteuiani, i.e., to create" (León Portilla 1974:385). These three terms were the closest Aztec thought came to designating what is today referred to as "shaman" or "artist" (León Portilla 1974:392).

The task of generating a Chicana/o process of human liberation that draws from Chicana/o notions of reality was a fundamental tenet of Theater of the Sphere. This task, it was felt, could be accomplished only through a process of extended struggle, motivated by love rather than hatred.[9] The struggle of El Teatro Campesino was carried out by means of a program of reeducation and training whose goal was to achieve human integration or the condition of the Spherical Actor.

Theater of the Sphere: The Twenty Steps

The process of achieving human integration (becoming "a complete human being" or "the Spherical Actor") within the universe translates—within *Pensamiento serpentino*—into learning to evolve or move in harmony with life, with the people in one's immediate environment, and with the cosmic movement.[10] The rationale for the process of achieving human integration was born from a desire for empowerment that encompassed all human dimensions, after having recognized the limitations of seeking only political empowerment. A 1975 Teatro Campesino flyer describes the need to cultivate *poder* (power), not framed strictly as political power, but as the emergence from colonization in all of its forms, be they political, cultural, racial, or spiritual. The Teatro Campesino conceptualized *poder* as the very essence of the United Farm Workers' rallying cry *Sí se puede* [Yes, we can!] Theater of the Sphere emerged as a pedagogy of the oppressed, offering self-empowerment through a process of relearning and reascertaining a Chicana/o humanity.

The process of relearning involved the elaboration of a human pedagogy and performance described here in sequential order (which the linearity of discourse demands) although carried out in many ways simultaneously. At the core of the Theater of the Sphere are the "Twenty Footprints of God," or the symbolic representation of "Man's Spiritual Pilgrimage." The Veinte Pasos constitute a holistic training that engages and synchronizes the entire field of mutually determining human forces designated as the mind, the body, the heart, and the soul. The dimension of the "soul" is something of a cumulative force, akin to "creative spirit," or the unity of elements attained in the Spherical Actor. Each of these human forces or dimensions corresponds to five of the Twenty Steps, or Footprints, each named for one of the twenty Mayan days of the month used in the sacred year, or *Tzolkin*, consisting of a succession of 260 days. The twenty days of the mind, body, heart, and soul diagram (fig. 1) serve to illustrate how the twenty steps and the mind, heart, body, and soul are considered—at one level—distinguishable but not separable. They are fused and exist in relationship to each other. Theater of the Sphere seeks to strengthen the individual and group awareness of that fused relationship through an integration of the various spheres.

It was Domingo Martínez Paredez who transmitted the names and meanings of the twenty days to Teatro Campesino members, pointing out that they

symbolize a process of human evolution. With this in mind, the Teatro
Campesino ensemble transposed these Mayan twenty days into a program
designed to foster human capacities and potentialities. The Twenty Steps can
be described as a program of reflection and exercises leading through various psychophysiological stages of transformation. Each of the Twenty Steps,
or days, has a number and a meaning linked to both a corresponding human state achieved through a specific exercise program and to a geometric
figure illustrative of that concept or human state. This affirms the inextricable
linkage between mathematics, humans, and the sacred, or god. The meanings of the twenty days are as follows:

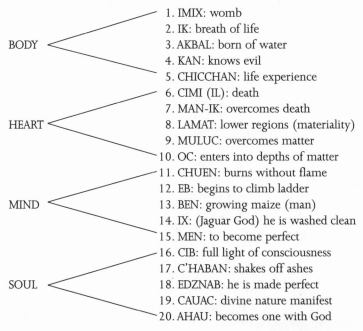

BODY
1. IMIX: womb
2. IK: breath of life
3. AKBAL: born of water
4. KAN: knows evil
5. CHICCHAN: life experience

HEART
6. CIMI (IL): death
7. MAN-IK: overcomes death
8. LAMAT: lower regions (materiality)
9. MULUC: overcomes matter
10. OC: enters into depths of matter

MIND
11. CHUEN: burns without flame
12. EB: begins to climb ladder
13. BEN: growing maize (man)
14. IX: (Jaguar God) he is washed clean
15. MEN: to become perfect

SOUL
16. CIB: full light of consciousness
17. C'HABAN: shakes off ashes
18. EDZNAB: he is made perfect
19. CAUAC: divine nature manifest
20. AHAU: becomes one with God

Out of this general scheme, El Teatro Campesino developed a complex
pedagogy of human transformation. In consultation principally with maestro Martínez Paredez and also Andrés Segura, each of the Twenty Steps was
developed into a thought and action complex involving philosophical reflection and corresponding physical exercises. Former ensemble member Olivia
Chumacero describes the process: "What we would do was spend the whole
day on just one of the Veinte Pasos in order to be able to capture and understand everything that evolved around that particular symbol, number, and

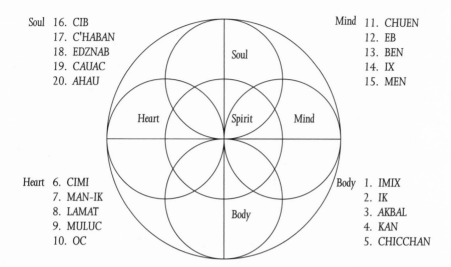

Soul 16. CIB
      17. C'HABAN
      18. EDZNAB
      19. CAUAC
      20. AHAU

Mind 11. CHUEN
      12. EB
      13. BEN
      14. IX
      15. MEN

Heart 6. CIMI
       7. MAN-IK
       8. LAMAT
       9. MULUC
      10. OC

Body 1. IMIX
      2. IK
      3. AKBAL
      4. KAN
      5. CHICCHAN

Figure 1. Mind/Body/Heart/Soul Diagram

the part of your body to which it corresponded. We then took it from there to very specific theater games and exercises that would reflect and focus on that particular theme" (interview, 8/18/1989). The goal was to cultivate a consciousness of a particular human state and to internalize it while ultimately seeking to achieve a mastery of the entire system of interlocking signs. Training toward sphericality was at once an individual, group, and social and ecological undertaking, given that the individual capacity for action and response only exists in relationship to group and social, environmental, and cosmic forces. Within the process represented by the "Twenty Footprints of God" there is a progression from a series of five steps associated with the body, to a series of five steps associated with the heart, to a series of five steps associated with the mind and intellect, to the highest and final series of five steps associated with a holistic awakening of the body, heart, and mind to its inherent spirituality. The progression within the Veinte Pasos is a pro-gression or development that envelops all human dimensions and reality at large. This development is described in a Theater of the Sphere document (albeit in male-centered language) (Chumacero, n.d.): "He must learn to move with his body, mind, and heart simultaneously. He must learn to move as a sphere. Once he becomes aware of his 4-directions, his yolteotl, his sphericalness, he becomes in tune with himself and recognizes that he is a vibration of energy moving through space recreating itself as a tiny manifestation of El Creador, Dios [the Creator, God]."

In order to provide a more concrete understanding of the actual process of becoming spherical, I offer here some examples from the Veinte Pasos. I do so only by way of illustration and not with the intention of delivering a usable Theater of the Sphere handbook or manual. Like other dimensions of Chicana/o oral culture—such as dance, music, or healing—Theater of the Sphere is something that can be transmitted only *physically*. Hence what follows can stand only as a signpost.[11]

The journey through the Theater of the Sphere begins with a prebeginning called "*gel*," or "nothingness." Prior to and at the conclusion of a day's action or thought, performers meditate on their infinite potential while in an absolutely motionless state. On one level this meditation serves to create focus for what follows. On another level, it prefigures the desire and capacity to tie back to the cosmic center represented by Step Twenty (*ahau*: becomes one with God). The first step of the Veinte Pasos is imix, represented by a dot within the sphere, a zero and a point within it. Imix refers to the pregnant womb in Mayan, a womb with a fertilized egg from which birth will follow, ideally the birth of a complete human being. In the Teatro's words: "Your HEART is the FERTILIZED EGG inside the WOMB of your BEING. YOUR potential. It is up to you to give yourself BIRTH."[12] El Teatro Campesino developed various exercises to cultivate a sense and understanding of imix, all of them centered on the fertilized egg, human heart viewed as the center of each individual's sphere. Ensemble members made an effort to focus on what was considered a performer's sphere of energy. In the Teatro's understanding, every individual is conceived of as a luminous being composed of a spherical field of energy that can be controlled and directed if the individual is in tune with her or his center or heart and body.

To begin with, various individual warm-up exercises are performed to both loosen the muscles and circulate blood to all parts of the body, thereby awakening the energies enclosed in the body. This is followed by group warm-ups for the purpose of gathering all the individual energies into one or a group focus. More specialized exercises are then undertaken as a group in order to sharpen each individual's sense of heart and circulation in every part of the body.[13] Among the goals envisioned are the capability to feel the presence of the heartbeat in every individual body unit (such as the eyes, the soles of the feet, the skin covering the skull, the spine, the jugular vein, etc.) and then throughout the entire body at once. Among the many exercises corresponding to imix is one in which the individual begins in the fetal position with arms wrapped around the knees and the feet flat on the floor. From this position the participants rise and open to form a "tree of life." Another exercise consists of pacing forward with hands holding down the lower back (hands open and pointing down) in order to be led by the body's midsection, or "center of creation."

In addition to such exercises performed by individuals, imix also progresses to exercises pertaining to the interaction of two or more spheres of energy. Such exercises seek to sharpen the individual's ability to react and to influence the actions of others, as well as to anticipate others' movements. This ability can be used to oppose others' energy or to harness it by moving parallel to it. In either event, the idea is to never move contrary to the lines of energy, but in the direction of the energy flow. For example, one person (A) comes forward and is met by another (B), who grabs A's wrist, moving with that person and in the direction chosen by that person, but then B manages to incline A toward the floor, using A's own energy to bring A to the floor in a spherical motion. A comparable exercise is described in the following parallel-car exercise:

> Picture two cars moving at the same speed. The idea is to move with the same pace and in the same direction. Now with human beings, you must move at the same speed and direction as your opponent. You must be willing to open your sphere of energy and expose it to your opponent. He in turn will do the same and this will allow you to feel and sense his moves before he actually makes them. It's up to you to move a second sooner than him so that your sphere will *engulf* his sphere.

The second "step" of the Veinte Pasos centers on the concept ik: breath of life. Ik refers to the breath of life bestowed in the womb. Significant here is the number 2 as duality, in combination with a consciousness of the dual nature of respiration, involving inhalation and exhalation. This duality is seen as well in the beats of the heart. The challenge to individuals consists of cultivating their sense of the duality of all things, beginning with the body. Fully aware of the all-important element of contradiction which exists in reality, members of El Teatro Campesino likened ik to the "law of dialectical materialism." Within the physical reality of the body "it refers to our entire dualistic nature. We have a left side and a right side, an up and a down." Ik is also conceptualized as the splitting of imix (the point/number 1/fertilized egg) into two cells through contrary forces. The two cells, although separate, are at the same time unified.

A key Aztec concept applied and studied at this point is that of Nahui Ollin, or "movement through union of opposites," symbolized graphically by two lines that interlock and go in opposite directions within a circle (symbolizing the same concept as the Chinese yin-yang circle). Various exercises explore that human duality and seek to illustrate how the play of two contradictory sides resolves itself in circular motion: "The circulation of your blood from the heart. The circulation of your torso at the hips and neck. The circulation of your hands at the wrist. Your head at the neck. Your eyes in their sockets, etc." The performers must mentally, emotionally, and physically explore the various movement directions possible for the body: in two directions, four, six, and finally in the circular direction that encompasses all others. Achieving awareness of ik involves attaining consciousness of one's contradictions.

Although vast in its applications, breath serves as the symbolic focal point within the concept of ik. In one flyer the direct relationship between ik (breath of life) and performance is briefly stated: "Your soul breathes. That is why breathing is so important to actors. Because breath is a spiritual matter—more spiritual than material. And it has everything to do with the spiritual power of a performance." Exercises corresponding to ik focus on the contradictions of the body. Among them, for example, are various rotational exercises concentrating on the four major parts of the body (head, trunk and lungs, thighs and legs, hands and arms) as well as exercises dealing with opposing forces in the body. The exercise known as "serpent dance," for example, works on the contradictions of the body and consists of a group stomp in circular motion, weight alternating from left foot to right foot using a rhythm of three stomps per foot.

Within the third step of the Veinte Pasos—akbal: born of water—a triangular relationship is established with the first two, connoting the synthetic quality of life, the dynamics of life elements coming together even as they appear to fall apart. It is the synthesis of the thesis and the antithesis and as such traces the completion of a movement, such as the thrust of blood from the heart, or the movement of vision formed through a synthesis of left eye and right eye. Exercises corresponding to akbal focus heavily on the dynamics of physical movement and the movement through life, which is said to spiral, returning at intervals to the same point on a different plane.

The fourth step, or day, of the sacred calendar is named kan, which means serpent (as in kukulkan: feathered serpent). As the fourth step is in the process of human evolution, it is associated with the human state designated as "knows evil." Since knowing evil (the negative) presupposes knowing the positive, it is suggestive of a balanced or stable state. Stability or balance are

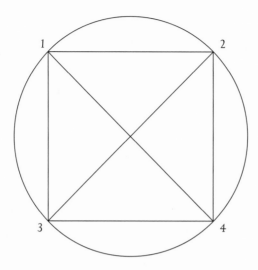

Figure 2. *Kan Closes the Triangle*

also inherent in the number 4, which represents numerous things, such as, the four seasons, the four human races, the four quadrants of the planet, the four winds, the four elements (earth, air, fire, and water), the four cardinal points, the cross, as it stands for Quetzalcoatl (*kukulkan*) itself. *Kan* is also said to represent the illusion of the material world, where things seem to be stable but are actually in motion and in evolution. Cultivation of *kan* requires various exercises that focus on balance; for example, the entire body is balanced on the head, hands, buttocks, but most of all on the feet, where one-fourth of the body's bones are located. Geometrically speaking, *kan* closes the triangle within the circle into a square, as in figure 2.

The fifth step, *chicchan*, means "to gather your life experience." In performance terms this signifies presence or stage presence, which is a human state achieved through combining the previous four steps. Performers are called on to "sense the whole presence of your being from inside out." *Chicchan* involves the capacity to practice "free flowing exercise" through awareness of total bodily being (presence). The reality of "gathering life experience" is rendered geometrically by the pyramid, which is formed by pulling upward from a central point within the square (*kan*), as in figure 3.

At the conclusion of the first five steps, the performers should have reached an understanding of the body-sphere. This is described in a Theater

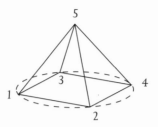

Figure 3. *Gathering Life Experience*

of the Sphere workshop flyer as follows: "As actors, our body must have the total freedom to move around in all directions with balance and grace. It must be well-tuned, flexible, and ready to be used on or off the stage. We stress the importance of using music, dance and their aid in developing rhythm and movement."

It should be pointed out that the exercises developed by El Teatro Campesino for the Veinte Pasos were both developed and supplemented by a great deal of individual and collective improvisational exercises. Olivia Chumacero recalls:

> What you would do specifically was to do an improvisation. Let's say you were working on number five (*chicchan*). You take the ones that you've done before, say "breath of life," "born in water," so you can create an improvisation in which you are dealing with a certain aspect of your life experience, but it's not verbalized. You can use the symbol of breathing; you can make sounds but not make a language with it. Or you can use the symbol of water, which is fluid and therefore that would kind of put an emphasis on how you could move your body or associate our body movements to water. "Knows evil" is to react in the positive/negative way because when you know evil you know the positive as well. So you would take all these elements into yourself and say, "Okay, I'm going to do an improvisation on when I was a kid and I almost drowned a dog." Something real specific, real concrete. You would do an improvisation but it would be totally abstract. But you would know and the people around you would know what you were dealing with because we had already gone through these other steps. Then we had all those physical exercises as well that go through each one of the Veinte Pasos. (Interview, 8/18/1989)

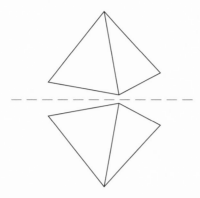

Figure 4. Cimi

On completion of numerous exercises pertaining to facets of the body, an exploration of human emotionality was undertaken, corresponding to steps six through ten of the Veinte Pasos. Those activities pertaining to emotions (called "the heart") were described as follows:

> Within our work, we have discovered that we have to experience and control the whole spectrum of our emotional makeup. Within every human being, there are opposing forces constantly at work. These opposing forces or emotions (love-hate, fear-courage), are what make our life dynamic. There is nothing wrong with being emotional so long as we are in control and can return to the center where all emotions are neutralized. As actors, we must be able to cry and then laugh at the next moment. We must develop trust in ourselves, as well as in others. (El Teatro Campesino [n.d.], Workshop)

The training of the heart and the emotions begins with number 6, cimi, which means death. Death here refers to the need for death of the ego, or old self, as preparation for the rebirth of a new self whose consciousness extends beyond the self (in number 7); number 6 (cimi) also involves cultivation of a consciousness of self as actor, audience, and member of the ensemble simultaneously. In practical terms it refers to the mobilization of the creative spirit so as to effect a collective meeting of minds, hearts, and bodies among all involved in any given action or performance. In Mayan, 6 also means cauac or "that which emerges from itself." This describes the process

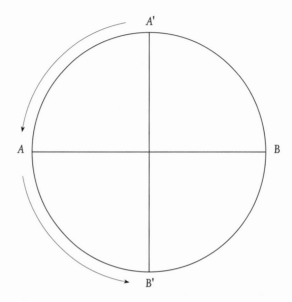

Figure 5. *Nahui Ollin Circle Exercise*

of extending beyond the self, or "ego death," which is called for. Cimi uti-
lized various trust exercises involving one immobile person who is lifted by
the group from a lying to a standing position. The immobile person then
is left to fall backward and is caught by the others. This concept is represented
geometrically by a diamond shape—which is nothing more than the image
of a pyramid emerging mirror-fashion from another pyramid, as in figure 4.

Cimi is followed by man-ik, the number 7, which represents "to overcome
death," or rebirth of the new self through emergence out of the formerly
static self of cimi. This involves the projection of pairs of emotional opposites
(in numerous exercises) and the experience of the entire spectrum of emotions. In the work of performance it implies the acquisition of an understanding (through experience) and control of emotional states (love-hate,
courage-fear). This includes the capacity to express any emotion without
being captured by that emotion, so as to be able to return to one's emotional
center. In this scheme of things, emotions are considered a type of energy
vibration that can be tapped and applied in all forms of acting. Man-ik typically involves exercises conducted in a circle in order to probe emotional
opposites. These exercises are named "Nahui Ollin Circle Exercises" and can
involve two, four, or more people. Participants position themselves at the

quadrants (A, A', B, B') of the circle. As they move counterclockwise, they emotionally move from a positive emotion (e.g., self-confidence) to a negative one (e.g., self-pity), to a positive and back to a negative, as in figure 5. This movement from emotion to diametrically opposed emotion is performed using all conceivable emotional pairs.

Number 8 is *lamat*, which means "lower regions" (or materiality). It refers to the capacity to materialize the interplay of emotions (the contradiction or change of emotions) into the materiality of physical motion. It thus stands for two opposing emotional forces (*cimi* and *man-ik*), which result in a third force (a physical motion). *Lamat* involves numerous exercises that translate emotions into the materiality of physical motion. Emotions are expressed not in words but through appropriate motions, sometimes in combination with sounds.

The number 9 is *muluc*, "to overcome matter." *Muluc* represents the state of balance in a person's emotional makeup. This is in turn described as the ability to express emotion without the use of physical motion. One of the ways in which this is manifest is through the capacity to affect others (such as an audience) through one's emotions, yet without moving. The emotions are what move. Mastering *muluc* also enables actors to share intuitively in a common emotional state, hence vastly enhancing the process of ensemble collaboration.

The final step within the five steps pertaining to the emotions (number 10) is called *oc*, "to enter into the depths of matter." In practice it refers to the capacity to gather one's emotional experience into a point of realization or whole emotional awareness. This involves an awareness not only of emotional qualities and emotional strengths but of emotional weakness or weaknesses. The importance of discovering weaknesses should not be minimized. "It's being able to pull yourself out of your being and watch your body dance to your emotions." An example of an *oc* exercise (i.e., pertaining to emotional development) is called "I remember you" and seeks to sharpen emotional imagination. Participants form a circle; two of them enter the center and participate in an emotional interchange. Each speaks to the other as if she were his hated or beloved or feared teacher, parent, lover, or whatever.

The third set of steps within the Veinte Pasos pertains to the mind, or the intellectual development of the individual. Instead of continuing with a detailed step-by-step description of the remaining Veinte Pasos, I consider it preferable to pursue the analysis on a different plane. What is particularly significant is the cyclical element that exists within the twenty-step progression. For example, the "preparation for birth of the new self," which is step 1 of bodily training, is repeated in the first step of the emotional series (number 6). Both are a preparation for birth, yet in different dimensions or levels. "Preparation for birth," or "infinite potential," occurs a third time at the beginning of the mind series (*chuen*, number 11: burns without flame). Similarly, step 2 (ik: breath of life) of the body series returns within the number 7 of the emotional series and number 12 of the mind series. The second step within each five-step grouping or series has to do with an understanding of duality and opposites: ik (number 2) deals with bodily oppositions; *man-ik* (number 7) correspondingly deals with emotional contradictions; *eb* (number 12) pertains to intellectual contradiction. In other words, ik happens all over again, but at a different level each time.

This cyclical correspondence or circularity is also expressed by the regular repetition of the geometric symbols within the Veinte Pasos: on completion of the first five steps and their symbols, the symbols repeat themselves beginning at number 6; and they do so again at steps 11–15 (the mind series) and again at steps 16–20 (the steps pertaining to the soul). This is not surprising, given that the concepts pertaining to human development at the level of *body* subsequently repeat themselves at the level of *emotion*, then *mind* (intellectuality) and finally *soul*. These developmental concepts or steps can be schematized as follows:

1. Infinite potential; preparation for birth (bodily, emotional, mental, spiritual)
2. Unity of opposites (bodily, emotional, mental, spiritual)
3. Materialization (into movement, emotion, thought, spirit)
4. Balance (of body, emotions, intellect, spirit)
5. Gathering of experience; realization of total self (bodily, emotional, mental, spiritual)

It is by virtue of the passage of the body, emotions, mind, and soul through each of five steps or stages that the Spherical Actor is formed. The cyclical nature of the Veinte Pasos appears to affirm the intimate structural correspondence that exists between body, heart, mind, and soul as well as the reality of their unity (ideally) as a field of mutually sustaining forces. A consciousness and realization of the full potential of these human forces in synchrony is the foundation for human sphericality. The Theater of the Sphere is described as follows: "It is the unity (*unidad*) of the elements that we covered before—the body, heart, and mind all working together. This leads us into improvisations with creative focus, where people are communicating and interacting as different characters on a more spherical level, as true human beings (El Teatro Campesino [n.d.]:*Workshop*).

The immensely sharpened sensitivity of the Spherical Actor allows for immediate and appropriate response to and even anticipation of changing situations, an ideal within improvisational acting. In this regard the geometric image of the Sphere is again a metaphor or blueprint for human action: because it is round it readily moves and responds to outside forces. It responds to those outside forces by virtue of its own field of energy:

> The Sphere has an energy. Energy is acting upon it from the outside and energy is acting upon it from the inside out. It rolls, it moves, it sways. To me that symbol is like an unending source of energy because when the ball stops moving it still has the same potential: once you move it, touch it, affect it, it rolls. And that is like a symbol of your life. If you're at rest that does not mean that you don't have any energy or that you're not thinking. . . . Also as you move in time you're moving in that spherical way. In your lifetime. Because you do things in cycles, and you hopefully reflect on what you did over here at another time. As you continue in your movement it is a Sphere. I don't see my life in a flat plane or in one line. Because it's the extension of all the other lives that are around me. So the Sphere encompasses many aspects. The ones that you can touch and those you can't. And your reasoning and your will. (Chumacero interview, 8/18/1989)

The three human dimensions of body, heart, and mind achieve highest integration and hence sensitivity in the dimension of "soul" (steps 16–20). As a consequence, the dimension of soul represents a cumulative force, akin to "creative spirit." In other words, Mayan knowledge (myth, religion, science, art) expressed in the Theater of the Sphere can be said to have a pedagogical function, which cultivates the powers in each human's whole being for effective action in the world. Olivia Chumacero variously describes this kind of preparation, or Sphericality, as a type of "will-power" based on "enlightenment" or "consciousness." The "will-power" that is cultivated within the Spherical Actor also necessarily implies a goal in the outer world and a relationship to it:

> Each one of us acts like a ball because those things that are on the outside affect us every day, we react to it. We move *against* or *away* from it or *with* it, you know, all those different things. And we do that all the time, all the time. When you are a Spherical Actor then you are conscious of your actions. You are *conscious*, you have a *goal* in mind. You are *aware* of why you want to do that. You use that energy; you don't just let the energy push you and take you *y ya*; *sino que* [and that's it; instead] that energy comes in and you have your *own* will to be able to bring out in a positive way, or in a way in which it will make you *move* in a positive way or *act* in a positive way in this world. (Interview, 8/18/1989)[14]

The whole of reality and the relationship between its component parts is rendered through the symbol of the sphere. The sphere, functioning at once as a metaphor of transcendence and of the dailiness of applied communal life (including the life of each individual), became the central organizing principle within the Teatro's program of self-education. The sphere is among the most basic of universal mythological symbols representing the workings of life. It is considered a primordial symbol of that which is experienced constantly in reality. On the one hand it suggests a completed totality and, as such, the potential for a new beginning. The sphere is a sacred circle or sacred hoop, a fundamental symbol of Native American culture. The circularity of the sphere parallels the circularity of all cycles, such as the day cycle, the lunar cycle, the human birth-death-birth life cycle, the seasons, the cycle of time, the cycle of the generations, and the circle of all life, which is one. In addition, the sphere or circle is also considered a symbol of the entire solar system: the sun is a sphere; the planets are spheres; the moons are spheres. Time and space sphere (i.e., curve). The atom and its parts move in spherical fashion. In their movement or orbits the heavenly bodies in our solar system all trace out a sphere—around their own axis and in relation to each other and around the sun. Within the human being, life begins in spherical form: as a zygote encircled by the womb. Within this view of things, every human is viewed as essentially spherical; each person has a spherical presence or aura. ("Around every person there is a sphere, an aura. The immaterial part of you; this radiance. . . . There's an emotional-spiritual presence" [Valdez 1984e].)

Those who engage in the process of Theater of the Sphere strive to coordinate their individual circles or spheres within the universal circle of forces at work in the larger life process. The Sphericality of the performer extends (ideally) not only to the audiences but to two other intersecting performance spheres. In other words, the Performer's Sphere is construed not as self-contained, but in permanent exchange with three other Spheres: audience, society, nature and cosmos. This is illustrated in figure 6.

Theater of the Sphere: The World of Performance

The preceding discussion of the Veinte Pasos and of the Spherical Actor needs amplification. Although the training of the Veinte Pasos is directed at creating a Spherical Actor (defined as a complete human being), that Sphericality should not be understood in any way as sheer inwardliness or an exclusively internal or personal process. Achieving the highest state of consciousness within the Veinte Pasos in no way signifies a state of splendid isolation. Rather it is a state attainable only through engagement in this world, by which I

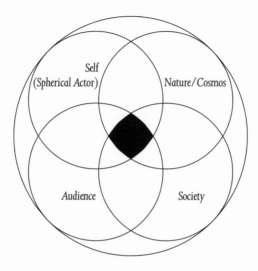

Figure 6. The Performer's Sphere

mean not only the world of the stage, but also the natural world and the social-economic-political world of human institutions. Some discussion of the relationship between the Spherical Actor and these other realms of the Theater of the Sphere is in order. In this section I discuss what could be called the intersection of spheres: the relationship between the world of the Spherical Actor, the theatrical world, the natural world, and the social formation (the sphere of performance, the sphere of nature and cosmos, the sphere of community).[15] My primary focus will be on the different dimensions of Theater of the Sphere manifested through the work of performance. In conclusion I also examine elements of the controversy created by the Theater of the Sphere project. Critical controversy accompanied the stage manifestations of Theater of the Sphere from beginning to end. It is perhaps beneficial to consider both the controversial dimensions and the promise that Theater of the Sphere holds in our time and for future generations.

To begin with, I would like to elaborate on how the Teatro Campesino approached the theatrical world. Application of the Theater of the Sphere had an impact not only on the individual performer, but on ensemble spirit, audience relationship, and the creation of performance pieces. The Teatro Campesino's conceptualization of its relationship to audiences, for example, relied on the fundamental principles of Theater of the Sphere. In fact, functioning "spherically" by definition includes audiences and all other elements of the environment. (The Spherical Actor always functions in the public sphere.) The Teatro Campesino's vision of "completeness" in the human being—meaning the realization of a person's infinite potential—included a very particular understanding of how effective, or Spherical, action functions; of how it is that one affects others. That understanding in turn has as its basis a particular understanding of energy transfer or power. It is a form of "reception theory." El Teatro Campesino's view of human energy as the sustaining force of life corresponds to that within Mayan philosophy that views energy not only as the first cause and basis of human life, but as the basis of all movement or transformation. This concept of energy is considered synonymous with spirit or power. The terms "spirit" or "power," "creative force" or "energy," are virtually interchangeable within Native American thinking throughout the Americas:

> The heart of Mexican philosophy and religion consists of knowledge about the force, process, or creative power which is called *Wakan Tanka* by the Sioux and *Ketche Manito* by Algonkian peoples. The various Indian names for this "foundation of all" are usually translated into English as "the Great Spirit," "the Great Mystery," or "the Creator." I myself prefer to translate *Ketche Manito* as the "Great Creative Power" because, in its ultimate form, it is a process of creativity, of potentiality, of unfolding, of becoming, rather than being a "superman" or a "super-spirit." All things can or do possess *manito* ("creative power") according to Algonkian peoples, and *Ketche Manito* is simply a way of referring to the mysterious source of *manito*. (Forbes 1973:53)

In the Teatro's conception and in that of Native American philosophy, all human interaction is viewed as an exchange of spirit, which equals energy transmitted through human vibration. The theatrical dimension of human interaction is no exception, and the goal of theatrical and life performance is considered the exchange of spirit and energy. This exchange is the force within the heart, the mind, the body, and the soul (see figs. 7 and 8). Theater is regarded, above all, as an inspiring (i.e., inspiriting) process. A Teatro Campesino document from 1976 defines the purpose of theater in terms of a "transference of energy":

> It is the purpose of teatro to infuse the people with *energy*, with *spirit*.
>   The actor must find his internal source of ENERGY. ENERGY-VIBRATION—we must communicate ENERGY.
>   The individual must "vibrate" and feel his energy. He must communicate this energy to his fellow actors. A company of actors must set up a flow of

energy between them—a vibration—and then
communicate this vibration to the audience.
    COARSE TO FINE VIBRATIONS determine the
quality of the communication—*the transference of energy.*
    Energy must be fluid (light) in order to flow
from one place to another, from one person to another.
    The aim is to discover BEING in people.
    The idea is to illuminate a person's life by uncovering
the presence of the CREATOR.
    El "CAN" el SI SE PUEDE, EL PODER! (*El Teatro Campesino.*
Renacimiento [6/7/1976])

This same vision of performance is later expressed by Luis Valdez (Dunsmore
de Carrillo 1977): "Spirit, you see, is at the very heart of the arts." In Valdez
(1984a) he expressed the same understanding:

> That's another way to describe what our work has become: it's an exploration
> about our human being, about humanity. What is it? And there is a link
> between what the flesh does and what the spirit does. And so when an actor
> is on, when he's out there doing stuff, these radiations are coming out that
> affect the audience. It's not just a question of watching a story; it's a question
> of being *there* and inspiriting people, inspiring people to grab life, to come
> alive again.

In this view of things, energy is differentiated into three distinguishable
but interrelated human spheres or types: the emotional, the intellectual, and
the physical. There is physical or bodily energy, emotional energy, and mental or intellectual energy. When and if the infinite potential (power) of these
three merge, then the cumulative force of "spirit" (soul) or "inspiriting" is
said to take place. The process of inspiriting corresponds to the transference
of human energy formed through the process of the Veinte Pasos. A Spherical Actor is an integrated and conscious human being, in control of (1) the
physicality of a performance; (2) the emotionality of a performance;
(3) the intellectuality of a performance; and (4) their interrelatedness, or
Sphericality. The inspiriting intention behind any performance, viewed as a
transference of that confluence of human energies, involves the generation
of an emotional response, an intellectual response, and a physical response
within one's audience.

    The Teatro Campesino additionally had a very specific understanding of
how the process of inspiriting happens; of how emotional, intellectual, and
physical energy is transferred to audiences. In essence that understanding

could be referred to as a model of communication or pedagogy that is central within the Theater of the Sphere. Communication or effective human action is conceptualized as the transmission of three distinguishable but interrelated forms of energy: emotional, physical, and mental. A schematic of the Theater of the Sphere (figure 7) illustrates how each human energy sphere grows out of the others, just as each unit in the progression of the Veinte Pasos emerges from what came before. What this circle also illustrates is the impossibility of separating any of the elements.

Nonetheless, the prerequisite for any and all communication is considered to be motion, viewed as a fundamental human vibration or life energy. That essential human vibration has primacy within the sphere. The first source of any performative communication is considered the vibration of an individual's being. It is perhaps useful to note that the vibration of being is understood as something drawn from the realm of spiritual energy, which is in us all. Reference to that energy source as a unified "realm" (called Hunabku in Mayan thought) simply suggests a belief in the essential sphericalness, or connectedness of all energy within the creation. Luis Valdez (1984b) describes that "realm" in the following terms: "Where does that vibration come from? Well, that is the mystery of life. What does that vibration consist in? My basic philosophy is that in the midst of all matter there is in fact no 'thing'; it is energy that is there. When you finally get down to it, it is spiritual energy. And when you finally get to the essence of that spiritual energy it is belief."

Belief within El Teatro Campesino came to be regarded as faith in oneself arising from the conviction that the "Creator" or "Creative Power" (power, energy) is present as infinite potential within the individual. That kind of belief was learned not only from Mayan philosophy but from the oral tradition generally and from a direct involvement in the United Farm Workers movement, whose determination ("energy") and political struggle was rooted in this very belief system. Hence César Chávez and the United Farm Workers of America received the Teatro's 1985 Feathered Serpent Award "for creating the spiritual ground from which El Teatro Campesino grew in the struggle for social justice in America" (inscribed on award). That spiritual ground of the UFW is the working-class Mexican belief system that contextualizes all human endeavor and creation as part of the greater creation. This could be described as a sacred conception of production as opposed to the dominant mainstream secular view of production, which is mechanistic and individualistic.

Theater of the Sphere is in essence an integrative model of human communication and learning. Primary human vibration (called "energy in mo-

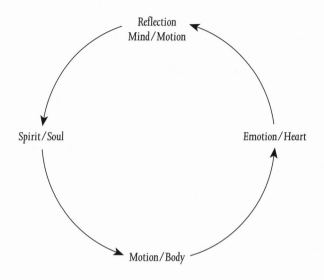

Figure 7. The Theater of the Sphere

tion, moving through space") in the Theater of the Sphere communication model or "inspiriting" process is said to be accompanied by "emotion." An emotional flow is considered the channel which then facilitatei "notion" (intellectual discourse, intellectual communication). Not only is notion (i.e., mental activity, reflection) said to follow upon emotion but it is considered almost impossible without the presence of that emotional flow. The pedagogy of Theater of the Sphere departed radically from the very dispassionate, rationalized, and rationalistic (i.e., based on reason) forms of communication (teaching and learning) practiced in American higher education, where body, heart, mind, and soul are not united but divided into "faculties" or departments. Valdez (1984b) describes the importance of the emotive impulse within the Theater of the Sphere. Its importance to audience receptivity and communication is prime: "Nobody can teach and nobody can learn unless there is an emotional exchange. I cannot get ideas across to you unless I have some kind of feeling for you. Now it could be positive, it could be negative. But there has got to be some emotion. If I feel nothing for you, I'm not going to communicate with you, and you're not going to communicate with me. We don't receive . . . You communicate best with those people that you touch emotionally."

The totality or Sphericality of the "inspiriting" process of human performance for the Theater of the Sphere can be summarized thus: motion (human vibration) is the foundation; out of that motion is generated emotion. Out of emotion comes notion (ideas). The circle spirals around and out of notion comes motion again, that motion among actors, but also motion among the audience members. Of course these four aspects should in no way be regarded as separate entities but rather understood only as unified aspects of any action.

The Teatro believed that only those ideas communicated on an emotional beam (and of course physically and spiritually) would motivate the audience to thought or action. Within the Teatro Campesino these four elements of Sphericality (motion, emotion, notion, spirit) were also at times referred to as →effect, →affect, →reflect, and →inspirit which leads again to →effect, →affect, →reflect, →inspirit (note: these four aspects do not follow each other but interplay constantly and simultaneously). An actor's presence and power are said to depend on how totally she or he inhabits her or his sphere on stage and is able to project the energy of total presence. A performer's movement can and should result in a certain emotional state of being, which can and should result in a certain reflection back to a new movement. It is when performances succeed in establishing that quadruple flow of energy ("spirit") with audiences (spiritual response, physical response, emotional response, intellectual response) that the circle widens and the Sphericality, or totality, of communication is established. The Theater of the Sphere hence emerges as a theory and practice of communicative action. What is communicated is conveyed through spirit. This movement is shown in figure 8, which illustrates how spirit is the extension of energy, the successful communication of energy.

The better developed the performer is, the better that person will be able to communicate energy. The well-rounded, or Spherical, actor, is also a successful ensemble player (not a self-centered actor) and has, as well, the ability to work in all realms of theatrical production (such as set design and music).

The same Theater of the Sphere principles involved in the performance of a play found application in the conception of those plays. The Theater of the Sphere informed all aspects of theatrical activity: performer training and performance, as well as the creation of performance pieces. In reference to Theater of the Sphere, Olivia Chumacero states: "It was the backbone of everything we did" (interview, 8/18/1989). In essence the productions staged by the ensemble sought to accomplish various things at once: the enactment or interpretation of a slice of Chicana/o reality; a style of characters and acting and thematics that was typical of the Rasquachi Aesthetic (see chap. 1).

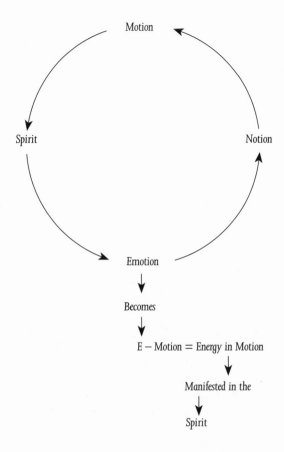

Figure 8. Spirit is the Extension of Energy

The Veinte Pasos—in combination with the Rasquachi Aesthetic—were used to construct the slice of Chicana/o reality chosen for theatrical elaboration. From the Rasquachi Aesthetic of the *carpa* came the style of the characters and of acting, as well as the basic thematics and their bipolar structure. Yet the artistic balance of the parts, the relationship between them, the interpretation or construction of that slice of reality, and the performance philosophy and orientation of the piece were based on Theater of the Sphere.

The levels of response (physical, emotional, intellectual, and spiritual) that Teatro Campesino performers sought to trigger in audiences were also applied in the creation of performance pieces. The overarching goal within

plays was to cover the four aspects of life and human development represented by the Veinte Pasos: the Body, the Mind, the Heart, and the Soul.
These aspects had to be found in all performance pieces—although not necessarily in the progressional order of the Veinte Pasos. In the 1980 version of
Fin del mundo, for example, the experiences of the main character—Reymundo
Mata—to a large extent reflect the Veinte Pasos. The play is divided into
two acts with ten scenes in the first act and thirteen in the second. Each
scene epitomizes one of the steps of body, soul, mind, and spirit. In other
words, the main thrust of the narrative in each scene corresponds to one of
the Veinte Pasos.

Plays such as the various versions of Fin del mundo or La gran carpa de la familia
Rasquachi were based on the Veinte Pasos skeleton or framework. Ensemble
members felt that a successful play was one that harmoniously combined all
the aspects of the Veinte Pasos in its development. Steps from the Veinte Pasos
often provided the conceptual focus for the improvisational work of collective playwriting. Improvisations of scenes were at times initiated with reliance on one of the Veinte Pasos. Chumacero (interview, 8/18/1989)
describes the process: "When we had a particular play that we wanted to
focus on or start creating off of, we didn't have to start from scratch because
we would know: Okay, we're going to work on imix today? Okay? And
you didn't have to start explaining from the base—'Well, it means this, and
then. . . . '—because you had gone through the workshop you had a sense
of what imix represented, so you started creating with that in mind."

The Theater of the Sphere encompassed more than the Veinte Pasos (as a
performance training and playwriting grid). It also included a program of
dissemination (the hosting of Theater of the Sphere workshops) and a program of study that embraced indigenous languages, poetry, philosophy, and
dance. Particularly influential were the oral and written teachings of
Domingo Martínez Paredez, Ignacio Magaloni Duarte, and Virgilio Valladares
Aldaco—all of whom, incidentally, take issue with and refute many of the
findings of the Mesoamerican studies establishment. Also important were
primary documents such as the work of Nezahualcoyotl and other indigenous poets, the codices, and in particular the PopolVuh. A great deal of what
was learned came not through the vehicle of print culture, however, but
through oral traditions of danza, through lived experience in indígena communities in the United States and Mexico, and through the pláticas by elders or
maestros such as Andrés Segura and Domingo Martínez Paredez.

Various elements from those teachings are palpable in all Teatro
Campesino productions of the 1970s. The 1980 Fin del mundo, for example, is
a farce grounded in indígena knowledge. The play follows the trials and tribu-

lations of a *rasquachi* underdog figure—Reymundo Mata—and his sidekicks (Vera and Huesos)—throughout his hilariously funny afterlife. If we look at the humorous elements seriously, an entire philosophy of life and death emerges, an *indígena* philosophy. What is dead is shown to be alive, and vice versa. The complementarity or even blurring of life and death are manifest. In other plays, such as *La gran carpa de la familia Rasquachi*, *indígena* teachings subtly inform the orientation of the piece but at times are manifest through the appearance of mythical beings such as Quetzalcoatl or Guadalupe.

Since indigenous knowledge (of science, art, philosophy, and "mythology") is often physically inscribed and transmitted—in ritual masked dance and pageants—the Teatro Campesino cultivated and enacted these on a regular basis. These included the Chorti Mayan *Baile de los gigantes* (adapted from a description by Maya scholar Rafael Girard); the *danzas* of the Conchero tradition (an entire cycle of dances performed under the guidance of Conchero captain Andrés Segura); as well as the *Pastorela* and *Cuatro apariciones de la Virgen de Tepeyac*.

Since the *Pastorela* and *Cuatro apariciones* are discussed in chapter 1, I will here elaborate only on the Conchero dances and *Baile de los gigantes*. Although these two dance practices come from different traditions—the Concheros are Aztec, the *Gigantes* are Mayan—the objectives of these and most other ritual dances are similar. In general, ritual dance seeks to promote a cosmic integration of the cosmic planetary movement, the individual, and the immediate and larger human community. Dance is felt to constitute a harmonizing force; humans expend force or energy on the representation of a particular dimension or understanding of human and planetary life and situate themselves within that understanding. Each dance representation manifests an understanding or blueprint of life dynamics or a dimension of life dynamics. Numerous Conchero dances, for example, are named after particular deities or "myths" that represent not individuals but relational complexes and principles pertaining to life and creation. Dances constitute vessels of indigenous scientific thought concerning all movement in the cosmos. Maya scholar Felipe Fernández thus indicates: "Ser danzante es comprender los complicados ritmos del cosmos y tener la facultad de exteriorizarlos mediante los movimientos del cuerpo del ser humano ... la danza verdadera es ciencia y conocimiento del cosmos" (To be a dancer is to comprehend the complicated rhythms of the cosmos and to have the capacity to exteriorize them through the movements of the human being ... true dance is science and a knowledge of the cosmos) (in Segura 1973:25–26).

The Mayan *Baile de los gigantes* functions in this same way. The *Gigantes* is a solstitial dance, which after colonization was made to coincide with the Day of San Juan, June 24, in order to appease Spanish Catholic authorities. The "Historia" (as the Chortis call the *Baile de los gigantes*) is a physicalization of the mythic portion of the Mayan "Bible," or *Popol Vuh*. Maya scholar Rafael Girard (whose research into the dance provided the basis for the Teatro Campesino's performance) describes the scientific knowledge preserved in this dance:

> What "The History" [*Baile de los gigantes*] offers us is not solely a mythical account; it sums up the native knowledge of theogony, cosmogony, and astronomy as well as the arithmetic and time-reckoning procedures employed during the Great Period of Maya civilization. Therefore, every single thing pertaining to its presentation is carried out according to a program that is exceedingly carefully laid out beforehand in harmony with the mathematical mentality that is so characteristic of the Maya. (1979:284)

The vast scientific, religious, mathematical, and humanistic knowledge is represented in the Historia as an allegorical struggle between the hero gods Hunahpu and Ixbalamque, who, together with their parents, the seven Ahpu, struggle against the giants named Vukup, Cakix, Zipacná, and Caprakan and the forces of Xibalba (the Black Giant and his henchmen). For a detailed description and discussion of this allegorical struggle I refer readers to Girard (1979). In the Teatro Campesino's conception of the piece, as in the Chortis', the drama is performed, on the one hand, to impart scientific knowledge. On the other hand, it offers protection to the community from the high concentrations of solar energy when the sun is at its zenith (around June 24). If not redirected, that solar energy is said to trigger violence and mental harm. Valdez describes both the effects of solstitial solar energy and the purifying effect of the *Baile de los gigantes*:

> And if in your person you have spiritual impurities, say you are given to anger or envy, that solar energy, like putting too much water in a bottle, breaks open the individual and he goes out and does something he is sorry for. June 24th is a notorious day for people killing each other. They take guns to each other, and they don't even know why. So *El Baile de los gigantes* is a purification for the performers and for the whole tribe as well. It shows the good forces fighting against the bad forces, and by concentrating on the action, the people go through the struggle, in a sense, and it liberates them from their bad feelings. It is cathartic, but it is also in direct relationship with the mathematical knowledge of reality. (Shank 1974:62)

The Teatro Campesino performed the *Baile de los gigantes* publicly at the 1974 Quinto Festival de los Teatros Chicanos y Latinoamericanos convened at the Mexican pyramids of Teotihuacan (Shank 1974). In subsequent years the

Ritual Mayan solstitial dance Baile de los gigantes *performed by Teatro Campesino at 1974 TENAZ Festival at the pyramids of Teotihuacan (Mexico City). Courtesy of Olivia Chumacero Archive.*

Teatro continued to perform the ritual dance, although rarely in public. It was commonly performed on the forty acres of land that the Teatro purchased in San Juan Bautista in the hopes of establishing a farm commune and performance school. Although a few farm animals were acquired, neither the farming project nor the performance school was established. Property ownership, however, definitely facilitated the work of the Veinte Pasos. Olivia Chumacero comments: "The 40 acres allowed us to work at the creative process. It gave us a space where we could be on land without having limitations. It gave us the freedom to continue to do our creative work" (interview, 8/18/1989).

Theater of the Sphere: Liberation or Mystification?
The Teatro Campesino's comprehensive Theater of the Sphere project did not receive attention from the press or academic criticism. Yet, the Teatro's 1974 performance of the *Baile de los gigantes* as well as subsequent Teatro Campesino plays manifesting an indigenist orientation certainly came under heavy criticism. That criticism targeted these public performances without acknowledging the larger Theater of the Sphere project. They critiqued textually, that is, without consideration of the intense collective exploration process and training dimensions of the Theater of the Sphere, without an understanding of *indígena* culture, and without discussion of the larger project's merit or potential.

Still, we do well to consider the controversy that arose around these Teatro Campesino performances. One festival eyewitness described the response to the *Baile de los gigantes* performed at the 1974 Quinto Festival: "there was a feeling among most festival participants that theatre should deal more directly with social-political problems, that it should designate the oppressor and the oppressed, that it should clarify the issues of the class struggle" (Shank 1974:66). One cannot but wonder whether this view extended to *all* communities that practice ritual or only to El Teatro Campesino. In other words, did most festival participants feel that ritual should be abandoned in the Americas? Or only that it should be abandoned by El Teatro Campesino? Were only performance forms that "designate the oppressor and the oppressed" considered valid or acceptable? Although critics were quick to cite what they considered missing from *Baile de los gigantes*, very few attempted to comprehend, let alone consider valid, the intricacies of the scientific, mathematical, and astronomical knowledge it enacted. Most critics simply categorized it and disqualified it as "religion."

At the same festival, the Teatro Campesino performed a version of *La gran carpa de la familia Rasquachi* in which the mythological contextualization of the reality of social struggle was apparently not convincing. Critic Yvonne Yarbro-Bejarano (1979) provides an interesting discussion of the controversy that arose around this performance. Various critics refer to the Teatro's use of *indígena* knowledge as "mythical theater," as a "mystical tendency [which] proves evasive and distracts attention from essential problems," as a "re-encounter with the past" that "seems a bit romantic . . . divorced from reality," as a "return to the past," or as an idealization of indigenous civilizations (Yarbro-Bejarano 1979:181; *Tía Cleta* 1974). Yarbro-Bejarano, however, goes on to discuss how the Teatro did (by 1977) manage to "place cultural and mythical content in the social and historical context of Chicanos today" (1979:184).

I would venture to say, however, that the presence of *indígena* knowledge or "mythology" was far more than a matter of "content." The Teatro Campesino did not regard the cultural and mythical in any way separate or outside of the social and historical context of Chicanas/os. The challenge, however, rested with convincingly bringing the holistic Theater of the Sphere to life within performance practice. What critics overlooked was that the Teatro Campesino did not perceive indigenism (i.e., the Theater of the Sphere) as an alternative to anti-imperialist struggle, but rather as a way to differentiate and refine that struggle. The Veinte Pasos, for example, were considered a path toward establishing a humanistic foundation within that very struggle. Yarbro-Bejarano (1979) points out that the Teatro never abandoned a direct concern with the enactment of social struggle. Yet critics generally disregarded the political and scientific rationale behind the Teatro's efforts to integrate indigenous knowledge and social struggle. Its emancipatory potential was not explored.

Various assumptions concerning indigenism and *indígena* culture combined to enable much of the criticism directed at El Teatro Campesino in the 1970s. Interestingly, these assumptions are prominent within a great deal of ethnographic and anthropological research as well. Most notably, a dichotomy or binary opposition is constructed between a supposedly past indigenous reality and the present Chicana/o reality, between a supposedly remote "mythical" *indígena* past and contemporary reality. Hence, efforts that link the two or that assume a continuity or dialogue between them are deemed escapist, anachronistic, or out of touch with what is considered "real" (the "contemporary"). This conceptual separation or opposition is in line with interpreting figures such as Quetzalcoatl or Guadalupe as existing in a supposedly supernatural or mythical realm, that is, as phenomena somehow outside the realm of the daily flesh-and-blood particulars of human life. This intellectual reification of the metaphoric imagery of myth enables the analytical separation of such figures from what is considered our "reality." (Thus the argument against the stage presence of Quetzalcoatl, for example, is usually cast in terms of "divine intercession" or the "out there" intervening in the here and now.) In the *indígena* and Teatro Campesino understanding, however, these "mythical" figures constitute the very blueprints of reality in which we all live. They are regarded not as remotely "mythical" but as contained within the very flesh-and-bones of Chicana/o (and all other) life and experience. In other words, Quetzalcoatl and Guadalupe, by definition, are present inside of living beings and life (the "Living Quetzalcoatl") or not at all; they are interpretive symbolic expressions of human or natural processes and potentiality.

Furthermore, the Teatro constructed *indígena* knowledge and science as something pertaining equally to past, present, and future, not just a thing of the past. The Teatro saw contemporary Chicanas/os and Mexicanos as directly rooted in *indígena* culture and history. The Theater of the Sphere constituted a sustained effort to build on the American roots (or at times fragments) of a Chicana/o "cultural way of being" through recourse to that native ancestral culture.

Some Marxist critics were most vehement about the construction of *indígena* culture as a static thing of the "remote" or "mythical" past. One of the most widely circulated and representative critiques (in the estimation of Teatro Campesino members) is an unpublished essay by Jorge R. González (n.d.). Like various other critics, González dismisses all discussion of "spirituality" as mystification. He immediately identifies and equates the "spiritual" with organized religion or the institution of the Church and rejects it. What is more, he views the Teatro's concern with spirit, body, heart, and soul reductively as "only" a concern of the spirit. González dichotomizes the Teatro into a group once engaged in struggle but "which now draws its basic beliefs from mystical books" and which "now turns to heaven as the primordial source of 'liberation.'" He also dismisses Mayan civilization and indígena culture as elite "cruel theocracies" and as something from the distant past.

What critics did not perceive is that the Teatro Campesino's reappropriation and cultivation of indígena (i.e., Mayan and Aztec) knowledge happened to a large part through living contact with indigenous teachers in Mexico, through contact with flesh-and-blood contemporary indígenas who lived in extreme conditions of oppression. Those indígenas have nothing to do with "cruel theocracies" or "mystical books." El Teatro Campesino studied the marginalized oral tradition of indígena communities and maestros such as Andrés Segura or Domingo Martínez Paredez.

The Marxist critique of Teatro Campesino (by González and others) assigned absolute primacy to economic struggle. The prevailing view was that struggle within the social formation had to fall within the category of class struggle. Forms of struggle outside the economic struggle of the labor market (and established politics) enjoyed no credibility. In other words, economic liberation was put at the center of all discussion and even separated from other related arenas of oppression and liberation. González (n.d.) expresses this view: "Our people don't need to be told to commend ourselves to the gods. We've done that for too long and with no results. We need now to commend ourselves to our power as the real producers of so much of the wealth that exists. . . . Mao Tze Tung also put his faith in his people . . . He understood that economics is the primary motivational force of people."

The primacy assigned to economics essentially relegates all other realms of human experience and domination to the domain of mystification. Such categorical denial of the value or need for human spirituality and other forms of endeavor stands in clear contrast to the values underlying many popular struggles of American people of color. The intellectual fragmentation that constructs an opposition between "organized struggle," "class consciousness," "historical veracity," "struggle for liberation," and spiritual concerns or popular (not necessarily institutional) cultural values is at odds with the popular religious and political sentiment behind a Martin Luther King or a César Chávez. These popular leaders and their movements were propelled by an amalgamation of the spiritual, political, emotional, and economic. The United Farm Workers (from which the Teatro Campesino emerged) always march behind the banner of the Virgin of Guadalupe. César Chávez furthermore explained his prolonged fasts (like those of Mahatma Ghandi) as spiritual undertakings aimed at fortifying him and others in the process of organized struggle. The possibility of counterhegemonic movements—such as the successful Indianization of the Catholic church through the Guadalupan deity, or movements such as the Theology of Liberation—go unperceived when the preoccupation with so-called objective conditions for liberation is conceptualized as divorced from other cultural considerations. Olivia Chumacero (oral communication, Santa Barbara, 12/1/1990) describes the conflict between the Teatro Campesino and some Marxist critics: "Staunch Communists accused us of living in a reality separate from the 'real' environment. The main contradiction with Marxists is that they are absolute. There is no other aspect to their analysis of life but the material."

The controversy between the Teatro Campesino and some Marxist critics, however, was not in any way a strictly Marxist versus non-Marxist debate. The issues at stake here had in the past been at the core of the Marxist debate itself. Eurocommunist Antonio Gramsci's critique of Trotsky and of Lenin in the 1930s centers on some of these very same issues. Gramsci, for example, critiques classical Marxist analysis of domination and then-current models of liberational praxis (1971). Among other things, Gramsci sought to rid Marxist theory and practice of its economistic reductionism. He viewed the mechanistic-economistic view of humans as a degradation of the producing subject to the level of a mere mechanical function.

The Teatro Campesino clearly regarded the Theater of the Sphere as a model of human liberation indispensable to the larger social struggle. It provides a holistic, integrationist model of the human being, a model that seeks to decolonize and fortify Chicanas/os at the emotional, spiritual, intellectual, and physical levels of existence. As such the Teatro Campesino's Theater of the Sphere project was a deeply humanistic enterprise, for it grappled with the question of creating a new humanity as it sought to create a just society. The Teatro's philosophical treatise *Pensamiento serpentino* repeatedly affirms the need for a Chicana/o cultural reconstitution and reclamation, as it affirms the need to struggle for justice. In this regard it in some ways parallels Gramsci's attempts (in criticizing Lenin and Trotsky) to provide for the genesis of a new humanity, to create a theory for overcoming human alienation and not just domination. Nor did Gramsci assume that the overcoming of human alienation would occur automatically.

As a model of human liberation, the Theater of the Sphere proposes that we cannot wait for the big social revolution and the new society before we begin conceiving of a new humanity. It places the beginning of a new humankind in the present and affirms that the process of human liberation will always have to begin from within oppression. The Teatro's Theater of the Sphere project seeks to maximize the potential of the collective by trying to work against human fragmentation and the degradation of work common in the theatrical mainstream (see chap. 4) and in the larger society. Through the Theater of the Sphere, the Teatro Campesino laid the foundation for a new model of cultural politics, a model for human integration outside of the dominant institutions that Chicanas/os cannot control. This corresponds as well to Gramsci's insistence on pushing beyond schematizations of the world in terms of class relations, while affirming the political and human importance of cultural forms of resistance.

In summary, the Teatro Campesino's Theater of the Sphere can well be considered a model for a Chicana/o liberational praxis. Although it was designed to foster human wholeness in the context of performance, performance was not conceptualized in any way separate from daily life within the social formation. The performance training provided by the Theater of the Sphere project was intended to enhance and foster a Chicana/o cultural way of being and its concrete expression both on and off the stage. It could conceivably be transposed to all other types of work activity.

The Teatro's militant affirmation of the indígena ancestral heritage can be appreciated only in the context of the Chicano movement's insistence on decolonization, and the movement's affirmation of Chicana/o cultural and historical distinctiveness. The intense reclamation of Mayan and Aztec knowledge was a direct response to the historical Euro-American institutional denigration of the Chicana/o people and the ever-present threat of cultural assimilation, at the same time that it affirmed a Chicana/o axis. While conceptualizing a Chicana/o distinctiveness it provided a weapon against Euro-American cultural dominance or intrusion which Chicanas/os experience daily in the schools and universities, the media, and related agencies of social control. Although theoreticians like Gramsci have pondered how it is that individuals and groups shall reconstitute their worlds from within a social system that systematically denigrates life, few sustained examples of countercultural education have emerged with the scope and depth of the Chicana/o Theater of the Sphere.[16] With its insistence on the indivisibility of the human being, the Theater of the Sphere fosters a utopian vision of humankind and a culture-bound program for cultivating human wholeness and self-awareness within the larger political struggle.

The concern with human wholeness and human regeneration and integration characteristic of the Theater of the Sphere must also be understood in the context of the sociohistorical era of violence and resistance in which it emerged: it was the height of the Vietnam War, the United Farm Workers movement and all civil rights struggles. Pensamiento serpentino, the Teatro's philosophical poem, which addresses the four human aspects—heart, body, spirit, and mind—does so in the context of a call for Chicana/o decolonization and social liberation. The urgent need for Chicana/o social liberation and concomitant cultural, spiritual, emotional, and physical self-recovery is continually situated (by the ensemble) in the global context of the Vietnam War and not in an abstract, essentialist reality. The Teatro Campesino—farmworkers' theater—was deeply conscious of the human devastation brought on Vietnamese men, women, and children by the profit-seeking U.S. industrial-military complex, as well as the ravages suffered by the largely minority farmworkers in the United States at the hands of agribusiness—ravages perhaps best illustrated by the farmworker's life expectancy of fifty-four years.

These two seemingly unrelated social struggles—of the Vietnamese peasantry and of the Chicana/o farmworkers—are shown in their interrelatedness in the Teatro's play *Vietnam campesino*. *Soldado Razo* similarly thematizes the trauma felt in Chicana/o barrios as a result of the Vietnam War, where a disproportionate 25 percent of the American casualties were Chicano. In this global context, the Theater of the Sphere—especially the program of the Veinte Pasos—emerges to affirm the spiritual, physical, mental, and emotional attributes of all human life. It does so against the tide of human carnage of the Vietnam era. Just as Gramsci in his prison notebooks addresses the "spiritual death of man" as well as the emotional dimensions of humankind, the Teatro points to the damage suffered by the human spirit and heart when they inflict violence upon others. *Pensamiento serpentino* names the U.S. bombing of Hanoi as an example of such self-violence. Correspondingly, the process of Chicana/o decolonization is said to involve countering acts of hatred and violence with a philosophy of nonviolence. Becoming Chicano would ultimately involve acts of love (vis-à-vis *all* humankind) and cultural self-affirmation.

Along these same lines the treatise *Pensamiento serpentino* specifies that Chicana/o decolonization must necessarily restore the colonial terms imposed on us to their original meaning. Jesucristo becomes Quetzalcoatl and Guadalupe becomes Tonantzin in a reversal of the colonization process. Such a redefinition of terms is a political, spiritual, and emotional restoration process, a coming to self.

The Theater of the Sphere project must be contextualized further as part of the intense anti-imperialist discourse of the 1960s, which included a widespread reconsideration of colonialism and the application of the "internal colony" model to Chicana/o reality. The worldwide discussion of economic and cultural imperialism was indeed led by Third World intellectuals as well as by people of color in the United States. André Gunder Frank's *teoría de dependencia* (dependency theory [1969]) went hand in hand with a reconsideration of classical works on colonialism and on the colonial mentality, including works such as Memmi (1967), Fanon (1967, 1968), or Guevara (1968). Viewed in this intellectual and political context, the Theater of the

Sphere is generated by the need of Chicanas/os to impose a new meaning, a Chicana/o interpretation of Chicana/o historical experience, in the face of the widespread American institutional practice of deprecating minority cultural practices.

The program of the Veinte Pasos is in no way divorced from the politics of the Chicano movement, from a political program and political action. Yet it is an expansive view of politics, one that includes the human spirit and heart. It is a restorative project, a healing project, in some ways closely related to forms of *curanderismo* (Mexican folk healing). *Curanderismo* conceives of humans as consisting of three related spheres: the material, the spiritual, and the mental. Health is defined as a harmonious balance between a person's physical, psychological, and spiritual existence. The Teatro Campesino's Veinte Pasos resembles *curanderismo*'s objective of reestablishing integral harmony within human beings. It does so, however, not in the manner of crisis intervention (as does *curanderismo*) but as an ongoing program of self-development.

Although the complexities and far-reaching implications of the Theater of the Sphere project cannot be treated in one chapter (or be adequately conveyed in writing), the present exposition should serve to reveal its significance as a liberational pedagogic model with the Chicano movement. As a comprehensive program of *action* it responded to Chicana/o social alienation through a sustained collective effort to construct an alternative Chicana/o praxis. That praxis self-consciously affirmed the value and presence of the much-deprecated *indígena* in contemporary life and sought to reconstitute Chicana/o humanity by actively nurturing the *indígena* body of knowledge—a knowledge divided in Western "learning" into science, art, religion, medicine, and so on. We stand to benefit from a re-vision and reencounter with the Teatro Campesino's program of countercultural education embodied in the Theater of the Sphere project. As we move into the twenty-first century, society's institutions—in particular, educational institutions—continue to protect and privilege white male upper-middle-class ethnocentric (and Eurocentric) definitions of knowledge and systems of learning. In this context the cultural politics of the Theater of the Sphere counterpose an alternative pedagogy with an alternative conception of reality and human beings and a vision for a new humankind. The Veinte Pasos affirm, for example, that all mental learning must necessarily find physical expression, that it must pass through the portals of human experience in order to become real. As in all oral culture, and in contradistinction to mainstream institutional education, learning within the Theater of the Sphere has a high somatic component: it is a process that engages the *whole body*. It simultaneously educates the four human aspects—body, mind, heart, soul—through physical means, unlike mainstream school learning, which seeks to educate (read "train") persons through mental means that relegate the body to "physical education" classes. By contrast, the Veinte Pasos are not only an intellectual program but an integrated bodily program. This integrated focus reaffirms its native pedagogic quality, its essential tie to the oral tradition. This alternative holistically grounded pedagogical model is at the heart of ritual dance, for example.

The collective undertaking that was the Theater of the Sphere went into the suspended state with the dissolution of the Teatro Campesino ensemble after 1980. After Luis Valdez turned his sights to mainstreaming (see chap. 4) it became impossible for the ensemble to continue working on a collective basis. Members went their separate ways and the Theater of the Sphere project as well as collective theatrical performance were discontinued. Most ensemble members, however, continued to meet regularly in the context of *danza* (ritual dance) under the guidance of Conchero *capitán* Andrés Segura of Mexico City. That practice is carried out to this day by former Teatro Campesino ensemble members.

Although *danza* was originally an activity practiced as part of the Theater of the Sphere project, the other key practices, such as the Veinte Pasos, have not enjoyed further cultivation in the absence of an institutional setting such as that formerly provided by El Teatro Campesino. Most former Teatro Campesino members view the economically austere 1980s and the 1990s as a time when basic survival supplanted a concerted preoccupation with alternative programs such as the Theater of the Sphere. To be sure, the Theater of the Sphere is a form of study and human development that requires a lifetime. It is conceivable that this project will be resumed in another time and place, under different circumstances.

Although the Teatro Campesino's Theater of the Sphere never enjoyed widespread dissemination, it stands as an alternative human educational model, which may well be regarded as prefigurative for any construction of democratic alternative institutions in the future. As we move into the twenty-first century, the need to imagine and implement prefigurative institutions remains a challenge to all who perceive a need for comprehensive change in our society. What appears certain—given the increasing ecological and human devastation on the planet—is that true change will not be just a matter of externals and property relations. The Theater of the Sphere project, developed as a collective project spanning over a decade of the Chicano movement, stands as an important humanistic contribution of considerable emancipatory potential.

Diane Rodríguez (standing) and Socorro Valdez (Skeleton) in 1978
La Carpa de los Rasquachi (European tour). Courtesy of
Diane Rodríguez Collection. Photograph by Ferdinand Schuster.

3. Toward a Re-Vision of Chicana/o Theater History: The Roles of Women in El Teatro Campesino

Introduction

In the summer of 1980 I witnessed a performance of El Teatro Campesino's *Fin del mundo* in Europe. That production marked the end of the ensemble known as El Teatro Campesino, a group that represented a way of performing and a way of living, both intimately linked. Closely associated with the United Farm Workers Union, the theater troupe emerged in 1965 as part of the Chicana/o labor and civil rights struggles of that era. After disassociating itself from direct union involvement, El Teatro Campesino remained a spiritual, cultural, and ideological standard-bearer of the Chicano movement. The spirit of group commitment was still evident in the 1980 production of *Fin del mundo* and contributed to the rare power of that performance, power that was visibly transmitted to German and French audiences despite language and cultural barriers. Standing ovations ensued in a frenzy of enthusiasm such as I had never witnessed from a German theater audience.

Among the male characters, the most expressive was a Pachuco youth, nicknamed "Huesos" (Bones). Huesos controlled the audience and the motion on stage. How astonished I was to discover backstage after the performance that the extraordinary Huesos was played by a woman, Socorro Valdez. Her performance was unforgettable. Yet her presence in the Teatro has never been noted by scholars or historians of Chicana/o drama. Her talent, as well as that of the other women (and men) I saw perform, has always been subsumed under the general heading of El Teatro Campesino, with individual credit going to its now-well-known director, Luis Valdez.

The history of women's participation in the long tradition of Mexican theater in the Southwest constitutes a neglected cultural legacy whose contours have yet to be mapped. The contributions and struggles of the women in El Teatro Campesino are a part of that rich legacy that, once exposed, will alter the established version of Teatro history. To illustrate, I will comment in general terms on the body of writing about El Teatro Campesino since its founding in 1965. I will not reiterate specific findings but rather will indicate some characteristic orientations and omissions in Chicana/o theater criticism and history, which in many cases predetermined researchers' findings.

Speaking generally, the history of El Teatro Campesino since its founding in 1965 has been canonized as the history of the life and times of Luis Valdez. Like history in general, Teatro history has largely been reduced to a chronology of the doings of one individual, its director. The nature and significance of Valdez's contributions have never been examined in relationship to the contributions of the anonymous others. The reality of collective creation in the Teatro has been noted by some researchers, but that has not altered their overriding historical framework, based on the great-man concept, similar to the hierarchical division of labor with a supposedly omnipotent boss at the top.

It is a way of looking at the world. It is a way of writing history. The tendency to place individuals at the center of history constitutes a radical oversimplification by which the dynamics of life process are filtered out, and only names, dates, and places are left behind. By creating monuments to individuals, we eclipse the memory of group achievement and feel dwarfed by all those "great men" instead of learning of the strength we have through community and collaboration. Although Luis Valdez indeed functioned as director to the group, virtually all Teatro Campesino creations were collectively created. In literature on El Teatro Campesino, that collaborative activity is either overlooked entirely or considered to be of secondary importance. Yet references to "Luis Valdez's Actos" or to "Valdez's characters" or to "his teatro"[1] are descriptive inaccuracies reflecting the age-old method of conveniently subsuming the work of a group of people under the name of one man.

Jorge Huerta, in numerous articles and a book (Huerta 1982), has extensively chronicled the history of Chicana/o theater groups, including El Teatro Campesino. Huerta's significant book examines the themes of Chicana/o theater as a reflection of greater sociohistorical forces that generated dozens of teatros. Furthermore, he offers a vivid and comprehensive description of Chicana/o theatrical productions for the period 1965–1980. Huerta's perspective on the history of El Teatro Campesino has become something of an official version, shared by countless other researchers.

Underlying his pioneering treatment of Chicano theater history is the great-man conceptual framework; despite recurrent mention of a "collective process," "collectivity," and "collective authorship," Huerta does not deliver a usable description of the actual steps involved in the process of collective authorship, nor a broader sociocultural framing of that collective process so common among Chicana/o theater groups. The group dynamics of theatrical creation are subsumed under the individual rubric of Luis Valdez, thereby reducing the terms "collective" and "improvisation" to something that happens under the aegis of a genius. Huerta (1982:17) writes: "But few of the dramatic efforts that are now available in print approximate the quality of Valdezian actos. Perhaps the success of this creative genius' collaborations with his ever-evolving troupe is due to the fact that Valdez is a poet, playwright, actor and director who can see all of the elements necessary for effective theater and who can transpose those visions to the stage." The qualities of "creative genius" as well as the capacity to "see all the elements necessary for effective theater" and "transpose those visions to the stage" are ascribed solely to Valdez, as if the anonymous "ever-evolving troupe" possessed no genius or vision or human agency.

In reality the creative process drew from the vision of all Teatro Campesino members. Teatro veteran Olivia Chumacero describes the writing of a play:

> We used to develop our scripts as we went along, from the improvisations. . . . Sometimes, like when we were doing La carpa, which was in corrido form, we had nights in which people met who wanted to work on writing the versos for the corrido. Smiley and I would go, along with different other people who were interested in writing. We'd sit down with Luis and work at it that way too. First we would talk ideas, about where we wanted to go in the piece. And then we would write different verses or whatever, and then select from that. Or then we would talk about what we wanted to say, then we would do an improvisation and he [Luis Valdez] would watch. (Interview, 1/19/1983)

Olivia Chumacero describes this intensely collaborative way of working, which encompassed not only the writing of individual plays, but all facets of theatrical activity:

> It was a collective way of working. We made our own costumes, we built our own props and sets . . . we did all the work collectively, which meant that at a certain time we all took time to make the props, or to make the set. At a certain time we all took time to clean up. All the work was done in that way. Of course the person or persons who were more knowledgeable in a certain area were responsible for that area, but everybody had to help. Ves? [See?] What is amazing is that we were in contact with each other almost 24 hours a day—all the time. (Interview, 1/19/1983)

In spite of this collective reality, theater historians', anthologists', and critics' fixation on a great man snowballed into an account that distorted the simplest facts. Anthologies of Chicana/o theater, for example, usually name only Luis Valdez as the author of works that were in fact collectively authored (see for example Cárdenas de Dwyer 1975, Castañeda Shular et al. 1972, Harth and Baldwin 1974). Luis Valdez has also contributed to this myth by republishing the collectively authored *actos* as his "early works" (Valdez 1990). The most widely anthologized *acto*, *Soldado razo*, runs without exception under Valdez's name. Yet Olivia Chumacero recalls that this *acto*, like all others, was written by various members of the ensemble through the process of collective improvisation:

> Once we were working on *Soldado razo*, working on the idea. In fact I remember we were going to do this *acto* specifically for the moratorium against the war in Vietnam. . . . *Entonces* [Then] there was a girl in the Teatro who told us what had happened in her family. . . . And so the *acto* is based on a real story. Well, Luis introduced the *calavera* [skeleton] character into one of the improvisations; and Phil [Esparza] did the *calavera* in the improvisations. He started doing various numbers. And we immediately thought that this is a great tool to use in this *acto*. And it worked. I remember that was when Luis actually wrote the dialogue that the mother and the son have in the letter . . . for the rest of the *acto* we were working off improvisations that we were doing. Luis was teaching at the university and he didn't have as much time to help put it together. So I remember that he wrote that part. But all the other parts were done collectively. Everybody's ideas, everybody's input, the improvisations. Luis functioned as sifter. . . . We were like an experiment, you know. We were the experiment and we would just keep going and he would just keep taking from that. That is how we worked, and it was great. You know, it was really great, because people had to be on their toes, people had to think, people had to have this information within them, too. You had to draw from yourself, from where you were coming from. Things came out from you, from what you thought, from what you had experienced in life. . . . It was your life. (Interview, 1/19/1983)

The vital facets of history that become blurred or erased by the great-man perspective are the very forces that shape the "great individuals" and sustain them in a position of prominence. The special contributions of women are among those facets that are absent in the writing of theater history. Nonetheless, the actual dynamics of the creative process in El Teatro Campesino are blurred by Jorge Huerta's linear vision (chronological and text-centered) of a "great man" directing the anonymous masses of actors. Teatro members who devoted ten or more years to that intense collective undertaking—Olivia Chumacero, Roberta Delgado, Lupe Valdez, Rogelio Rojas, Philip Esparza, Diane Rodríguez, José Delgado, to list only a few—are not even named in Huerta's history. Daniel Valdez is introduced simply as Luis Valdez's "younger

brother Danny"; the extraordinary Socorro Valdez only mentioned in passing as "his multitalented sister" (Huerta 1982:22,209). Huerta's admiration
for Valdez appears limitless and eclipses that for all other ensemble members:
"Valdez' world encompasses more than his critics can comprehend"; or, "The
pressure might have stopped a lesser man" (pp. 183,178). With regard to *La
gran carpa de la familia Rasquachi*—a collectively authored work—Huerta tells us:
"but *La gran carpa de los rasquachis* was his [emphasis mine] tour de force and
there was nothing that could stop him from dancing" (p. 206). Indeed, Valdez
is portrayed as a figure so great that we can barely hope to grasp the nature
of his genius: "Valdez was dancing his way to truth in a way no intellectual
could understand" (p. 205). Other members of El Teatro Campesino are never
quoted, nor are their opinions in any way included for the sake of adding
profile or even contrast to the frequently quoted views of Luis Valdez. Yet
these names stand for the variety of human forces, interactions, contradictions, clashes and resolutions that constitute Teatro history.

Only by learning to ask new questions will a new Teatro history emerge
that incorporates voices and issues long overlooked or buried. Playwright
Bertolt Brecht (1976:252) picks at new veins of historical truths with his
questions in a poem:

Who built Thebes of the seven gates?
In the books you will find the names of kings.
Did the kings haul up the lumps of rock? . . .

Every page a victory.
Who cooked the feast for the victors?
Every ten years a great man.
Who paid the bill?

So many reports.
So many questions.

Without an understanding of the collision and merging of forces, without
an account of the daily life processes and struggles, of the living circumstances of performance, Teatro history becomes a promenade through a wax
museum.

In the years since the European tour of *Fin del mundo* I have explored the
dynamics of El Teatro Campesino and other *teatros*, combining fieldwork,
extensive interviews with members and former members of El Teatro
Campesino, day-to-day living experiences with the women and men of
El Teatro Campesino in California, and research in the Teatro Campesino
archives. During my two years of research residence in San Juan Bautista,

the base of operations for El Teatro Campesino, I developed an understanding of the day-by-day behind-the-scenes creative process that predated that final production of Fin del mundo and especially the roles of the women in that process.

Women have constituted a distinct force within the Teatro Campesino and, by extension, within the history of Chicana/o theater. Yet in Teatro history, as in history writing in general, the participation of women is often overlooked. The course charted by these women is rich in contradictions and human potential. By presenting these conflicts and contradictions and their resolutions in all their human breadth, I hope to rectify the history of El Teatro Campesino so that process—the full range of human action, including women's contributions—becomes visible. Thus in seeking to reconstitute a portion of the unwritten history of Chicana/o theater I focus here primarily on the women, and the roles they played—both on- and offstage.

In researching and reconstructing Chicana performance history, my richest—and most exclusive—source of information has been female performers themselves. It is through interviews—collected over a ten-year period—that I have begun to develop an understanding of the life, work, and struggles of Chicana performers. None of these women—including the women of the Teatro Campesino—had ever been interviewed before.

I view this chapter as collectively written. It could never have been written without the intense participation and reflection of the women whose life and work are examined here. In order to express the reality of collective authorship, I have chosen a collective presentational format rich in quotations from the oral histories I have collected. In integrating as much of women's testimony as possible, I furthermore reflect a feminist commitment to honor women's words, to validate the notion that a woman's experience is best described in her own words, in spite of what researchers may think to the contrary. The focus on women's experience should also serve as a corrective to the hundreds of existing works of exclusively male focus. Consultation with male members of El Teatro Campesino on the participation of women elicited scant results; their tendency was to pass over the topic in as few words as possible before changing the subject altogether. It was the women who most eloquently addressed what has been their own historical experience.

In this chapter, theoretical perspectives are elaborated implicitly rather than explicitly. I do not privilege theory and the theoretical as the most important or most significant way of knowing or communicating; what I do privilege is women's own words concerning their own life experience. Careful attention to women's experiences must provide the grounding for any theory we construct and for any categories of analysis we apply. Putting women at the center of analysis does not simply mean that we now include subjects who were formerly excluded. Rather, the inclusion of women's experience will fundamentally alter the way in which performance history or other history is written.

The experience of these women not only illustrates the struggle by women in El Teatro Campesino and other *teatros* but in many ways parallels efforts by women *outside* the theater. Their stories interest us precisely because they are not the stories of "creative geniuses" but the stories of all women.

The Roles of Women in El Teatro Campesino

Within the vast body of critical writings on El Teatro Campesino, critics have overlooked the history of women's participation. The amply documented and discussed repertoire of El Teatro Campesino has been viewed principally from the perspective of genre: documenting the company's development of various theatrical genres, from the *actos* to *mitos* to *corridos*. A different historical configuration appears, however, when we focus on the roles of women in El Teatro Campesino.

Throughout the course of El Teatro Campesino's dramatic evolutionary process, the female roles have remained fairly constant in all the genres: variations of the same three or four types or categories. These characters are defined in a familial or age category: mother, grandmother, sister, or wife/girlfriend. Note, for example, the cast of characters in the 1970 *acto Huelguistas*. Whereas the male characters are named according to place of origin or by workplace function (e.g., Campesino Tejano, Campesino Coyote), the women are described in terms of age and marital status (Campesina Casada, Campesina Viejita [Married Campesina, Old Campesina]). These designations are irrelevant to the nature of their statements in the *acto*, however. In addition to the familial or age category, all women are also assigned one of two sexual categories: whores or virgins, a categorizing evident since the early period of the *actos*. Wives, sisters, girlfriends, and mothers are made to fall chiefly into either the whore or the virgin category. Although some degree of mixing and matching can occur—such as with the "whore-mother" character of Chata in *Fin del mundo* (1980)—women fall into only one of two categories: good woman or bad woman.

This reductive characterization continues after the period of the early *actos*. In the remarkable dream parody, *La gran carpa cantinflesca* (1972), for example, the female characters recede entirely during most scenes. The cultural and political disputes between the generations are carried out by the father and two sons. In the play's final part, consisting of a farcical reenactment of the

Chicano movement, the daughter Cantinflucha enters and makes the comical but characteristic remark: "What about Chicanas, vato? Or do we get only bit parts in this revolutionary carpa? I have a script too!" This line strongly signals an awareness within El Teatro Campesino of the gender oppression within the Chicano movement: Women were expected to participate in political activity, but not as leaders. The double standard relegated women to bit parts. The Teatro Campesino's apparent awareness of the problem did not, however, make an impact on the group's portrayal of women. In La gran carpa cantinflesca the Chicana's "script" is nonexistent and her role is concluded shortly after her bit part.

Depending on the circumstances of any given Teatro Campesino play—all of which have male protagonists—the handful of available female traits are mixed or matched to create the desired effect. The acto of Los Vendidos presents a somewhat different—but equally troubling—projection of Chicana women. It features one Chicana woman secretary (and five males) in speaking roles. The Chicana is sent from Republican governor Ronald Reagan's office to recruit a token Mexican for the administration. She anglicizes her name (from Jiménez to JIMenez) and upholds the conservative Republican politics. Although the acto Los Vendidos creates a space for Chicanas as speaking political subjects, her politics is that of a vendida (sell-out). This acto replicates the male colonial ideology that created the term "malinchismo"; that term and that ideology assign historical responsibility for "selling out" (or collaboration with the enemy) to female subjects. Like the bulk of the Teatro Campesino female characters, Miss JIMenez of Los Vendidos also engages only in activities which are accessory to those of males.

Women's roles do not enjoy the dramatic space necessary for the unfolding of a full character. In their confinement, women do not evolve beyond a single dimension. With the exception of La Virgen de Tepeyac, all Teatro Campesino plays have males as their focus. The female figures are those affected by men; they are peripheral, the ones to whom things happen. Never is the world seen through the eyes of a woman. This is reflected in the very titles of the works, which usually carry the name of the male protagonist. Even in works of an almost epic scope, such as La carpa de la familia Rasquachi (1973), later renamed La carpa de Jesús Pelado Rasquachi, women are male-centered and limited to being victims or satellites of men. Whereas the three Rasquachi brothers are endowed with various personal ambitions, Rosita Rasquachi's single intent is to not lose her boyfriend:

(Children gather around Pelado and complain about going to Mexico)
Joe: Oh no, Papa. I want to join the Marine Corps!

Scene from 1980 Fin del mundo European tour. Left to right: Rogelio Rojas, José Delgado, Yolanda Parra (as Newscaster), Olivia Chumacero (sitting), Diane Rodríguez, Socorro Valdez. Courtesy of Olivia Chumacero Archive.

Louie: I want to make some feria!
Macario: I want to go to college!
Rosita: What about my boyfriend!
(El Teatro Campesino 1973:22)

In the exciting 1980 European production of Fin del mundo, female characters in the show felt like carbon copies of those from earlier Teatro plays: there was the saintlike, wilting wife; the sleazy whore; and the grandmother figure. Compared with the male characters, the women were one-dimensional and insignificant. In Valdez's winter 1981 play about the 1860s California Chicano social bandit Tiburcio Vásquez (Bandido!), the historical figure's legendary quest for social justice becomes insignificant as Valdez highlights Vásquez's quest for women. All three women in the play are his satellites and are defined solely in terms of men. The high-browed Rosario is wife to Leiva and lover to Tiburcio Vásquez; California Kate is a madam; and Rita Madrid is a "feisty camp follower" competing with Rosario for the love of Vásquez. Much of Rita's dialogue centers around wooing Vásquez: "You were mine years before you even met that weak, little bitch! I knew back in New Idria she couldn't hack being your woman. . . . I'm the woman you need, Tiburcio. I'll ride with you until the day we die, even if they hang us, so long as it's together" (Valdez 1981:90).

Socorro Valdez in characteristic expression as Huesos ["Bones"] in Fin del mundo, *1980 European tour. Courtesy of Olivia Chumacero Archive.*

In a perceptive article exploring the roles of women in the Teatro de la Esperanza, Yvonne Yarbro-Bejarano points to the ideological problems of having individual protagonists—male or female:

> The question concerning main characters goes beyond the fact of being male or female. It is actually part of a larger question of special interest in political theater, namely, what is implied by having a main character at all. There has been much discussion of the classical Lukacsian idea of the protagonist who incarnates the clash of antagonistic social forces. Instead, people have begun to wonder whether the inclination in theater to create heroes does not imply a tendency to envision social problems as the problems of an extraordinary individual, usually male. (1981:8,10)

Individual heroes as protagonists also create dramatic problems. The overpowering centrality of one character creates limitations of dialogue, space, and action in the development of other characters. In Teatro Campesino plays there is invariably a main male character, although balanced by other male characters (such as in Fin del mundo, 1980, or La gran carpa cantinflesca) or by allegorical figures like La Muerte or El Diablo (such as in La carpa de los Rasquachis). Female characters fill the spaces in between.

In my interviews with Teatro women I explored the genesis of these roles, the women's views of them, and women's development across time. Without exception the women placed these roles within the context of their own personal development. The stereotyped roles found in the work of El Teatro Campesino to some extent reflect the stereotyped views of Chicanas in society at large. The women who joined the company in the 1970s inherited these stereotypical female roles. Roles were to some extent preestablished and were never submitted to scrutiny by male members of the Teatro. Nor did the women question these roles at the time, principally because of their youth. Most women entered the Teatro in their teens, when their consciousness of themselves as women and of their roles as women in the theater was not highly developed. Teatro member Diane Rodríguez described the women's early passivity:

> At the beginning we were playing various types, like the supportive wife, you know, or the virginal type, like an icon, literally she was just a statue— and that was a character; that was one of the main roles. We were playing these roles, we let that happen. And we had some input. But where were we, as women, at that point? Somehow at that point we didn't have the consciousness and we played these cardboard roles. Or maybe we did have some consciousness but we didn't know how to get it on the stage. There was something that was not as strong as it is now, of course. There is more of a consciousness of women—in oneself—that there wasn't then. (Interview, 6/7/1980)

Socorro Valdez, who performed her first Teatro Campesino role at age fifteen, also said that her youth prevented her from questioning the female roles: "I was growing up, you know. So for me to confront Luis [Valdez] at that time and say: Look. Your writing about women is no good . . . well, that is not where I was coming from; he was much older than me and had more life experience. But he didn't have female experience" (interview, 3/1/1983).

Furthermore, efforts to address the politics of Chicanas/os as a whole during the 1960s somehow precluded any special consideration of women's roles or problems. A discussion of gender issues was given very low priority. Diane Rodríguez recalled how the importance of the show did not allow the women's roles even secondary consideration: "It seems that because we have always worked for a certain goal, we have overlooked some things. I admit that. I admit it very much . . . we perform his [Luis Valdez's] view of women, basically. Now there is some input. But in order that the show go on . . . well, we have said: Okay we'll go with this and we have performed these roles. . . . We have talked about this and I think all of us are very conscious. But I don't think that we have found the answer yet either" (interview, 6/7/1980).

Putting women's issues second, or discounting them altogether, was common among leftist groups of the 1960s and the 1970s in the United States and around the world. The liberation of people in general was considered the chief priority. It is ironic that those engaged in struggles for human equality were slow to recognize that class struggles and ethnic struggles would not necessarily better the lot of women. The women of the Chicano movement of the 1960s and 1970s who raised women's issues were accused of being divisive. The situation was equally touchy for women in El Teatro Campesino, despite the ensemble's history of perpetual transformation.

Gradually, with the development of a consciousness as women, the confinement of these roles became increasingly apparent and increasingly frustrating to the women. Socorro Valdez, the youngest of the group, lamented:

> It was like walking the same path over and over. There was the mother, the sister, or the grandmother or the girlfriend. Only four. You were either the novia, la mama, la abuela, or la hermana. [The girlfriend, the mother, the grandmother, or the sister]. And most of the time these characters were passive. The way those females are laid out are for the most part very passive and laid back, y aguantaban todo [and they put up with everything]. I think that is what really chewed me up at the time. (Interview, 3/1/1983)

The women's dissatisfaction with these roles led to one of the longest and deepest struggles in the development of the Teatro Campesino. I would even venture to say that the question of women's roles became the most enduring contradiction within the company, a contradiction paralleled in various ways within the Chicano movement. It was a contradiction between what was, on the one hand, a constant process of renewal in the form of new performance visions and experimentation, and what was, on the other hand, a static clinging to well-worn stereotypes of gender roles. The Teatro Campesino repertoire, with its strong progressive strides in the treatment of labor issues, of Chicano culture, of historical issues, consistently demonstrated stagnation in its treatment of women.

Resistance to change was in some ways anchored in the makeup of the company, which had been predominantly male since its founding. Socorro Valdez describes how the women struggled to be viewed and treated as equals:

> At one time there was only three women in the whole darn thing: Olivia Chumacero, myself, and a third I don't remember. That was a real interesting time. We were either going to remain members of the company, or just be "the women of the company." That made a real difference, you know, because I hated to be put into a mold like "These are the ladies of the Teatro." Aw shut

Scene from 1980 Fin del mundo *European tour. Left to right: Diane Rodríguez, Yolanda Parra, Olivia Chumacero; Socorro Valdez in background. Courtesy of Olivia Chumacero Archive.*

up! Don't give me that! They would separate you without needing to. And so Olivia fought for her own, as I did. You know we were both very young. We both ended up in the role of fighters because that's what was needed to get the men's heads to a place where they would be able to discuss something with you. We would have open meetings where the shit would fly across the room. . . . But I know how important those three women were at that period, because there was no other female voice in the company." (Interview, 3/1/83)

Administrative and decision-making power was, to a large extent, in the hands of the men. In time, women learned to question the division of labor along gender lines:

We even got down to questioning who was going to be telling who what to do; because I personally got very tired of being under the thumb of a man. We had a male touring manager. We had a male booking agent. We had a male director. We had a male stage manager. We had a male everything. And there are women there who are just as strong. . . . I could pick up a house if I had to, you know. . . . But they just never thought I could. And it was up to me to show them that I could. There was no fault to bear, just responsibility. (Socorro Valdez interview, 3/1/1983)

The patriarchal organization of El Teatro Campesino reinforced the aspect of male dominance in administrative matters. Luis Valdez typically worked

Socorro Valdez performing in an acto created for the 1976 United Farm Workers
Second Constitutional Convention. Courtesy of United Farm Workers of America.

with persons much younger than himself. And the relationship between the
members of the ensemble, a group that worked and lived together, was definitely
a familial one. The group was officially defined as a familia; Luis Valdez was
the symbolic father, or person in charge. The rest of the company was much
younger. Olivia Chumacero describes the relationship as follows:

> When I joined the company I was nineteen, you know. He [Luis] was much
> older, thirteen years, whatever. For me it wasn't a problem. Within my reality
> it was always the oldest person that was in charge. That is just part of the
> culture—even if the older person is only two years older than me: that was
> the person you respected and that was the person who was in charge. But that
> didn't mean that you didn't have a mind, or that you didn't think, that you
> didn't express what your opinions were on everything. (Interview, 1/19/83)

Luis Valdez's paternalistic role presented a problem for Yolanda Parra, who
joined the company in 1977. Parra initially accepted but eventually rejected
the obedient daughter role, both on and off the stage:

> Luis did not treat one as an adult. . . . The most dangerous thing with me and
> Luis is when he gets that parent/daughter thing with me. . . . It's very easy to
> fall into that: whatever the man says, and yielding, yielding, yielding, not
> questioning. I have been trained really good that way. But somewhere along
> the line I start thinking, "Wait a minute." There comes a point—and I don't

know what starts it exactly . . . but you start to think. About you and about your position, your own honor, your own dignity . . . and then you ask yourself: Well, why am I doing this? And the answer is: Well, because *he* said. Well, does *he* know what *I'm* feeling? Can he tell *me* how to live? (Interview, 12/21/1982)

The process of changing the portrayal of women, of developing fuller roles and images of women, was perceived by the women as a challenge both in theatrical terms and in terms of human dignity. Yet the men did not share that sense of urgency in the women's challenge. Perhaps it was alarming to the patriarchal structure of El Teatro Campesino. Socorro Valdez describes the challenge created by women:

Luis has seen a lot of stuff through the work that the women have done in this group. They've always given him a little . . . to *challenge* him. And there were times in the group that the women were just outraged. We'd say, "What are you doing? I'm sick of playing mothers! I'm sick of playing sisters!" (Interview, 3/1/1983)

As the women developed, so did their desire to create more integrated female characters, female characters possessing many traits and not just the flat mother, sister, whore figures typical of the Teatro Campesino repertoire. Yolanda Parra recalls the limited roles forced on female actors:

There is this constant stereotypical portrayal of women. His women charac-ters are virgins, whores, or mothers. Is there anything else? No. But you see, women don't come like that. Women are *all three*, not one or the other. And they are more things; they are men, too, and they are children. It's not just three separate things. Like: "I'm all virgin!" . . . Who's going to buy that? See, that's a real problem. (Interview, 12/21/1982)

The question of redefining female roles, however, met with passive resis-tance. For one thing, it never really found acceptance as a problem. Far from being taken up as a challenge, it was treated as an unnecessary provocation. Women's efforts to dramatize a new vision of women were frequently coun-tered by a subtle form of ostracism—the suggestion that they write their own plays. The collective spirit clearly suffered a collapse when gender roles were questioned. Suddenly an individual solution was suggested for what was a collective problem. That response was indicative of the lack of ensemble commitment to the creation of adequate roles for women. Women of the Teatro view that resistance—on one level—as a function of the men's not having "female experience." But a more complex dimension of that resistance is also articulated: the narrowness in men's perception of women is linked to the narrowness in the men's self-perception: "He [Luis] can't experience women any other way except as a man. And no one else can do that either, unless they are willing to *stretch their own image of themselves*" (S. Valdez interview, 3/1/1982).

Male resistance to female self-determination within the Chicano movement, however, should not be personalized or considered the special problem of this or that man or group. In truth, it is not unique to El Teatro Campesino. Male supremacist ideology and practice, in all sectors of society, have been the focus of extensive discussion and investigation within the women's movement. A prime manifestation of that ideology is the inability to accept women beyond their biological roles: wife/mother/lover. It is a form of blindness that prevents many from perceiving the vast spectrum of experiences that in reality make up womanhood. The virgin/whore dichotomization of women is the distorted projection of male supremacist ideology. Maintenance of male power *needs* a fragmented (i.e., nonthreatening) image of women. Although various women in the Teatro Campesino ensemble were a living antithesis of the male stereotypes of women, there is virtually no evidence of a new understanding, or "stretch." The women's self-image remained at odds with the images of those unable to see women in their wholeness; the issue of women's roles was consistently deflected.

The growing desire of some Teatro Campesino women to create and try out roles with greater depth to some extent coincided with Luis Valdez's gradual striving to assume greater power within the organization. That striving was not without implications for the women engaged in redefining the roles of women. Casting decisions became the exclusive right of Luis Valdez. And casting decisions became a conscious or unconscious tool in the perpetuation of the classic stereotypes of women. In the last Teatro Campesino ensemble production (Fin del mundo, 1980), the female lead character of Vera—companion to the drug addict Reymundo Mata—was played in the highly incongruous but characteristic ingenue style. This was the result of a casting decision: a novice actress was chosen over the more experienced Teatro women. As in so many productions, a role that promised a great deal delivered very little. Yolanda Parra, an experienced *teatrista*, recalled:

> The one role that all of us women tried out for was the role of Vera, the pregnant wife-girlfriend. Unfortunately, that role was handled by a very weak actress. . . . She was *physically* maybe suited for the role: a pretty face. But in terms of *guts* I think that Olivia or Diane were much better suited. . . . It was a real hurt for us, because we would try to coach her: "Don't act like such a clinging vine! Leave us a little bit of pride!" It had the makings of a wonderful

role, but it didn't get developed. Luis cast her in that role. (Interview, 12/21/1982)

The same practice of casting weak female actors in pivotal roles was repeated in subsequent roles, to the detriment of the plays as a whole. The production of Rose of the Rancho, which inaugurated the Teatro Campesino Playhouse (1981), featured a wilting Juanita character in the play's center. That role was the result of a casting decision and of playwriting. A powerful and expressive female actor in the role of Rose might well have created a character highly incompatible with the general thrust of this lightweight melodramatic comedy. The drama seeks to entertain and to attract a broad audience by offending no one. As such, it follows a stereotyped entertainment formula: the weak Mexican Juanita character and her rancho are saved by an Anglo whom she then marries. All live happily ever after.

The same novice who played the Rose character then played the principle female role in Luis Valdez's Bandido! (1981), a play about the 1860s California's Chicano heroic outlaw, Tiburcio Vásquez—with predictable results. The historical figure's legendary quest for justice becomes insignificant as Valdez highlights Vásquez's quest for women.

Casting decisions were at times even based on the female actor's skin color, as evidenced in the play about the Indian deity Guadalupe, Las cuatro apariciones de la Virgen de Tepeyac. This play occupies a very special place in the history of El Teatro Campesino. The women of the company regarded playing the revered Mexican deity Guadalupe-Tonantzin as much more than a "role." It was an honor and a deeply spiritual undertaking. As was shown in chapter 1, it is not the Roman Catholic institutionalized version of Guadalupe that gives the pageant its power, but rather, the adoration of Guadalupe-Tonantzin as the Native American deity that she is: the symbol of a cosmic force. The role of Guadalupe is perhaps the one female role that was loved by all the women of the company. Unlike other roles, it represented a tribute to female potentiality. Yet the role also fell prey to stereotyping. An unspoken casting taboo altered the appearance of the goddess. Yolanda Parra tells of the alteration.

In the Virgin de Tepeyac they should have a real Indian-looking woman because that's the whole point. She appears to Juan Diego in the image of an india, and I mean hard-core stone-ground Mexican-Indian. . . . But the women they pick for the role look like little Spanish madonnas. I've always thought Olivia Chumacero would make a great Virgen de Tepeyac, because there is a certain amount of ovaries that go into that part. You're talking the guts of the Universe there. You're talking somebody who can really feel the power. (Interview, 12/21/1982)

Control over casting decisions provided a kind of insurance policy for the director. It assured that the roles would be played in accordance with his view of women. Within the three or four role types available to women, only certain predetermined women could play certain predetermined roles. Just as female roles in plays had become cemented, women also became stereotyped along rigid lines *offstage*. A vicious circle of typecasting was created. In the words of Socorro Valdez:

> As it were, the actresses that were "soft" offstage and just *muy buenas, muy muy buenas* [tame, real, real tame] got the "soft" roles. And the ladies that were *medias cabronas* [the ones who wouldn't take shit from anyone] and had a beer and cigarette hanging out of their mouth, well you know what role they got. . . . I always ended up with that other stuff. (Interview, 3/1/1983)

Women were divided basically into "soft" types and "hard" types—into good and bad. Yet this division did not go unquestioned. What is more, it deepened the women's understanding of themselves and of their roles. In the words of Socorro Valdez:

> Now I know these choices. And I know there were moments in the group when there was to be a "girlfriend." Well, can Socorro be the girlfriend? No, Socorro can't be the girlfriend. Socorro is either the old lady or she is the jokester. But I was never seen in this company as a "soft" woman, because they confuse softness and hardness and they attach those two things to strength or weakness. But there is no such thing in my mind. . . . You can't put those two things together like that. They fluctuate. (Interview, 3/1/1983)

El Teatro Campesino continued to reenact all varieties of virgins, mothers, and sleazy whores throughout the decade of the 1970s. This is not to imply that the women stayed in the company in the position of martyrs. There were various other dimensions of activity that made the experience very rewarding. The flowering of creative capacities afforded by the collective process within the Teatro was seemingly limitless, as long as it did not pertain to the expansion of women's roles. Even the eventual entry of women into administrative positions did not trigger a modification of the portrayal of women on the stage.

Any theater history that places women's experience at its center will have to include categories such as childbearing and child-care. The rigid views of gender roles both on and off the stage created a special set of problems peculiar to women in the theater. These problems illustrate the close relationship between the private and the public spheres in theatrical life.

One obstacle women had to overcome was the negative response of many to the very presence of women in *teatro*. The prejudice against female actors manifested itself even among Teatro Campesino supporters:

> It got wild when people started saying: Those broads are nothing but a bunch of *tú sabes* . . . *que actrizes ni que actrizes* [you know . . . actresses, my foot]. Only *guys* could be actors. For some reason we were still *only* women. . . . Somehow or other. Critics of the Teatro, people that were close to the company, people that were around: they wondered what kind of women we were. We were just cheap broads. Now the idea is different; but traditionally women in theater— even way back to the dark ages—were considered just whores. (S. Valdez interview, 3/1/1983)

In many cases, Chicanas also encountered parental resistance to their work in theater. Olivia Chumacero tells of this situation: "It's been eleven years since I left the house . . . but when my parents think of the theater they think of loose women. In Mexico, if you are into the arts in this way *eres mujer de la calle* [you're a woman of the street.] . . . Women have it harder and they have to be strong" (Chumacero/Rodríguez interview, 6/7/1980).

In the course of time, motherhood also became an issue affecting the participation of women in El Teatro Campesino. Many critics have commented on the intimate relationship between daily life and art for Teatro Campesino members. Yet none have mentioned that if a woman's life included childbearing, her days as an agent in theater history were numbered. Childbearing and childrearing were considered incompatible with theatrical touring. Rather than accept elimination from the company, however, women struggled to demonstrate that touring with children was possible and necessary:

> We wanted to have more say in certain decisions. For instance: touring and babies. How about taking babies out on the road? So-and-so couldn't travel because she had a baby. Now that's ridiculous. Olivia was one of them . . . the forerunners of the mothers in the company. They had their babies . . . and they proved it, not only to themselves or their in-laws or their parents, but to Luis, that it could be done. They proved that women—even now—with all the pressures of motherhood could be seen performing on the stage and then breast-feeding their kid in the van the next hour. It was possible. It wasn't easy. . . . I use Olivia as an example because she just trudged right through it in the best way she knew how. And it wasn't always easy for her . . . I don't have any children but I do know how I want to be now that I've *seen* how they could do it. They proved certain things for me. And that was during the *hard*

times when we had to go cross-country to New York in one van, and the baby
diapers and all that. . . . You know, that was a hell of a point that women
made. It affected me a great deal to see that. The company had to make it
possible for children to go with us. That's what it had to do. Staying home had
to be a matter of *choice* and not a matter of having children. That point was
very important: the establishment of an acting mother. (S. Valdez interview,
3/1/1983)

Although acting mothers became a common thing in El Teatro Campesino, a policy of equal sharing in child-care responsibilities was not established. Each couple with children had to work out its own strategy for
dealing with the added responsibility of child care. Particularly in the case
of infants, primary or sole responsibility usually rested with the mother. As
such, acting mothers found themselves with a workload disadvantage in the
company. In the women's or men's testimony there is no mention of difficulties in the establishment of an acting father.

Breaking the Mold: Creating New Pathways

Having devoted a good deal of attention to the limitations imposed on
women and female characters on the stage, I would now like to examine the
other side of that long-smoldering contradiction. The efforts—of *some*
women—to break through the confinement of stereotypical female roles
had, to some extent, been thwarted. Yet their determination and consciousness remained unaltered and became a compelling force in other directions.
New avenues had to be explored. From the backstage perspective of theater
history, I witnessed dramatic breakthroughs, some of which had immediate
consequences for centerstage action, while others had their impact in areas
of less visibility.

Let us briefly follow the strivings of Socorro Valdez, whose breakthroughs
have been dramatically inspirational. The first role that Socorro ever played
in the company was the grandmother. I offer her own recollection of that
activity:

I was fifteen years old—my first role in the company was that of an old lady
about eighty years old. And I jumped on it real quick because it was character,
it was character work. It was real big, broad acting. That was my point of
beginning. And so when I played my first character I immediately relied on
my strength. And the old lady I played was by no means a whining old lady.
She was a very powerful character . . . maybe the way I'm going to be when
I'm eighty, because I don't see myself coming from a weak place. (Interview,
3/1/1983)

Although that performance is not noted by historians of Chicana/o theater, it is alive in the memory of all *teatristas*. Olivia Chumacero recalled: "Socorro, for example, created the mother and grandmother characters in the Teatro. She was sixteen years old and she used to do the most fantastic old lady that you had ever seen. Incredible. Really incredible: *el movimiento, la forma, el estilo de hablar, las expresiones* [her movements, her form, her style of talking, her expressions] everything. It was wonderful" (interview, 1/19/1983).

In spite of the vitality of the performance process, the female roles became stagnant after they began to repeat themselves in various guises for over a decade. Socorro Valdez described how she resolved to break the mold:

> At the time there were no men in the group who could be made to play *pachucos*, or old men, etc. And it was important to play the men's roles well, because the truth is that Luis writes for men. He always has. His point of view is male and it will always be so. But it was kind of strange that he had no men to play the men. So I figured "Hell, what's holding me back? Just let me put on a pair of pants and jump into it and see." And in fact I ended up playing men better than the men . . . It wasn't that I was trying to *get* the role; I was trying to *establish* the role within the group. Those characters of men needed to be played. But unfortunately the men in the group at the time were not able or capable or free or whatever the problem was. (Interview, 3/1/1983)

Assuming a male role represented a major step in the exploration of new possibilities as a performer. And that step was an outgrowth of the living, creative impulse that had become frustrated within the narrow confines of stereotyped women's roles. The male roles enjoyed a major part of the lines. For Socorro, a male role was a new adventure in role playing: as a male she was now in an *active* position. In the Teatro Campesino repertoire, action was typically centered around male protagonists, with female characters generally functioning as auxiliary figures. The women figures were those *affected* by men; they were peripheral—the ones *to whom* things happened. Not that the reverse would be desirable. The overpowering centrality of one character (usually male) creates limitations on dialogue, space, and action in the development of other characters. In Teatro Campesino plays in which the main character (male) has been balanced by other characters, those other characters are also invariably male (such as *Fin del mundo*, 1980, or *La gran carpa cantinflesca*) or they are sexless characters like La Muerte (Death) or El Diablo (the Devil) (such as in *La carpa de los Rasquachis*). Female characters fill the spaces in between.

Socorro Valdez's appropriation of male roles provided an opportunity for her to stretch her own self-image, to grow: "[The female roles] are very limiting.There is the mother type, and then there is the 'mutha': the whore type, sleazy cheap. There is always the mother, the sister, the girlfriend, or the grandmother.That's very limiting.And that's one of the reasons I dove so deep into aborting the fact that I was female and only female. I needed exploration in my work" (interview, 3/1/1983).

The exploration and imagination involved in the creation of new characters in El Teatro Campesino were considerable.To play a role or character did not mean to follow a script or another person's directions. It meant literally to *create* a character by improvising it to life, bringing it to life virtually from scratch. That included the creation of the dialogue and the movement through the improvisational process. Playing each role entailed a degree of creative responsibility for performers very unlike that of dramatic traditions within print culture, whose fixation rests with written scripts. To perform a play was to *generate* a play. Even the classic *actos*, which have been adopted by Chicana/o theater groups throughout the United States and by groups in Latin America, were never rehearsed by El Teatro Campesino using a script. Contrary to popular belief—and contrary to the spirit and practice of the oral performance tradition—the published collection of *actos* does not represent a "definitive" collection of texts. The concept of "definitive" is not at all applicable within the oral performance tradition, in which plays change markedly with every performance—based on the improvisational fancy of the performers and their relationship with that evening's audience. Olivia Chumacero described the process: "When the *actos* book was done, no scripts existed. Félix Alvarez went around with a tape recorder asking people what their lines were so that he could write it down and put the *acto* book together . . . even though those lines changed a lot as we went along, depending on who was doing the character and depending on the situation. The parts would change a lot" (interview, 1/19/1983).

Teatro Campesino plays were clearly collaborative exercises that changed with each performance and with each rehearsal. Much of theater criticism and theater history divorces these pieces from the human beings who created them. Yet the texts uttered did not exist separately from those people. They did not exist as a fixed text in "dramatic literature" fashion. The text alone is not even half the story. For much of Chicana/o theater it holds true that academic textual analysis cannot unfold or reveal the artistry involved. Socorro Valdez described her view of bringing expression to a "crude image," that is, a role: "The roles are like an old rock, but crack that baby open and you have intricate, intricate layers of evolution. *That* is what has been my goal: to take these very crude images that were there, that have their own form of artistry, and break them open so that the inside is expressed. It makes me work harder, it makes me push more to get inside of a *cholo* or to get inside of that *campesino* who seems so obvious" (interview, 3/1/1983).

Writing a Teatro Campesino history from the perspective of women and discarding historical accounts that subsume the work of a group of people under the name of one man or a male "genius" has implications that extend beyond questions of gender. Subsuming the work of a group of people under the name of one man implies individual authorship, a hallmark of *print culture*. A history of El Teatro Campesino through the eyes and voices of women clearly demonstrates that the work of El Teatro Campesino fits squarely within *oral culture*, or the oral performance tradition, which is radically different from the print culture model of theatrical production.

In the centuries-old oral performance tradition, plays emerge from the collective improvisation process. Performances are stored in the human memory and not in scripts. This is an entirely different tradition than that of print culture, where a script is created by an individual writer and constitutes the starting point (not the result) of a lengthy improvisational rehearsal process. Within the oral performance tradition, actors create their characters, their spoken lines and actions. The responsibility and function of actors are clearly very different within oral culture than they are in print culture.

The role of "director" of El Teatro Campesino similarly had a function much unlike that within print culture or mainstream theater. The dynamics of oral performance and collective authorship created a process in which the "director" was in fact more often engaged in taking direction than in giving it. The director was the person directed by the actors' creativity. This relationship of reciprocity prompted Yolanda Parra to indicate that "Luis Valdez was created by El Teatro Campesino" when historians of the theater always put it the other way around. In her words:

> He [Luis] pulled a lot of stuff out of them and they gave him a lot of material, tons of material in the improvisations. And you see that material appear even in shows like *Zoot Suit*. He took characters that had been developed within the group in a collective situation. As director he might come out and say, "This is the situation." But then it was the actors that made it happen for him. . . . In a lot of ways Luis was created by El Teatro Campesino. The unquestionable loyalty of the members also created him. (Interview, 12/21/1982)

Given the extraordinary acting skill of Socorro Valdez, it would be no exaggeration to speak of her as a leading figure in the history of El Teatro Campesino. In the entire history of her work with the Teatro Campesino, however, Socorro Valdez never played a lead female part—only numerous male leads. That is a startling fact considering not only Socorro's almost leg-

endary talents as a performer but also her yearning to explore various roles.
Yet the stereotyped casting within the company eliminated her, and other
women who looked like her, from various female leads. There was sadness
in her voice when she indicated that she was never allowed to play Our Lady
of Guadalupe in La Virgen de Tepeyac:

> I never even got close to it. They wouldn't let me . . . I could never have the
> role . . . because Luis doesn't see me that way. They see the Virgen de Guada-
> lupe as a very soft, demure, peaceful, saintly, ingenue type. The really incred-
> ible part was when it turned out that I have too many teeth. I was told "You
> got too many teeth. The Virgen didn't have that many teeth." It appears the
> Virgen de Guadalupe had no teeth. I thought to myself: "That is the stupidest
> thing I ever heard of!" *Apoco estaba molacha la Virgen de Guadalupe?* [Are you going
> to tell me that our Lady of Guadalupe was toothless?] (Interview 3/1/1983)

The truth, however, was that Socorro did not meet the standards of beauty
that had been set for the dark-skinned deity, La Virgen Morena: Socorro has
strong *indígena* features and dark brown skin.

This also partially explains how she and other Teatro Campesino women
ended up creating numerous roles that camouflaged their natural appearance.
In addition to the male roles, they created numerous sexless characters.
Socorro's portrayal of La Muerte—in *calavera* (skeleton) costume—became a
classic. She commented: "In all these years I was always under heavy makeup
or under heavy costume, you know. And one role that I pretty much made
my handle was the *calavera* because it was sexless; it was of neither sex" (interview, 3/1/1983). The sexless roles became numerous, and they were
pursued as a creative outlet by women seeking to escape the confinement of
female roles. Olivia Chumacero created the Diabla (Devil) during the *corridos*
dramatizations of the 1970s and also the Angel role and San Miguel in *La
Pastorela*; Yolanda Parra's performance as San Miguel in *La Pastorela* (1981) is
remembered by many as one of the finest renditions of that character.
Socorro Valdez first created the *mago* (magician) role in the *Pastorela*. Several
women also played male roles, but not as consistently as Socorro.

In the course of seeking new channels for creativity, Olivia Chumacero
and Socorro Valdez also began directing. Socorro directed many productions
of La Virgen de Tepeyac. Teatro Campesino women, initially still heavily influenced
by the prevailing ideology of gender oppression, performed and created
socially approved images and stereotypes of women, images born of the male
imagination. Yet as these women left their teens and twenties, their emancipatory demands engendered the creation of new characters.

Today former *teatristas* are still clearing new pathways for sharing their theater expertise, and most of these paths lead back to the Chicana/o community. Yolanda Parra left El Teatro Campesino and is doing theater work with children: "I believe that an artist who does not feed back to the community he or she comes from, is nowhere. It's very easy to say: 'I'm my own little artist; I'm my own little island' . . . I don't think that's the way it should be. Every artist has a responsibility to the community, to put back some of that energy. The community gave me what I am . . . and I feel that there is no greater joy than to be able to feed back" (interview, 12/21/1982).

Olivia Chumacero has also developed alternative pathways for applying her acting and directing expertise. She performed with the Teatro regularly until 1980, while also pioneering in theater work with children of Chicana/o migrant workers. She continues to do that work today, in addition to conducting drama workshops in centers for battered women and for youth in drug prevention centers. She has also taught drama courses at the University of California at Santa Cruz and UC-Santa Barbara. In 1990 she finished her training in filmmaking at UC-Santa Cruz and has made documentary films. Olivia's work can serve as a model for the application of theater skills in ways that directly benefit disenfranchised sectors of society. Like most of the former Teatro Campesino members, Olivia is strongly committed to doing theater work that gives to the community from which it has drawn. In a similar vein, Diane Rodríguez now works primarily with the sociocritical comedy group Latins Anonymous.

The paths taken by Socorro Valdez, Olivia Chumacero, and Diane Rodríguez provide us with but a few examples of the new roles that women have assumed and created, in an effort to break the mold of distorted and fragmented images of Chicanas. But at different times and in different ways virtually all the women have consciously engaged in the effort to create new spaces and models in which they and other women—and men—can move. Many have managed to transform old frustrations into new options. These are women who are keenly aware of the possibilities within themselves—as performers and as human beings. The history of El Teatro Campesino must include the history of its contradictions and of the emergence of women who have charted new territory for subsequent generations.

An Epilogue: Chicanas Onstage in the 1980s

The long history of El Teatro Campesino's collective work had ceased entirely by 1980. When Luis Valdez went to Hollywood and then to Broadway, the members of the ensemble for the most part went their separate ways. El Teatro Campesino still exists on paper, as a largely dormant production company whose name is attached to an occasional production in the hope of imbu-

ing it with the aura of the distinguished but defunct ensemble. Yet the name
El Teatro Campesino no longer stands for an acting ensemble that is strongly
committed to specific cultural and social ideals; Luis Valdez has long since
left the arena of alternative theater and is committed to mainstreaming—a
process he sometimes likens to a narcotic injection: "I see it as mainlining
into the veins of America" (Martín 1983).

I would like to focus attention on Luis Valdez's major stage creation of the
1980s, a production entitled Corridos. The show enjoyed considerable box
office success both in San Juan Bautista (1982) and at the Marines' Memorial Theater of San Francisco (1983). It also traveled to the Old Globe Theater in San Diego and the Variety Arts Theater in Los Angeles in 1984. Corridos
harvested the critical acclaim of the establishment press and received virtually all Bay Area theater awards for the 1983 season. In 1987 Corridos premiered as a PBS television special film. As will be shown in chapter 4, the
stage production of Corridos and the subsequent filming of that production
can serve as model cases for hypotheses concerning Chicana/o mainstream
entertainment products.

Since his departure from alternative theater, Luis Valdez has described his
artistic goal in terms of creating cultural products with mass appeal, as opposed to playing primarily for Chicana/o audiences. The redefined audience
relationship has of course necessarily brought on a considerable change
in what could be termed artistic orientation. Corridos is very unlike anything
ever produced by the Teatro Campesino ensemble. A careful examination
of the Corridos production reveals that the shift in audience alliance—a shift
away from Chicana/o community audiences and toward Euro-Americans
and middle-class Americans—had immediate effects on the type of work
produced.

Here I wish to explore only the representation of women in the mainstream stage production Corridos. A brief examination of Corridos corresponds
with the trajectory of the present inquiry: the stated goal of Corridos is "to
explore the relationship between men and women" (narrator). Let us examine the results of this exploration especially as they pertain to women.
I also want to look at how the corrido itself is represented. As will be shown,
the Valdezian construction of woman and of the corrido tradition are closely
related.

The corridos (traditional narrative ballads) chosen for the stage performance
were "Rosita Alvirez," "Cornelio Vega," "Delgadina," and a Luis Valdez weav-
ing of "La Rielera/La Valentina/La Adelita" entitled "Soldadera." What then,
is the nature of the relationship between men and women? One prominent
feature common to these corridos is the murder of a woman. One exception

Olivia Chumacero in 1979. Courtesy of Rogelio Rojas Collection.

is "Cornelio Vega," where a man is murdered "por amar a una mujer [for loving a woman]." Valdez himself indicates in an interview (Martín 1983): "Hay un tema central que tiene que ver con la violencia en contra de las mujeres que desgraciadamente es real, hasta hoy en día. Es parte de nuestra historia como es parte de nuestro presente" (There is a central theme having to do with violence against women that unfortunately is real, to this very day. It is part of our history as it is part of our present). The theme of violence against women, however, is in no way treated as an issue or a problem. To the contrary: it is used as a comic element or simply as a dramatic climax. And through the very choice of *corridos*, violence against women is assigned a prominent and almost exclusive role in "the relationship between Mexican men and women" (narrator). In fact, relationships between males and females seem to exhaust themselves in violence. In the San Francisco production, the *corrido* of "Doña Elena y El Francés" (Doña Elena and the Frenchman) was added; Doña Elena is of course shot by her husband. In an effort to establish a kind of equality between the sexes, a *corrido* in which a woman murders her husband was also added: "El corrido de Conchita la viuda alegre" (The Ballad of Conchita, the Happy Widow). The heavy focus on shooting and blood projects the image of Mexicans as a bloodthirsty, vengeful crowd, a people quite busy killing each other. In spite of the abundance of existing *corridos* in which no one is murdered, only *corridos* with violence between men and women are dramatized. The desire to exploit the dramatic tensions of violence clearly takes precedence over the desire to provide a balanced portrayal of people and of their ballad tradition.

Left to right: Diane Rodríguez, Olivia Chumacero, and Rosa María Escalante, in Don Juan Tenorio (1982). Courtesy of Olivia Chumacero Archive.

The excessive violence in the vision of relationships between men and women is not startling, given Luis Valdez's mythical and violent vision of what he terms "basic human experience." Within that vision, historical process is put in terms of the sexual imagery of rape. And, by implication, sexual experience is likened to the historical process of raw conquest. In his own words:

> We who are of the Third World and are victims of colonization have been subjected with the rest of the world to the phenomenon of Europe for the last five hundred years. These people left that section of the world and they went out and conquered other vast sections of the world. Now conquest and that warriorlike stance is not peculiar to this period of history, it has been all throughout the history of the human race and also in the Americas. Perhaps what is upsetting us is that we are still in this period, that we are still stuck. The modern Genghis Khan is still with us and he came from Europe in all of his forms. He came in a particularly masculine form. In the case of the Spanish he came in iron armor. The male erection made flesh, if you will, "*Chíngate, Cabrón!*" [Fuck you, you bastard]. If I may refer to the basic mythical experience of the male in the sex act—that is what it takes. In order to do your stuff as a man, you have to have armor and a spear and you have to penetrate and the more you penetrate the better it is. *Dime que no* [Tell me that's not true]. On the other hand, there is the other part which is just as natural which is the female experience which is "*Vente, Cabrón*" [Fuck me, you bastard]. Those two fit together. I am not trying to embarrass you. I am talking basic human experience. (*Califas* 1982:43)

Related to the presence of violence is the Corridos production narrator's statement that the corridos portray types such as la coqueta (the coquette) or el valiente (the brave-but-foolhardy). The type that emerges in the course of staging a corrido, however, is very much a result of dramaturgic interpretation. Attaching one label to a corrido figure involves a choice by which one characteristic, among many possible ones, is singled out. It is the essence of stereotyping. One example of this procedure can be seen in the decision to characterize the figure of Rosita Alvirez as a coquette. Instead of focusing on the hija desobediente (i.e., the mother/daughter relationship), she is portrayed as a sexually loose and reckless woman. Highlighted action includes, for example, Rosita seductively lifting her dress in front of a mirror and flashing her legs. At the dance, Rosita is staged as lewdly flirtatious and then seems to "get what she deserves." In other words, her provocative behavior seemingly justifies Hipólito's violence against her. Rosita could also have been typed as the hija desobediente, the disobedient daughter, however, to highlight the mother/daughter relationship. Yet that relationship, and the traditional Mexican value of a mother's advice, is sabotaged from the outset by the willful decision to portray the mother as a stumbling drunkard.

The dramatization of "Tierra sin nombre" distorts the corrido text by projecting a male fantasy of female submissiveness. Its plot consists of a love triangle: a woman loves two men and finally chooses one over the other. At the wedding she is murdered by the man she did not choose. The dramatized corrido distorts the text in various ways. For example, the successful suitor is portrayed as a rich, "handsome" Spanish-type gentleman whereas the rejected man is cast as a barefooted indio-campesino (Indian-farmworker) type. It is through a dramaturgic sleight of hand that the female character is subtly maneuvered out of legitimately choosing between two men based on emotional considerations. She bases her decision on money (class) and looks (race); she chooses the rich, tall, "handsome" man, who symbolically throws around a bag of coins. But is it really her decision? Cast in the ingenue mold, the female character cannot resist the advances of the good-looking rich man. He actively pursues her and she passively submits, her eyes lowered in shyness. We are left with the stereotype of the passive yet opportunistic Mexican woman. None of that is in the original corrido text. As a comment on the nature of relationships between men and women, and as a comment about women, the stage portrayal projects a male fantasy of female submissiveness. Throughout the show the narrator emphasizes the point that "corridos are macho in viewpoint." Commentary such as that would appear to indicate that the images of men and women we see before us simply represent a retrograde Mexican tradition. That is also what the script indicates to us when we are told that "the corridos are reproduced with loyalty to the corrido tradition." Such statements seek to equate what corridos are with what is in reality one interpretation of them. A sharp distinction between the two must be drawn, however. Otherwise, not only a number of female and male corrido characters are stereotyped but also the entire corrido tradition. The images of women for sale, women as passive victims, women as drunkard mothers are not a creation of the corrido tradition but a projection of the Corridos production.

Valdez's emphasis on so-called machismo could easily have been balanced by the inclusion of other neglected non-sexist corridos, such as "Juana Gallo," "Agripina," "El corrido de las comadres," or "María y Julián," all of which provide multifaceted, narrative ballad portrayals of women. "Juana Gallo" graphically describes the heroic actions of a young female warrior in various battles of the Mexican Revolution. Agripina—heroine of the corrido bearing that title—also engages in battle.

The longest single performance segment within the Corridos production is entitled "Soldadera," a pastiche of three famous corridos about women. It is of special interest because Luis Valdez conceived it as a corrective to his own interpretation of the corrido tradition as "macho:"

> In search of some justice to the true role of women in Mexican history, we now go to the period most aficionados consider to be the high point . . . of the corrido: the Revolution of 1910. . . . And there we find three legendary songs about three legendary women—La Adelita, La Valentina, and La Rielera. . . . These, together with a character inspired by the dispatches of an American journalist riding with Pancho Villa back in 1914, a man by the name of John Reed, now combine to give us a portrait of Mexican woman at war. (Valdez 1983:59)

"Soldadera" is of further interest because Socorro Valdez played a lead female role. For Socorro the piece marks another breakthrough in her career as a performer. After 1980 she went to Hollywood in search of other acting opportunities. Her return to San Juan Bautista was not unconditional. She demanded to play a role that she had long been denied. In her words:

> He [Luis Valdez] put the corrido together and he wanted me to play the role, because I had been after him for a length of time. You know, I wanted to play a young girl. And I didn't want makeup on my face. I didn't want lipstick. I didn't want false eyelashes or fake boobs or nothing. I just wanted to be myself up there, just wanted to be the Indian person that I am . . . I came back to him [Luis], but I said: "That's it. No more masks, no more calavera face, no more calavera bones on my face. None of that shit. I'll go out there in a plain cotton dress and I'll have those people going." (Interview, 3/1/1983)

And she did, in truth, have *Corridos* audiences going. Her stage presence and commitment to the work at hand were unique within the cast. Yet, the strength of her performance was diminished by the script's vision of women.

What is Valdez's vision of the women of the Mexican Revolution? One of the striking features within "Soldadera" is that it is not female characters such as La Adelita, La Valentina, and La Rielera who address women's role in history. The production does not draw from even *one* female testimonial source concerning the Mexican Revolution of 1910. Nor were historians of women consulted. The result is a highly superficial and distorted portrayal of women's participation in the Revolution, and from a white male perspective. The "true role of women in Mexican history" is—ironically—narrated through the agency of a white male character. The character of John Reed (author of *Insurgent Mexico*) does most of the talking in the piece entitled "Soldadera." Mexican women are thus positioned in such a way that a white male speaks of their experience for them. What could be more contradictory and counterproductive than to foreground and privilege a white male subject even as you propose to do "justice to the role of women in Mexican history"? John Reed, the only Anglo in the production, also functions as a white savior: he is the only male in the production who does not engage in violence against women. He is a heroic Anglo man who speaks gently and protects Elizabeta (Socorro Valdez) from her brutal Mexican companion.

Reed's manner stands in strong contrast to that of the three *soldaderas* (the soldier women of the Mexican Revolution) and the Mexican men. The verbal exchanges between these men and women are almost exclusively aggressive or abusive. Men and women fall into the categories of conqueror or conquered. Some effort is made within "Soldadera" to demonstrate diversity in women—but that diversity is external: La Valentina is the hip-swaying, hard-nosed companion to the colonel. In the San Juan Bautista production she also displays a strong inclination toward attire highly unsuited to the rigors of the Mexican Revolution: spiked-heel boots and skintight pants. La Adelita carries a rifle; La Rielera (Socorro Valdez) is a gentle-souled Indian woman who follows men. The semblance of diversity collapses entirely when the women engage in dialogue. Their contribution to the narrative line consists entirely of discussions concerning the finding and losing of men, about following men, about holding on to men. There is nothing in their dialogue or actions to reveal any depth in their character nor an understanding of the revolution around them. Mexican women are not shown in their true roles as thinking historical agents but only as helpmates to men.

John Reed, for all his talking, provides no insight into the social forces within the Revolution. He has been edited in such a way that he portrays battles without causes. All discussion of social forces, of the colonial bondage that Mexicans sought to overthrow, has been eliminated from his narration. The Mexican Revolution, and history in general, are reduced to a backdrop, a foil for song numbers and centerstage chatter. La Rielera (the railroad woman) engages in only two activities: sleeping with her man, Juan, and making tortillas.

The Valdezian portrayal of *soldaderas* constitutes a distorted simplification of the historical role of these women, for although some women did cook for men on the revolutionary campaigns, many women also fought in battle; and many joined the revolutionary forces on their own. By positioning women within the shadow of John Reed, Valdez most clearly articulates his conscious or unconscious view of them as insignificant. It is fair to conclude that Luis Valdez's "search of some justice to the true role of women in Mexican history" was conducted less than halfheartedly, for it produced highly questionable findings. The professed search amounted to little more than a rhetorical device aimed at paying lip service to women's presence in history. Notwithstanding the vast critical acclaim that greeted the piece, with it the stage portrayal of Mexican women reached a new low.

The deplorable representation of Mexican and Chicana women is a chronic weakness and signature of Luis Valdez's mainstream productions, such as Zoot Suit, Corridos, or the film La Bamba (1987). In Zoot Suit, which earned widespread recognition as a landmark play and movie in the 1980s, we again encounter the stereotypical dominant mother, the whorelike Bertha, the virginal Della, and a white savior, here Alice Bloomfield. Most lamentable, the true historical role of Chicana Josefina Fierro in organizing the Sleepy Lagoon Defense Committee in 1942 in behalf of the zoot suiters was completely erased. Valdez supplants her in the play and film by a white female character. Chicana/o community leader Bert Corona sharply criticizes Luis Valdez's distortion of the facts:

> In 1942, Josefina Fierro, as national secretary of the Congreso Nacional de los Pueblos de Habla Española, carried out two very significant actions. One was the formation of the Sleepy Lagoon Defense Committee (contrary to the distorted version in Luis Valdez's play Zoot Suit) which conducted the public defense of the twenty-two Mexicans who were tried for the death of one. Josefina traveled all over the nation, assisted by Luisa Moreno, to develop the broad national campaign against the racist and divisive indictments and yellow journalistic press descriptions of the Hearst Press. . . . It is to be

deplored that Luis Valdez could find insufficient drama in the true facts about the Defense of the Sleepy Lagoon and *Zoot Suit* victims, that he had to rely upon Hollywood gimmicks of a fictitious melodrama between two persons [Alice Bloomfield and Henry Reyna] that never took place in order to tell his story. (1983:16)

Truth and substance have taken a backseat to melodrama in *Corridos* as well. In spite of the production's undeniable entertainment qualities—the visual effects, the dancing, musical direction and performance, the fast pace—it is entertaining without being thought-provoking. What is worse, *Corridos* affirms Hollywood images of men in sombreros and on horseback engaged, for the most part, in violence, and colorful señoritas defined in terms of men. The tradition of such images and their marketability in the entertainment business has been described by Luis Valdez:

Now there was a time when this country reveled in Latino images— commercially—and that was in the 1940s of course, parallel with the Zoot Suit era. . . . The U.S. . . . turned its attention to Latin America and said, "How can we sell more movies in Latin America?" And obviously they said "Let's put more Latin images on films, but let's make them 'safe' images." So what we ended up with was Carmen Miranda. What we ended up with was the Latin Night Club and Rhumbaing down to Rio or what have you . . . Desi Arnaz came out of that era, you know. But nothing came from the Mexican Revolution . . . at least not during World War II. (*Califas* 1982:46–47)

With *Corridos*, the Mexican Revolution has now entered the ranks of safe (i.e., caricature), commercial "Latino" images such as those projected by Desi Arnaz, Carmen Miranda, and various others. The media may well revel in these well-worn images, now marketed by Valdez as "New American Theater." Some may thrill at the visibility the show provides for so-called Hispanics. Others may take pride in seeing Mexican Americans perform in what is known in show business circles as legitimate theater. But El Teatro Campesino in the 1960s set the standard to demand more than that.

The highly visible professional Chicana/o productions of recent years offer little that is inspirational or alternative. With regard to the representation of Mexican and Chicana women, productions such as *Zoot Suit*, *Corridos*, or *La Bamba* are nothing short of devastating. It would appear that the absence of a collective work context has left Luis Valdez wholly unrestrained in giving expression to his fragmented vision of women. The division of labor inherent in professional theater and commercial film, with its hierarchy of personnel and constant turnover of hired actors, does not foster discussion or the development of a critical consciousness, let alone disagreement or a challenge to established models. The production team recruits from a generation of actors for whom the portrayal of Mexicans on stage is not an issue. In my conversations with the cast members of Corridos it became apparent that the images of women (and men) the production projected were not a matter of particular concern. In the absence of a group of female actors who have learned to question and reject shallow roles, the emergence of a broader vision of women within the new Luis Valdez productions seems unlikely.

El Teatro Campesino is now the name of a small administrative apparatus that puts on an occasional play in which the spirit of group commitment and the performance energy characteristic of Teatro Campesino ensemble is altogether missing. The tight-knit acting ensemble has been displaced by actors who do their jobs and then return to Los Angeles in search of the next gig. The model for the new organization comes from business administration. Theatrical production is streamlined: actors act, the director directs, administrators administer. In the arena of glittering lights, the struggle to establish new women's roles has dissipated. Yet far from the limelight we can perceive the efforts of Chicanas who continue to explore and create dramatic alternatives for women. The dream to represent the vast spectrum of Chicana womanhood on the stage will in time find creative expression. After the Corridos production Socorro Valdez described her dream of representing the vast spectrum of Chicana womanhood on the stage:

> I'll tell you what my dream is—one of my dreams. And I know I'll get to it because it's a driving thing in me . . . My dream is to be able to do a theater piece on the phases of womanhood. It's something that has not been done yet. All the times that I've seen women's programs or women in this or women in that, it somehow has never been quite satisfactory for me, you know. No one can take womanhood and put it into one thing. But that is precisely what I want to do. I want to put womanhood into every form that I can express: in singing, in crying, in laughing, everything. That role is not yet there. That role has not been written. Maybe it has been written in a Shakespearean way. But I don't relate to those European images of women. . . . Women are obviously in a type of great void. They are balanced, but in terms of the way the world looks at us they've put us in this position where we've accepted the condition of doing one role instead of many. If there were some way of taking that and putting it into words that are theatrical, I would like to do that. I don't believe a man is going to write that. I don't believe that for one single minute. And I sure can't sit around and wait for Luis to write that role. (Interview, 3/1/1983)

The activities of several of the women from El Teatro Campesino—Olivia Chumacero, Socorro Valdez, Diane Rodríguez, Yolanda Parra—and the work of Silvia Wood in Tucson, Arizona; Nita Luna from El Teatro Aguacero in New Mexico; the women and men of El Teatro de la Esperanza; Ruby Nelda Pérez's or María Elena Gaitán's one-woman shows; the plays by Estela Portillo Trambley, Denise Chávez, Cherríé Moraga, and more recently by Josefina López, Edit Villareal, and Evelina Fernández, all mark the entry into a new cycle of theatrical activity for Chicanas.[2] We are not without inspirational models, nor without the example of women who question and who strive to reclaim a fully human female identity on stage. We would do well to acknowledge that activity in the writing of theater history. A quantitatively different historical account emerges when we attempt to recover the silenced history and reconceptualize the established historical record, when we aspire to discover marginalized voices and perspectives. The history of women's participation in theater history is of far-reaching significance in and of itself. Yet it is but one of the possible correctives to the monolithic great-man vision of human activity, which has obscured many aspects of history.

Zoot Suit at Mark Taper Forum. Left to right: Roberta Delgado, Danny Valdez, Edward James Olmos, Evelina Fernández, Tony Plana, Abel Franco, Lupe Ontiveros. Courtesy of Mark Taper Forum.

4. El Teatro Campesino: From Alternative Theater to Mainstream

Introduction

At its inception in 1965, El Teatro Campesino consciously viewed itself as working outside of the dominant (i.e., commercial) theater performance practice, which goes by names such as the mainstream, show business, or legitimate theater. There was always an awareness within the Teatro of being an underdog's or poor person's theatrical form of oppositional expression: an alternative form of cultural practice with a world view antithetical to that of white establishment theater. The entire Chicana/o theater movement that burst forth in the 1960s and the 1970s aimed to serve the interests of Chicana/o communities whose needs and struggles were in no way addressed by the mainstream theater machinery characterized by elitism and commercialism. TENAZ (Teatro Nacional de Aztlan), the umbrella organization of the Chicana/o theater movement, formulated the alternative mission of Chicana/o theaters in its 1973 Manifesto:

> Theater is the voice of the barrios, of the community, of the downtrodden, the humble, the "*rasquachi*." ... We, the workers of Teatro Nacional de Aztlan, are dedicated to the life struggle. ... The organization, TENAZ, will work with all oppressed people; it must develop a human and revolutionary alternative to commercial theater and mass media. It is necessary that we work together with all the liberation theaters wherever they may be, particularly in Latin America. The creation of theaters as community organizations will serve as a tool in the life-struggle of LA RAZA. (Rodríguez n.d.:83)

This sentiment is also expressed in the "Notes on Chicano Theater" in the Teatro Campesino's *Actos*, its only published anthology of early skits: "Chicano theater, then, is first a reaffirmation of LIFE. That is what all theater is supposed to be, of course; but the limp, superficial, *gringo seco* productions in the 'professional' American theater (and the college and university drama departments that serve it) are so antiseptic, they are anti-biotic (anti-life). ... It [commercial *gabacho* (Euro-American) theater] reflects a characteristic

'American' hang-up on the material aspect of human existence" (Valdez 1971b:1). Luis Valdez's introduction to the *Actos* similarly affirms Chicana/o theatrical creation as antithetical to that of mainstream America: "Our rejection of white western European (gabacho) proscenium theater makes the birth of new Chicano forms necessary" (Valdez 1971a:5). The rejection of "white western European proscenium theater" was common to the entire Chicana/o theater movement of the 1960s and the 1970s.

More fundamental than that rejection, however, was a shared vision of why and for whom Chicana/o theater was being performed. A strong commitment to "liberation" and the Chicana/o "life-struggle" (TENAZ Manifesto) implied a social and political alliance between performer and spectator unlike that found in the world of mainstream theater. It was a vision of theater art generated and sustained by an immersion in the history of Chicanas/os in the United States and an alliance with Chicana/o socioeconomic and cultural struggles of the 1960s and the 1970s. The strong alliance between Chicana/o performers and working-class audiences in the arena of Chicana/o alternative theater is of paramount significance. That alliance constituted the basis for the choice of aesthetics, production material, performance sites, acting style, and so on. In the case of alternative theater the alliance was with working-class barrio audiences and farmworkers. Given the primacy of the *audience* within Chicana/o performance, it would be fallacious and distortive to examine its trajectory in terms that separate audience and performance. Chicana/o drama cannot be conceptualized as an "autonomous" work of art to be examined as an autonomous literary artifact. This holds true for alternative Chicana/o drama as well as for mainstream drama.

The early Teatro Campesino was a theater of farmworkers for farmworkers. It was situated outside of the hegemonic mainstream theater industry by virtue of its close affiliation with the labor struggles of the United Farm Workers (Levy 1975). That alliance determined both its practical and its aesthetic goals in the initial years. For one thing, the working-class reality of its members (farmworkers) and audiences entailed a reliance on the Mexican popular performance tradition, whose trajectory and techniques differ vastly from those of mainstream American theater (see chap. 1). For the Teatro Campesino as well as the other Chicana/o theaters, the decision to serve barrio and farmworker audiences—that is, working in the context of an alternative aesthetic—also entailed a commitment to work under conditions of severe material deprivation, both on- and offstage. Motivated primarily by a desire to better the lives of their audiences, the ensemble typically performed without giving much thought to material gain. Minimal proceeds from performances forced Teatro members to wage a constant struggle for group and individual survival. The struggle for survival waged by Teatro Campesino ensemble members was essentially no different from the work-ing-class struggle for survival of its audiences.

Under these austere economic conditions, Teatro Campesino perfor-mances were typically of very high energy and very low production value: lighting and sound equipment were unheard of; props, costumes, and make-up were makeshift and minimal; acting skills had been acquired in the course of negotiating a hard life and not from specialized training. Specialists such as stage managers were unheard of. For the early Teatro Campesino the site of each performance was a matter of improvisation dependent on where audiences could be found. "If the *Raza* [Chicanos] will not come to the the-ater, then the theater must go to the *Raza*." This statement by Luis Valdez (1971b:4) epitomized the Teatro's determination to be an integral part of Chicana/o life. Early Teatro Campesino performance sites included the backs of flatbed trucks, the roadside adjacent to agricultural fields, or any hall or union meeting where Chicana/o workers congregated. Against all odds El Teatro Campesino thrived and evolved into a seasoned ensemble with en-thusiastic supporters in the United States, Latin America, and Europe. By 1970 the ensemble stood as a symbol of excellence and commitment within the worldwide alternative theater movement.

In this chapter I document and analyze the Teatro Campesino's transfor-mation from an alternative Chicana/o ensemble to a mainstream production company patterned after "white western European proscenium theater." The sudden success of Luis Valdez's and El Teatro Campesino's *Zoot Suit* on main-stream American stages marked a turn in Chicana/o theater, which had tra-ditionally maintained a separatist stance vis-à-vis commercial or mainstream theater. Although the *Zoot Suit* success of the late 1970s, as well as its filming by Universal Studios in 1981, engendered a great deal of pride in Chi-cana/o communities, it also triggered a great deal of skepticism and critical discussion concerning the underlying significance or price of that success. Skeptical critics were particularly wary of what might be the deleterious ef-fects of "show business" upon Chicana/o theater as an alternative institution with a commitment to barrio audiences. The turn away from the arena of alternative theater seemed to signal an abandonment of commitment to the life and struggles of the Chicana/o community.

In my analysis I hope to weigh both the benefits and the drawbacks of mainstreaming by looking primarily at the *Zoot Suit* experience and its aftermath. Existing discussion of the phenomenon of Chicana/o theater in the mainstream has been for the most part of a journalistic nature, usually in the context of production reviews. In addition to being highly superficial

(and written, for the most part, from a non-Chicana/o perspective), jour-
nalists have focused on dramatic pieces or on Luis Valdez as autonomous
artistic entities, without consideration of the Teatro Campesino *ensemble* and
the larger relations of production and without weighing the social and material forces that influence the production of theatrical spectacle or the relationship between theater spectacle and audience. I seek to integrate these
perspectives in my discussion of the mainstreaming process. My exploration
of Chicana/o performance activity at the crossroads of alternative and mainstream theater proceeds from the premise that El Teatro Campesino can be
understood only if we look at the broader sociocultural and political context articulated through a living relationship with audiences. As I shall demonstrate, the relationship with audiences is pivotal to Chicana/o theater
practice and to any analysis of it.

The dynamics of theatrical mainstreaming set in motion by *Zoot Suit* has
continued to this day, most recently by the staging of Luis Valdez's *I Don't Have
to Show You No Stinking Badges* at the Los Angeles Theatre Center (1986) and San
Diego's Lyceum (1987) and also with the PBS TV filming of *Corridos* (1987)
and then *La pastorela* (1991). I will focus on the dramatic and social dynamics
that gave rise to the mainstreaming experience heralded by *Zoot Suit*. I explore
the Luis Valdez productions immediately following *Zoot Suit: Rose of the Rancho*
(1977 and 1981), *Bandido!* (1982), and *Corridos* (1983, 1984). These were all
experimental pieces, and the overriding goal of the experimentation was the
development of new dramatic material to launch onto mainstream stages.
Unlike *Zoot Suit*, these pieces have generated embarrassed silence instead of
lively debate among the Chicana/o intelligentsia and the community in general.[1] Virtually nothing has been written on any of the pieces that followed
Zoot Suit, nor on recent mainstream productions. I hope to break that silence
and stimulate new discussion.

The theatrical mainstreaming process is very much in need of critical inquiry. It is a process of particular interest to Chicanas/os and other people of
color working in theater arts and entertainment in general. We must also take
a broader perspective and recognize that there are valuable lessons to be
learned by the Chicana/o population as a whole from the mainstreaming
experience of its own "elite"—be it in the areas of, for example, theater,
education, politics, film, or business. It is not accidental that the entrance of
Chicanas/os into mainstream theater is a phenomenon of the 1980s. The Chi-
cana/o demographic explosion and the meager social gains won as a result
of the Chicano movement have somewhat altered the historical options available to some sectors of our people who have become upwardly mobile. The

sudden emergence of a Chicana/o middle class in the 1980s brought with it an unprecedented participation in white mainstream institutions for merly off-limits for reasons of race, class, and gender. The challenge to Chicanas/os working within mainstream institutions is and will remain an uneasy and contradictory one. On whose terms do we enter? Once we become part of mainstream institutions, whose interests do we serve? In the wake of the Chicano movement and the community consciousness it championed, the epithet *"vendida/o"* ("sell-out") is commonly attached to those Chicanas/os who have been assimilated into mainstream institutions without benefit to Chicana/o communities. As we move into the twenty-first century and witness the increase of Chicanas/os in positions of power, we need to understand the dynamics of Chicana/o involvement, the choices made and the reasons behind them. We will need to take inventory and make an assessment concerning whose interests have been served and what the implications of that may be for future action, both on- and offstage.

Chicana/o theater productions, like Chicana/o films or any other Chicana/o media that engage in the large-scale marketing of Chicana/o images, must be held accountable. What vision do they advance for the future of Chicana/o communities? What ideological purpose is served by the mainstreaming project? Mainstream institutions and Chicana/o individuals working within them need to feel the pressure of minority needs. This chapter is a contribution toward the critical understanding of alternative and mainstream Chicana/o theater as they pertain to minority needs. In this case it is the need to see constructs of our own reality: images that reflect the lives and human potential of the Chicano peoples in the United States, images that will promote our understanding of ourselves, images that will foster self-determination in an era of continued bondage. It is to be hoped that a critical exchange of ideas between Chicana/o researchers, Chicana/o theater artists, and Chicana/o community members will in time help advance the collective potential of our people in addition to making Chicana/o culture more accessible to all non-Chicanas/os.

In my analysis of the Teatro Campesino transition from alternative theater practice to mainstream I rely on numerous sources, none of which are to be found in research libraries. During an extended research residency with El Teatro Campesino I occupied the role of participant-observer at numerous preproduction meetings, production meetings, rehearsals, and Teatro Campesino board meetings. I have also witnessed various productions both in the United States and Europe, as well as backstage and societal realities that helped shape those productions. I also had access to secondary sources

such as newspaper reviews and articles, production notes, diaries, and pho-
tographs from members of the Teatro Campesino. My richest source of insight has been the endless hours of informal conversations and formal oral
histories I conducted with the cast, crew, and directors of Teatro Campesino
productions.

El Teatro Campesino in the Mainstream

The presence of Chicanas/os in the Euro-American mainstream entertainment industry—be it in theater, film, music, or other branches—is not a
recent phenomenon. The untold story of that Chicana/o presence includes
names such as Anthony Quinn, Lupe Vélez, Joan Baez, Linda Ronstadt, and
Vicki Carr, to name only some of the most notable ones. Yet the reality of
mainstream pressures to assimilate or "pass" in most cases motivated artists
to discard their ethnic identities and project a Euro-American image. It was
only in the course of the Chicano Movement and its push to affirm ethnic
pride while denouncing inequality that some Chicana/o performers—such
as Anthony Quinn and Joan Baez—"came out" and proclaimed their Mexican ancestry.

The impact of that climate of militant affirmation of ethnic pride in time
came to be felt within some mainstream entertainment institutions and
funding agencies as well, even if only marginally. When such militant ethnic
demands became felt, they usually translated into economic or political concessions. Economic concessions meant tapping into the new "Hispanic market." Political concessions meant halfheartedly heeding minority demands
that publicly funded institutions serve all constituencies.

It was in the wake of that heightened ethnic awareness and protest against
exclusionary practices that the Mark Taper Forum for the first time opened
its doors to a staging of a Chicana/o play: Zoot Suit. No other Chicana/o plays
were commissioned in the ten years following, however. Universal Studios'
subsequent decision to fund the filming of Zoot Suit (albeit on a severely limited budget) can also be interpreted as a timid and halfhearted effort to target a new and growing minority audience. Among the documents included
in a 1981 Universal Studios marketing report entitled "Positioning Zoot Suit"
is one that indicates that "the Hispanic market is the fastest growing minority in the country" and that "the moment is ripe for advertising in the Hispanic market" (Guernica 1981:xii). Luis Valdez was certainly conscious of
the new mainstream opportunities available in the 1970s: "I think what inspired Universal Studios to do the film, was the realization of the number of
Hispanics in the Southwest, Chicago, and New York that has grown within

the last 25 years. The question is whether a Chicano theme that is as Chicano as *Zoot Suit* can reach out to everybody" (Pérez 1981:8).

It is important to note that the efforts to gain entry and establish a foothold in show business are a story not only of glory but also of failure. In the case of El Teatro Campesino, the *Zoot Suit* experience motivated not only the complete transformation of the ensemble but also its eventual dissolution. That dissolution constitutes a phenomenon attendant on mainstreaming and is a development that has been entirely overlooked by critics although it is one of the chief lessons to be learned from the mainstreaming experiment. I wish to examine both the success and the failure of the contradictory mainstreaming process, its possibilities and limits.

In order to understand this double-edged sword it is first necessary to reexamine the Teatro Campesino years preceding *Zoot Suit*. For many, *Zoot Suit*'s breakthrough into the mainstream seemed meteoric and startling. For others it seemed like the "logical" culmination of the Teatro Campesino's years of successful performance. In reality, what appeared to be a sudden entry into the mainstream was neither "sudden" nor was it a "natural" culmination. It marked one more step in a process that had been initiated and in the planning stages since before 1977. It was neither a "natural" thing nor a "logical" next step, but rather the outcome of a deliberate decision, which involved a radical departure from what had been El Teatro Campesino's performance philosophy since 1965.

Not all members of the Teatro Campesino ensemble shared the new mainstreaming vision; in retrospect it seems evident that even those who did advocate mainstreaming were not entirely aware—nor could they have known—of the implications of that choice and of its consequences, which included the ensemble's dissolution. It is a process no Chicana/o acting ensemble had ever had to confront. We have a great deal to learn from the process itself and the outcome of this experimental project. In examining that project I also seek to shed light on the larger network of social relationships in which it is embedded.

The full-fledged entry into the mainstream heralded by *Zoot Suit* was in fact the success side of deliberate efforts at mainstreaming that go back to 1976. It was then that El Teatro Campesino toured Europe with *Fin del mundo* and then filmed a PBS television special entitled "El Corrido" (televised in November 1976). In the same year, Teatro Campesino received an offer to participate in a major motion picture starring Richard Pryor, entitled *Which Way Is Up?* We can infer that the film's producers approached the Teatro because the film had a farmworker context as backdrop to the comedic whodunit plot. Teatro

Campesino's involvement in the lightweight film was auxiliary. Luis Valdez did some consulting, writing, and acting. Ensemble members Daniel Valdez, Diane Rodríguez, and Ernesto Hernández had acting roles.

The impact of these two projects on the company's development cannot be underestimated. José Delgado (1977:24)—an ensemble member—describes that impact in an official Teatro Campesino stocktaking essay published in the 1977 TENAZ Festival program: "In a sense the group is at a pivotal point in its history. A Public Broadcasting System (PBS) television special, a tour of Europe last Fall [1976], and involvement with a major motion picture have inspired a move toward a new direction that will draw inspiration far beyond previously self-imposed limitations." Since the Teatro had already been to Europe three times, we can assume that the "move toward a new direction" was inspired more particularly by the involvement in a major motion picture and the PBS special, both of which were fairly lucrative and provided a previously unknown exposure to the mainstream world.

That exposure proved tantalizing to some members of the ensemble and motivated a turning point. It is noteworthy that the striving for "new directions" was coupled with a somewhat negative assessment of the group's past, perceived in retrospect as limited. The reference to "previously self-imposed limitations" (emphasis mine) merits some attention because it provides a clue to the company's future trajectory. Statements concerning the "new direction" provide insight into what some had come to view as limitations. The new direction is described as the goal of reaching mass audiences, partially inspired by the fact that the PBS special "El Corrido" had reached an estimated fifty million people. By comparison, the company's former mission of playing primarily for Chicanas/os—that is, with Chicana/o needs in mind—could only appear "limited." The 1977 Teatro Campesino essay (Delgado 1977:29) repeatedly indicates who the new targeted audience or constituency is, the "unsympathetic millions": "Our new community is huge and requires us to go beyond movement politics and performing to sympathetic audiences. The real challenge is to conquer the hearts of those unsympathetic millions of Americans who are perhaps unfamiliar with what we represent as a people or cause."

Significantly, the "new direction" for El Teatro Campesino and what is attendant to that new direction emerges from this redefined audience relationship. The decision to focus on "those unsympathetic millions of Americans" instead of "performing to sympathetic audiences," of course, necessarily meant a change in what could be termed dramatic orientation.

The "unsympathetic millions of Americans" have needs different from those of Chicanas/os and as such would place a different set of demands or expectations on the ensemble's creative efforts. Projected changes in the company's work plan were described as follows: "Our experiences have taught us that if we wish to communicate to a larger audience our sense of art must become more refined. The characters we portray must be well-rounded, our material more detailed and profound. The images of Chicano Culture and the world around him must be true and subtle" (Delgado 1977:29).

This description of a new performance aesthetic certainly implies a distancing from the Teatro's Rasquachi Aesthetic, which suddenly was no longer perceived as "subtle," "detailed," or "refined" (see chap. 1). Other elements of the "new direction" are described as a desire "to work with more non-Chicano actors, actresses and technicians in the future." The company's shift in audience alliance—a shift away from Chicana/o community audiences and toward the unsympathetic white audiences—had immediate effects on the company's sense of collectivity. The new exposure to mainstream relations of production, which only allow for individual achievement and not the work of collectives, heightened the sense of the individual's importance, thus diminishing the perceived value of collective creation and collective struggle. This new validation of individuality is described in that same Teatro Campesino essay:

> How has all of this affected the internal make-up of the group itself? I would say that there is more of a focus on developing individuals within its structure and more recognition for individual accomplishment.
>
> A company is being born and developed. A company of actors, directors, costume designers, technicians, recording artists and an administrative staff. (Delgado 1977:29)

As will be seen, the new individualism evolved into a division of labor previously unknown within the company. The response to the question: "What lies ahead then for this company?" is: "I think the group will be doing more television, if the programs are Chicana/o in nature and will make ourselves available by offering professional help whenever possible. It does not mean that we will stop performing live Chicano Teatro for Farmworkers. That would obviously be a big mistake" (Delgado 1977:29). The performance of "live Chicano Teatro for Farmworkers" did, however, cease entirely almost as soon as the new direction was taken. It was clearly not feasible to pursue two contradictory artistic visions.

Rose of the Rancho: Validating Chicana/o Oppression

The new artistic vision of El Teatro Campesino, tentatively formulated in Delgado's 1977 essay, began to take dramatic form with the first staging of the play Rose of the Rancho in that same year. This first El Teatro Campesino staging of Rose enjoyed only a limited run (June 25, 26 and July 1–9) and was dedicated to the 180th anniversary of the San Juan Bautista Mission. Although the piece was not produced as a mainstream commercial production, it was conceived as an experimental staging, a trial run from which a mainstream production might emerge.

For those familiar with the company's history or reputation this melodramatic piece seemed a highly unusual choice. In the Los Angeles Times, Dan Sullivan—who, along with Silvie Drake, had reviewed El Teatro Campesino's performances since they began—asked: "and what is El Teatro Campesino doing with a play like this?" He answered not in his own words but with a quote from Luis Valdez: "'Well,' says El Teatro's jefe, . . . 'Sometimes harmony can be as interesting as alienation'" (Sullivan 1977). The "harmony" to which Luis Valdez alludes is that between Anglos and Chicanas/os established in the play through the marriage of the Mexican principal character (Juanita) to an Anglo suitor who wins out against the Mexican suitor and saves the day.

The play represents a radical departure from El Teatro Campesino's alternative trajectory for various reasons beyond the new interracial "harmony" it professes. For one thing, it marks the first time ever that the Teatro performed material neither developed by the ensemble nor belonging to the repository of traditional Mexican miracle plays. Rose of the Rancho was written by David Belasco and Richard Tully and performed very successfully on Broadway in 1906. Although the play was shortened by ensemble members César Flores and Luis Valdez—and produced by Valdez—it maintained the same fundamental thrust, the same dialogue, the same plot line, and the same flighty melodramatic style as the original.

Rose of the Rancho is set in California of the 1840s, the period of westward expansion when Anglo land-grabbers moved in to seize titles to Mexican ranches. The melodrama centers around the competition for the hand of the beautiful and capricious Juanita. Juanita and her family—like many other Mexican families—are about to be dispossessed of their rancho. Land-jumper Kinkaid plans to register the rancho in his name. (Such seizures became legally possible under the U.S. laws that came into effect in 1846, when California was taken from Mexico by the United States.) As an act of resistance, Mexican families refuse to register their lands with a government they do not recognize. This much is made clear in Rose of the Rancho. Yet such acts of resistance to Anglo domination are made to appear outmoded, intransigent, and self-defeating. Central within the plot line is U.S. government agent Kearney, who outwits land-jumper Kinkaid and saves Juanita's family *rancho* by registering it against her family's wishes. Juanita thereupon eagerly agrees to marry the benevolent Anglo who has saved the *rancho* and the *rancheros*, in spite of themselves. All live happily ever after.

Both artistically and ideologically speaking, the play is questionable. It is not resistance and Mexican self-determination that are validated. What is validated is the new Anglo law requiring Mexican landholders to register their land deeds with the U.S. government. The "white savior" (government agent Kearney) symbolizes the new regime. It is he whom Juanita (who symbolizes Mexican California) embraces wholeheartedly, while rejecting her Mexican suitor, Don Luis de la Torre. Indeed, a rejection of all things Mexican is very much a part of Juanita's flighty character. The "larger destiny" she envisions for herself has to do with marrying an Anglo. Her statements to that effect are repeated verbatim from the 1906 play:

> Mamacita, listen first, *por favor!* I . . . I want a larger destiny . . . that's it! That's what I want . . . a very larger destiny than to be married and to go live in Monterey. Oh! I have dreamt, lazily of living in a *gringo* city . . . like San Francisco . . . of living in a wooden house with a gringo husband. Of going to the play every night and of loving very hard all the time and doing nothing but loving and not getting old and brown and having so many children like the Spanish! (Belasco et al. 1936:77)

Even the historical fact of *being Mexican* is eradicated through the ideology of "Spanish" California affirmed throughout the play. Juanita (and others) consistently refer to themselves as "Spaniards." She embodies the stereotypical "Spanish señorita," complete with rose in hair and fan. Such fantasy heritage works hand in hand with some of the more striking historical distortions contained in the play. Lt. Samuel Larkin, for example, is portrayed as a hero leading the state militia which will save the Mexicans in spite of themselves. Larkin was actually a carpetbagger who opened the path for General Fremont's expedition. In the same vein, "white savior" Kearney provides us with an explanation of the Mexican-American War—in talking to his beloved Juanita—that justifies U.S. aggression by portraying Mexico as the aggressor: "My dear young lady, I regret it as much as you that Mexico fired on our troops and ceded you in consequence. But why not make the best of it?" (Belasco et al. 1936:76). Juanita does make the best of it and ethnic differences are easily resolved in the happy-end melodrama.

The *Santa Cruz Sentinel* of July 3 indicated that *Rose* was "a story of the 1840's, and of a *señorita's* decision between the old Mexican tradition and the rising

tide of Americanization" (Beebe 1977:25). Juanita's assimilationist choice—
portrayed with much merriment and music—places this piece entirely outside the tradition of Chicana/o alternative theater. Unlike all prior Teatro
Campesino dramatic activity, this piece was devoid of any inspirational perspectives for Chicanas/os—be they social, spiritual or other human perspectives. Recourse to *Rose of the Rancho*, a theatrical product tried and tested in the
American mainstream, was remarkable for the Teatro Campesino—as was the
recourse to melodrama. *Los Angeles Times* critic Dan Sullivan (1977) concluded:
"It wouldn't do, though, to examine the play too closely for political overtones. Basically this is a second-generation melodrama, smoother than 'Curse
You, Jack Dalton,' but still heroes and villains stuff, with a pretty girl as the
reward."

We might well ask what motivated this curious revival of a problematic
turn-of-the-century melodrama. And what motivated its uncritical adoption,
given the Teatro's history of alternative drama? What appeared incomprehen-
sible to the *L.A. Times* makes sense only as an early attempt to "conquer the
hearts of those unsympathetic millions of Americans." It was a piece tailored
to the tastes of those unsympathetic to Chicana/o socioeconomic and cultural struggles for self-determination. Its assimilationist ideology, its light
melodramatic format, its boldly stereotypical characters certainly assure instant accessibility to a mass audience unfamiliar with anything Chicana/o and
perhaps unwilling to learn. The portrayal of ethnic and economic conflicts
which were—as *Rose of the Rancho* would have us believe—fortunately resolved
a long time ago, assures instant palatability to today's white audiences. It was
perhaps the very formula that made it such a success on Broadway at the turn
of the century. With *Rose of the Rancho* one other projected goal was realized:
the desire "to work with more non-Chicana/o actors, actresses and technicians in the future" (Delgado 1977:25). The play featured—for the first time
in a Teatro Campesino production—various Anglo actors and technicians.

Rose of the Rancho most certainly constitutes a first probing step into mainstream American theater. Although it was not successfully launched onto a
mainstream stage—it was performed in the San Juan Bautista Breen House—
it was an experiment aimed at attracting and appealing to non-Chicana/o
audiences. The results of the experiment are difficult to gauge, given the
play's very short run. But evidently it was considered a worthwhile experiment, since the play was revived five years later. *Rose of the Rancho* was restaged
again in 1981, as the inaugural play of the Teatro Campesino Playhouse in
San Juan Bautista. What appears particularly noteworthy is the play was directed by a Euro-American, Frank Condon.

The New Professionalism: Zoot Suit in the Mainstream

After the 1977 staging of *Rose of the Rancho* the Teatro Campesino resumed work on *Fin del mundo* in hopes of converting it into a "hit." In the words of ensemble member (and later producer) José Delgado: "We didn't travel in 1977 specifically because we wanted to do something that was going to be a hit. We thought it was going to be *Fin del mundo*" (Delgado and Esparza interview, 8/10/1983).

As the ensemble began working on *Fin del mundo*, a parallel activity was initiated by Luis Valdez, who perhaps had a different notion of where the next "hit" would come from. Valdez (through Delgado) offered his services to the prestigious Los Angeles Mark Taper Forum; the offer *excluded* the ensemble. José Delgado recalls: "I had written a letter to Gordon Davidson suggesting the idea of maybe Luis directing *The Shrunken Head of Pancho Villa* down in Los Angeles. It didn't have to be Teatro Campesino actors. It could be L.A. talent. All he would be interested in doing would be directing it. That was the proposal that was originally sent out" (Delgado and Esparza interview, 8/10/1983). Luis Valdez's offer to work independently of the Teatro Campesino collective was certainly also in keeping with the new plan to "focus on developing individuals."

Gordon Davidson did not respond to the proposal until months later when the idea of *Zoot Suit* emerged. Delgado described the steps leading up to the *Zoot Suit* idea:

> Meanwhile what happens is that the tenth anniversary of the Mark Taper Forum was taking place that April [1977]. That's when we first met with Gordon [Davidson]. We asked him if he got the letter. He says: "Yes, I got the letter, we have to talk." We came back to San Juan; Diane [Rodríguez] and I went back down to Los Angeles to do more research. We found the files, Carey McWilliams's files at UCLA, stayed there for about three or four days, gathered as much information as we could, brought it back, showed Luis the stuff. He got all excited about it and came up with the title for this piece that he was going to write called *Zoot Suit*. . . . Gordon was very excited and interested in the idea. From there it went into the hands of the Mark Taper Forum. (Delgado and Esparza interview, 8/10/1983)

The plan to launch a "hit" under the auspices of the Mark Taper Forum marked the beginning of a growing division of performance interests within the Teatro Campesino company. On the one hand, there was the mainstream project *Zoot Suit*, while most ensemble members continued to work as a collective within the Rasquachi Aesthetic. Luis Valdez was individually commissioned to write the play *Zoot Suit*, while the Teatro Campesino ensemble prepared for a second European tour of Fin del mundo. Delgado describes the ensemble's new divided work situation: "Meanwhile as Luis was directing Zoot Suit in L.A. what happened to us is we came back to San Juan Bautista and started to deal with the whole problem of trying to continue the work in San Juan without Luis. That was when he handed us, basically, the company as it existed at that time. This was in 1978" (Delgado and Esparza interview, 8/10/1983).

While Luis Valdez began the work of writing Zoot Suit (June–Dec. 1977) under the auspices of a Rockefeller Foundation Playwright-in-Residence grant, the Teatro Campesino ensemble worked on the third version of Fin del mundo for touring after the European tour. In the spring of 1978 the ensemble embarked on a Southwest tour of Fin del mundo and then a European tour of Carpa de los Rasquachis. Although the ensemble was in Europe during the first ten-day run of Zoot Suit—"Baby Zoot" as it is known in the company—they returned in time to attend Zoot Suit's second opening at the Mark Taper Forum's main season on August 17, 1978. After that the ensemble resumed its U.S. tour and returned in time to catch the Zoot Suit opening at the Aquarius Theater in Hollywood on December 3, 1978. Most ensemble members participated in the Fin del mundo tour, but a few did participate in the Zoot Suit project. Roberta Delgado did the initial research for the dances of the period and then acted as assistant to the choreographer in subsequent productions. In the Broadway production she also played the role of Henry Reyna's sister Lupe. Diane Rodríguez and Socorro Valdez had minor acting roles. Phillip Esparza became associate producer.

Although the ensemble's participation in the final Zoot Suit production was minimal, much of the play was in fact the product of the ensemble's prior collective creativity. Much of the play had been generated through the collective improvisation process by ensemble members in San Juan Bautista— prior to the Mark Taper production. Hence a play that ultimately was credited to one individual was, in fact, in large part created by the Teatro Campesino ensemble. Ensemble member Olivia Chumacero (interview, 1/19/1983) describes it in this way: "Luis Valdez has drawn from our collective work even years later. The first time that I saw the play Zoot Suit, "Baby Zoot" at the Mark Taper forum, I sat there and I could tell you who the people were who had improvised the blocking and the types of scenes that Luis used. I could sit there and tell you: 'Socorro thought of that' or 'So-and-so put that together' or 'This person improvised that particular blocking.'"

Zoot Suit drew much inspiration from the work of many people. Beyond the various elements that can be traced to particular individuals, Zoot Suit is very much a product of the general Teatro Campesino conglomerate performance style: the Rasquachi mixture of style and performance genres—vignettes of action, song, dance, dialogue—in rapid and smooth transition, which is in turn a hallmark of the Mexican popular performance tradition (see chap. 1). What is new is their application in a context of high-tech mainstream theater.

The extent of *Zoot Suit's* success exceeded everyone's wildest expectations. The initial Mark Taper Forum production with a ten-day run (April 1978) sold out almost immediately. What ensued was a series of successful restagings: first a main stage production at the Taper's 1978 season, then a production at the twelve hundred–seat Aquarius Theater in Hollywood, which opened on December 3, 1978, and ran for almost ten months. The Hollywood production broke box office records for a play originating on the West Cost; the New York production (1979) was the first Chicana/o play in several decades staged on Broadway. Although *Zoot Suit* closed on Broadway after only five weeks—due to poor turnout and an unfavorable critical response—it signaled the beginning of a process that has come to be known as "mainstreaming." The desire to launch a hit in the mainstream initiated a process that ultimately transformed the Teatro Campesino ensemble entirely. One symbolic and material indicator of that transformation is the fact that the Teatro Campesino ensemble members were all laid off, for the first time in that company's history, at about the time that *Zoot Suit* opened on Broadway (spring 1979).

Before discussing the nature of the impact of the mainstreaming process on the Teatro Campesino ensemble, it is perhaps illuminating first to examine the play *Zoot Suit* and the impact of the mainstreaming process on the various productions. An examination of relations of production in the mainstream and of the impact of those relations on artistic creation is of particular relevance in any discussion of mainstreaming. From its original scripting as "Baby Zoot," to the Mark Taper main stage, to the Aquarius, and then to Broadway and film, *Zoot Suit* underwent a number of transformations. These transformations—rewritings and restagings—can be viewed as a response to changing relations of production: those conditions of artistic practice include the numerous factors and persons that influence productions, be they collaborators such as producers, investors, designers, choreographers; be they questions of physical environment such as theater size and location; be they variables of social and artistic environment. In the course of its performance life, *Zoot Suit* went through five performance sites (including the film set) and at least nine rewritings, three of them for the film version alone. It is of course not possible, or perhaps even desirable, to understand what motivated each and every change throughout the various productions.

What is more relevant is a general understanding of each production, of its significance and of the principal developments and changes as Zoot Suit moved from its initial staging at the Mark Taper Forum to ever-larger houses in Hollywood and Broadway.

Zoot Suit's five performance sites trace a progression representing various *degrees* of mainstreaming. These sites range from the less commercial Mark Taper Forum to the highly commercial Broadway stage (the Winter Garden Theater). Houses such as the Mark Taper Forum are somewhat less subject to economic pressures of the market, for they are heavily subsidized by government and foundation grants, as well as individual arts patrons, which augment box office income. As a nonprofit theater, the Mark Taper Forum is viewed as providing a community service. The Mark Taper Forum furthermore relies economically on a large subscription audience, which buys into productions with little or no knowledge of their merit or orientation. For-profit Broadway stages, on the other hand, subsist entirely without subsidy. As such they are more susceptible to marketing pressures and mount productions first and foremost with commercial considerations in mind. As will be seen, such differences in performance sites even within the mainstream of so-called professional theater involve a different set of work conditions and place a different set of expectations or demands on productions.

What follows is an analysis of the six major Zoot Suit scripts, including the film version. Zoot Suit went through considerable changes each time it moved to a bigger performance venue. In each of those scripts the Sleepy Lagoon Murder Case took on a different configuration. Zoot Suit dramatizes the 1942 Sleepy Lagoon Case in which twenty-two pachuco youths were unjustly convicted of criminal conspiracy in connection with the death of a Chicano youth named José Díaz. In a gripping series of chronological and spatial leaps, Zoot Suit links the events surrounding the case, the trial, the youths' two-year imprisonment while awaiting appeal, as well as scenes from the day-to-day lives of some of the pachuco youth. Although the facts of the case would suggest the use of a group protagonist, Valdez created an individual protagonist in the form of Henry Reyna and his companion, the archetypal "El Pachuco." In later versions the prominence of the El Pachuco character matches that of Henry Reyna, the leader of the 38th Street gang under mass indictment for murder.

It is fitting that Zoot Suit should be born and premiered in Los Angeles where the infamous Sleepy Lagoon Case was initiated and tried. What led up to the trial was the pervasive racism against the Chicana/o citizenry of Los Angeles, which found its wartime outlet in the form of U.S. Marine riots brutalizing pachucos and other Chicanas/os in the barrio. The main story line of the play *Zoot Suit* remained constant throughout all versions: it is a story of racism and classism against Chicanas/os in 1940s Los Angeles as manifest in the Anglo system of justice and law enforcement. The role of the press and the police in sustaining that system is highlighted. Luis Valdez (1978b) has described the climate of those times, which fostered the mass trial of twenty-two youths for one murder, as well as the subsequent U.S. Marine riots in the barrios: "Public resentment against the zoot suiters grew, compounded by a certain 'wartime hysteria.' In 1942, as the federal government mounted extensive campaigns to encourage patriotism and spur the World War II defense efforts, those who were out of step with majority customs or who jarred cultural norms and dress codes, were often abused" (Valdez 8/13/78).

From the onset, Luis Valdez chose to mitigate the hard historical reality of racial violence by adding a fictitious love story between a white woman (Alice Springfield—later changed to Bloomfield) and Chicano protagonist Henry Reyna. This contrived love plot—the love triangle between Alice, Henry, and his girlfriend, Della—is a highly problematical element within the play, competing with and at times even supplanting the historical realities being portrayed. It is not surprising that the Alice/Henry/Della love story had trouble fitting into the play's trajectory and underwent more revision than any other element within *Zoot Suit*. The first draft is a case in point. In it, Alice has the first and last words in the play, including a highly patronizing, trivial, and lengthy closing monologue directed at an absent Henry Reyna. Alice—one of the play's white saviors—is the most prominent speaking subject. Her prominence contrasts markedly with the shadowlike presence of Della, Henry's Chicana girlfriend, who is present only as a mute body constantly snubbed by Henry. In the final scene she is even knocked to the ground by Henry—only to bounce back inexplicably in the end as Henry's girlfriend ("she embraces him from behind and he responds").

It is significant that the first draft of *Zoot Suit* was rejected by the Mark Taper Forum, on the grounds that it was too "realistic." It was through such institutional pressure that a second *Zoot Suit* was written.

The second draft (dated 2/28/78) was the first one actually performed. It had a very limited (ten-day) run in the New Theater for Now series of the Mark Taper Forum. In this second draft, the prominence of Alice Springfield was somewhat reduced, perhaps because of the introduction of the archetypal El Pachuco character, who opens the play by slashing an overblown facsimile of the newspaper front page with his switchblade and emerging from the slit. El Pachuco, the *bato loco*, or the *cholo* (streetwise dude) had been developed in earlier Teatro Campesino *actos* and plays such as *Bernabé* and *Fin del mundo*. In *Zoot Suit* Edward James Olmos was an unforgettable presence as

El Pachuco. His sensual sliding gait, his staccato speech and honeyed speaking voice were among the characteristics that gave him a distinctive personality. The first spoken words in this version of the play are in *pachuco* Caló—the *pachuco* idiom. He speaks Caló throughout the play—a language shunned by the Mexican middle-class let alone Anglos. In spite of his charismatic presence, however, the archetypal El Pachuco character is not present in many scenes. It was only in later versions of the play that his presence became central or even dominant within the play.

A second important feature of the second draft is the introduction of the villainous Press, or Reporter, character, who illustrates and personifies the key position played by the Hearst newspapers in swaying public sentiment and motivating the rioting against Chicanas/os in general and *pachuco* youth in particular. In various scenes the Press is shown telling sensationalist stories. Interspersed are the alternative versions of such stories told by El Pachuco, by Della (who relates the events at Sleepy Lagoon), and others. Hence, the antagonism between the Chicana/o community and the white establishment press constitutes a strong and effective through-line in "Baby Zoot," as this first staged version came to be known. One of the play's most memorable and striking features—illustrating the confluence of oppressive forces—is the use of the Press character as Prosecutor during the Sleepy Lagoon Trial.

From the very beginning, *Zoot Suit* made generous use of music, in characteristic Teatro Campesino fashion. Frequent dance sequences, performed for the most part in nightclub scenes, are key in establishing the Chicana/o musical ambience of the 1940s. The play highlights the music of Lalo Guerrero ("Chicas Patas Boogie," "Los Chucos," "Vamos a Bailar"), who was popular in the 1940s, but it also features the Big Band sound of Harry James ("Sleepy Lagoon"), Glenn Miller ("In the Mood"), the Dorseys, and Benny Goodman—all popular among Chicanas/os of that era. Choreographed sequences also feature the various dances popular in the 1940s and the 1950s: *pachuco* versions of the mambo, *danzón*, swing, jitterbug, boogie.

"Baby Zoot" is not without its weaknesses, however. Among them is the abundance of superfluous scenes, discussions, and characters, which detracts from the play's movement instead of enhancing it. Another problem is the final scene, which dangles without any conclusion (in the earlier *Zoot Suit* the outcome of the trial, the acquittal, is revealed to us from the start). "Baby Zoot" also suffers from the excessive use of violence. As if in a diplomatic effort to balance the instances of violence against Chicanas/os by whites, Valdez punctuates the entire play with numerous instances of violence among Mexicans. For example, the two brothers, Henry and Rudy Reyna, are stopped from fighting each other by their father. Rudy and Joey fight over Bertha. At the police interrogation, Valdez has a Chicano detective (Galindo) beat up Henry Reyna. Furthermore, Rudy Reyna is shown hitting (and presumably murdering) a man with a big stick at Sleepy Lagoon. (Did he murder José Díaz?) We are, in addition, told that Henry Reyna stabbed a prison guard in San Quentin. Violence among Chicanas/os is everywhere: Henry Reyna and his cousin Ramon Gilbert almost have a fist fight. Bertha and Lupe are stopped from fighting. Henry and Rafas go at each other with switchblades. Some audience members might well have wondered whether Mexicans are not in fact a bloodthirsty lot who belong behind bars.

In the use of violence, dramatic effects took precedence over historical accuracy. In the play, for example, the switchblade plays a prominent role and we quickly associate the switchblade with *pachuco* youth. Interestingly, it is historically documented that the 38th Street Gang (or *pachucos* in general) did not carry switchblades. It is a curious historical twist that the eight surviving defendants of the Sleepy Lagoon Case filed suit in 1979 against Luis Valdez and others involved in the production after seeing *Zoot Suit* at the Mark Taper Forum. They settled out of court and, ironically, were awarded financial participation in the proceeds from the play and the movie (Trombetta 1981).

In spite of such shortcomings, *Zoot Suit* represented a rare theatrical event featuring characters and situations with which Chicanos could identify. Audience response was so enthusiastic that the initial ten-day run at the Mark Taper Forum sold out almost immediately. The instant success of that production motivated the Mark Taper Forum to open its main season that same year with an eight-week run of *Zoot Suit* (August 17–October 1). That run also met with an overwhelming response, breaking single-day sales records for the theater. Almost $18,000 in tickets were sold on the first Sunday tickets were offered for sale. Among those waiting in line were Lupe Leyvas, the real-life sister of the play's protagonist, "Henry Reyna" (Henry Leyvas), who died of a heart attack in 1971. Lupe Leyvas commented: "The truth is finally being told. I was there when they arrested my brother. I went to the police station and they said: 'You want to see your brother?' He was handcuffed to a chair, his face was bleeding and he was unconscious. They ruined him, his pride, everything about him" (Miller 1978). The day tickets went on sale Lupe Leyvas, her brother Rudy, nieces, nephews and cousins purchased 121 tickets for $879.50. The play very clearly spoke to a need in the Chicana/o community to see realistic images of its own history in the entertainment world.

As *Zoot Suit* moved on to the Mark Taper main season it underwent further changes. Speaking in general terms, the play took on more abstract effects, moving away from the strong stage realism of the earlier version. To give but one example, many elements of the stage set that were originally depicted in realistic fashion—such as the Henry Reyna home complete with plants that were watered—eventually took on an abstract quality. Real furniture, for example, was converted into the symbolic medium of newspaper bundles. As the *Zoot Suit* production continued its run, the remaining elements of a realistic stage were eventually replaced by one-dimensional planes constructed of black mylar with silver trim. That effect gave the Broadway production in particular a highly surreal dimension, a quality reinforced by the large *pachuco* shadow backdrops introduced into the set. These changes may very well reflect one of the major tensions connected with the play: the challenge of merging historical documentation and dramatic effect.

The tension between theatrics and historical narrative remained visible throughout all *Zoot Suit* productions and was a source of considerable controversy in the establishment press as well as in the Chicana/o community. Dan Sullivan of the *Los Angeles Times*, for example, had problems with the play's "construct of fact and fantasy" as announced by El Pachuco in his opening monologue. Sullivan (1978) stated: "Fiction and fact blur here, and all we know is that this is how it *felt* in the barrio. That is no small thing to know, but we would like more hard documentation." Between the two productions at the Mark Taper Forum, Valdez described his move away from realism as a move away from "documentary" and toward "dramatic narrative" ("As I go back into a rewrite, I'll make it into more of a dramatic narrative, rather than a documentary" [Benitel 1978:34]).

The new streamlined Mark Taper script remained essentially the script used in subsequent productions (at the Aquarius Theater and on Broadway) although there were some significant alterations in the actual *staging* of the script. The new script that emerged (dated July 11, 1978) greatly improved the play's flow. Cumbersome scenes (such as the long and pointless posttrial socializing at the Sleepy Lagoon Defense Committee office) and various superfluous characters (such as Ramón Gilbert and the anarcho-syndicalist Villareal) were eliminated. Although the second Mark Taper script was greatly streamlined, some critics noted a loss of passion as well. *Variety* (8/11/1978) noted that "the show has been Mark Taper-ized to the point where it no longer has any emotion, impact or soul . . . dry as a conservative newspaper that takes no sides in controversies." Similarly, another reviewer noted: "The current version is more theatrical, better constructed and technically superior. But somewhere in the re-doing a measure of fire and passion was lost. This rendition is probably more commercially acceptable but the rough, unedited original had a bite and flavor that needed no gloss to hit with a deep emotional impact" (Goldsmith 1978). Longtime Teatro Campesino sup-

Zoot Suit at Mark Taper Forum featured stage furniture and props constructed with newspaper bundles. Left to right: Enrique Castillo, Paul Mace, Arthur Hammer, Mike Gómez. Courtesy of Mark Taper Forum.

porter Sylvie Drake (1978) on the other hand wrote about the "new improved version" in the *L.A.Times*: "For whatever price it is paying in gloss and slickness, *Zoot Suit* has gained enormous size and theatricality."

Unlike previous versions, the Mark Taper main season production (and subsequent versions) does not reveal the Chicana/o youths' acquittal until the next-to-the-last scene, thereby maintaining dramatic suspense throughout. Although this version eliminates the pithy El Pachuco/Press debate scene—a scene in which El Pachuco exposes a great deal of the society's racism as well as the opportunism of the Press—that omission is made up for by a brilliant change in design: all conceivable stage furniture and props are constructed with newspaper bundles. All chairs, the judges' bench, prison

Zoot Suit at Mark Taper Forum. Left to right: Rose Portillo, Danny Valdez, Evelina Fernández, Edward James Olmos, Rachel Levario, Mike Gomez. Courtesy of Mark Taper Forum.

cots, and other furniture are conspicuously lugged onstage, by the Reporter, a newsboy, and other characters. When Henry is interrogated, he sits on a newspaper bundle. Henry's mother removes newspaper pages from the clothesline instead of clothes. Henry's prison cell is made of newspaper handcarts wheeled in around him. These effects are tied together by the giant facsimile (with sensationalist headlines) used as a backdrop in front of which all the play's action unfolds. The Press's overpowering physical presence—in the form of newspapers—makes a palpable statement concerning its powerful role (and its close collaboration with the authorities) in the Sleepy Lagoon Case, in inciting the Marine riots, and in the lives of Chicanas/os in general.

As in previous versions, the second Mark Taper production features the press reporter doubling as prosecutor, thus underscoring the unholy alliance between the judicial system and the media. The third pillar in this alliance is law enforcement officials. This alliance is further accentuated through the doubling of Police Sergeant Smith as Court Bailiff and the tripling of Police

Lieutenant Edwards as Judge Charles and Prison Guard. The complicity of press and police within an oppressive social system is stunningly illustrated by Police Lieutenant Edwards's racist press release proclaiming that Mexicans have a genetic propensity for violence dating back to their "Aztec bloodlust." It hardly comes as a surprise when the *pachucos* are convicted of murder.

The second act unfolds episodes from the *pachuco* youths' two-year imprisonment as they await the appeal, the so-called zoot suit riots in Los Angeles, and the winning of the appeal, which is juxtaposed with the victory of World War II. New as well are references to World War II and connections established between the Sleepy Lagoon case and the greater context of the war. Woven into the final scene is another unconvincing exchange between white social activist Alice Springfield and Henry Reyna. Like some earlier versions, the fourth rewriting concludes with a victory celebration scene at the Reyna home in the barrio. Yet the victory does not signify a story with a happy end. In the midst of the merriment El Pachuco interjects that trouble will resume as soon as the celebration ends. In his omniscient way, El Pachuco foreshadows the segment in the final scene in which we witness continued police harassment and racism in the barrio.

Although the play does not diminish the importance of the Sleepy Lagoon victory it does situate it within the larger context of continued oppression. The personal or individual fate of Henry Reyna becomes secondary and recedes behind a broader social panorama. At the play's conclusion, three contradictory but possible ends to his life are mentioned; they are capsule statements representing the potential success or failure of *pachuco* lives.

During its main stage run at the Mark Taper Forum, *Zoot Suit* broke the Taper's box office record, taking in a total of $357,843.[2] Audience enthusiasm was matched by that of the critics. The City of Los Angeles, with the exception of the *Herald-Examiner* critic, seemed swept by *Zoot Suit* fever. Mayor Tom Bradley even proclaimed a *Zoot Suit* Week (November 13–20, 1978). Interestingly the most dissenting voices were the New York City critics who came west to view the play. Their negative response was a portent.

Zoot Suit's success at the Mark Taper Forum inspired the producers (Center Theater Group/Mark Taper Forum) to transfer the production from the 740-seat Mark Taper Forum to the 1,200-seat Aquarius Theater in Hollywood. Although the Aquarius is owned by the Mark Taper, the move meant a departure from a heavily subsidized tax-exempt theater (nonprofit) with a subscription audience of twenty-five thousand people to a sink-or-swim commercial stage dependent wholly upon the sale of tickets ranging in price from twelve to twenty dollars. What ensued made theater history. *Zoot Suit* played to capacity audiences for months, setting a new Los Angeles attendance record for a play originating on the West Coast. What was—and has remained—unique about Zoot Suit is that it succeeded in attracting barrio audiences, that is, persons who do not normally attend theatrical productions, in large numbers.

For the Chicana/o community the staging of Zoot Suit was of particular significance because it marked the first time that a Chicana/o play with a predominantly Chicana/o cast had gained entry into a white establishment theater. More significant, there was a deep sense of satisfaction among Chicana/o audiences at seeing images on stage that to some extent critically reflected upon the Chicana/o experience in this country. Zoot Suit at the Mark Taper Forum in Los Angeles clearly spoke to a need in the community and the community response was enthusiastic. It should not be overlooked, however, that a great deal of the momentum behind that response was also, in part, due to the existence of a loyal Teatro Campesino following as well as to the attraction of the play's central pachuco figure—as one of those highly distinctive and maligned Chicana/o street dudes of the 1940s and the 1950s who organized within neighborhood clubs. El Pachuco was rehabilitated during the Chicano movement and had been reconstituted as something of a positive antihero.

Part of the play's attraction can be ascribed to the fact that the very performance site (the Mark Taper Forum) stands where a Mexican barrio stood not long ago. What is more, the historical and human events portrayed hit at the heart of the Los Angeles Chicana/o and Anglo communities—a rare achievement for any regional theater. And it should not be overlooked that the Chicana/o community's pride and enthusiasm stemmed in part from the fact of Zoot Suit's near-subversive presence in a space commonly reserved for white elite entertainment: the Los Angeles Music Center. The play clearly possessed a magnetism for both white and nonwhite audiences that has not been equaled by any other Chicana/o production in the mainstream.

It should not be overlooked that Zoot Suit also opened new vistas to many Chicana/o performers. Many of the Chicana/o cast members who participated in the show had never worked in what is known as "legitimate" theater. Most had never worked in so-called professional houses. The exposure and experience they gained from the Zoot Suit production—and the prominence of that production in Chicana/o community consciousness—motivated many young artists to pursue a career in mainstream theater institutions, formerly considered politically or racially off-limits. The theater establishment, on the other hand, was jolted into recognizing the presence of Chicanas/os and the need to view the Chicana/o community as part of its constituency.

While *Zoot Suit* was still playing to capacity audiences in Hollywood, negotiations began between the Los Angeles producers and the Shubert Organization in New York for a Broadway production. A growing consciousness
of the Chicana/o and Latina/o market—if not of the people themselves—was
a motivating force behind the Shubert Organization's $700,000 investment
in a Broadway *Zoot Suit* staging with a weekly operating budget of about
$90,000. Barbara Darwell, head of the Shubert Organization's department
of sales and marketing, commented at the time: "We've been interested for
some time in finding a way to develop the Hispanic market in New York. But
until now we haven't had a product to induce them to come to the theater"
(Lawson 1978). Bernard Jacobs (*New Yorker* 2/19/79), co-owner of the
Shubert Organization, which owns twenty-two theaters, including the Winter Garden, where *Zoot Suit* was staged, indicated that the search for a "Hispanic" play had been on since *The Wiz*—Broadway's first successful staging of
an all-black musical—had finally tapped the "black market." The black market had been "developed" for the first time in 1975 through the nonmessage
all-black musical *The Wiz*. It opened to scathing reviews but became an audience success nonetheless. Two other black shows were running on Broadway at the same time as *Zoot Suit*: *Eubie* and *Ain't Misbehavin'*. The Broadway
production of *Zoot Suit* opened on March 25, 1979, in New York City's biggest theater, the Winter Garden, while *Zoot Suit* was still running at the
Aquarius in Hollywood. All of the lead actors were transferred to New York
from the Hollywood production, which continued its run with new leads
(Marcos Rodríguez as El Pachuco; Enrique Castillo as Henry Reyna). *Zoot Suit*
on Broadway, however, was not successful. It closed a mere five weeks after
it had opened, at a loss of $825,000. *Zoot Suit* in fact was the most expensive
nonmusical production in Broadway history.

Although it is impossible to state with any certainty why *Zoot Suit* did not
repeat its West Coast success, we can speculate about what went wrong. One
of the difficulties faced by the play with each change of theater was the suc-
cessively larger theater space, culminating in the huge fifteen hundred–seat
Winter Garden on Broadway. The Broadway aesthetic—generated partially
in response to the monstrous theater size—usually calls for a great deal of
slickness or ostentatiousness. One *Washington Post* critic has described Broadway in the following way: "The style is inherently exaggeration" (Coe 1979).
The Broadway *Zoot Suit* underwent some considerable changes, virtually all
of them in an effort to adapt visually and acoustically to the Broadway environment. Speaking in general terms, the Broadway staging enhanced its production values, as some critics noted: "Valdez is still making changes in the
New York version, highlighting the universality, making the music hotter and

the costumes flashier" (Herridge 1979). The *Washington Post* critic indicated: "The major leads of the 28-member cast . . . state that the Winter Garden production is planned to be 'more extravagant and costlier.' That may be helpful, but one recalls other regional creations fatally started up for Broadway inspection" (Coe 1979). Valdez himself commented on the increased embellishment: "We are polishing it to a great sheen" (Herridge 1979). This "great sheen" was perhaps the single greatest difference between the Broadway production and prior ones: richer costumes, heightened lighting effects, a bigger backdrop, a more pronounced symbolism in general. And although the sheen—or effects needed to adequately "fill" the cavernous Winter Garden theater—was perhaps a necessary adaptation to the Broadway environment, the embellishment in production values may well have overshadowed the play's actual substance.

The sense that the Broadway staging suffered from overproduction is the general consensus among the cast.[3] This, in fact, might have contributed, for example, to critic Richard Eder's (1979) view that the piece was "overblown and undernourished." The *New Yorker* also refers to the "grotesquely overamplified sound" (Gill 1979). Yet in spite of the play's embellishments it did maintain its basic thrust, plot, dialogue, and pace.

Like Eder, some establishment critics produced scathing reviews of the production. Yet their response to the play was triggered not by its cosmetic problems of overproduction but by other factors. Various New York critics resented the very subject matter of *Zoot Suit* because of the guilt it evidently made them feel. That sense of discomfort manifested itself in critical backlash ("We are being sermonized at, and suddenly we feel that Roots III is being directed at our guilt regions again" (Bondy 1979). One critic put it quite succinctly: "White Americans will be uneasy" (*Daily News* 3/28/1979). And who wants to attend a Broadway play that will make one feel uneasy?

The dramatic portrayal of white powerholders abusing Chicanas/os provided the cue for defensive anger and retaliation in some critics. The *Daily News* critic is a case in point. He indicated that the play was "a slanted neo-rabble-rouser, abrading ethnic emotions, presented in unnecessary hyperbole, terminal exaggerations. . . . The plot is almost totally stereotypical anti-American establishment." The same critic then told us that if we put all of the play's factualness aside and viewed it all as fiction—that is, if we performed the impossible feat of "putting aside" what the play was saying, the play's actual substance—*then* it would be a great play. In his own words: "But let's take *Zoot Suit* out of its unfairness as factual drama and see it as pure fiction: on that level it is riveting drama told with tough, bitter, and ruthless wit, performed with consummate acting and direction by a cast of virtually unknown professionals" (*Daily News* 3/28/1979).

One of the most often heard stories in connection with *Zoot Suit* (especially from Luis Valdez) was that the critics killed it in New York. In reality critical opinion was divided, with more positive reviews than negative. The positive reviews should not be overlooked, even if some very pivotal reviews—such as those in the *New York Times* and *The New Yorker*—were hostile. Interestingly, all West Coast reviews of the New York production were as positive as ever. There was clearly an East/West divide. What then did New York critics dislike about *Zoot Suit*?

Although different elements of the play were criticized in the various reviews, there are recurring statements to the effect that the play employs too many clichés, too much rhetoric; that it is simplistic, overly sentimental, and sententious; that the characters and political arguments are too black-and-white, too cardboard. "Agitprop" is commonly used as a put-down. Critic Walter Kerr in the *New York Times* (4/1/1979) formalistically dwelled exclusively on the play's language flaws, unable to look beyond the "stale phrasings," the "bloodless rhetoric": "He [Valdez] is utterly unable to resist a cliché, possibly even to recognize one." Michael Feingold in the *Village Voice* (4/2/1979) also focused on language: "In fact, he [Valdez] is not primarily a writer, and one of the things wrong with *Zoot Suit* is that the writing gets clumsier as it gets closer to seriousness, instead of the reverse. It bogs down in platitude, which may come partly from the fact that English is not Valdez's primary language, and in overstatement. . . . the clunky sententiousness of the language offends me."

In attempting to determine what displeased the critics about *Zoot Suit* I found the tone of their reviews as revealing as their arguments. The tone in the negative reviews is one of hostility and defensiveness mixed with an air of condescension that is perhaps reserved only for upstarts—indeed minority upstarts and from the West Coast. In understanding the critical response, two very significant realities must be kept in mind. One is the critics' sense of self-importance as gatekeepers and self-appointed spokespeople for the East Coast Great White Way aesthetic. They reserve the right to make pronouncements on theatrical quality, to declare what is good and what is below standard. That attitude, combined with *Zoot Suit*'s tremendous publicity campaign and the buildup preceding the opening, did not sit well with many critics. We can only imagine how some critics felt when *Zoot Suit* exploded onto the New York scene with a tremendous publicity campaign ($15,000 weekly) announcing the arrival of one of the greatest plays ever—indeed a "New

American Play"—to Broadway's biggest theater. Various newspapers commented on what they called the "Ballyhoo about this work." *Drama-Logue*
wrote: "The big news is the advertising campaign. . . . Clothing stores are
doing zoot suit windows and there are plans to have 'trendsetters' photo-
graphed wearing zoot suits to fashionable discos. NBC is doing a half-hour
special on the play, and major New York banks are being asked to enlist their
support in underwriting theatre tickets for students" (Cole 1979). Another
critic indicated: "But I am concerned over the 'hype' surrounding the play
and its author. In recent articles in major newspapers and magazines, much
praise and publicity have been lavished on Valdez and *Zoot Suit*" (Otten 1979).
Another critic drew a direct connection between the media hype and his
"disappointment": "*Zoot Suit* is a disappointment perhaps in part because of
the hype that preceded its arrival here" (le Sourd 1979).

Zoot Suit arrived with such a splash that some critics must have felt eclipsed
in their roles as guardians of public opinion. The response was predictable.
Various reviews were written in that "I'll show *them*" attitude of condescension, unfairly condemning the play lock, stock, and barrel with insufficient
supporting evidence. What follow are examples of this tendency:

> There is inadequate material for making organized theater of *Zoot Suit*. A
> porridge of dates and facts, lectures and slogans, a romance, a trial, plus
> showy dance numbers and incidental drama—weakly written, directed, and
> played—it is, more than anything else, a "living newspaper" play out of the
> 30's. (Gottfried 1979)

> I regret to say that it does not seem to me to be major-league theatre.
> (Hughes 1979)

> It's filled with Good People and Bad People. The former are Chicanos and the
> latter are Anglos. . . . the writing is honest, but in the hands of such incom-
> petence it turns out phoney—verbal posturings and inflations that couldn't be
> worse if Valdez' intentions were sheer hack. (Kauffmann 1979)

> Zoot Suit turns out to be mediocre or worse all down the line—book, acting,
> production. (Currie 1979)

> The playwright's treatment is leaden, superficial and as emotionally mani-
> pulative as the cheapest agit-prop of the period. . . . not really meant for the
> Great White Way. (le Sourd 1978)

> Zoot Suit at the Winter Garden makes for a better fashion show than it does a
> play. . . . This treatment of the prosecution of Los Angeles Chicanos for the

Sleepy Lagoon Murder in 1942 grinds its ax so monotonously that it can cause an Excedrin headache by the second act. (Sharp 1979)

A simplistic show . . . Poorly written and atrociously directed. . . . *Zoot Suit* is flat and boring child's play. (Watt 1979)

Zoot Suit . . . is a great deal of loose material draped over a spindly form. (Eder 1979)

One critic, insensitive to how offensive expletives can be when taken out of their spoken context, even availed himself of *pachuco* or Mexican derogatory terms in reviewing *Zoot Suit*: "The characters are caricatures . . . the action is spasmodic, inconsistent . . . the staging by Luis Valdez is as *pinche* as his dramaturgy. The acting is hard to evaluate, since the writing is mostly *pendejadas*" (Simon 1979).

Some critics found the "mixture of styles" characteristic of the Teatro Campesino style (and of the Mexican oral performance tradition) distasteful, although some praised *Zoot* despite this supposed shortcoming:

Playwright Luis Valdez has tried to shape this tale as a mixture of myth, documentation and fantasy, but he never gets past the Abc's in any category. (Kalem 1979)

The kaleidoscopic barrage of styles with which Valdez dramatizes all this may not be a masterpiece of form, but a strong emotion and elegance is somehow shaped by this barrage, and we're seeing the image and energy of a culture that's never been seen on a Broadway stage before. (Kroll 1979)

Zoot Suit . . . is overblown and undernourished. It is a bewildering mixture of styles—realism, stylization, agitprop and plain showbiz gaudiness—that clash and undermine one another. (Eder 1979)

The political arguments of *Zoot Suit* are presented in stilted and paper-thin terms. (Eder 1979)

One critic, however, did see value in Valdez's Rasquachi eclecticism, indicating that the "mishmash" did "compose a theatrically vivid unity" and "stirring outcry against racial bigotry":

On the face of it, it is crude stuff. Its method harks back to the Living Newspaper of the New Deal days. It also employs certain vaudeville and sideshow techniques. There are smatterings of Brecht's "alienation effects." All these—call it a mishmash if you will—nevertheless compose a theatrically vivid unity, mounting to a stirring outcry against racial bigotry and the cruel mass stupidity which such hysteria engenders. (Clurman 1979)

An additional source of irritation for some New York critics was the fact that a good amount of the advertising campaign targeted the Puerto Rican and Latina/o population, thereby triggering a defensive attitude of ethnic polarization in some critics, perhaps a sense that this play was not really for them. The New York Times—in a tone of indignation with racist overtones—reported on how the producers were "reaching out to the Hispanic community": "They have two Spanish-speaking people taking ticket orders on the phone, and one Spanish-speaking person in the box office. They are also paying for ads in the newspaper El Diario and the magazine Nuestro and for commercials on radio station WADO and television channels 41 and 43. The 'Anglo' advertising, meanwhile, is minimal" (Corry 1979).

Months prior to the show's opening the New York Times quoted Mark Taper Forum coproducer, Ken Brecher, concerning all the special preparations in advance of the Broadway Zoot Suit production: "No one preparing for a Broadway show has spent so much time in the South Bronx as we have. . . . We have already decided that the ushers and box-office people will be bilingual. It's very important to make these people [Latinos] feel at home in the theater" (Lawson 1978). Brecher and Phil Esparza sent out forty thousand mailers, accompanied by a personal letter, to Puerto Rican families. They visited with community organizations and enlisted their help. (The community self-help organization CHARAS, for example, formed a "Barrio Brigade" of youths to distribute promotional materials.) Through the Theater Development Fund and group sales it was possible to see Zoot Suit for as little as $4.50.

Another major factor contributing to the negative critical response was the East Coast/West Coast competitive posture that exists in theatrical circles as well as other institutions. The aggressive condescension cultivated particularly by members of the East Coast theater establishment toward West Coast theater was evident even among Zoot Suit's own producers: the East Coast Shubert Organization (represented by Bernard Jacobs) and the West Coast Mark Taper Forum (represented by Gordon Davidson). A considerable East/West divide was clearly visible in their very first face-to-face meeting in New York, which culminated in Jacobs's patronizing comment: "For the West Coast, Gordon does a great job" (New Yorker 2/19/1979). The effort to prove one's own coast superior to the other is also manifest in territorial statements such as that by Mark Taper Forum artistic director Gordon Davidson: "New York is no longer the generator of theater in America, but the receiver" (Thompson 1979). Such a statement, trumpeted in the New York Times ten days before Zoot Suit opened—along with all the other media hype—might well have negatively predisposed the very provincial and ethnocentric New York critics toward the West Coast's *Zoot Suit*.

It is striking that the same *New York Times* launched not simply *one* scathing review of *Zoot Suit* (by Richard Eder on opening night, March 26, 1979) but *two*. The second scorched-earth review (by Walter Kerr) was published one week after the first review (April 1, 1979). The *Los Angeles Times* was quick to respond: "For this West Coast observer, however, *Zoot Suit* has, ironically, never seemed in better shape. It fits neatly into the stage of Winter Garden, with an assurance and focus refined well beyond all three of the previous L.A. versions" (Drake 1979). In an opening night review in the *Washington Post*, critic R. L. Coe (1979)—as if responding to Gordon Davidson—stated: "The Los Angeles stage, though lively enough, remains strongly New York–oriented." With characteristic colonial hubris, another New York critic prefaced his review with a reference to California as a "cultural wilderness": "Out of a monied paradise but cultural wilderness steps a character of mythic proportions" (Lewis 1979). The inane privilege of belittling the *other* coast was no doubt a factor in some critics' reviews.

Some very positive reviews (*Wall Street Journal, Variety,* the *Washington Post*, *Daily News, Newsweek,* to name a few) were issued as well, however. Virginia Woodruff of Channel 10 (3/25/1979), for example, praised the production lavishly: "Once in a while a play fairly exploding with passion and vitality, one simply yet flawlessly staged, comes along." *Newsweek* published a patronizingly glowing review: "Any drama-school freshman can see *Zoot Suit*'s flaws of structure and tone, but these should not obscure the guts, flash, class, sweetness, pride, pain, humor and sheer vitality of the enterprise" (Kroll 1979). Audiences who saw the play on Broadway responded with wild cheering and standing ovations uncharacteristic of audience reaction on the Great White Way. Many critics noted this fact. *Zoot* clearly touched a chord in New York audiences, although they did not come out in the numbers needed to float the play.

As one might expect, Chicana/o critical response to *Zoot Suit* was of an entirely different order. Chicanas/os were, first of all, much more concerned about and appreciative of the play's *content*, while the New York critics took issue with the play's *form*, often indicating that the form cheapened the political thrust. (We might well wonder to what extent the play's politics caused them to take exception with the form.) Chicana/o critics and the West Coast press showed themselves in possession of a different aesthetic and social sensibility as well as different tolerance levels when it came to viewing on stage the naked realities of racism. In reference to the New York critics Luis Valdez

indicated that they found fault with Zoot Suit because they felt it was still re-
belling. That no doubt was a factor in the critics' response.

Chicana/o critical opinion, although heavily focused on content, was to
some extent divided. Most Chicana/o critics shared the enthusiastic audience
response of the Los Angeles and New York audiences. Critics such as Antonio Burciaga and Jorge Huerta praised the play, speaking to its historical significance—as a mainstream performance—its merits as a theatrical spectacle,
and its social relevance as a document exposing an important chapter in
Chicana/o history. Jorge Huerta (1982:183) discusses Valdez and Zoot in
nothing but superlatives ("Valdez' world encompasses more than most of
his critics can comprehend"). In the process, however, he fails to examine
what might be considered the shortcomings of Zoot Suit or contradictions in
the mainstreaming process. His discussion ends with an overly optimistic
flourish of predictions that have failed to come true: "The Teatro Campesino
would continue to perform in this country and abroad; Zoot Suit would pack
the houses in every major center of the Mechicano population" (p. 183). In
fact, the Teatro Campesino ensemble never again performed in this country
or abroad. Nor did Zoot Suit "pack the houses in every major center of the
Mechicano population."

Critics Yvonne Yarbro-Bejarano and Tomás Ybarra-Frausto, on the other
hand, focus heavily on what they consider the play's numerous problems,
while not commenting on what one might consider the play's virtues.
Ybarra-Frausto and Yarbro-Bejarano (1980) deliver an interesting ideological analysis of Zoot Suit, focusing above all on the pachuco character. Their focus
on some aspects of the play's ideological thrust, however, happens almost
entirely at the level of script. The authors disregard entirely the play's theatricality, the function (ideological and other) of—for example—the music
and dance sequences, other significant performance elements, and audience
response. A disregard for the economic realities governing all Broadway productions, furthermore, leads them to state, contradictorily, that they do not
at all criticize Luis Valdez for going to Broadway, yet they decry the commercialization of the piece (i.e., the heavy advertising campaign, the high price
of tickets, etc.). Yet Broadway, in fact, is the quintessential commercialization
of theater and going to Broadway necessarily involves working within a specific set of economic terms. The critique ends with a summons to Chi-
canas/os in theater: to follow the "alternative of taking nourishment from
our popular roots. That way we will reclaim the mass communications media, radio, television, Hollywood and Broadway, not as individual artists, but
as a popular theatrical movement" ("Ofrecemos esta crítica de la obra para
continuar la discusión, para que se plantee la alternativa de volver a nu-

trirse de la raíz popular en contra de la imitación de Valdez. Y así vamos a recuperar los medios masivos de comunicación, la radio, la televisión, Hollywood y hasta Broadway, pero no como artistas individuales, sino como un movimiento teatral popular") (Yarbro-Bejarano and Ybarra-Frausto 1980:56).

Yarbro-Bejarano and Ybarra-Frausto put their finger on one of the chief contradictions of the mainstreaming project: the conflict between "popular roots" and "popular theatrical movement" (which are based in collectivity), and the dimension of individual ambition and success. In spite of *Zoot Suit's* contradictions, however, there can be no doubt that as a theatrical product its merits by far surpassed those of average Broadway fare. As a play depicting a highly racist era of American history it did present an alternative reality in a theater world that ordinarily specializes in superficial entertainment glorifying the status quo.

The question remains: What are the problems Chicana/o theater faces when it becomes a Janus-faced undertaking, one face looking to the Great White Way and the other to Chicano reality and the needs of Chicana/o communities? Public response to a play will vary significantly, depending on what any given public expects from theater or Chicana/o theater. Many New York critics were overwhelmed by the historical and political reality presented in *Zoot Suit,* for example, while Chicana/o critics Yarbro-Bejarano and Ybarra-Frausto faulted what they considered the "diluted historicism" of the piece.

Most Los Angeles and New York critics—along with various Chicana/o critics—found El Pachuco (Edward James Olmos) extraordinarily impressive while Yarbro-Bejarano and Ybarra-Frausto did not comment on Olmos's extraordinary performance, or El Pachuco's function as a theatrical device. They viewed him wholly as a mythical character who they felt stood in contrast to—and eclipsed—the play's historical dimensions. Although I share their uneasiness concerning the tension between "fact and fantasy," between the mythical and the historical, in *Zoot Suit* I do not view the mythical El Pachuco character as competing with or supplanting the historical figure Henry Reyna. As a theatrical device, the mythical El Pachuco has a twofold function. On one level, he is Henry Reyna's doppelgänger (*cuate*), his alter ego, or super-ego, always at Reyna's side and visible and audible only to Reyna. Dramaturgically speaking, the El Pachuco/Henry relationship allows us to listen in on Henry's dialogue with himself, his *internal* struggle, without having to turn it into dreary monologues directed at the audience.

Throughout the play, El Pachuco and Reyna are seemingly at odds. They represent the dialectical unity of opposites, united in contradiction, providing the two sides of every story, two opinions on every discussion, two pos-

El Pachuco and pachuco Hank Reyna in Zoot Suit at Mark Taper Forum (Los Angeles). Left to right: Edward James Olmos (El Pachuco), Danny Valdez (as Hank Reyna). Courtesy of Mark Taper Forum.

sible reactions to every action. At times El Pachuco utters what Henry is think-ing and cannot express without editorializing; at other times he serves as the voice of historical experience repeatedly warning Henry not to expect jus-tice in a society without justice. He goads Henry to do things he might not want to do, to think things he had not thought. He serves as a mirror of Henry. El Pachuco's colors—red and black—as well as his frequent associations with mirrors and smoke tie him symbolically to the Aztec deity Tezcatlipoca. He embodies the voice of wisdom, of conscience, of the school of hard knocks. The connection between Chicano and Indio is thus established. Henry Reyna and El Pachuco are not necessarily *separate* entities but a carefully construed duality within one Chicana/o youth. To view El Pachuco only as a separate mythical character and as an "evasión de lo histórico concreto" (evasion of the historically concrete) is to disregard the theatrical complementarity of El Pachuco and Henry Reyna.

El Pachuco's second important function as a theatrical device rests with his role as omniscient master of ceremonies facilitating the play's presenta-tional mode and its many transitions. He allows us to move smoothly in and out of the past. With a snap of his fingers, a wave of his arm, or a turn of his body El Pachuco changes scenes, flips us into a courtroom, or into the Reyna home, beckons dancers onto the stage, flirts or kids with the audience—breaks through the play's dramatic climaxes, turns tragic moments into humorous ones, or injects cynicism into lighthearted moments. As a com-mentator *outside* the action he serves as a perpetual distancing device (what Brecht calls a *Verfremdungseffekt*), which forces us to *reflect* on the theatricality of what we are seeing, instead of allowing us to be unthinkingly *absorbed* by the action. By extension, El Pachuco's "mythical" position outside the play's particulars allows the play to give expression to many positive human dimen-sions of *pachuco* life: in his extravagance El Pachuco symbolizes imagination, fantasy, aspiration, defiance; he is downtrodden yet courageous and inde-pendent, a proud symbol of the barrio.

The use of *pachucos* in *Zoot Suit* opened the door to another lively contro-versy. Some Chicana/o critics felt that the play glorified *pachucos* and that his-torically speaking *pachucos* were nothing to be proud of. Richard García, a Chicano historian, published an essay in which he sought to prove that *pachucos* were a reactionary element in the Chicano community and that their cultural pride was expressed mainly through criminal violence and extrava-gant dress. For García *pachucos* were essentially hoodlums. The *Los Angeles Times* (García 1978) published his view: "Most pachucos ended up dead, in prison, or alcoholic. The current celebration of an underclass of dropouts and failures is damaging . . . The pachucos were lumpen—groups of chronically unemployed and often delinquent youths." García made the same mistake the Hearst press did in the 1940s: he interpreted what was a hip fashion among youth—el tacuche (zoot suit)—as something synonymous with gangsterism. Indeed the play Zoot Suit endeavors to illustrate that the attire was worn by noncriminals as well. The term "pachuco" came to be a generic term for "hip youth" dressed in a distinctive fashion. Some were organized in neighborhood clubs; others not. Some were delinquents; most were not.

El Pachuco and the play Zoot Suit must also be understood within the historical context of the 1970s: as part of the Chicano movement's revalorization of traditionally maligned sectors within the barrio or within Chicana/o working-class reality. Such a revalorization of the pachuca/o—a conscious crediting of what can be considered his or her admirable dimensions—must be seen in the general context of cultural nationalism and the Chicano Movement's intense debate concerning Chicana/o identity. That debate includes artists' responses to Octavio Paz's denigrating interpretation of pachuquismo in The Labyrinth of Solitude, a text widely read by Chicana/o intellectuals in the 1960s and the 1970s. Contrary to Paz, Valdez describes El Pachuco's positive potential: "The need to stand up and just rebel, to say no, is to provide a new possibility: it's to bring a new consciousness into being" (Orona-Córdova 1983:110). The revalorization of the pachuco was one of a number of redefinitions that, among other things, gave us the word Chicana/o in its current usage. Such redefinitions of "outsider" or "underdog" figures occurred in Chicana/o art, in Chicana/o literature, in Chicana/o theater. Indeed, much of the moving force for the new Chicana/o literature of the 1960s came from former pachucos: José Montoya, Raúl Salinas, Ricardo Sánchez. Being a pachuco during one's youth was not incompatible with developing into a responsible adult. United Farm Workers founder and president, César Chávez, was a pachuco. This is not to say that pachucos were all great kids. Nor does Valdez portray them as innocent angels. But they were not necessarily criminals either. What should not be overlooked, however, is that the heavy focus on pachucos in Zoot Suit gives the play an overbearingly masculine bent.

Yarbro-Bejarano and Ybarra-Frausto (1980) concur with García's and Ron Davis's highly negative view of pachucos and also deplore the fact that Valdez does not depict the pachuco as a productive member of the labor force. The expectation that Valdez portray his Sleepy Lagoon characters as members of the work force is perhaps an unrealistic expectation for a play focusing primarily on these youths' incarceration. Valdez, however, does emphasize Henry Reyna's (and his brother's) enlistment in the armed forces—which, to this day, unfortunately represents one of the few avenues open to young Chicanos seeking "dignified" work or job training.

Zoot Suit is most problematic with regard to its gender politics and construction of the historical past. As has been shown, Valdez's gender politics and his construction of history are intertwined. Both are steeped in a dominant ideology that has traditionally assigned Chicanas/os a passive role in history. In the opening monologue of Zoot Suit, El Pachuco refers to the play as "a construct of fact and fantasy." That of course can be understood in any number of ways. Does it mean that all the historical facts presented are true and simply presented in an imaginative way? Or does the intermingling of fact and fantasy signify that important facts are modified or even falsified? To what end? What constitutes historical "fact" anyway? Recent theory of history teaches us that *any* writing of supposed "facts" involves a good dose of fantasy, in their selection, organization, and the rhetorical strategies by which they are conveyed. The choices Valdez made in the selection, organization, and delivery of historical fact in Zoot Suit are very much in need of examination.

It is where historical facts are imperceptibly altered or tailored to suit fantasy or marketing needs that the drama is at its weakest and the play's ideological thrust most questionable. The two major Anglo figures in Zoot Suit signal a particular orientation in the selection and organization of historical facts, that is, in the construction of Chicana/o history. Alice Bloomfield (Springfield in an earlier draft) and George Shearer (a lawyer) function as "white savior" figures such as are present in virtually all Luis Valdez productions since he decided to mainstream. In Zoot Suit the white saviors figure most prominently: they organize the Sleepy Lagoon Defense Committee; they visit the beleaguered "boys" in prison; they instruct the young Chicanos on how to fight the system; they profess faith in the system; they occasionally patronize the young Chicanos; and they win the case for them on appeal. Chicanas/os are not shown in a position of self-help, nor as agents in their own destiny. In Zoot Suit, the Chicana/o community as a whole is strikingly absent in the defense of the *pachuco* youths.

It is interesting that this was not a feature of Zoot Suit initially. In the first version, a Chicano movie star (the character named Ramón Gilbert) is prominent in raising support and funds for the legal appeal. This figure disappears in subsequent versions where there are, however, references to Chicanas/os helping out. By the time Zoot Suit appeared on Broadway and in the film version, Alice Bloomfield and George Shearer were bigger than life and references to barrio leaders and activists in defense of the *pachucos* had all but vanished.

The prominence of the white saviors constitutes a very particular kind of distortion of historical fact, or a reshaping of historical fact along specific lines. It corresponds to the dominant ideology's traditional view of Chicanas/os as passive subjects who simply let history happen. The truth of the Sleepy Lagoon case is not the story portrayed in the film *Zoot Suit*. In fact the Los Angeles Chicana/o community was not a peripheral element in the Sleepy Lagoon case, but the moving central force. For one thing, the role occupied by Alice Bloomfield in the movie was—in historical fact—occupied by Chicanas, namely Josefina Fierro and Luisa Moreno. Chicano historian and activist Bert N. Corona—who was also a member of the Sleepy Lagoon Defense Committee—speaks to the vital role played by these two women:

> In 1942, Josefina Fierro, as national secretary of the Congreso Nacional de los Pueblos de Habla Española, carried out two very significant actions. One was the formation of the Sleepy Lagoon Defense Committee (contrary to the distorted version in Luis Valdez's play *Zoot Suit*) which conducted the public defense of the twenty-two Mexicans who were tried for the death of one. Josefina traveled all over the nation, assisted by Luisa Moreno, to develop the broad national campaign against the racist and divisive indictments and yellow journalistic press descriptions of the Hearst Press. . . . It is to be deplored that Luis Valdez could find insufficient drama in the true facts about the Defense of the Sleepy Lagoon and *Zoot Suit* victims, that he had to rely upon Hollywood gimmicks of a fictitious melodrama between two persons [Alice Bloomfield and Henry Reyna] that never took place in order to tell his story. (1983:16)

Although a real "Alice Bloomfield" (named Alice Greenfield McGrath) does exist, she did not occupy the savior role attributed to her in *Zoot Suit*. In reality she was a paid employee of the Sleepy Lagoon Defense Committee and was not hired until months after the very long first trial ended. Needless to say, the romantic involvement between Alice and Henry, so prominent in *Zoot Suit*, never existed. Historical fact notwithstanding, Valdez even places Alice at the play's center: "In Alice Greenfield McGrath [named Alice Bloomfield in the play and movie] we finally discovered the mainline of the play. It was her relationship to the boys" (Valdez 1978a).

The role of the Los Angeles Mexican American community in the defense of the Sleepy Lagoon defendants is correspondingly obscured in the film. Yet the community's role was central. One Sleepy Lagoon case attorney, George E. Shibley (1979)—after whom the *Zoot Suit* character of attorney George Shearer is patterned—in 1979 publicly stated that "*Zoot Suit* does perpetuate some seriously damaging distortions of the realities of the Sleepy Lagoon murder case." He elaborated on these serious and damaging distortions: "Chief among these distortions are the myths that the Mexican-Americans themselves had little or no part in the organization of the Sleepy Lagoon Defense Committee; that no ethnic group other than Jews came to the aid of the 22 defendants; that the case was won almost singlehandedly by the unmarried heroine, Alice, whose Jewish identity impelled her to set up a defense committee, hire a lawyer, and then fall in love with the chief defendant, Henry Reyna." Shibley goes on to point out that Chicanas/os were "active and indispensable" in organizing the defense and that the appeal was in reality fought by a team of at least five lawyers (not one), including a lawyer retained by the Mexican Consulate.

Luis Valdez's decision to create white savior characters that eclipse the role of the Chicana/o community has considerable ideological implications. Most significant, it implies that the Chicana/o community is unwilling or unable to be an agent in history, to act on and in its own behalf. It paints a picture of Chicana/o helplessness. For help, the impotent Mexican community must turn to whites. Such highlighting of white saviors is not accidental, and this choice of characters certainly raises another question: To what extent does this distortion constitute a Valdezian attempt to ingratiate himself with the powers that be? Is it a means of making the *Zoot Suit* project more "palatable" to whites, be they producers, theater administrators, critics, or audiences? Is this the kind of concession the mainstream requires? Is it anticipatorily accommodationist on the part of Valdez? One New York critic saw in Valdez's use of white characters in dominant roles a form of "calculation." In reference to the white characters of George and Alice that critic points out that "the former [is] implicitly, the latter explicitly, Jewish . . . on the assumption, I daresay, that most of our theatergoers are Jewish and that buttering them up is good for business" (Simon 1979).

The white savior dimension of *Zoot Suit and* its male-centeredness certainly served to weaken the film and had a direct impact on its exploitative gender politics. As it is, the Chicana characters are largely inconsequential or shallow because they stand in Alice Bloomfield's shadow. Beyond that, Chicanas fall into the standard Teatro Campesino categories of (a) being auxiliary to males and (b) consisting of one of two types: the virgin or the whore, the long-suffering mother or the "cheap broad" (see chap. 3). Della Barrios is Henry Reyna's virginal girlfriend who puts up with everything. Bertha is her counterpoint: the woman who sleeps around. This shallow one-dimensional representation of Chicana women is of course intensified by denying recognition to Chicana historical figures such as Josefina Fierro or Luisa Moreno, and by transferring that recognition to a larger-than-life fictional white female savior. Such blatant erasure of Chicanas as historical agents is not unique to Zoot Suit, however. It parallels the widespread erasure of Chicanas from Chicano historiography and other forms of discourse.

The weakness of Chicana roles in Zoot Suit went virtually unperceived by critics. Valdez's gender politics was either altogether ignored or referred to only in passing. Chicano theater historian Jorge Huerta fleetingly indicated: "Valdez's treatment of the women has also been the concern of all the women I have talked to who saw the production" (1978). Unfortunately, Huerta did not elaborate on what women said or on the nature of Valdez's treatment of women. Teatro Campesino ensemble member Roberta Delgado—who carried out the initial research into pachuco dance styles of the 1940s and choreographed the dance sequences for the early Zoot Suit—similarly indicated that the women's roles were consistently questioned by Chicanas who attended the postperformance colloquia at the Mark Taper Forum: "When we were doing Zoot Suit we would have these symposia when we were at the Taper. They were discussions. You know, Chicana women would always ask about the women's roles" (interview, 7/21/1983). In spite of this feedback, the hegemonic and exploitative portrayal of Chicanas in Zoot Suit—involving active historical distortion—remained unaltered throughout all productions.

Zoot Suit's critics, however, did not focus on the ideological and political significance of a play in which Chicanas/os are portrayed as a passive entity and as people whose only hope for social change rests with the intervention of white saviors. Questions such as the portrayal of the Chicana/o community or of Chicana women were also certainly of no concern to the New York critics who panned Zoot Suit.

Zoot Suit closed on Broadway due to various factors largely unrelated to its good or bad points. It is of course impossible to single out only one or two reasons why Zoot Suit did not enjoy success in New York. Various factors have been discussed here, such as many critics' defensive reactions vis-à-vis a highly touted West Coast play, a play that furthermore exposed a chapter of racism in this country and that was created and performed by newcomers to the Great White Way. But the critics are not omnipotent and many plays are successful in spite of negative critical opinion. Although we can surmise that the critics kept a portion of the traditional white audience from seeing the play, Puerto Rican and black audiences do not read critics like Clive Barnes, Martin Gottfried, or Richard Eder. These are the "nontraditional" audiences Zoot Suit producers were hoping to attract or develop. Yet Latinas/os did not attend the production in sufficient numbers to keep the play going. The unstated but existent boundaries of segregation in this country have kept Broadway almost exclusively white, notwithstanding the handful of successful black productions. Broadway is not a space frequented by Latinos and they were understandably reticent, even after several thousand discount ticket coupons were distributed. Furthermore, *Zoot Suit* did not hold the same kind of attraction for them as it did for Chicanas/os on the West Coast.

Bernard Jacobs, *Zoot Suit* coproducer and president of the Shubert Organization, speculated as to why *Zoot Suit* did not enjoy success: "What went wrong? I would criticize the marketing, not the play. The Hispanic community didn't support it sufficiently. The community's leaders were wonderfully supportive, but the troops weren't ready yet. The first attempt is inevitably a failure. There will be a successful Hispanic play some day. It took about 10 black plays before we got a successful one" (Lawson 1979). Of course the expectation that a Chicana/o play should appeal mainly to Puerto Ricans and not especially to white theatergoers is a curious assumption.

Chicanas/os on Broadway: To Be or Not to Be?
The entry of people of color into white mainstream institutions is a contradictory undertaking. What follows is a discussion of some of the attendant tensions as well as a tentative assessment of prospects for Chicanas/os and Latinas/os on Broadway or in Hollywood.

Zoot Suit did not open new paths for Chicana/o stage productions on Broadway. In fact, no Chicana/o play has been produced on Broadway in the more than ten years since *Zoot Suit*, even though we may be sure that many Chicana/o performers, and some playwrights, have their eyes set on that goal. Having seen Broadway from the inside, through the *Zoot Suit* experience, it might be well to consider whether Broadway provides the performance conditions to which Chicanas/os should aspire. Those conditions include economic and aesthetic pressures that mutually inform each other.

Zoot Suit brings home some economic lessons. Behind the glittering lights and potential stardom turn the powerful wheels of cutthroat economic realities, which can force even the best of plays out of business the day after opening night if reviews are bad—or shortly thereafter if box office figures indicate a loss. Broadway certainly ranks among the most expensive and risky of theater enterprises. It demands a highly specialized division of labor and demands a highly polished look, both of which are capital-intensive. It prefers big names—actors, choreographers, costume designer, director—which are expensive. *Zoot Suit's* running costs were $85,000 weekly. By opening night $700,000 had been invested. Given the negative reviews, the play normally would have been closed immediately. Instead the producers invested another $125,000 for advertising and operating expenses in hopes that nontraditional (read minority) audiences would show up. Zoot Suit closed after five weeks at an $825,000 loss.

Had it played off Broadway, costs would have been significantly lower and Zoot Suit might well have reached more New Yorkers because the time and money pressures would not have been so acute. Broadway may well be a self-defeating enterprise for Chicanas/os—and for non-Chicanas/os as well. Capital-intensive and risky at once, those aspiring to the Great White Way are working with a theater machinery so cumbersome that serving a community can be only a distant consideration.

The economic demands of Broadway are such that they have fostered a very particular theater climate. Broadway's commercialism breeds a theatricality seeking mass appeal; lowest-common-denominator entertainment values are the norm. Such concessions, born of economic considerations, are perhaps the major reason behind the artistic decline of the Great White Way in recent decades. Luis Valdez was quite aware of this reality: "Even in Europe, there's more latitude and experimentation in the mainstream of those countries' theatre. This country, under the mothership of Broadway, has stagnated for the last fifty years. These are basically 19th century proscenium houses on Broadway. I understand that economics are involved and you cannot change them. It nevertheless is a stagnated tradition. . . . My feeling is that other forms belong on Broadway" ("First Hispanic-American Show on Broadway" 1979).

Luis Valdez's crusade to bring new forms to Broadway was in fact cut short by economic realities. Valdez nonetheless regards that short-lived presence as a triumph and a "cultural stand": "This is a cultural stand; like it or not, it's a real stand and America has got to come to terms with it. Because we're not going to go away" ("First Hispanic-American Show on Broadway" 1979). Given the "stagnant" quality of Broadway we might well wonder why Broadway is a theatrical institution worth penetrating. Why Broadway? Why not San Antonio or other centers of Chicana/o population thirsting to see theatrical images to which they can relate? Luis Valdez indicates why he has set his sights on Broadway: "Broadway is a little like electoral politics. I didn't come here because I thought it was the temple of art. I came because it's the marketplace. It tends to register national opinion" (Drake 1979). Although we can certainly agree that Broadway is a marketplace, it is but one marketplace and certainly the most remote of marketplaces for Chicana/o communities. Given the history of segregation on Broadway, it does appear more than doubtful that Broadway registers "national opinion"—a term both vague and hegemonically oriented—because "national opinion" has always excluded the opinions of those vast sectors of the population who do not control the media. Critic Clayton Riley (1979) described the very exclusive nature of Broadway: "The American theater in New York remains one of the nation's most rigidly segregated institutions, both on and off Broadway, and has been so consistently derived from the tundra of Shakespearean Nationalism that its usual creative portraits seldom touch even an approximate spirit of the true America. This devotion to a European ideal dishonors a presumably mature people and occurs at the cost of this city's identity and self-respect."

In pondering the relative merits of viewing Broadway as a Chicana/o mecca, it is worthwhile to consider the price—literal and figurative—for producing a Broadway play. *Zoot Suit*, although vastly overproduced to fit it to the Winter Garden Theater, seems to have come off relatively well, without making too many concessions. Yet it is difficult or impossible to guess what *Zoot Suit* might have been had it been produced outside the mainstream. Critic Gerald Rabkin (1979) wisely questioned whether it was possible for minorities to work in the mainstream without becoming like the mainstream. This is the contradiction inherent in minority participation in all mainstream institutions. Although Rabkin pointed out how the periodic injection of new ethnic vitality had invigorated Broadway in the past—using the emergence of Jewish American artists on Broadway in the 1920s and the 1930s as an example—he realistically indicated that such an entry onto Broadway was fraught with difficulties or was "enmeshed in a paradox" because Chicana/o and black theater "wants and deserves its share of the American pie, but it is also aware that much of its vitality springs from its role in forging cultural pride and self-identity, in its special relationship to its communities." The question is how to work inside the mainstream "without losing your source of cultural strength by submitting to the values of a culture you reject. . . . If you want Broadway and Hollywood's approval, can you help dancing to their tunes?"

Broadway and Hollywood are discursive spaces that have not reflected the values or culture of Chicanas/os. We cannot, however, fault artists who seek to penetrate and alter that discursive space, who seek to make it more inclusive or responsive. Yet that greater inclusivity or responsiveness will not necessarily alter corporate theater's raison d'être: a profit motive, which thrives on maintaining the economic status quo. If Valdez succeeded in pushing the boundaries, we must also recognize that his incorporation into the mainstream deeply transformed him as well. Although *Zoot Suit* tells a Chicano

underdog's story and showcases numerous Chicana/o cultural practices and
talent, it also manifests numerous artistic choices tailored to appeal to white
mainstream America. Valdez's politics of artistic representation directly reflects his contradictory self-positioning.

Zoot Suit signaled to many Chicana/o artists that the mainstream was indeed something to which to aspire. Yet the glory of Broadway is a double-
edged sword. Chicana/o artists in the future will have to weigh the benefits
and drawbacks of working under the "mothership of Broadway"—if that opportunity should ever arise. In the decade since Zoot Suit Broadway has demonstrated an unwillingness to embark upon any further "Hispanic ventures."

Zoot Suit: The Film

The Broadway closing did not signify the end for Zoot Suit. The play continued running to packed houses at the Aquarius Theater in Hollywood and the
film was under negotiation. Valdez faced considerable obstacles in finding a
movie company willing to bankroll a film conceived, written, directed, and
acted by Chicanas/os. Such a film had never been made in Hollywood. There
were plenty of offers to buy the idea and the title Zoot Suit but an unwillingness to allow Luis Valdez to write the screenplay and direct the film. The major
factor behind the film industrialists' skepticism was that Valdez had never
before directed a film. New York critics' hostile response toward Zoot Suit
also raised questions concerning the film's marketability. Universal Studios
ultimately decided in favor of the project. Luis Valdez managed to secure artistic control of the film. As a result, Universal Studios was highly skeptical
of the project and unwilling to make much of an investment in it. As a consequence, the film had to be shot in only fourteen days and on a budget of
$2.5 million—one-fourth of what a mainstream film normally cost at the
time. Any discussion of the artistic merits or shortfalls of the film must necessarily take such material factors into account. The film was created with
financial constraints although certainly not as severe as those facing many
"alternative" films.

Although Luis Valdez was able to negotiate a good amount of artistic control over Zoot Suit and although the film stands as a Luis Valdez product, working in the context of the Hollywood film industry necessarily meant
relinquishing control of some critical dimensions of the production process—such as cinematography and editing. The extreme division of labor
within the mainstream film production process—with its intricate system
of individual credits, of taking credit for "your own" private contribution—
no doubt places limits on how much a director controls, especially a first-
time director totally unfamiliar with the technological side of film produc-

tion. It is perhaps neither useful nor possible to determine who was responsible for what was in *Zoot Suit*. In attempting to understand and assess the mainstreaming process, however, an examination of the basic material conditions underlying the product that emerges on the silver screen is indispensable.

Zoot Suit—the first Chicano feature-length Hollywood film—can be analyzed from a number of perspectives. What is of particular relevance within the present inquiry is an examination of the transformation of *Zoot Suit* as it entered the new discursive space of the Hollywood film industry. I would like to explore the relationship between the Chicana/o mainstream film practice (*Zoot Suit*) and the Hollywood film space. In terms of Luis Valdez's goal to mainstream—that is, to reach a mass audience and to create a product with mass appeal—the film medium obviously constitutes the most effective means of reaching that mass audience. What changes did *Zoot Suit* undergo as it transferred from the stage to the mainstream mass medium par excellence? Given that *Zoot Suit* was the filming of a stage play it is perhaps illuminating to examine the changes made as it went from a stage play to a screenplay, as it moved from one set of relations of production to another.

One very significant reality of the mainstream film apparatus is that its prime goal is to make money. The marketing of any film is a prime consideration from the moment of its inception. This is true of the corporate theater as well, but even more so of the film corporation because *more money is at stake*—in the form of potential profits and investment capital. The search for a winning box-office formula, the pressures to *appeal* to audiences are greater and those pressures have a presence that underlies all aspects of artistic creation. That is a vastly different set of relations of production than in the arena of alternative theater and alternative film, where mass appeal is not a pressing criterion in the formulation of a work's aesthetic.

As a spectacle, *Zoot Suit* made the transition from stage to screen elegantly. The film has an undeniable intensity, a captivating pace, and smooth flow throughout. It certainly does not have the overly static quality characteristic of so many "filmed play" productions.[4] As *Zoot Suit* made the transition from stage to screen some very significant changes occurred, however. Although the filmed story is a filming of the play, using essentially the stage set as a movie set, the screenplay differs markedly from its theatrical predecessors. *Zoot Suit* on film was not intended as a filmed stage show or "Great Theater Masterpieces on Film" production. The absence of on-location shooting accentuates the nonrealistic quality or artificiality of the narrative and accentuates the presentational mode. That artificiality creates a heightened symbolic texture and, as such, allows for a greater distancing from actual historical events. In the film version, historical events recede even more because of the heavy foregrounding of the personal or individual dimensions of historical events; that is to say, the Sleepy Lagoon case becomes even more heavily translated into the story of one man's life. In the program notes for the stage productions of Zoot Suit Valdez indicates that the production is "not a documentary but an imaginative dramatization." In the film version elements of imagination displace historical documentation even further. In an interview concerning the film, Luis Valdez indicated that "the whole Sleepy Lagoon Case is told in Zoot Suit in terms of the personal struggle of Henry Reyna" (Orona-Córdova 1983:108). Once again, Luis Valdez insisted on a male-centered vision of the world. He also pointed out that all sociohistorical events were experienced in one's internal life as much as in one's "external social life." Although I fully agree that the workings of one's internal life are as much history or historical reality as "external social life," in the film the balance weighs far more heavily to the side of the internal life than it did in the stage productions, where the internal life was in closer touch with external social life or historical events greater than the individual.

Nor is Henry Reyna's internal struggle in the film successfully linked to history, that is, as a process of achieving greater consciousness of the world and of his role in that world. Instead Reyna often seems only to burrow deeper and deeper into himself. His prison scene in solitary confinement is a prime example. When Reyna speaks with El Pachuco in the stage version's solitary confinement scenes, they argue concerning social justice and the chances of the impending court appeal. Then El Pachuco draws him out of prison to witness the marines beating up zoot suiters in Los Angeles. In the film version, by contrast, their dialogue in the solitary cell only fleetingly touches on the realities of the judicial system or the impending appeal. Instead, the dialogue focuses on the nuclear self, entirely divorced from sociohistorical realities. At the climax of the film's solitary confinement scene Henry asks the fundamental questions: "Where am I? What am I doing here?" The response given by his other self, the pachuco, is of a vague existentialist sort: "You're here to learn to live with yourself, Hank. You're a marijuana dreamer floating in a night of unfulfilled phantasies."

More than anything, such statements are oddly circular and inward. What is more, they consistently subordinate historical reality to a self-absorbed individual psyche. At the conclusion of that scene Hank Reyna acknowledges the pachuco as an integral part of himself, a dimension of his own personal struggle. His subjectivity is constructed in the narrowest of individualistic terms: "Sabes que, ese. I've got you all figured out. I know who you are, carnal. You're the one who got me here. You're my worst enemy and my best friend. Myself. So get lost."

Similarly, the *pachuco* at another point tells Henry: "San Quilmas [San Quentin] was made for self-victimizing suckers like you, Hank." By blaming the victim or assigning self-blame ("You're the one who got me here"), a kind of psychic struggle in the context of the Sleepy Lagoon case is foregrounded to the near exclusion of the sociohistorical struggles epitomized by that extended court battle. Examples of this tendency to personalize by dehistoricizing abound in the film. This tendency constitutes a weakening of the play's social thrust. Translated into viewer response, the film's personalization of events no doubt allays the white American audiences' potential sense of historical responsibility—that is, guilt—when viewing the racist injustices portrayed in the larger story. After all, this mess is Henry Reyna's *own* fault. This point is made several times. The yellow journalism of the Hearst Press, the racist judicial system and complicit law enforcement agencies, and the nation dedicated to wartime hysteria are all indirectly let off the hook.

There is another very striking feature of the film which—unlike the stage versions—tends to downplay the seriousness of each historical event as well as the story's overall historical thrust. That feature is the overly prominent and often gratuitous use of music, singing, and spectacular exhibitionist dancing. The film begins with a flashy and prolonged dance sequence and is frequently punctuated with dance and music. Chicanas/os would appear almost to live at dance halls. Dance, song, and music not only frequently serve as transitional devices, at the beginning and end of scenes, but often leave very little space for dialogue and action, which appear sandwiched in between. Numerous substantial scenes from the stage version—such as the court scene—appear in abbreviated form in the film. Music and dance effects supplant much of the dramatic narrative of the stage version. The effect of this is an accumulation of fast, hectic filmic scenes, which slow down appreciably only when Henry is intensely engaged in very personal matters, such as his love dialogues with Alice or Della, or when Henry explores the depths of his own personality in solitary confinement, or when the defendants first meet with their benevolent white savior lawyer. These highly personal or inwardly directed scenes constitute the play's chief focal points or points of visual repose. These are the emphasized scenes, where the spectator's attention is allowed to linger, not only because these scenes are long but also because the camera *and* the characters are static. It is significant that these are the only scenes not disrupted by music, dance, or singing. The more historically oriented scenes, by contrast, are often introduced by or capped with a flurry of dance, thereby heightening the film's entertainment value but diminishing its historical thrust.

The same tendency is observable in the "zoot suit riots" scene in which El Pachuco is stripped of his zoot suit by U.S. Marines. The lighthearted tone of that scene is set by the preceding dance scene, which leads directly and even blends into the highly stylized "riot." The historical import of the 1943 riots—in Los Angeles hundreds of U.S. servicemen entered the East Los Angeles barrio (with police protection) to freely brutalize Chicanas/os—is lost entirely by virtue of the happy tone set by the upbeat dance prelude and through the riot's overstylization. (In early drafts of the screenplay this was depicted with far greater realism.) Along the same lines, the film version of Zoot Suit added a trio of female singers, who appear in numerous scenes and whose function is purely decorative. It is a characteristic Valdezian objectification of women. In its function as satellite and clinging vine of El Pachuco (the women often physically cling to him) the female trio strengthens the movie's frivolous dimensions and diminishes its impact as a medium of sociohistorical understanding and critique. Equally gratuitous are a number of additional song and dance numbers added to the film strictly for their entertainment value. The long "Handball" song in prison as well as "Marijuana Boogie" are two prominent examples.

Missing from the film are the newspaper bundles formerly employed as furniture, the newspaper handcarts representing a prison cell, newspapers as a constant *visual* presence symbolizing the press's pervasive influence and its hand-in-glove relationship with the law enforcement and judicial systems. Also omitted is the very significant stage scene in the barrio that follows the defendants' release from prison. That omitted scene shows the renewed harassment by the police. It is the same type of police harassment that led to their initial arrest. The play implies that the Sleepy Lagoon case did not change society, that the barrio suffers from the same police brutality as before. That scene effectively dispels the notion that the acquittal constitutes a happy end. In the movie this scene is dropped entirely. At the movie's end El Pachuco states: "A happy ending. But life ain't that way." Yet no particulars are explained, there is no elaboration of what he means. It is left at that, in the abstract. The play's hard-hitting conclusion, the concreteness of continued police harassment in the barrio—which resonates with relevance for Chicanas/os today—is thus eliminated in the film. In its place the film features a litany of possible versions of how the *individual* Henry Reyna lived out his life. Again, the film's focus supplants social structures and the collective picture in favor of showcasing one individual.

Arriving at a fair assessment of Zoot Suit as a film product can only be as contradictory as the film itself. On the one hand, it can be argued that the transition from stage to screen changed Zoot Suit from semidocumentary dramatic narrative to a heavily melodramatic musical, which obscures the play's more hard-hitting historical and social dimensions. The film's considerable increase in purely entertaining elements and the corresponding decrease in attention to the disquieting elements of historical reality can well be interpreted as an effort to broaden the movie's mass appeal and as a concession to the film industry's spectacle formulas. Another prominent mainstream entertainment formula in the film and stage versions is, of course, the fictitious love triangle between the protagonist Henry Reyna, the white woman Alice, and Reyna's Chicana girlfriend, Della.

The film marks the end of a long series of rewrites of the original stage version. By the time of the film (1981), issues of class and racial inequality had receded considerably as the entertainment spectacle and Henry Reyna's inner world become foremost. Gender inequality—far from being an issue in the film or the plays—was reproduced by Valdez. The mainstream concessions evident in *Zoot Suit* the film signify a political and artistic retreat by the once politically vocal Chicano cultural activist Luis Valdez.

These observations concerning the dilution of a play in the mainstream for the sake of mass appeal constitute but one perspective on *Zoot Suit*, however. We must conjoin any negative dimensions of critique with a positive recognition of the work's undeniable qualities: we can applaud the making of a movie in which young Chicano (i.e., male) filmgoers see images of themselves, in a series of events relevant to them (in spite of the specifics of their construction), images of underdogs portrayed sympathetically on the silver screen, as well as positive images of a culture given visual representation in film (music, dance, language forms, dress). For young *Chicanas*, however, it is of course a somewhat different matter. Still, *Zoot Suit* certainly is a far cry from Chicana/o exploitation films such as *Boulevard Nights, Walk Proud*, or *Borderline*, released in Hollywood at about the same time.

Notwithstanding the value of *Zoot Suit* in affirming a chapter of Chicana/o history, of Chicano identity and cultural pride—in a general sense—the film (and the staging) reflects the contradictions of competing interests experienced by all Chicanas/os who work in mainstream institutions. The film in particular reflects strong accommodationist tendencies. Those tendencies are certainly at odds with the image of struggle and political commitment that we formerly associated with Luis Valdez and that he still cultivates in his media appearances. Those familiar with his prior work measure him against the Teatro Campesino standard and consequently expect more of him. Regardless of what we have come to expect of this or that person, however, each and every Chicana/o performance stands as a public spectacle representing a particular set of interests which we must submit to scrutiny. Although we can only speculate about whether the elements of Zoot Suit critiqued here were conscious or unconscious responses to the world of commercial entertainment, there unquestionably is a correlation between Luis Valdez's mainstream ambitions and changes in artistic orientation and practice. We of course are entitled to evaluate such products with the same rigor we apply to Chicana/o cultural products outside the mainstream.

The new commodification of Chicana/o culture by the mainstream entertainment industry—initiated in the late 1970s and even more visible with crossover musicians such as Los Lobos and Linda Ronstadt, for example— must be a matter of vital concern to the Chicana/o community and those engaged in cultural criticism. As more Chicanas/os rightfully demand their place in the nation's institutions we will need to both monitor that entry and develop a consciousness concerning the extent to which diversity of race, gender, and class is accommodated by those institutions; we need to examine and discuss how minority individuals will assert their otherness in the nation's white institutions of privilege. Or will minorities find acceptance only at the expense of relinquishing community interests and ethnic identity? These are some of the questions that arise as we witness the entry of Chicanas/os into mainstream theater, into mainstream educational institutions, into mainstream politics, film, business, and much more. We need to cultivate a critical consciousness concerning our own institutionalization and incorporation.[5] In the poem "Los They Are Us," José Montoya alerts us to the dangers and reality of the "us" becoming the "they." The poem describes the unfortunate human transformation that can take place as the doors of mainstream opportunity open for a select few people of color, who then proceed to serve dominant interests and no longer the interests of the community from which they came.

Mainstreaming and the Dissolution
of the Teatro Campesino Ensemble
The most far-reaching of choices made by Luis Valdez in his ambition to mainstream was his decision to separate from the collectivity of the Teatro Campesino ensemble (collectives cannot mainstream). That decision guided his subsequent efforts to transform (or dismantle) that collective ensemble into an administrative apparatus ("production company") geared to facilitate his mainstream ventures. This little-known and never-publicized side of events is as much a part of the mainstreaming story as the publicly visible events such as Zoot Suit on stage and film.

The present exploration of the mainstreaming process and its impact on the Teatro Campesino ensemble is based both on a study of stage productions and on a study of the many dimensions of theatrical work invisible to audiences: behind-the-scenes dimensions of theater such as production meetings, rehearsals, budget priorities, the artistic and life experiences of cast members, and work conditions. Just as we cannot claim to understand auto production by examining automobiles, nor the production conditions of garment workers by examining the garments, theatrical production cannot be grasped fully by viewing stage productions. The stage product is but the publicly visible dimension. All stage production, however, is embedded in a set of institutional conditions that shape it and that intersect with the broader set of socioeconomic and cultural conditions.

To date critics of Chicana/o theater have focused exclusively on the public face of El Teatro Campesino, largely disregarding its internal workings and the everyday negotiations within the company that shaped its changing identity. The conversion of El Teatro Campesino after 1980 from a collective ensemble to an administrative unit or production company cannot be understood without such behind-the-scenes analysis. Those internal workings and realities in some ways contrast markedly with the public image cultivated through selective public statements and press releases for public consumption. They are the 90 percent of theatrical life behind the 10 percent that is public performance. It is very important that the very "private" dimensions of the Teatro Campesino story be made public so that we may come to understand the nature of that experience, formulate an informed assessment of it, and thus participate in the necessary critique of Chicana/o mainstream products. It is also to be hoped that such a critique will directly benefit theater workers who contemplate either mainstream or alternative stage work.

The success and failure of the *Zoot Suit* experience cannot be measured solely in terms of the play itself but also with regard to its broader repercussions. For one thing, the play served as an eye-opener in Chicana/o circles, inspiring some Chicanas/os to seek work in the mainstream while perhaps also awakening the slumbering mainstream. In addition to the influence it had upon Chicana/o artists and on the mainstream world in general, it also had considerable impact closer to home: within the Teatro Campesino company itself. The success or failure of the *Zoot Suit* experience will have to be measured as well in the context of its short- and long-term effects on the Teatro Campesino ensemble.

For a period of time during the *Zoot Suit* production the Teatro Campesino continued its work without Luis Valdez and the few ensemble members who participated in *Zoot Suit*. The Teatro Campesino continued its work of creating and performing theater pieces in the United States and Europe throughout the various stagings and the filming of *Zoot Suit*, from 1977 to 1980. El Teatro Campesino specifically worked on a new production of *Fin del mundo*—the third version of that piece—in 1977 and initiated the first annual Día de los Muertos festivities in San Juan Bautista that same year. Also in 1977 the *Pastorela* was performed as well as the traditional *Las cuatro apariciones*. In 1978 the company embarked upon a Southwest and Northwest tour of *Fin del mundo* and a European tour of *La gran carpa de la familia Rasquachi*.

The fact that the ensemble toured Europe and carried out other activities while Luis Valdez prepared further stagings of *Zoot Suit* and its subsequent filming is indicative of, if not a rift, then at least a plurality of interests and pursuits within the company. Later that plurality of interests became even more pronounced. For a time the company came to encompass two contradictory theatrical aesthetics and goals, which were largely irreconcilable and in a state of tacit antagonism. One sadly symbolic expression of the tension between the old Teatro Campesino and the new came when *Zoot Suit* opened on Broadway in 1979. In a kind of throw-away gesture, the entire Teatro Campesino company in San Juan was laid off for the first time in its history. The individual success of Luis Valdez and the ensemble's sudden layoff coincided as a palpable but also symbolic harbinger, of changes motivated directly and indirectly by the *Zoot Suit* experience. The layoff was but one of the fundamental changes that had begun to make themselves felt even while *Zoot Suit* was in production. Although this layoff in itself might seem insignificant, it marked the beginning of a process of radical change within the company, a change that could be characterized as the push to transform the alternative ensemble of El Teatro Campesino into a "professional" theater company or production company.

I use the terms "corporate theater," "commercial theater," and "mainstream" interchangeably. Each accents a different aspect or dimension of theatrical activity, but they essentially signal the same phenomenon: the systematic commodification of cultural performance acts. The decision to go after a mass audience, to enter the so-called mainstream sector, cannot be seen simply as a *quantitative* change, a simple change of workplace from performing for a limited audience or public to performing before a mass audience. That decision or change marks above all a *qualitative* change in the reasons for doing theater as well as in the changing attitudes toward the human labor involved in achieving those ends. I do not consider the qualitative change a matter of so-called professionalism, for the Teatro Campesino ensemble's professionalism—although it was of a different nature—certainly matched that of any commercial theater.

In examining the qualitative changes in the company in the tow of the decision to mainstream, I center my analysis around the concept of work. As I shall show, mainstreaming does not simply mean going to a different place to do theater; nor does it mean, primarily, enlarging one's audience or even becoming more "sophisticated" or "professional" (the Teatro Campesino ensemble was indeed both sophisticated and professional). Mainstreaming entails, above all, buying into particular forms of human labor and cultural production, participating in the systematic commodification of cultural performance acts—both of these radically different from what had been practiced within El Teatro Campesino since its founding. Nor are the forms of human labor practiced within mainstream theater in essence "theatrical" and particular to the theater. Instead these work forms and the work rationale correspond to economic forces and structures at work within the U.S. labor market at large: they are corporate and industrial work forms that have everything to do with the larger system of socioeconomic relations. Theatrical production invariably reflects the material relations of production under which it is carried out. This essential relationship will be illustrated with reference to various post–*Zoot Suit* Valdez productions: *Rose of the Rancho, Bandido!*, *Soldier Boy, Corridos*, and *I Don't Have to ShowYou No Stinking Badges*. It is not my intention to deliver a full critique of any of these productions but rather to refer to them to illustrate certain observations pertaining to the company's development.

The process that led to *Zoot Suit* (in Hollywood and on Broadway) and to the dissolution of the Teatro Campesino collective ensemble is a process involving the adoption of a different set of attitudes toward human labor, toward work and production—in all of their theatrical and economic senses. It is a story of both a theatrical and a human transformation rooted in the dialectical interplay of individual and collective artistic visions within changing relations of production and social contexts. We cannot overlook that the mainstreaming project was born in the decade that saw both the decline of the Chicano movement's communitarian spirit and the rise of widespread individualism and personal ambition in Chicana/o intellectual, artistic, and political life. That rise in individualism and personal ambition is a symptom of the historical emergence of a Chicana/o middle class.

It is ironic that the radical efforts within the Teatro Campesino company to become bigger and better through mainstreaming in time brought about the ensemble's dissolution and the establishment of a largely dormant production company or administrative apparatus. *Zoot Suit* marked the breakthrough to the targeted mass audience. But after the breakthrough came the retreat. There can be no doubt that Zoot Suit's success in West Coast mainstream theater constituted for many a validation of the push to reach the unsympathetic millions of Americans. It motivated a few of the members of the Teatro Campesino company to embrace some, if not all, elements of the commercial stage and to strive to introduce such elements into the work activity of El Teatro Campesino.

As early as 1978, when the play Zoot Suit was in production, mainstream elements began slowly to make inroads into the ensemble, largely at the urging of Luis Valdez. In that year, for example, nonensemble actors were invited to audition, a mainstream recruitment and casting tool never before practiced by El Teatro Campesino. Throughout its existence the membership of El Teatro Campesino comprised persons who shared a humanistic vision of and commitment to socioeconomic causes. Prospective members went to work with the Teatro and eventually became members after a trial or transition period during which they acquired or polished their collective ensemble skills, that is, the performance orientation and style characteristic of the company (see chap. 1). Membership was, so to speak, earned through a period of organic apprenticeship. The company possessed a unified social vision and artistic homogeneity until the 1978 production of La gran carpa and Fin del mundo, when so-called method and other actors reared in television, film, or the mainstream stage were invited to audition for some parts. The practice of auditioning marked the first change in the terms that defined how people were going to work together. For the ensemble—bred in collectivity—the mainstream competitive practice of auditioning signaled the onset of qualitative change the long-term effects of which could not be anticipated.

In the short run, auditioning created a mixture of incompatible performance styles in the company. A disparity in acting styles as well as performance mission made itself felt within the cast. Teatro Campesino ensemble members and outside actors came from extremely different life experiences and artistic backgrounds. A vast discrepancy in social, cultural, and political experience, consciousness, and mission separated the ensemble members from the auditioned members. In the words of Olivia Chumacero:

> It's like this. I did a lot of talking with those people from L.A. who came here for auditions in 1978. I would talk about the Farm Workers Union. I would talk about the American Indian movement. Anytime I would talk about movidas políticas [political movements] that were happening, their response was: "What's that? Who's that? When did that happen?" It's not that they were not interested, probably. They just didn't know. They were actors. They were learning the discipline of acting. They were complete specialists. Their complete

energy and their time was concentrated on that. Theirs is an entirely different reality. When I met those people and they were going to do the acting in *La carpa de los Rasquachis*—that was a piece that we had developed as an ensemble—they had to portray the campesino reality. I went and sat in at a couple of rehearsals when I was able to move a little more [after an accident]. I remember once the actors wanted to know exactly how do you cut grapes, how do you do the actual work of campesinos. This was their "character study." They didn't know because they had never been in that situation in their entire lives. It's understandable, but it shocked me to see these people representing a life that they knew nothing about. And if somebody were to interview them in Europe and ask them about the Farm Workers Union—because they were representing the union in the piece—well, they would have very little to say. That upset me. (Interview, 1/19/1983)

In 1979 actors were once again auditioned, this time for a European tour of *Fin del mundo*. It was in that production in fact that auditioned actors outnumbered Teatro Campesino ensemble members for the first time. The considerable differences between auditioned actors and Teatro Campesino ensemble members had both short-term and long-term effects upon the company. In the short term those differences meant strained relations within the cast and the company as a whole, due to the awkwardness of combining quite antithetical acting techniques. Perhaps the most striking immediate difference was the auditioned actors' utter inability to work collectively through the Rasquachi Aesthetic centered around improvisation. With Teatro Campesino ensemble members, collective memory, improvisation, physical spontaneity, and elements of unpredictability were cultivated skills and the very basis of *all* performance. Ensemble member Olivia Chumacero described the discrepancy between ensemble members and the new "method" actors from Los Angeles:

In fact during the last *Fin del mundo* [1979] one day he [Luis Valdez] came in and he was totally frustrated with the development of the piece because half of it was ensemble and the other half were actors from L.A. Well, we would get going improvising with each other. But we would have a very hard time with the other people. I guess we were clashing. He [Luis Valdez] would see us act one way and they would act another way. We were acting in two different styles. It was obvious. It was very obvious to those of us working in the piece. And Luis used to get so mad. Whenever we wanted to, we improvised and changed lines. Then these people [the actors from L.A.] would have a heart attack if you didn't give them the *exact* word which was in the script and which was their cue. If you said the same thing, for example, but changed the word order of a sentence, then they could not come in and say their lines because you did not give them the right cue; it was crazy. But that's what Luis wanted to do. And I had a hard time working with actors who acted like puppets, actors who refused to think. (Interview, 1/19/1983)

The logocentrism of the auditioned actors was not necessarily the product only of a "refusal to think" bred in the theatrical mainstream but also the antithesis of the Teatro Campesino's Rasquachi Aesthetic, which demanded the integrated use of the entire body (not just words) to convey meaning. In any event, the beginning of what Chumacero calls the "actors from L.A." signaled a rupture within the Teatro Campesino company as well as a change in the company's work philosophy, in which performance was not a specialized activity carried out only onstage. The Teatro Campesino ensemble had always been keenly conscious of the continuity between life on and off the stage. Stage work was but one dimension of the overall cultivation of a performer's human potential as well as sociopolitical awareness and involvement. Other dimensions included a collective self-education process (see chap. 2), a consciousness of historical and class community and of one's sense of belonging to and participating in the life of a community. It was the antithesis of the philosophy of the Los Angeles actors, who only acted, who viewed the role on stage as the extent of their human performance commitment. They were actors trained within the division of labor and specialization characteristic of mainstream theater. Chumacero commented with eloquence on the relationship between the Teatro Campesino ensemble's sense of responsibility within a human collective and its performance or acting philosophy:

Within El Teatro there had been some degree of unity between the work done in the teatro and the world outside of that. I know that it is good for people to evolve their skills and their art. I know that it is good for a musician to have the time to rehearse, to practice. I know that these things are essential. I know that the painter must have time to paint. And the actor must have time to practice acting. But I do not accept the fact that you should isolate yourself from the reality around you and from the things that are happening around you—to the point that you know nothing about it because you have given yourself so totally to one thing.

You are in this world not as an individual. You are supported by every other human being that is around you and by the different types of work that they do, you know. You are collectively living in the world; and you are responsible for the space that you use, for the food that you eat. For everything you carry a responsibility, not the other person. You. Every individual. When I first started reading Tolteca philosophy, I saw that science, religion, music, and art were an integral part of everyday life—which is what they should be. I know that you must take time within different disciplines in order to learn something. But that does not mean that you should disregard everything else around you. That would be like saying: "O.K. Take care of me. I don't know anything. All I know how to do is one thing. So feed me. Clothe me."

One lives in a community. You use the streets. You pay taxes. You eat food that's full of poison. . . . There may be a child next door that is getting abused. Wake up. Wake up. And for all the time that you spend on your art, you still need those people. You need the audience, for example. You need people. You use people. You use people so that they can appreciate what you do. They are the ones that put the value upon what you do. (Interview 1/19/1983)

A keen awareness of a responsibility toward self and society—including other performers, audiences, and the greater community—and a consciousness of the "unity between the work done in the *teatro* and the world outside of that" had always characterized the Teatro Campesino. The company's spirit of collectivity was entirely inimical to the type of specialization or division of labor that are standard in mainstream theater. Within the Teatro Campesino's collective work mode, all members shared in all facets of production activity. The ability to work in various realms of theatrical production (performance, the creation of plays, sets, props, costumes) was in fact highly valued as characteristic of a "Spherical Actor" (see chap. 2). As Chumacero described the situation, auditioned actors coming from the mainstream subscribed to an entirely different type of work and social philosophy. And their presence had an impact upon the company's work and practice conditions.

The changing composition of the Teatro Campesino ensemble—and the attendant changes in the company's relations of production—also became evident in 1979–1980 when *Fin del mundo* toured California for three weeks and then Europe for six months. Although collective ensemble energy and Rasquachi Aesthetic were still palpable in that production, it was maintained only with a great deal of difficulty. Temporary hires outnumbered ensemble members in the cast and their presence posed new problems arising from the tensions between the new actors' individualistic work ethic and the old-time ensemble members' collective work ethic. Tour manager José Delgado describes the problems created by the new breed of Chicana/o actors:

[Those who were not ensemble members] . . . had hardly traveled out of state, let alone out of the country. They brought a lot of internalized aggression and attitudes toward Europeans on tour. . . . They really started to understand who they were . . . and understand who they were as individuals, too. But unfortunately at the expense of everybody's good feelings and well-being. It was very difficult for me because I had to be on top of everybody's problems, and also on top of our agent's problems, who was very disillusioned with the company. Eventually he just backed off; he ended up going back to Paris and said: "You deal with them." The fact [is] that they were so problematic, but also so American, which he hadn't expected. He expected more of what he had already defined as being Chicano, which was basically the company as it existed in the early to mid-seventies: people who are willing to experience everything and be more accepting. That wasn't the case this time. I even had to settle a fight between this guy who had his own definition of what "professional" was—and other members of the cast. It was totally ridiculous. Ultimately I just said: "Forget it, God damn it; just do the work." (Delgado and Esparza interview, 8/10/1983)

The division-of-labor work mode characteristic of the "professional" mainstream theater world gradually found even broader implementation within the Teatro Campesino company. The kind of "professionalism" and alienated labor in the mainstream world, although not fully experienced or understood, suddenly was embraced by a few long-standing ensemble members. The experience of working with people from the outside and the success of Zoot Suit exerted a powerful influence. Olivia Chumacero describes the transition:

The composition of the Teatro Campesino was changing and people changed with it. In 1978 the Teatro Campesino had auditions for the first time; that was for the European tour. A group of people came in to work with the Teatro regularly for the first time. Those people were like the beginning of the actors from L.A. It sounds like a science fiction story. But people change: the regulars from the company changed during that tour to some extent. Some wanted to have résumés, glossy 8" x 10" pictures. Some wanted to have an agent. The transition was spreading. So even the nucleus of the company had been affected—in different places and at different times.
(Interview, 1/19/1983)

Zoot Suit was a transformative experience above all for Luis Valdez and the few members of the ensemble who assisted him in the Zoot Suit production (Phil Esparza, José Delgado, and Roberta Delgado). Chumacero recollects:

The people that went to work with Luis on Zoot Suit were changed by the experience too; because they were in a big city, in a metropolis like L.A. They were in a reality in which drama was respected as an official form of work. If you said you were working at the Mark Taper, it meant something. And so everybody changed. Everybody that worked with Luis on that piece changed. Luis changed. There was suddenly a lot of talk about being "professional," about *really* being a "professional," about *really* doing *teatro*, about *really* writing, about *really* being a technician. I mean *really*. None of this playing around stuff any more. It was suddenly "*real*."

Dramatic experiences change a person all the time. And Luis, well I think he enjoyed the way a director is treated within that method of work, *en esa clase de trabajo*. He also enjoyed the fact that there wasn't so much time "wasted," because his main character didn't have to miss a rehearsal to go finish a prop, you know. Or it was never the case that a musician was missing because he was working on the set or because he was in the office trying to book the tour. That kind of thing. He could say: "From nine to five o'clock these people are going to work with me on acting, on putting this piece together. And they have nothing to worry about, nothing, absolutely nothing, except how they are going to be acting." (Interview, 1/19/1983)

In his sustained quest for mainstream institutional self-legitimation, Luis Valdez wholeheartedly embraced a new system of cultural production. Luis Valdez—as the celebrated author and director of *Zoot Suit*—thoroughly felt the allure of success. The experience may be compared to that of a child given complete freedom in a toy store: for the first time Valdez enjoyed the luxury of a stage manager; of light, sound, and other technicians; of elaborate stage sets; of costume designers and makeup specialists; of complete control over the actors; and of a big budget at his disposal.

This is the world Luis Valdez set out to replicate in the small town of San Juan Bautista when he returned from *Zoot Suit* in 1981. As a first step in that direction he purchased a packing shed with the money he made on the film and converted it into a theater. As a second step toward "legitimacy" he negotiated to make it an "Equity house," one governed by the Actors' Equity Union, a symbol of mainstream professionalism. (Of course the Teatro Campesino ensemble members were not Equity actors.) Through a series of subtle and not-so-subtle communications, Luis Valdez then signaled to members of the Teatro Campesino ensemble that the collective performance style cultivated by the company for almost twenty years was not good enough. In the *L.A. Times* he even spoke of the "retarded artistic growth of some of the members of the company" (Drake 1980). As Olivia Chumacero implies, the company's Rasquachi Aesthetic was thrown into question and even invalidated because it was not the professionalism of corporate mainstream theater. Luis Valdez's disavowal of the ensemble, his denial of all but one kind of "professionalism" (that of the mainstream) indeed took on grotesque proportions. In 1982 he stated: "If you're not professional, you're not considered to be legit, you know. And if you're not legitimate, I guess you're illegitimate theater. We were illegitimate theater for quite a few years and were happy being that. I suppose in that sense, too, things have changed" (Engstrom 1982).

Ensemble members were quickly urged to retool artistically or to ship out. Although some made halfhearted efforts to retrain in the new performance style of the mainstream, the ensemble for the most part was skeptical about the "actors from L.A."; that is, the new acting technique was perceived as essentially lifeless and expressionless. Most ensemble members were also unwilling to relinquish what they perceived as the ensemble's Mexican and Chicana/o performance foundation and its strength: the Rasquachi Aesthetic grounded in the Theater of the Sphere. The new mainstream relations of production contradicted all principles and procedures of the collective tradition of performance. Most ensemble members kept their distance from the new mainstream-type production pieces launched by Luis Valdez (*Rose, Bandido, Soldier Boy, Corridos*).

All these factors contributed to the mutual distancing process that ensued between the Teatro Campesino collective ensemble and Luis Valdez. Within two years the longtime ensemble members were, so to speak, mothballed and decommissioned into a new administrative category called the "core group members"—a group without any administrative or artistic authority. All production decisions passed into the hands of Luis Valdez and a few professional administrators, made possible under the auspices of a 1980 NEA Institutional Advancement Grant. Productions henceforth were staged almost exclusively with auditioned actors from Los Angeles.

The term "mainstreaming" masks the complexity and implications of the dominant process of theatrical production and the possibilities for people of color within that process. It is a process that involves a qualitative leap in terms of aesthetics and relations of production. For Luis Valdez, the move from the domain of El Teatro Campesino into the mainstream was a move from an alternative subsistence-level organization to an upper-middle-class cultural institution embodying the nation's dominant cultural practices and interests. To some extent that move entailed a shift in class and ethnic allegiance and identification. Although there is much speculation as to the *degree* of assimilation that mainstream institutions demand from persons of color, one does not make the passage unaltered. We might also speculate concerning the degree to which minorities in mainstream entertainment alter or have an impact on mainstream institutions. In the case of Luis Valdez, the passage was deeply assimilatory: it entailed abandonment of the Mexican and Chicana/o popular performance aesthetic based on collective creation and the corresponding adoption of Euro-American corporate proscenium theater practices based on a division of labor and individualism. It was, as well, the switch from the collectivity of oral culture to the individual authorship of print culture.

It is significant that the Teatro Campesino departure from the Mexican and Chicana/o collective performance tradition also coincided with an economic dependency ushered in by the decision to seek the financial assistance of grants. These grants, which the Teatro collective had refused for fifteen years, suddenly became pivotal to the Teatro's institutionalization and (ironically) instrumental in triggering the company's chronic economic crisis after 1980. Grants (and the conditions attached to them) further facilitated the Teatro Campesino's radical turnabout in relations of production after *Zoot Suit* and the corresponding radical alteration of the company's social relations of production. Aside from the economic dependency that comes from grants, foundations also exercise control over artistic production through the various conditions attached to them. The example of the NEA Institutional Advancement Grant ($150,000 annually for three years) first awarded in 1980 is symptomatic. Institutional Advancement grants were awarded preferentially to "organizations that have developed from populist origins," according to A. B. Spellman, director of NEA's Expansion Arts Program. He added: "What they needed next was assistance to gain a firm administrative footing" (Drake 1980). Hence, institutional *advancement* was almost explicitly defined by the NEA as the transition into the dominant relations of theatrical production: the adoption of a strong administration with a hierarchical division of labor characteristic of corporate theater. Luis Valdez anticipated the various problems that would be associated with grants in a 1970 statement: "Above all, the national organization of teatros Chicanos would be self-supporting and independent, meaning no government grants. The corazón de la Raza cannot be revolutionized on a grant from Uncle Sam . . . there is yet a need for independence for the following reasons: objectivity, artistic competence, survival" (Valdez 1971b:3–4). In 1975 Valdez expressed a similar distrust of grants, while describing the difficult alternative of living without them. It was at that time that Ruth Maylese of the NEA urged the Teatro Campesino to apply for grants under which they could receive thousands of dollars. Some Chicano companies had received as much as a hundred thousand dollars. In spite of the allure of Foundation money, the Teatro decided as a matter of principle not to apply for any grants from foundations, espe-

cially government-funded ones. In the following years the Teatro Campesino survived, as in years before, through a combination of various auster-
ity measures that included handouts from compassionate families, tours to
distant places, and a frugal lifestyle. That position changed vis-à-vis grants
by 1980.

The 1980 NEA grant to the Teatro Campesino, like other grants, such as
the massive Ford Foundation Hispanic theater grants of the 1980s, was
an assimilationist vehicle. These grants facilitated the "advancement" of
Chicana/o theater ensembles into white establishment formations or appa-
ratuses. Through its Institutional Advancement Grants the NEA provided
heavy incentives for an "advancement" synonymous with mainstream institutionalization and for the dismantling of theater companies and practices
rooted in working-class collective performance traditions (their "populist
origins"). The NEA grant awarded to El Teatro Campesino in fact stipulated
that the entire first phase (nine months) of the three-year grant be spent
developing a long-range administrative plan, thus securing a hierarchical
division of labor.

As a participant observer with the company during the grant's implementation I had a firsthand opportunity to observe its effects. The influx of money
radically altered the relations of production and the artistic thrust of the company. The Teatro Campesino's long-standing economic principles of minimal
but regular income, of sharing, of mutual aid, of collective belt-tightening
and collective creation, sacrifice, and survival in difficult times were supplanted by a new economics and forms of human relations based on hard-
nosed capitalist business management practices.

The Teatro Campesino collective process was irrevocably altered by the
adoption of business management practices. Chief among them was the new
"professional" division of labor, principally between a well-paid administrative bureaucracy, a second tier called the "creative staff" (in charge of artistic decisions), and the third tier of hired "professional" actors (who rarely
received a living wage). The longtime Teatro Campesino ensemble members
were assigned to a fourth, very marginal, category named (ironically) the
Core Group. The members of the core group were Olivia Chumacero, José
Delgado, Roberta Delgado, Phillip W. Esparza, Adela González, Julio
González, Andrés V. Gutiérrez, Ernesto Hernández, Luis Oropeza, Rogelio
Rojas, Diane Rodríguez, Luis Valdez, Lupe Valdez, and Socorro Valdez. The
bylaws (rights and responsibilities) of the core group were never worked out;
by 1985 the category was abolished altogether.

The differential treatment of individuals, inherent in the new Teatro
Campesino's hierarchization (conditions of artistic practice visible in all

mainstream industries), produced a corresponding decline in the company's overall morale. The decline in morale had everything to do with the new set of relations of production adopted from corporate theater. Work became organized along structures and rationales antithetical to the collective oral tradition of the Teatro Campesino ensemble. Whereas all members of the ensemble had participated collectively in all aspects of production and in decisions pertaining to production, the new Teatro Campesino production company introduced forms of specialization (a division of labor) that replicated the artistic and decision-making disenfranchisement of actors that was prevalent in corporate theater. Within the Teatro Campesino company, a sense of the *creative process as a whole* was lost, as that process became fragmented. (This is the essence of "alienated labor.") Under the new structure actors had no control over major artistic decisions; the administration had no control over the stage process; and the artistic staff was caught between the reality of artistic creation and the economic dictates of the administration.

The changes in work organization and work rationale are visible, even palpable in the post-1980 mainstream stage productions of the new Teatro Campesino production company: the energy of those productions has in no way approximated the intensity, energy, and flow of the old Teatro Campesino ensemble. The new actors who come as temporary hires have no stake in or concern for the overall process of creation or for an artistic vision. It cannot surprise us that these actors simply cannot perform with total involvement— involvement in the company, and involvement with other actors. The noneconomic work incentives that drove the ensemble (such as social responsibility, tradition, pleasure in the work itself caused by the spirit of cooperation and collectivity, and the opportunity for collective human development of all members of the group) became a thing of the past. Most of the auditioned actors I spoke with in fact had never heard of El Teatro Campesino prior to their stint in San Juan Bautista. In the words of one of the lead actors in *Soldier Boy*: "I never heard of Teatro Campesino until I came to San Juan. My agent urged me to come here. She said Luis was hot right now" (oral communication, 11/21/1982). Olivia Chumacero comments on the nature of the motivation among the new breed of actors:

> The technicians that come here now, the actors that come here now, the stage managers that come here now, the directors that come here now . . . all the people that come here and work for low wages do it because the Teatro Campesino has a name. That name looks good on résumés. But that name was acquired through years of sacrifice, by all the sacrifice of all the people that gave before these people came. These people that you see here now—with

rare exceptions—are not the ones who made El Teatro Campesino. It was all those people before; those people who sacrificed, created, who gave their time, their hearts, everything. (Interview, 1/19/1983)

The post-1980 Teatro Campesino work and production relations manifest that general breakdown of the labor process—that Harry Braverman (1982) calls "the degradation of work." The breakdown, or degradation, is said to be inherent in the division of labor, in differential pay rates, in the presence of a management team whose chief job is to increase work output. It cannot surprise us that antagonism arises between those who act and those who manage them. What became visible after 1981 (when a set of administrators was installed for the first time) was administrative efforts to maximize self-importance and authority while minimizing the importance of all "temporary hires," that is, the artists. The weight of the new administrative cadre (consisting of an executive director, a press director, an executive secretary, a producer, and a production manager) was ponderous. At an October 10, 1983, board meeting, administrative operating expenses were totaled at $240,857, while artistic production costs totaled $146,000. Very revealing is the final statement of thanks in the 1983 Annual Report, which indicates: "None of these achievements would have been possible without the dedication and hard work of Producer/Production Manager (name), Tour Producer (name) and Press Director (name)." Not even one word of appreciation for the work of numerous actors, musicians, and other artists who worked below minimum wage is expressed.

It is instructive to witness how the NEA's Institutional Advancement Grant in fact even further jeopardized El Teatro Campesino's ability to function after 1981. What was supposed to be a three-year grant from NEA was frozen under the Reagan administration after only one year of funding. El Teatro Campesino did receive $120,000 (of the first year's allocation of $150,000) and succeeded in matching that sum with contributions from other granting agencies and private benefactors. Two things were accomplished with the money in 1980–1981: (1) the warehouse purchased by Luis Valdez with his Zoot Suit profits (and rented to the Teatro Campesino, Inc.) underwent the first phase of its conversion into a theater space; (2) the Teatro Campesino carried out an ambitious administrative and technical staff expansion program. The sudden freeze of funds in 1982, however, left the organization in the lurch, economically speaking, and with an expensive administrative apparatus almost impossible to sustain. Economic pressures spiraled as the production company sought to fulfill the conditions of granting agencies, to pay administrators, to pay its overhead, and to launch productions requiring considerable investment capital. Fund-raising became a major preoccupation.

The staging of productions as investments further dictated a great deal of what happened or did not happen. For example, the negotiations surrounding the *Corridos* production (negotiations for a theater space, for investors, for the private benefactors) involved a protracted series of postponements, delays, and waiting periods. In the interim, the playhouse in San Juan went dark and all creative activity ceased. In time, the Teatro Campesino production company not only failed to duplicate the *Zoot Suit* success, but entered into spiraling cycles of economic problems—exacerbated by the fact that the company's hope for economic solvency—the *Corridos* production—emerged in the red after the Los Angeles run (in 1984). The administrative apparatus installed under the NEA Institutional Advancement grant ultimately had to be pared down. It is indeed ironic that the grant, which, in the words of Elizabeth Weil, Director of the NEA challenge grant program, was supposed to "enable these institutions . . . to become more financially and managerially independent" (Drake 1980) was in some ways instrumental in ushering in dependency and economic destabilization. In any event, the decision to mainstream created a new, strict business orientation in the company. Money became prime in the mediation of social relationships and those relationships suffered correspondingly.

The radically altered social relations of production had an impact not only on the fabric of human and stage relationships but also on aesthetic choices and the staging of dramatic works. In the absence of collective creation, the Teatro Campesino production company embarked upon a search for individually authored plays. Between 1981 and 1985 the following were produced: *Rose of the Rancho* (1981), *Soldier Boy* (winter 1982), *Don Juan* (fall 1983), in addition to plays written by Luis Valdez—*Bandido!* (1982), *Corridos* (1983), *Badges* (1985). The pieces developed were felt to have the potential for mass appeal (i.e., economic success). All of these productions reflect the new mission, aesthetic, and work relations of the Teatro production company. As Eagleton (1976:48) points out: "every literary text in some sense internalizes its social relations of production . . . every text intimates by its very conventions the way it is to be consumed, encodes within itself its own ideology of how, by whom and for whom it was produced." Luis Valdez made no secret of the fact that his post–*Zoot Suit* productions were directed at middle-class audiences (the economic backbone of mainstream corporate theater) and at unsympathetic white Americans. This is, for the most part, a privileged class of people—whose very privilege rests on social relations of inequality.

The Teatro Campesino's mainstream plays correspondingly avoid the discourse of social inequality. That is most certainly one way of encoding an "ideology of how, by whom, and for whom it was produced" (Eagleton 1976:48).

Although this is not the place for an in-depth analysis of the various post–Zoot Suit plays produced by Valdez and the Teatro Campesino production company, I would like to point to some striking commonalities among these productions. Taken as a body of work, they constitute a radical departure from both the aesthetic and the social vision of the work produced collectively by the ensemble—indeed even a departure from Zoot Suit, which was still to a large extent shaped by the collective vision. In contrast, the post-1980 productions reveal an ideological adherence to certain conventions: (1) they foreground middle-class characters, not the masses; (2) they avoid engaging controversial social issues. When they do surface, the issues are trivialized; (3) they center largely on the individual sphere of existence, the workings of the emotional or mental private life of a person or a small group of persons; (4) they use humor only in the form of light wit and no longer as a satirical or parodistic tool that critiques power. Valdez came to rely heavily on standard "funny" genres such as melodrama and sitcom and no longer on the biting satire of the humorous conventions described in chapter 1; (5) they often feature a white savior; (6) they demonstrate a politics of gender even more problematic than in the earlier period; and (7) they are in the English language, not in Spanish or bilingual. The only exception so far is Corridos, which provides a running English translation (projected as slides) of all the ballads. In what follows I would like to highlight how these conventions are manifest in various post-1980 productions.

The very lighthearted spirit of the era of mainstream productions was heralded by the revival production of the proassimilationist melodrama Rose of the Rancho (discussed earlier in this chapter). Rose—chosen as the inaugural play for the new El Teatro Campesino Playhouse in 1981—features middle-class characters and a happy end replete with a white savior who rescues and marries the Mexican girl Juanita. Valdez's selection of this piece as the inaugural piece for the Teatro Campesino Playhouse, as well as the selection of a Euro-American to direct it, visibly reinforced the play's and the company's new proassimilationist ideology. The Teatro Campesino collective was not invited to perform at the inauguration of the Teatro Campesino Playhouse. Olivia Chumacero's comments reflect the sentiment of many ensemble veterans at that time.

When Luis came back from *Zoot Suit*, he bought a warehouse from the money he had made. He bought the Teatro Campesino building. It's his building. And that warehouse was transformed into a *teatro*. And the first piece that was done in the teatro, in the new building, was *Rose of the Rancho*, which was not written by us, nor was it directed by Luis. That was one of the saddest times for me . . . because during all the early years we always used to talk about having our own *teatro* some day. We used to really talk about it *all* the time; and we would talk about the things we were going to do; we were going to do this and we were going to do that. And here finally we had a *teatro* and the building was named El Teatro Campesino. It opened in 1981 and it opened with a piece that was not an original Teatro Campesino piece; it opened with a visiting director [Frank Condon]; and it opened with a cast brought in from Los Angeles. Todo este tiempo [All this time] that we had been working and desiring and dreaming of this . . . it was . . . it was like finally getting something you had craved and then somebody coming along, and taking it away from you. It was such a strange feeling. You know, it felt good to have a *teatro*, it felt good to see the building, it was good to see such a transformation. But somehow it wasn't our *teatro*. . . . Seeing the inauguration of the Teatro was like the final change. Seeing that was the culmination of the change, the end of an entire period. There was no more imagining, there was no more talking about it. There it was. I saw it right in front of me. The Teatro Campesino that we had always struggled to maintain had come to an end. The entire process of creation changed totally. (Interview, 1/19/1983)

The inaugural *Rose of the Rancho* production (apparently a Luis Valdez favorite) was restaged once again in 1989.

After *Rose of the Rancho*, the company staged Luis Valdez's *Bandido!*. The Luis Valdez melodrama of Californian social bandit Tiburcio Vásquez bears a strong similarity to *Rose* in its treatment of history. The 1981 play is set in California in the 1873–1875 period, a quarter of a century after the Gold Rush and the Mexico-U.S. War. As in *Rose*, history is trivialized and hence distorted. In *Bandido!*, social activist Vásquez, who fought against Anglo encroachment and injustice until his hanging, is recast by Valdez as a libertine and a bandit (hence, the title). Both acts begin in a whorehouse setting with Tiburcio Vásquez surrounded by a group of prostitutes. At the play's opening Madame Kate refers to Vásquez as a "scurrilous libertine." Vásquez, for his part, talks only about stealing, thus living up to the play's title. Valdez sets up a melodramatic binary opposition of *simpático* bad guy (Vásquez as thief) and the good guys (law officials). In the process, the highly complex historical figure of Tiburcio Vásquez, who waged protracted warfare against the social outrages perpetrated on Mexicans in California, becomes "simplified" into a sex-hungry bandit.

In shaping the play Bandido! Valdez appears to have followed a mainstream entertainment formula: avoid controversy and keep things simple. The production's program notes reflect an unwillingness to raise "discomforting" questions. The front page of those notes is devoted entirely to describing Vásquez's exploits as a bandit. Those notes close with the statement: "the entire state of California mobilizes its [white] lawmen to bring the [Mexican] desperados to justice." (White saviors?) There is absolutely no discussion of the justice Tiburcio Vásquez was seeking. Valdez reduces him to a "horse thief and stagecoach robber—but with a romantic flair." No mention is made of why Vásquez took to banditry. The program only fleetingly mentions that "Vásquez was caught in the grip of historical circumstances and emerged a horse thief." The effort to avoid anything that might seem confrontational to Euro-Americans is so extreme that the history of Mexicans (and others) in nineteenth-century California is wholly distorted by omissions. Is this Valdez's idea of how to please "the millions of unsympathetic Americans"?

His efforts at individual authorship in Bandido! suffer from other dramatic weaknesses as well. In the words of Bandido! musical director Francisco González (oral communication, 7/18/1988, San Juan Bautista): "One of the problems with Bandido! is that it never jibed. What you ended up with was a mishmash of ideas that didn't come together. There is so much about stereotyping that the piece becomes a stereotype."

To the press, Valdez explains Bandido! as a contribution to the "mythology of the conquest of the West." The idea was to put Tiburcio Vásquez among legendary "heroes" like Jesse James, Black Bart, and Wyatt Earp. Yet in this Chicano "western" the Mexican still gets hanged at the end. Valdez also reaffirms his desire to reach a mass audience with this piece: "I want it to work for a broad audience, not only nationwide, but also for Europe and Latin America" (Stone 1982). It is ironic that when the Teatro Campesino's longtime European booking agent from France came to see Bandido!, he found the piece too broad to be of any interest in Europe. A European tour never materialized.

Other post-1980 productions are equally problematic. The 1982 production Soldier Boy (written by Judith Shiffer Pérez and Severo Pérez) was produced by Luis Valdez in winter 1982. Again, history (World War II) is the backdrop to this family psychodrama. It takes us through a series of emotional upheavals and adjustments experienced by one family whose son returns a hero from the front. In keeping with the new aesthetic, the play features a middle-class family that speaks only English. Like *Bandido!* or *Rose* this piece avoids engaging larger social issues in which the family is immersed. Instead it places at its center the emotional father-and-son-like attachment that is formed between a boy and his uncle (because the boy's father is at war).

Luis Valdez's *I Don't Have to Show You No Stinking Badges* takes a similarly narrow focus: it features one day in the life of a Chicana/o (or "Hispanic"?) middle-class nuclear family. The parents work as bit players (usually maids and gardeners) in entertainment industry plays and movies; the son is an upwardly mobile student at Harvard. He visits his parents in Los Angeles and experiences considerable emotional upheaval concerning his social role and identity. Again, however, the larger social picture is blurred as we focus primarily on the young man's mental processes. In a tangential way *Badges* has to do with many issues, most especially with an uncritical quest for social legitimation. None of the issues raised are developed, however, since the theatrical sitcom format a la "I Love Lucy" forbids any sustained treatment of anything. At regular intervals we are distracted by funny and absurd moments.

Corridos on stage (1983–1984) and screen (1987) features a return to material from the Mexican popular performance tradition developed earlier by the Teatro Campesino ensemble. *Corridos* consists of a collection of dramatized narrative ballads, most of them drawn from the period of the Mexican Revolution. The *Corridos* production is billed as a Luis Valdez script. *Corridos* plays upon the expectations of a mass audience with regard to Mexicans. The production is at its best when it comes to musical and dance performance. It is at its worst when it comes to acting skills, gender politics, and the foregrounding of a white savior character (John Reed).

In Broyles-González (1990), I have published an extensive critique of both the stage and the film productions of *Corridos* (see also chap. 3). In my critique I elaborate on how the *corrido*—a working-class oppositional cultural practice—is converted by Valdez into something that reproduces the dominant culture's distortions of the Mexican population of the United States. The considerable contradictions operative within Valdez's politics of representation lead him, for example, to position a white upper-middle-class male (John Reed) in the role of speaking subject in a production that professes to "do justice to the true role of women." In addition, John Reed functions as the white savior found in so many of Luis Valdez's mainstream productions. Reed is the only male in the production who does not engage in violence against women. In fact, he at times must even intercede and "save" a Mexican woman from the violence of her Mexican companion. The gender problematics of the *Corridos* production resurfaces in later Valdez productions such as *La Bamba*. In her recent book on Chicana and Chicano film, Rosa Linda Fregoso discusses the disparaging images of women in *La Bamba* (Fregoso:1993).

In 1992 the Teatro Campesino production company took a bold and unprecedented step by producing and touring two one-act plays written by two women and directed by Socorro Valdez: *Simply María* by Josefina López, and *How Else Am I Supposed to Know I'm Still Alive* by Evelina Fernández. Although this touring production represented largely the work of women, the Teatro Campesino's publicity material highlighted above all the accomplishments of Luis Valdez. Consequently, publicity materials at various performance sites did not even mention director Socorro Valdez and also often eliminated any mention of one or both female playwrights. (Such was the case with the University of California at Santa Barbara's publicity posters, for example.) That tour was followed by plans for a Frida Kahlo movie by Luis Valdez. The film production company withdrew from the project, however, following the bad publicity generated by a protest by Chicana and Latina actors. The protest and press conference at the Beverly Hills Hilton were directed against Valdez, who cast a white woman in the role of Frida while not auditioning Chicana actors for the role. Chicana actor Rose Portillo of *Zoot Suit* fame commented:

> When I first heard of the project, I knew that as an actor and as a Chicana, I would be overlooked. I had worked with Luis Valdez in "Zoot Suit" (I played Della in L.A., New York and the film) and hoped I would receive, at least, a courtesy call. But I was not surprised by its absence. I've been around, working in and out of this industry for 15 years. (Portillo 1992)

All of these Luis Valdez productions created for the mainstream and within mainstream relations of production encode within themselves their "ideology of how, by whom, and for whom they were produced" (Eagleton 1976:48). They are productions that expressly aim to please a particular segment of the population. This they accomplish through a turn to light melodramatic genres, through a turn inward (psychologizing), through avoidance of the burning issues of our day. At the same time, various accommodationist conventions make their appearance. These conventions, evidently geared to making productions more "palatable" to Euro-American and middle-class audiences, include the white savior convention, the use of middle-class protagonists, and an embracing of proassimilationist tendencies and of the stereotyping of Mexicans so popular in the dominant culture.

Perhaps the most telling feature of this entire set of productions created with an eye for mass appeal is that none of them are particularly inspirational, artistically or otherwise. They are of a bland sort, with little or no force of conviction. Nor are they energized by that sense of urgency that informed the work of the Teatro Campesino ensemble. It is a new era of institutionalization, an era of Chicanas/os in the mainstream. The creation of Chicana/o cultural products within the mainstream discursive space poses considerable challenges, many of them generated at the contradictory intersection of aesthetic imagination, cultural integrity, and economic pressure.

Conclusion: Whither El Teatro Campesino?

After 1980 the Teatro Campesino ensemble was transformed into a production company that disassociated itself from the Mexican and Chicana/o popular performance mode based on collectivity. Closely related to that transformation was the avoidance of controversial contemporary social issues and the turn to lighter, melodramatic, and even proassimilationist themes and forms. We witness these tendencies in productions such as *Rose of the Rancho, Bandido!*, or *Badges*. This disassociation is as much related to a conjunctural set of forces as it is to "free" artistic choice or "natural" development. The artistic choices and practices of performing groups such as El Teatro Campesino are very much related to shifts in the sociopolitical and economic environment of which performers and audiences form a part. The transformation of El Teatro Campesino must be seen, specifically, in relation to the dramatic changes in the social formation beginning in the late 1970s. For one thing, the rise of a new conservative political tide and the onset of economic recession along with widespread economic and social retrenchment policies during the Reagan and Bush administrations signaled the subsidence of the strong leftist sociopolitical fervor and activity of the 1960s and the early 1970s. Chicana/o efforts to break into mainstream performance and white mainstream institutions coincided with the strong decline of the Chicana/o theater movement and a new conservative political tide, with the rise of a new and small Chicana/o middle class, as well as with a sharp rise in poverty levels for the vast majority of Chicanas/os (see Acuña 1988, esp. chaps. 10 and 11). Luis Valdez was in the forefront, going with the times, just as he had gone with the leftist times of the 1960s. After the 1970s the formerly widespread dedication to alternative social ideals and public activism gave way to a new self-involvement, to individualism and personal ambition within the emergent Chicana/o middle class. The same Luis Valdez who characterized then-governor Ronald Reagan as

"Ronald Rajón" [Ronald the Liar] in an *acto* of the 1960s, personally invited President Ronald Reagan to attend the inauguration of the Teatro Campesino Playhouse in 1981. In 1983 Reagan reciprocated with an award honoring Luis Valdez for his contribution to the arts in this country.

The decline of the Chicano movement (and other liberational social movements) in the late 1970s also triggered a corresponding decline within the Chicana/o theater movement. It became difficult—if not impossible— for many Chicana/o theaters generated from the fervor of the Movimiento Chicano to sustain themselves in the absence of that movement and of white liberal enthusiasm. Significant as well is the dramatic increase in Chicana/o and Latina/o poverty levels throughout the 1970s and the 1980s, along with the continuing unequal access to education. Sheer survival has become increasingly difficult in the 1990s.

The most important sociohistorical factor that has helped open the doors of mainstream entertainment institutions or industries—within limits—to Chicanas/os, particularly in California, is not affirmative action but demographics: the advertising and entertainment industry's realization of the very high birth rate and population explosion among Chicanas/os, with demographic projections predicting a Chicana/o majority in California by the year 2030. Add to that the emergence of an affluent Chicana/o middle class and the industry's sudden awareness of the Chicana/o community's buying power, a previously untapped reservoir of dollar power. By the same token, some Chicana/o performers perceived what could be called a crack in the door of the entertainment industry. Prior to these new social realities, Chicanas/os were in no position to bring Chicana/o culture into the white mainstream.

The new mainstream course charted by Luis Valdez in the late 1970s no doubt in some ways represents an adjustment or accommodation to a changed sociopolitical and economic environment. What is not at all certain, however, is that the mainstream represents the only pathway for alternative theater groups at a time of crisis for all alternative institutions. Various veteran members of the ensemble indicate that the alternative nature of the company could have been preserved—although in modified form. The new directions set forth after *Zoot Suit*, however, led ultimately to a brand of Chicana/o theater modeled after the very theatrical model decried ten years earlier: the corporate theater of the white mainstream.

Change was always a constant with El Teatro Campesino. The company's elaboration between 1965 and 1975 of *actos, mitos, corridos* and mixtures thereof has been variously discussed and debated.[6] Its merger of Mexican popular performance techniques and repertoire with the Theater of the

Sphere project was groundbreaking and traditional at once. The new direction embarked on in the late 1970s, however, was qualitatively unlike any previous period of Teatro Campesino activity. At each prior stage of development the Teatro Campesino aesthetic was a direct outgrowth of Chicana/o working-class cultural and social ideals and strivings; it was always an aesthetic formulated from a dedication to changing perspectives within a broad Chicana/o humanistic vision. During the early period of performance, for example, the vision centered on contributing to the farmworker struggle for improved living conditions and human dignity. That vision then expanded to include related urban struggles and issues such as the war in Vietnam or the failures of the educational system. The Teatro Campesino ensemble's later work drew additional impetus from a revalorization and revival of the *indígena* heritage of Chicanas/os. That resulted in the Theater of the Sphere. The new direction adopted after the dissolution of the ensemble in the late 1970s, however, represents a leave-taking from any specific Chicana/o ideals. The Teatro Campesino production company's push into the mainstream is not primarily the result of any stated aesthetic, philosophical, or political orientation, but of a newly defined audience relationship, of a marketing strategy that became a goal in and of itself.

Of course, marketing to a mass audience is not an activity without philosophical, aesthetic, or political implications, even if they remain unstated or unconscious. What is different about the new commitment to mass marketing is that the idea of selling the theatrical product becomes the chief consideration; all other considerations become secondary. The question of what to sell to the "unsympathetic millions of Americans" increasingly became a trial-and-error guessing-game for the Teatro Campesino production company and was dictated by opportunity and devoid of an alternative artistic foundation. The radical shift in audience alliance—from alternative to mainstream venues—has signified a considerable loss of focus and a turning away from the Teatro Campesino ensemble's aesthetic, cultural, and social ideals. This state of affairs has persisted for years and is best illustrated by Luis Valdez's comment at a 1983 Teatro Campesino board of directors meeting (St. Francis Retreat, San Juan Bautista, 11/14/1983): "We're in business. The only question is: 'What will our product be?'" The foregrounding of the business side of things has taken precedence over and to a large extent eclipsed the formulation of artistic aims. The work presented at the Teatro Campesino Playhouse in San Juan Bautista correspondingly reflects the uncertainty of what the "product" will be. The playhouse has not succeeded in emerging from a state of ambivalence or semidormancy.

Few productions have been staged since *Zoot Suit*. At present the Teatro Campesino administrative apparatus occupies a good deal of its time with booking guest artists into the Teatro Campesino Playhouse. Although *Zoot Suit* was hailed far and wide as the harbinger of a new "professional" boom for El Teatro Campesino, it also marked the onset of a decline signaled by both the dissolution of the Teatro Campesino ensemble and the infrequency of Teatro Campesino theatrical productions. In the post–*Zoot Suit* period we have witnessed primarily the personal advancement of Luis Valdez, most recently through his hit film *La Bamba* (1987). Luis Valdez's ambitions as a dramatic writer, however, have not borne much fruit.

The lavish celebrations Luis Valdez staged marking the twentieth anniversary (1985) and then the twenty-fifth anniversary (1990) of the Teatro Campesino sought to create a smooth picture of continuity in a period of rupture and conflicting interests. They projected an image of constant growth and progress in a period of decline. More than ever, Luis Valdez is given to making statements to the effect that the Teatro Campesino ensemble still exists and that his production company is "playing in the streets." On the occasion of the Teatro Campesino's twenty-fifth anniversary (1990) he misleadingly indicated: "We will be embarking on projects in film and television. And we of course will always be a teatro. There will always be actos . . . done in the streets wherever the people are out on the streets" (Hernández 1990:7).

Similarly deceptive is the new publicity strategy that deals with the constant turnover in cast members. For public consumption, grant applications and painting a a false picture of continuity are carefully cultivated and advertised. Teatro Campesino ensemble veteran Roberta Delgado comments:

> It's [the Teatro Campesino] not the thing now that it was, that people think about it as. The most loudly touted part of the *teatro* doesn't exist anymore. The whole idea of there being a *company*. That's the most integral part of it. . . . I'm bothered as a person who was a part of that whole time period *before*. I'm bothered when I see a review in the paper that touts the "*members*" of El Teatro Campesino. Because those people aren't "members," to me. They're contracted players. They don't carry the knowledge of the aesthetics of the company. They don't carry a knowledge of the *concept* of the company. They don't know anything except that they're being paid to do the show, and they want to do the show because maybe they'll get something out of it. That's not a condemnation of where those people are, it's just that there's a difference in terms of commitment. To me the people who have been committed are still those who hold onto that core company membership, you know, and want to foster

certain things within the company, and want to see that aesthetically it goes in a certain direction. The point is whether that really is a possibility or not, or whether those of us who would like there to still be part of that *teatro* left are—I hate to say the word—*deluding* ourselves. The more I observe the machinations, the more I think that it's never going to be allowed to happen. (Interview, 7/21/83)

The artistic power and inspirational force of the Teatro Campesino material created collectively by the ensemble (and published as the "early works of Luis Valdez" [Valdez 1990]) have not been matched in the post-1980 period. There can be no doubt that the now-legendary and magical quality of the name El Teatro Campesino, its countercultural strength and international reputation, was a function of its rootedness in the oppositional working-class cultural practices of the Mexican popular performance tradition. A new flowering will perhaps come forth from those roots. Each generation of Mexicanas/os in the United States must deal with a changing reality and the struggles of its own time. In any event, a knowledge of the past and the present will provide the tools necessary to forge the future. It is to be hoped that the celebrations of the Teatro Campesino will in time lead to a rediscovery of those elements from its legacy with which we can construct a better future. Olivia Chumacero has expressed faith in the resilience of the cultural legacy forged by the Teatro Campesino collective:

Nobody can take away what you learned or what you created for yourself within El Teatro Campesino. Nobody can take that away. Nobody can remove what you have learned—nor keep you from applying it in life. And you may not have the scope or you may not have the impact of El Teatro Campesino in 1974—because that was a *group* energy. And it may take you a very long time to be able to have the place or situation to create that kind of impact again. But that does not mean that people are not wise to that kind of thing. (Interview, 1/19/1983)

Chronology

1962

César Chávez and Dolores Huerta found the National Farm Workers' Association (NFWA) in Delano, California, the beginnings of the first agricultural labor union in history.

Sept., 1965

NFWA joins the AFL-CIO Agricultural Workers Organizing Committee (AWOC) in what became a five-year strike against the Delano grape growers. That strike forged a national coalition of unions, students, people of color, consumers, and churches.

The 1960s into the 1970s

El Movimiento Chicano (the Chicano movement) becomes a part of the civil rights movement and gains national civil rights momentum through multiple local, regional, and national activities such as: the UFW labor and human rights struggles, establishment of La Raza Unida Party (1967), the 1969 First National Chicano Youth Conference, Denver's Crusade for Justice, the Los Angeles "Walk Outs," the trial of Los Siete de la Raza, El Plan de Santa Barbara (1969), El Plan Espiritual de Aztlán, El Plan de El Paso, and the Alianza Federal de Pueblos Libres (Federal Alliance of Free Peoples) in New Mexico. Independent Chicano schools are established in Texas, Colorado, and California. A national movement of Chicana/o theatrical activity emerges, along with youth organizations such as the Brown Berets and MEChA. Tensions between indigenist, nationalist, and Marxist philosophies.

Comparable movements among many U.S. racial and ethnic groups spring up (e.g., Black Muslim Movement, the Black Panther Party, the American Indian Movement, the Puerto Rican Young Lords).

Internationalist perspectives and momentum through Third World liberation struggles such as the Cuban revolution, Maoism in China, the Vietnam War—in the context of the Cold War. Political assassinations characterize and influence the era: Che Guevara, Patrice Lumumba, Ngo Dinh Diem, John F. Kennedy, Martin Luther King, Jr., Malcolm X, Fred Hampton, Robert F. Kennedy, Salvador Allende, the Wounded Knee siege. These inform later El Teatro Campesino productions.

Oct. 1965

César Chávez envisions the need for a farmworker performing group (a *carpa*) to inform the public about the strike. El Teatro Campesino (ETC) established as an organizing tool within the NFWA. Cofounders include Luis Valdez and Agustín Lira.

1966–1967
The NFWA and AWOC merge to form the United Farm Workers of America, AFL-CIO. The UFW leads the historic 280-mile march/pilgrimage from Delano to Sacramento (1966). ETC performs at nightly rallies for marchers. Farm labor *actos* developed include *Las dos caras del patroncito, Quinta temporada, Tres uvas, Schenley Contract, El achinique, Los mafiosos, La suegra, La causa, El grito de la union, La burra, La union de "No hay," La conquista del Perro-Minetti, La lucha de un pueblo, El mercante de muerte,* and *Huelga.* First national tour. The Village Voice Off-Broadway Awards Obie 1967–1968, "El Teatro Campesino for creating a worker's theatre to demonstrate the politics of survival." ETC performances include one in Washington D.C. before members of the Senate Subcommittee on Migratory Labor.

1967–1968
El Teatro Campesino separates from the UFW and moves to Del Rey, California, where it establishes El Centro Campesino Cultural. Thematic focus broadens to include multiple urban and rural issues. *Actos* include *Los vendidos, La conquista de México, The Militants, Acto on Welfare, A Day in Court, Los doctors, The Complex;* also Valdez's *The Shrunken Head of Pancho Villa.* Los Angeles Chicano high school student strikes for educational reform ("Blow-outs") inspire *actos* on secondary and university education such as *No saco nada de la escuela, Los ABCs, Juanito* (a puppet show), *El patrón, Acto on Education, The Orientation, El machete,* and *Máscaras del barrio.*
César Chávez fasts for twenty-five days in the continuing strike against grape growers.

1969
ETC moves to Fresno, California, and has its headquarters at an East Side church that also houses the Brown Beret Community Program. Performs *The Shrunken Head* and *actos* at the World Theatre Festival, Nancy, France. Los Angeles Drama Critics Circle Award, 1969, to "El Teatro Campesino for demonstrating the continuing vitality of theatre as an instrument of social change." Performances of *Calavera de Tiburcio Vásquez, Las dos caras del patroncito,* and other *actos* including *Dos vatos, El cuento de los zapatos, The Militants, The Commercial,* and *Bernabé.*
Fresno State College initiates Raza Studies, cochaired by Valdez, who teaches first Chicano Theater workshop. First influx of student performers into ETC.
First gathering of Chicano *teatros* (Fresno) and establishment of TENAZ (El Teatro Nacional de Aztlán).
ETC produces the award-winning film *I am Joaquin,* which receives "Best of Category" at the San Francisco International Film Festival, and is named "award winner" at the Independent Film Makers Festival.

1970
UFW wins the five-year grape strike, forcing growers to sign first contracts in agricultural labor history.
National Chicano Moratorium in Los Angeles protests the Vietnam War and the disproportionate Chicano fatality and recruitment rate. In response to the Vietnam War, the Teatro produces *Vietnam campesino, Soldado razo, Los vatos locos de Vietnam, El patrón, Chale con el draft,* and Valdez's *Dark Root of a Scream;* other performance pieces include *The American Dream, The Eight to Five Chicano, Bernabé, El mero Xmas de Juanito Raza,* and *Huelgistas.* (The Vietnam War ends in 1973.)
One group from ETC tours the midwestern and eastern United States, while the rest perform at rallies accompanying the thousand-mile UFW caravan protest from Calexico to Sacramento. ETC becomes the target of armed violence in Fresno County, and is fired

upon during a performance. Valdez teaches Teatro workshop at UC-Berkeley. ETC moves to storefront on Van Ness in Fresno, continues *actos*, and releases 45-rpm recording of *El Louie*.

First TENAZ Chicano Theater Festival (in San Jose).

Andrés Segura, ritual Conchero dancer and Aztec elder, visits ETC and strengthens the indigenous philosophical teachings within the collective. He also introduces the work of Maya teacher Domingo Martínez Paredez.

1971
ETC relocates to the rural town of San Juan Bautista, California. It is now composed primarily of university students recruited at Berkeley and other colleges. ETC performs in San Juan, and members live in a Gilroy storefront.

ETC travels to Mexico (performing *Bernabé*, *No saco nada de la escuela*, and *Soldado razo*), and visits Domingo Martínez Paredez, whose teachings intensify the exploration of Mayan philosophy and help shape the Theater of the Sphere.

Part of ETC tours the Midwest. First TENAZ workshop. First performance of *La Virgen de Tepeyac*. Los Angeles Drama Critics Circle Award, 1971, to "El Teatro Campesino for embarking in new directions which include exploring Chicano cultural roots and substantially refining their craft and techniques in the process." ETC continues to perform *actos*. Ten-day second TENAZ Chicano Theater Festival (Los Angeles). *Los Corridos* workshops. ETC publishes collection of *actos* entitled, *Actos, El Teatro Campesino*.

1972
Half of the ETC ensemble returns to the World Theatre Festival, Nancy, France, and performs actos, while the other half remains in San Juan Bautista and then tours the Southwest.

First production of adapted Tully/Belasco *Rose of the Rancho* at the Teatro Calavera in San Juan. Production of Emmy Award-winning TV Special, *KNBC Special: El Teatro Campesino*, which includes filming of *Los vendidos*. Production of *La gran carpa cantinflesca*, *El velorio*, and *La pesadilla de cinco pesos*. *Corridos* and *Dark Root of a Scream* performed at Inner City Cultural Center in Los Angeles.

Colombian actor/playwright Enrique Buenaventura visits ETC.

"Fiesta de los Teatros Chicanos" (third TENAZ festival) on the Orange Coast College campus.

ETC hosts TENAZ workshop in San Juan Bautista.

1973
Host to Peter Brook and his Center for International Theater Research for an eight-week summer workshop. A joint production of *Conference of the Birds* goes on tour. New York and Midwest tour of *La carpa de los Rasquachis*. Fourth TENAZ Chicano Theater Festival (in San Jose).

Theater of the Sphere is developed as a concept evolved from Aztec and Mayan knowledge.

Valdez publishes *Pensamiento serpentino: A Chicano Approach to the Theater of Reality*.

1974
ETC tours the Southwest. Collective purchase of forty acres of land in San Juan; beginnings of a land cooperative.

ETC performs *El baile de los gigantes* and *La carpa* at the ancient pyramids of Teotihuacan as part of the Fifth Annual Chicano Theater Festival (TENAZ)/Primer Encuentro, Mexico City. ETC performs La carpa at the Mark Taper Forum in Los Angeles, and goes on tour.

Pastorela performed as a puppet show.

1975

ETC tapes PBS television special for national telecast, El Corrido. First draft of Viene la muerte cantando. U.S. tour of Fin del mundo #1 (the version based on indigenous philosophy). ETC breaks with TENAZ after the Sixth Annual Chicano Theater Festival in San Antonio, because of a conflict between Marxist and spiritualist tendencies.

ETC continues short-lived efforts at an agricultural collective. La Virgen de Tepeyac performed.

1976

ETC produces full-length Fin del mundo #2 (the version with UFW thematics) for national tour. ETC produces music and narration for the UFW film Fighting for Our Lives, which is nominated for an Academy Award as "Best Documentary Film." Tours of Western Europe with highly acclaimed La carpa de los Rasquachis, a bilingual musical dramatic production. That play is reworked and produced for television as El Corrido. Performances include Actos y canciones and other actos. Performance at the UFW Second Constitutional Convention.

Pastorela performed in the streets of San Juan.

1977

Some ETC ensemble members participate in the filming of Which Way is Up, a Universal Studios production starring Richard Pryor. New acto promoting the UFW, El botón. Mafiosos performed. Second production of Rose of the Rancho. First San Juan Bautista Día de los muertos (Day of the Dead) celebration.

Luis Valdez commissioned by the Mark Taper Forum to write and direct a new piece entitled Zoot Suit. He develops Zoot Suit through months of improvisational workshops with the ETC collective.

ETC performs Pastorela and Virgen de Tepeyac. "Ahora es cuando" radio show for UFW. Eighth Annual Chicano Theater Festival, in San Diego, California.

1978

Valdez and the ETC collective begin to go their separate ways, as Valdez is occupied with Zoot Suit at the Mark Taper Forum. ETC directorial duties are assumed by Socorro Valdez and the collective. ETC tours the Southwest with Fin del mundo #3 (a calavera play), and then Europe (summer tour of six countries) with La carpa de los Rasquachis. For the first time in its history ETC auditions actors.

ETC ensemble members are laid off for the first time in the company's history. Valdez opens Zoot Suit at the Aquarius Theater in Hollywood, winning numerous awards, including the Los Angeles Drama Critics Circle Award for Distinguished Production, eight Drama League awards for outstanding achievement in theater, a Nosotros Award, and a Nuestro Magazine award.

Olivia Chumacero directs first Migrant Children's Theater Project. Children's production wins Best Children's Theater Award at San Jose International Children's Festival. ETC stages Virgen de Tepeyac and Pastorela.

Fin del mundo #3 tours Europe and northwestern and southwestern United States.

ETC ensemble members form Conchero ritual dance group "Xinachtli," headed by Andrés Segura [this group continues until the present].

Mill Valley TENAZ Seminar.

TENAZ Talks Teatro newsletter begins publication, edited by Dr. Jorge Huerta.

1979

Zoot Suit, by Luis Valdez, becomes the first Chicano play to appear on Broadway. Valdez acquires a produce warehouse in San Juan Bautista from Zoot Suit profits, and establishes Luis Valdez, Inc.

ETC stages La Virgen del Tepeyac.

Tenth Annual Chicano Theater Festival, in Santa Barbara.

1980

Ronald Reagan becomes president, initiating a twelve-year period of conservative Republican rule that dismantles or weakens social programs and widens economic stratification.

ETC tours California and then Europe (four months) with Fin del mundo #4 (in Calavera with a new storyline). This production combines for the first time an equal number of ensemble core-group members with auditioned actors. ETC hosts Día de los muertos in San Juan. Performs Pastorela.

Carlo Mazzone-Clementi conducts commedia dell'arte workshop for ETC.

Following Zoot Suit, El Teatro Campesino ceases to exist as a collective ensemble and is transformed into a production company which auditions actors for occasional productions. Unlike the collective, the new production company accepts grants, among them an Institutional Advancement Grant from the Ford Foundation. The process of radical transformation includes installation of an administrative apparatus (filled by persons not formerly associated with the company) and a slowdown in artistic production.

TENAZ Seminar, in Fresno.

What follows no longer refers to the Teatro Campesino collective ensemble that existed from 1965 until 1980.

1981

Valdez's produce warehouse is converted into a theater and opens as the Teatro Campesino Playhouse, inaugurated with Rose of the Rancho, directed by Frank Condon.

Zoot Suit filmed at the Aquarius Theater in Los Angeles. Reopens in 1982 and plays for three weeks.

Bandido! The American Melodrama of Tiburcio Vásquez by Valdez plays for one week.

Eleventh International Chicano Latino Teatro Festival in San Francisco.

1982

The hard-won Agricultural Labor Relations Board is dismantled by Republican governor Deukmejian.

Corridos workshop and production in San Juan Bautista (much of it dating back to Los corridos in 1971). Virgen del Tepeyac.

Soldier Boy by S. Pérez and J. S. Pérez.

1983

Corridos opens at the Marine's Memorial Theater in San Francisco. Pastorela performed at the San Juan Bautista Mission. Don Juan Tenorio laboratory workshop by J. Bierman and M. Griggs.

1984

Corridos opens at the Variety Arts Theater in Los Angeles and later at Old Globe in San Diego. I Don't Have to Show You No Stinking Badges opens in Los Angeles.

1987

Corridos is filmed as a PBS production. Valdez's La Bamba is released.

1988

César Chávez conducts a thirty-day hunger strike as a "declaration of non-cooperation" with pesticide poisoning of agricultural workers and consumers. Grape boycott continues.

1989

ETC presents Fin del mundo (four performances), Passion Play, Pastorela, Rose of the Rancho, as well as Food for the Dead and Simply María (one-acts by Josefina López).

1990

Pastorela is filmed as a PBS special. Productions of Virgen de Tepeyac, Simply María, and Valdez's I Don't Have to Show You No Stinking Badges (at Teatro Campesino Playhouse and Marines' Memorial Theater).

ETC celebrates its twenty-fifth anniversary.

1992

ETC tours How Else Am I Supposed to Know I'm Still Alive by E. Fernández and Simply María.

Notes

1. El Teatro Campesino and the Mexican Popular Performance Tradition

1. Some of those elements have been enumerated by Nicolás Kanellos (1978), yet they are inventoried in piecemeal fashion and not conceptualized as a unified cultural field.

2. Particularly relevant and illuminating with regard to "oral culture" is Ong (1982).

3. On Felipe Cantú's death in 1989, Valdez once again issued a similar orientational statement concerning Cantú: "He combined the styles of Brecht and Cantinflas" (Valdez 1989). Brecht and Cantinflas here can be understood as "something like Brecht or Cantinflas." Brecht, however, cannot be regarded as a direct or indirect influence on Cantú since, for one thing, Cantú's formation predated any entry of Brechtian influence into the Chicano theater movement—or even the existence of the movement. Furthermore, Cantú's formation precluded any exposure to print culture (such as to Brecht): Cantú could not read. It might, in fact, be realistic to study the influence of the *carpa* on Brecht; he resided in California during the heyday of the *carpa* (1941–1947).

4. Although the young Valdez certainly *read* Brecht and was in some way influenced by him, two facts speak to Brecht's very marginal influence: (1) the Teatro Campesino aesthetic *and* performance pieces were collectively generated from a farmworker collective ensemble steeped in the Mexican popular performance tradition and entirely unfamiliar with Brecht. In other words, they came from the Cantinflas tradition; (2) much of what Brecht generated in the way of technique, theory, and plays came, in his own words, directly from popular culture traditions, which have affinities and resemblances worldwide, even though they originated and evolved entirely independently of each other. Common to many peoples, for example, is a comedic tradition. Many elements that critics immediately identify as "Brechtian" are, in fact, native folk comedy techniques. Hence, many techniques of Mexican comedian Cantinflas or English comedian Charlie Chaplin show a relationship to Brechtian theory, although in fact they predate Brecht and were certainly never influenced by him. What is more, Brecht never took credit for "inventing" the techniques that scholars have come to identify solely with him. The much-discussed and quoted *Verfremdungseffekt* (defamiliarization technique), for example, was nothing new or original with Brecht. Brecht himself refers to this technique as a common one within popular culture—chiefly the comedic tradition—as well as within Chinese theater. In his *Arbeitsjournal* he indicates: "gewisse verfremdungen stammen aus dem zeughaus der komödie, das 2000 jahre alt ist" [certain defamiliarization techniques are derived from the arsenal of comedy which is 2000 years old] (Brecht 1973:912). In *Der Messingkauf* he similarly states: "Der Versuch, dem Publikum die darzustellenden Vorgänge zu verfremden,

kann auf primitiver Stufe schon bei theatralischen und bildnerischen Veranstaltungen der alten Volksjahrmärkte angetroffen werden" [The attempt to defamiliarize the events portrayed to the public is evident in primitive form in theatrical and pictorial events found at traveling fairs] (Brecht 1967:619).

Although critics have quickly seized on the reference to Brecht and other European sources (e.g., commedia dell'arte), Valdez himself was quick to see the European traditions in terms of the Mexican one. He reverses the relationship that critics falsely establish by indicating how very much like Cantinflas Brecht is, or how the harlequin echoes the popular Mexican performance tradition (represented by Cantinflas). In other words, Valdez will admit to parallels, but not readily to influence:

> Then what Cantinflas was doing up there on the screen was a direct reflection of that audience. They identified with him. They reveled with him because he was dealing very directly in his humor—especially in his early movies—he was identifying with the low man on the totem pole, he was the victim of fate, and yet trying to survive in his own way, using his wits; outwitting the rich, outwitting the powerful, doing a double-talk that everybody knew was nonsense but it was imitative of education, it was imitative of being powerful. And so he became a very popular hero, and a magical hero to watch. There is some of that character, of the Cantinflas character, of the harlequin character in Brecht's work, here and there. Some of them are sometimes women. Mother Courage is a female Cantinflas, in her own way; if she is portrayed in a certain way, you can get that tragic-comic quality about her. Certainly some of the central figures in Brecht's anti-military plays, such as Man Is Man, are Cantinflas types.
>
> I guess the closest way for American audiences to see that is in English music hall Chaplinesque terms. For me as a Chicano I saw that in Cantinflas terms. . . .
>
> I think Brecht derived the alienation effect from the ancient roots of the theater. To the extent that I am drawing from my own ancient roots, it is there too.

These quotations and a discussion of Brecht and El Teatro Campesino are found in Broyles (1983), here pp. 39–40.

5. An excellent account of these developments can be found in El País de las Tandas (1987); Alonso (1987); and Bryan (1985).

6. The primacy of orality, of the reliance on memory for cultural survival, can well account for the resilience of Native American cultures even after the mass destruction of codices. Such codices provided a visual rendering of traditional memorized tribal knowledge. In other words, tribal knowledge did not depend on the written word for its own reproduction. Rather, it depended on human memory.

7. In this regard, Williams's conceptualization of culture as tradition and practice is relevant:

> Cultural work and activity are not now, in any ordinary sense, a superstructure: not only because of the depth and thoroughness at which any cultural hege-mony is lived, but because cultural tradition and practice are seen as much more than superstructural expressions—reflections, mediations, or typifi-cations—of a formed social and economic structure. On the contrary, they are

among the basic processes of the formation itself and, further, related to a much wider area of reality than the abstractions of "social" and "economic" experience. People seeing themselves and each other in directly personal relationships; people seeing the natural world and themselves in it; people using their physical and material resources for what one kind of society specializes to "leisure" and "entertainment" and "art": all these active experiences and practices, which make up so much of the reality of a culture and its cultural production can be seen as they are, without reduction to other categories of content, and without the characteristic straining to fit them (directly as reflection, indirectly as mediation or typification or analogy) to other and determining manifest economic and political relationships. (1977:111)

8. Although it may appear far-fetched functionally to equate *relajo* and the seriousness of miracles, their closeness in the life of the oppressed is concisely elaborated by de Certeau, who convincingly describes the oppositional nature of the indigenous tradition of miraculous narrative (de Certeau 1984:16–17).

9. This essential characteristic of the Mexican comic sketch is pointed out by Ybarra-Frausto (1983), who reproduces such a sketch.

10. Diego Durán, *Historia azteca*, II, p. 233, quoted in Garibay (1971:93–94).

11. Quoted in Rojas Garcidueñas (1935:25).

12. Quoted ibid., p. 26.

13. "Overland Via 'Jackass Mail' in 1858: The Diary of Phocion R. Way," ed. William A. Duffen, *Arizona and the West*, II, summer 1960, quoted in Gibson (1967:6).

14. Angel Garibay (1971:95) tells us of a melodramatic genre similar to the opera or Spanish *zarzuela*, which has existed since pre-Columbian days and which is documented in the *Cantares mexicanos*:

Esta era de orden más bien melodramática. Quiero decir, tenía mayor semejanza con nuestras obras teatrales del tenor de la ópera o la zarzuela que con las obras propiamente dramáticas en el sentido moderno. No había recitados, sino que todo era más bien acompañado con canto. La más cercana de nuestras producciones literarias de hoy día es el bailete, que reúne en un solo impulso el canto, la música y el baile. [It was of a melodramatic type. That is, it bore a greater resemblance to theatrical pieces like the opera or the *zarzuela* than to properly dramatic works in the modern sense of the word. There were no spoken parts, everything was accompanied with song. The closest thing to it within our present-day literary productions is the *bailete*, which unites song, music, and dance in one sole impulse.]

Theater researchers have not explored this genre and its probable impact on Mexican performance history.

15. This is from autobiographical notes written by Mario Moreno in the 1940s, quoted by Monsiváis (1988:84).

16. The latter *acto*, like most, remains unpublished. Indeed it was improvised to meet the needs of the day's politics. It is described in detail by Valdez (1966).

17. This is reported by García Cubas (1950). This quote is a paraphrase of García Cubas by Bryan (1985:7).

18. This is affirmed by participants in the life of the *carpa*, such as Granados (1984:14)

and Ortega (1984:17).

19. For my comments concerning the indigenous interpretation of our Lady of Guadalupe from the oral tradition I am grateful to the teachings of my *abuela*, Leopolda Rodríguez de Verdugo, and to the teachings of maestro Andrés Segura, a spiritual leader of the Conchero ritual dance tradition of the State of Mexico.

20. The long trajectory of a "Hispanic" professional theater in the United States is treated by Kanellos (1990) and by Ramírez (1990).

2. Theater of the Sphere: Toward the Formulation of a Native Performance Theory and Practice

1. Dissertations include Diamond (1977); Flores (1980, published in 1990); Huerta (1974, published 1982); Vega (1983).

2. They were not constituted as "scripts" but transmitted through human memory. El Teatro Campesino's heavily mimetic and visual (i.e., non-language-based) performance pieces make their rendering in published script form almost impossible. The one volume of published *actos* (El Teatro Campesino and Luis Valdez 1971)—each transcribed from a single performance—constitutes the extent of Teatro Campesino's published legacy. Those *actos* were republished in 1990, this time wholly appropriated as the work of Luis Valdez.

3. In his landmark book on Mexicano verbal art, Charles L. Briggs (1988) describes how oral performance genres connect the imaginary world and the real world through constant juxtaposition within the process of interpretation. This process applies equally to the work of El Teatro Campesino in which the audiences' and the performers' own lifeworld is interpreted in light of the semi-imaginary stage world. Briggs describes this process:

> The artist uses the spoken word to transport her or his audience to another world. Skillful use of stylized language prompts the hearer to look beyond appearances to grasp the meaning with which the creator has imbued this world. Such artists also have the ability to "read" the "real" world in which their audiences live and thus to find the sorts of imaginary scenes and existential problems that will fit the experiences of their interlocutors. The interpretive task that confronts the artist is thus two fold—interpreting both an imaginary sphere and the perceiver's own world. But oral performance has a third component as well. The gifted artist uses stylistic devices in such a way that the form and content of the performance reflect the artist's view of the way these two worlds, imaginary and real, are connected. (1988:2)

4. Neither the Teatro's use of the term "god" nor its use of "religion" are used to designate any particular religious institution or dogma concerning any "god." The concept of "religion," for example, is conceptualized with reference to its Latin root *religiön* (conscientiousness, piety), which is equivalent to *relig(āre)*, to tie, fasten; the practice of religion is the practice of tying back to some kind of central point, some central cosmic center.

5. The conception of the indissoluble unity of spirit and matter is common to much of world mythology. In the Mayan understanding the "spirit" (*K'inan*) is equated with "energy" whereas that which is manifest (matter) is "*pixan*," also called "soul." These terms are explained at length in Martínez Paredez (1977), especially the first four chapters.

6. Unless this is understood, no intellectual critical practice can do justice to the mythological dimensions of Teatro Campesino plays such as *La gran carpa de la familia Rasquachi* or *Fin del mundo*. For example, the common intellectual reification of metaphoric imagery has led some critics to argue against the stage presence of Quetzalcoatl through arguments against "divine intercession"—as if Quetzalcoatl were an entity in any way isolatable as historical fact, in any way outside the human characters. Quetzalcoatl is a paradigm of the way reality is constituted. Humans are the "Living Quetzalcoatl" to which Teatro Campesino refers in Theater of the Sphere.

Quetzalcoatl functions—for the Teatro—much like Christ. Hence the Teatro frequently equated the two. They are viewed as ultimately representing something within us. There is also a correspondence between El Teatro Campesino's understanding of Christ/Quetzalcoatl and Campbell's:

> Now, according to the normal way of thinking about the Christian religion, we cannot identify with Jesus, we have to imitate Jesus. To say, "I and the Father are one," as Jesus said, is blasphemy for us. However, in the Thomas gospel that was dug up in Egypt some forty years ago, Jesus says, "He who drinks from my mouth will become as I am, and I shall be he." Now, this is exactly Buddhism. We are all manifestations of Buddha consciousness, or Christ consciousness, only we don't know it. The word "Buddha" means "the one who waked up." We are all to do that—to wake up to the Christ or Buddha consciousness within us. This is blasphemy in the normal way of Christian thinking, but it is the very essence of Christian Gnosticism and the Thomas gospel. (1988:57)

7. What I refer to as an invisible realm of culture is roughly synonymous with what Williams (1973) calls "structure of feeling." It determines the real power of language, informs the symbolism of dress, the taste of food, the feel of music, a relationship to the sacred, and much more. It is nothing immutable; indeed the essence of Quetzalcoatl is change, symbolized by the shedding of the serpent's skin.

8. I offer here Martínez Paredez's own exposition of the inextricable links between mathematics, humans, and the sacred in Mayan culture:

> Un análisis de esta manera de pensar respecto del mundo abstracto y concreto; nos lleva de inmediato al nombre del REPTIL de ese CAN que simboliza el gran todo, en sus diversas manifestaciones, resultando bastante curioso encontrar que este símbolo quiere decir lo cósmico; que es el número 4; que es Círculo y Cuadrado; que es agua, fuego, aire y representa el MOVIMIENTO, y por último el hombre se considera un ser serpentino, es CAN o CHAN. Por lo tanto, ahí se encuentra la clave de toda la estructura de esa concepción referente a ese modo formal de ser. El pensador maya observó que el reptil vive en la tierra, en el agua y en el aire, lo cual le demostró de manera palmaria esa identificación ideal, al establecer comparaciones entre la forma ondulante de la marcha del ofidio y la marcha del Sol y la Luna, que van cambiando de posición en zig-zag; observó el curso de las aguas; la forma en que las llamas se retuercen y parecen serpientes en brama; comparó los rayos producidos por el choque de las nubes y, él no hizo nada más que pensar en las FORMAS que semejaban a las del SIGNIFICANTE y les dio su SIGNIFICADO, hizo de ello un símbolo TOTAL, por esto al invertir la palabra CAN, nos da NAC-LIMITE.

Mas la detenida observación del desarrollo de estas especulaciones mayas, nos van llevando a ese pensamiento medular que gira alrededor de lo serpentino, que representa la aritmética y la geometría, ambas que también supieron combinar para llevar a cabo sin grandes tropiezos sus cálculos. Es así como también nos damos cuenta de la profusión de figuras en sus construcciones y en sus escritos jeroglíficos, cuya presencia no es simplemente decorativa, sino de valor algebraico. Esto denuncia algo sorprendente y que se refiere al uso de figuras geométricas como números, de acuerdo con sus respectivas posiciones en los grabados pétreos o en sus documentos. Y aquí está pues, esa integración de las formas, y la razón de sus monumentos piramidales. [An analysis of this way of thinking with regard to the abstract and concrete world immediately leads us to the name of the REPTILE, of that "CAN" that symbolizes the Great All in all of its diverse manifestations. It is intriguing to discover that this symbol signifies the cosmic; which is the number four; which is the circle and square; which is water, fire, air and that it represents MOVEMENT; and ultimately human beings are regarded as serpentine beings, that is, CAN or CHAN. As such, this provides the key to the entire structure of a conceptualization of being. Mayan thinkers observed that reptiles live on the earth, in the water, and in the air. That demonstrated in a clear way that this was an ideal basis of identification, in the establishment of comparisons between the undulating form of a serpent's movement and of the movement of the sun and the moon, which change their position in zigzag form; Mayan thinkers observed the movement of the waters; the ways in which flames writhe and look like serpents in heat; they compared the lightning produced by the clash of clouds. All that brought to mind the FORMS that resembled those of what was SIGNIFICANT and that gave everything its SIGNIFICANCE. Those thinkers created a TOTAL symbol. That is why when we invert the word CAN we get NAC=LIMIT.

An even closer observation of the development of this Mayan speculative thought leads us to that basic thinking that encircles the idea of the serpentine: arithmetic and geometry. Mayan thinkers understood how to combine both for the purposes of carrying out their calculations without error. As such we can also see the profusion of figures (numbers) in their architecture and in their written hieroglyphics. Those figures are not simply decorative, but rather have algebraic value. This reveals something startling, which has to do with the use of geometric figures as numbers, according to their respective positions within stone inscriptions or in Mayan documents. Hence, we see an integration of forms and the reasoning behind pyramidal monuments. (1976:172–173)

9. This coincides with the thinking of Che Guevara, who expressed the view that all revolutionary action must be propelled by a profound love and not hatred.

10. In Teatro Campesino usage, terms such as the "Creator" or "god" (usually rendered with the pronoun "he"), "Quetzalcoatl"/"Christ" are not anthropomorphic entities. Even historical figures such as Christ or Quetzalcoatl function as myths or stories. The myth of Quetzalcoatl or the myths of Christ both tell exemplary stories, which dramatize relationships (desirable and undesirable) between persons, within society and nature. They are metaphorical and symbolic of teachings concerning many life dimensions.

11. For those who seek to cultivate a more thorough understanding there are various possibilities: (1) consultation with former Teatro Campesino ensemble members who participated in the development of this aesthetic or philosophy of life, particularly Julio González and Olivia Chumacero. The latter occasionally teaches workshops on Theater of the Sphere and on the Rasquachi Aesthetic at the University of California at Santa Cruz and at Santa Barbara; (2) the Teatro Campesino Papers and Luis Valdez Papers housed (but inaccessible) at the University of California, Santa Barbara Library (Colección Tloque Nahuaque Unit).

12. Unless otherwise indicated, this and all subsequent Teatro Campesino quotations pertaining to the Veinte Pasos are derived from a notebook (handwritten and typescript) entitled "El coco serpentino," owned by Olivia Chumacero (n.d.). I thank her for making it available to me.

13. The word *sense* is used here in the most encompassing of ways, including physical sensation, feeling, perception, meaning, conscious awareness, mental capacity, judgment, and intuition.

14. Campbell (1988:57) similarly describes the relationship between the inner world and the outer world: "all of these wonderful poetic images of mythology are referring to something in you. When your mind is simply trapped by the image out there so that you never make the reference to yourself, you have misread the image.

"The inner world is the world of your requirements and your energies and your structure and your possibilities that meets the outer world. And the outer world is the field of your incarnation. That's where you are. You've got to keep both going."

15. It is interesting that these three spheres correspond to the three "spheres" of Kant, Weber, and Habermas: the aesthetic, the natural, and the moral. The Theater of the Sphere project integrates better than Habermas these three spheres into one, while Habermas's three spheres, for example, leave the aesthetic cut off from its political possibilities. Habermas, for example, would put Theater of the Sphere under the autonomous discourse of "expert culture" as a sphere of its own, while the Theater of the Sphere, in my assessment, allows a view of aesthetic, moral, and natural reintegration into an organic whole.

16. This construction of an alternative culture constitutes a tactic of alternative hegemony that Gramsci (1971) would doubtlessly have included within his concept of "war of position" as opposed to the physical violence of what he conceptualized as "war of movement." He regarded methods of "war of position" as molecular or covert advance (toward a new humanity) of the more progressive subaltern classes.

3. Toward a Re-Vision of Chicana/o Theater History: The Roles of Women in El Teatro Campesino

In its preliminary form, this essay was presented by invitation of the University of Arizona's Renato Rosaldo Lecture Series in 1982. A longer version, which included the discussion of the 1983 *Corridos*, was presented at the twelfth annual National Association for Chicano Studies Conference, 1984, in Austin, Texas. This paper appeared in published form in the proceedings of that 1984 conference, published in 1986 as "Women in El Teatro Campesino: "¿Apoco Estaba Molacha la Virgen de Guadalupe?" in *Chicana Voices: Intersections of Class, Race, and Gender*. Two important articles on Chicanas in the Teatro by Yvonne Yarbro-Bejarano appeared at roughly the same time (1985–1986) although not in time to include them in my own published pieces. The findings in this chapter on the women of El Teatro Campesino essentially date back to 1984. This chapter was republished in 1989 in *Making a Spectacle*, and is published here as a "historical" piece, with some changes. For additional elaboration on Chicanas in the Teatro see Yarbro-Bejarano (1985, 1986).

1. Similar phrases recur in writings on the Teatro. I have used these, from Cárdenas de Dwyer (1979), for the sake of illustration.

2. As a sequel to this chapter: Socorro Valdez discontinued all theatrical activity and her ties to the Teatro Campesino for a period of almost ten years after the *Corridos* production. In spring 1992 the Teatro Campesino produced and toured (mainly at university campuses) two one-act plays written by two women and directed by Socorro Valdez: *Simply María* (by Josefina López) and *How Else Am I Supposed to Know I'm Still Alive* (by Evelina Fernández). Although this touring production represents largely the work of women, the Teatro Campesino's publicity material highlights the past glory and accomplishments of Luis Valdez. In characteristic fashion, none of the publicity of the Santa Barbara performances mentions Socorro Valdez. The UCSB poster fails to mention Evelina Fernández entirely, while it includes a lengthy description of Luis Valdez and "his company." Nonetheless this Teatro Campesino production featuring the work of women was a welcome if long-overdue change.

4. El Teatro Campesino: From Alternative Theater to Mainstream

1. The handful of *Corrido* reviews by Chicanas/os are relatively brief. These include Burciaga 1983; Robles Segura 1983; Díaz 1984; Morton 1984; Sánchez 1985.

2. The previous high total of $337,512 was set by *For Colored Girls Who Have Considered Suicide When the Rainbow is Enuf* ("*Zoot Suit* Breaks Mark Taper Mark" 1978).

3. This has repeatedly been expressed to me in conversations with cast members.

4. Part of the reason is that the stage techniques of *Zoot Suit* were, in Luis Valdez's opinion, inspired by cinematic technique. As happens in film, the play *Zoot Suit* handles transitions with split-second timing. Instead of blackouts as transitional devices there is a continuous flow of action between scenes. These transitions—in the movie as in the stage version—are facilitated primarily by the omniscient *pachuco* character. The stage version was also immensely successful at achieving precise visual focus, although this feat is much more easily accomplished with a camera.

5. Very important dimensions of this complex problem are treated in an issue of the journal *Cultural Studies* (Fregoso/Chabram 1990).

6. This approach to telling the Teatro Campesino story is repeated in numerous articles, among them Yarbro-Bejarano (1979).

Bibliography

Unpublished Sources

ORAL HISTORIES
Cantú, Felipe. 3/22–3/25/1983. Interview. Fresno.
Chávez, César. 3/7/1993. Interview. La Paz.
Chumacero, Olivia. 1/19/1983. Interview. San Juan Bautista.
————. 3/22/1983. Interview. Fresno.
————. 8/18/1989. Interview. Santa Clara.
Chumacero, Olivia, and Diane Rodríguez. 6/7/1980. Interview. Strasbourg.
Delgado, José. 12/9/1983. Interview. San Juan Bautista.
Delgado, José, and Phillip Esparza. 8/10/1983. Interview. San Juan Bautista.
Delgado, Roberta. 7/21/1983. Interview. San Juan Bautista and Gilroy.
Lira, Agustín. 3/22/1983. Interview. Fresno.
Parra, Yolanda. 12/21/1982. Interview. San Juan Bautista.
Rodríguez, Diane. 12/28/1983. Interview. San Juan Bautista.
Valdez, Luis. 1/22/1983. Interview. San Juan Bautista.
Valdez, Luis. 5/5/1983. With María Emilia Martín. California Public Radio.
Valdez, Socorro. 3/1/1983. Interview. San Juan Bautista.

OTHER UNPUBLISHED SOURCES
Belasco, David, and Richard Tully. 1977. *The Rose of the Rancho*. Adapted by Luis Valdez and César Flores. TS. San Juan Bautista. Teatro Campesino Archives.
Cantú, Norma. 1982. "The Offering and the Offerers: A Generic Illocation of a Laredo Pastorela in the Tradition of Shepherds' Plays." Ph.D. dissertation, University of Nebraska.
Chumacero, Olivia. N.d. "El coco serpentino." MS and TS. Personal archive, Olivia Chumacero.
Diamond, Betty Ann.1977. "Brown-eyed Children of the Sun: The Cultural Politics of El Teatro Campesino." Ph.D. dissertation, University of Wisconsin, Madison.
Dunsmore de Carrillo, Patricia. 1977. Interview with Luis Valdez. Santa Barbara, 2/11. Tape recording, personal archive, Yolanda Broyles-González.
Flores, Richard R. 1989. "'Los Pastores': Performance, Poetics, and Politics in Folk Drama." Ph.D. dissertation, University of Texas at Austin.
Gibson, Rosemary. 1967. "The History of Tucson Theater before 1906." Ph.D. dissertation, University of Arizona.

González, Jorge. N.d. "Pensamiento serpentino: A Cultural Trampa or Is the Teatro Campesino Campesino?" TS. Personal archive, Yolanda Broyles-González.
Guernica, Antonio. 1981. "U.S. Hispanics—A Market Profile." Positioning Zoot Suit. Universal Studios.
Rose, Margaret Eleanor. 1988. "Women in the United Farm Workers: A Study of Chicana and Mexicana Participation in a Labor Union 1950–1980." Ph.D. dissertation, University of California, Los Angeles.
El Teatro Campesino. N.d. "Teatro Campesino Workshop." TS. Personal archive, Olivia Chumacero.
El Teatro Campesino Research Group. 1973. Notes. TS. Personal archive, Olivia Chumacero.
"El Teatro Campesino. Renacimiento." 1976. TS. 6/7. Personal archive, Olivia Chumacero.
Valdez, Luis. 1984a. Regents Lecture. University of California, Irvine. 10/25.
———. 1984b. Regents Lecture. University of California, Irvine. 10/26.
———. 1984c. Regents Lecture. University of California, Irvine. 10/31.
———. 1984d. Regents Lecture. University of California, Irvine. 11/1.
———. 1984e. Regents Lecture. University of California, Irvine. 11/2.
Valdez, Luis, and El Teatro Campesino.1975. "Huracán y el Poder." TS. 3/7. Personal archive, Olivia Chumacero.
Vega, Manuel de Jesús. 1983. "El Teatro Campesino y la vanguardia teatral: 1965–1975." Ph.D. dissertation, Middlebury College.
Woodruff, Virginia. 1979. Channel 10 Broadcast. 3/25. TS. Personal archive, Olivia Chumacero.

Published Sources

Acuña, Rudy. 1988. Occupied America: A History of Chicanos. New York: Harper and Row.
Alonso, Enrique. 1987. María Conesa. Mexico City: Océano.
Bakhtin, Mikhail. 1984. Rabelais and His World. Translated by Hélène Iswolsky. Bloomington: Indiana University Press.
Bandido program. 1981/1982. El Teatro Campesino Playhouse, San Juan Bautista.
Beebe, Greg. 1977. "'Rose of the Rancho' Offers Humor, Insight." Santa Cruz Sentinel (7/3), p. 25.
Benavídez, Max. 1993. "César Chávez Nurtured Seeds of Art." Los Angeles Times (4/28), section F, p. 1.
Benitel, Tomás. 1978. "Facing the Issues beyond Zoot Suit." Neworld 4:34–38.
Benjamin, Walter. 1966. "Der Autor als Produzent." In Versuche über Brecht, pp. 95–116. Frankfurt: Suhrkamp.
Bertolt Brecht Poems. 1976. Edited by J. Willett and Ralph Manheim. London: Eyre Methuen.
Boal, Augusto. 1976. "Categorías de teatro popular." In Teatro popular de Nuestra América, pp. 5–21. Cuernavaca: Cuadernos del Pueblo, Ediciones Mascarones.
Bondy, Filip. 1979. "Zoot Suit Collapses under Its Weighty Subject Matter." Patterson News (3/27).
Braverman, Harry. 1982. "The Degradation of Work in the Twentieth Century." Monthly Review (May):1–13.
Brecht, Bertolt. 1967. "Der Messingkauf." In Gesammelte Werke 16. Schriften zum Theater 2. Frankfurt: Suhrkamp.

————. 1973. *Arbeitsjournal*. Vol. 2. Frankfurt: Suhrkamp.

————. 1981. "Fragen eines lesenden Arbeiters." *Die Gedichte von Bertolt Brecht in einem Band*, p. 656. Frankfurt: Suhrkamp.

Briggs, Charles. 1988. *Competence in Performance: The Creativity of Tradition in Mexicano Verbal Art*. Philadelphia: University of Pennsylvania Press.

Broyles, Yolanda Julia. 1983. "Brecht: The Intellectual Tramp. An Interview with Luis Valdez." *Communications from the International Brecht Society* 12, no. 2:33–44.

————. 1984. "Hinojosa's *Klail City y sus alrededores*: Oral Culture and Print Culture." In *The Rolando Hinojosa Reader*, edited by J. D. Saldívar, pp. 109–132.(= *Revista Chicano-Riqueña*, XII/3–4).

Broyles-González, Yolanda. 1986. "Women in El Teatro Campesino: '¿Apoco estaba molacha la Virgen de Guadalupe?'" In *Chicana Voices: Intersections of Class, Race, and Gender*, edited by Teresa Córdoba et al., pp. 162–187. Austin: Center for Mexican American Studies.

————. 1989. "Toward a Re-Vision of Chicano Theater History: The Women of El Teatro Campesino." In *Making a Spectacle: Feminist Essays on Contemporary Women's Theatre*, edited by Lynda Hart, pp. 209–238. Ann Arbor: University of Michigan Press.

————. 1990. "What Price 'Mainstream'? Luis Valdez' Corridos on Stage and Film." *Cultural Studies* 4, no. 3:281–293.

Bryan, Susan. 1985. "The Commercialization of the Theater in Mexico and the Rise of the *Teatro Frívolo* (Frivolous Theater)." *Studies in Latin American Popular Culture* 5:1–18.

Burciaga, José Antonio. 1983. "Corridos—Sad and Happy Masks." *Hispanic Link* 5/15:4.

"Califas, Chicano Art and Culture in California." 1982. Final Report to the National Endowment for the Humanities. (4/18) TS. Oakes College.

Campa, Arthur. 1934. *Spanish Religious Folktheater in the Spanish Southwest*. (First Cycle). Albuquerque: University of New Mexico Press.

Campbell, Joseph. 1988. *The Power of Myth*. Edited by B. S. Flowers. New York: Doubleday.

Carballido, Emilio. 1988. "Editorial: El Eslabon." *Tramoya. Cuaderno de Teatro*, new series 14–15:2.

Cárdenas de Dwyer, Carlota. 1979. "The Development of Chicano Drama and Luis Valdez' Actos." In *Modern Chicano Writers*, edited by Joseph Sommers and Tomás Ybarra-Frausto, pp. 160–166. Englewood Cliffs: Prentice-Hall.

————, ed. 1975. *Chicano Voices*. Boston: Houghton Mifflin.

Castañeda Shular, Antonia; Tomás Ybarra-Frausto; and Joseph Sommers, eds. 1972. *Literatura chicana. Texto y contexto*. Englewood Cliffs: Prentice-Hall.

Clurman, Harold. 1979. "Theater." *The Nation* (4/21).

Coe, Richard. 1979. "City Cowboys and the West Coast Stage." *Washington Post* (3/25).

Cole, Doug. 1979. "New York, New York." *Drama-Logue* (3/2–8).

"Conference in Shubert Alley." 1979. *The New Yorker* (2/19), pp. 29–31.

Corona, Bert. 1983. "Chicano Scholars and Public Issues in the United States in the Eighties." In *History, Culture and Society: Chicano Studies*, edited by Mario García et al., pp. 11–18. Ypsilanti, Mich.: Bilingual Review Press.

Corry, John. 1979. "Broadway." *New York Times* (3/30).

Covarrubias, Miguel. 1938. "Slapstick and Venom: Politics, Tent Shows and Comedians." *Theatre Arts Monthly* 22, no. 8:587–596.

Currie, Glenn. 1979. "*Zoot Suit*: Damp Cracker on Broadway." *News World* (3/29).

[Also in the Times Herald (3/30/1979); United Press International.]
Daniel, Cletus E. 1981. Bitter Harvest: A History of California Farmworkers, 1870–1941.
    Berkeley and Los Angeles: University of California Press.
Day, Mark. 1971. Forty Acres: César Chávez and the Farm Workers. New York: Praeger.
de Certeau, Michel. 1984. The Practice of Everyday Life. Translated by Steven Randall.
    Berkeley and Los Angeles: University of California Press.
Delgado, José. 1977. "El Teatro." TENAZ Festival program, pp. 24–29.
Díaz, Katherine A. 1984. "Corridos: A Review." Caminos (Dec.), p. 12.
Drake, Sylvie. 1978. "Zoot Suit at the Taper." Los Angeles Times (8/18), part IV.
———. 1979. "Broadway Cool to Zoot Suit." Los Angeles Times (3/27), part IV, pp. 1–2.
———. 1979. "Zoot Suit Keeps Chin Up Despite Negative Reviews." Los Angeles Times
    (4/8), Calendar, p. 62.
———. 1980. "Endowment Challenge: The Gift That Keeps on Giving." Los Angeles
    Times (12/18), part VI.
Dunne, John Gregory. 1967. Delano: The Story of the California Grape Strike. New York:
    Farrar, Straus & Giroux.
Eagleton, Terry. 1976. Criticism and Ideology: A Study in Marxist Literary Theory. London:
    Verso.
Eder, Richard. 1979. "Theater: Zoot Suit, Chicano Music-Drama." The New York Times
    (3/26), part C, p. 13.
Engstrom, Paul. 1982. "El Teatro Campesino." Salinas Californian (4/29), p. 23A.
Fanon, Frantz. 1967. Black Skin, White Masks. Translated by Charles Markmann. New
    York: Grove Press.
———. 1968. The Wretched of the Earth. New York: Grove. [1961]
Feingold, Michael. 1979. "Truth in Melodrama." The Village Voice (4/2), p. 89.
"First Hispanic-American Show on Broadway: Zoot Suit. Luis Valdez Talks about
    the Show, the Critics, the Audiences." 1979. New York Theatre Review (May),
    pp. 22–23.
Flores, Arturo. 1990. El Teatro Campesino de Luis Valdez (1965–1980). Madrid: Editorial
    Pliegos.
Forbes, Jack. 1973. "Mexican Religion and Philosophy." In Aztecas del norte: The Chicanos
    of Aztlán, edited by Jack Forbes, pp. 48–69. Greenwich, Conn.: Fawcett
    Publications.
Frank, André Gunder. 1969. Latin America: Underdevelopment or Revolution. New York and
    London: Monthly Review Press.
Fregoso, Rosa Linda. 1993. The Bronze Screen: Chicana and Chicano Film Culture. Minneapolis:
    University of Minnesota Press.
Fregoso, Rosa Linda, and Angie Chabram, eds. 1990. "Chicana/o Cultural
    Representations: Reframing Alternative Critical Discourse." Cultural Studies 4, no.
    3.
Gabriel, Teshome. 1988. "Thoughts on Nomadic Aesthetics and the Black
    Independent Cinema." In Critical Perspectives on Black Independent Cinema, edited by
    M. Cham and C. Andrade-Watkins, pp. 62–79. Boston: MIT Press.
García, Richard. 1978. "Do Zoot Suiters Deserve Hoorays?" Los Angeles Times (8/27),
    part V.
García Cubas, Antonio. 1950. El libro de mis recuerdos, anécdotas y de costumbres mexicanas
    anteriores al actual estado social. Mexico City: Patria. [1885]
Garibay, Angel. 1971. Panorama literario de los pueblos nahuas. Mexico City: Editorial Porrúa.

Gill, Brendan. 1979. "Borrowings." *The New Yorker* (4/2), p. 94.

Girard, Raphael. 1979. *Esotericism of the Popol Vuh.* Translated by B. A. Moffett. Pasadena: Theosophical University Press.

Goldsmith, Len. 1978. "Zoot Suit: A Piece of Los Angeles History." *Daily Signal/Daily Southeast News* (8/18).

Gottfried, Martin. 1979. "Zoot Suit." *Cue New York* (4/27). [Also in *Saturday Review* (5/26/1979).]

Gramsci, Antonio. 1971. *Selections from the Prison Notebooks of Antonio Gramsci.* Edited and translated by Quintin Hoare and Geoffrey Smith. London: Lawrence and Wishart.

Granados, Pedro. 1984. *Carpas de México. Leyendas, anécdotas e historia del teatro popular.* Mexico City: Editorial Universo.

Guevara, Che. 1968. *El diario del Che en Bolivia.* Mexico City: Siglo Veintiuno Editores.

Hall, Stuart. 1988. "New Ethnicities." *ICA Documents* 7, pp. 27–30.

Harth, Dorothy, and Lewis M. Baldwin, eds. 1974. *Voices of Aztlán: Chicano Literature of Today.* New York: Mentor Books.

Hernández, Gina. 1990. "Que Viva El Teatro Campesino!" *Unity* (12/17), pp. 6–7.

Herridge, Frances. 1979. "Valdez Hopes His 'Zoot' Suits the B'way Audience." *New York Post* (3/23).

Horcasitas, Fernando. 1974. *El Teatro Náhuatl. Epocas novohispana y moderna.* Primera Parte. Mexico City: Universidad Nacional Autónoma de México.

Huerta, Jorge. 1978. "Tenaz Talks Teatro." *El Tecolote*, supplement, 1, no. 2.

———. 1982. *Chicano Theater: Themes and Forms.* Ypsilanti, Mich.: Bilingual Review Press.

Hughes, Catharine. 1979. "Mixed Bags." *America* (4/21).

Kalem, T. E. 1979. "Threads Bare." *Time* (4/9).

Kanellos, Nicolás. 1978. "Folklore in Chicano Theater and Chicano Theater as Folklore." *Journal of the Folklore Institute* 15, no. 1: 57–82.

———. 1990. *A History of Hispanic Theatre in the United States: Origins to 1940.* Austin: University of Texas Press.

———, ed. 1983. *Mexican American Theater: Then and Now.* Houston: Arte Publico (appeared as issue of *Revista Chicano-Riqueña* XI/1).

Kauffmann, Stanley. 1979. "Stanley Kauffmann on Theater." *The New Republic* (4/21).

Kerr, Walter. 1979. "Zoot Suit Loses Its Way in Bloodless Rhetoric." *The New York Times* (4/1), part 2, pp. 3, 20.

Kroll, Jack. 1979. "Heartbeats from the Barrio." *Newsweek* (4/9), pp. 85–86.

Lawson, Carol. 1978. "Zoot Suit Seeks Hispanic 'Sí'." *The New York Times* (12/27).

———. 1979. "'Loose Ends' Is Title—and Situation." *The New York Times* (4/25).

Leggett, John C. 1991. *Mining the Fields: Farm Workers Fight Back.* Highland Park, N.J.: Raritan Institute.

León-Portilla, Miguel. 1959. "Teatro Nahuatl Prehispánico." *La Palabra y el Hombre* 9:13–36.

———. 1974. *La filosofía náhuatl.* Mexico City: Universidad Nacional Autónoma de México.

le Sourd, Jacques. 1978. "Two Openings: One Sizzles, One Fizzles." *Reporter Dispatch* (4/1).

———. 1979. "Californian Drama Zoot Suit Tells of Chicano Oppression." *Standard Star* (3/26).

Levy, Jacques E. 1975. *César Chávez: Autobiography of La Causa.* New York: W. W. Norton.

Lewis, Barbara. 1979. "*Zoot Suit*: Black Experience with Chicano Accent." *New York Amsterdam News* (4/14), p. 25.

Limón, José. 1977. "Agringado Joking in Texas-Mexican Society: Folklore and Differential Identity." *The New Scholar* 6:33–50.

———. 1982. "History, Chicano Joking, and the Varieties of Higher Education: Tradition and Performance as Critical Symbolic Action." *Journal of the Folklore Institute* 19:141–166.

———. 1983. "Folklore, Social Conflict, and the United States–Mexico Border." In *Handbook of American Folklore*, edited by Richard M. Dorson, pp. 216–226. Bloomington: Indiana University Press.

———. 1982–1983. "Texas-Mexican Popular Music and Dancing: Some Notes on History and Symbolic Process." *Latin American Music Review* 3–4:229–245.

McWilliams, Carey. 1939. *Factories in the Field: The Story of Migratory Farm Labor in California*. Boston: Little, Brown.

———. 1973. *Southern California: An Island on the Land*. Salt Lake City: G. M. Smith: Peregrine Smith.

María y Campos, Armando de. 1939. *Los payasos, poetas de pueblo*. Mexico City: Ediciones Botas.

———. 1956. *El teatro de género chico en la revolución mexicana*. Mexico City: Talleres Gráficos de la Nación.

———. 1985. *Pastorelas mexicanas: su origen, historia y tradición*. Mexico City: Editorial Diana.

Martínez Paredez, Domingo. 1960. *Un continente y una cultura. Unidad filológia de la América prehispana*. Mexico City: Editorial Poesía de América.

———. 1964. *Hunab Ku: síntesis del pensamiento filosófico maya*. Mexico City: Editorial Orión.

———. 1976. *El Popol Vuh tiene razón. Teoría sobre la cosmogonía preamericana*. Mexico City: Editorial Orión.

———. 1977. *Parapsicología maya*. Mexico City: Porrúa.

Matthiessen, Peter. 1969. *Sal Si Puedes: César Chávez and the New American Revolution*. New York: Random House.

Memmi, Albert. 1967. *The Colonizer and the Colonized*. Boston: Beacon Press. [1957]

Miller, Marjorie. 1978. "*Zoot Suit* Pulls the Nostalgic and the Curious." *Los Angeles Times* (7/31), part II, pp. 1–2.

Mines, Richard, and Philip L. Martin. 1986. *A Profile of California Farmworkers*. Giannini Information Series, no. 86–2. Oakland: Giannini Foundation of Agricultural Economics, University of California.

Monsiváis, Carlos. 1988. *Escenas de pudor y liviandad*. Mexico City: Editorial Grijalbo.

Morales, Miguel Angel. 1987. *Cómicos de México*. Mexico City: Panorama Editorial.

Morton, Carlos. 1984. "Critical Response to *Zoot Suit* and *Corridos*." El Paso: University of Texas at El Paso Occasional Paper Series, no. 2.

Nelson, Eugene. 1966. *Huelga: The First Hundred Days of the Great Delano Grape Strike*. Delano, Calif.: Farm Worker Press.

O'Conner, John. 1967. "The Theater: Shades of the 30s." *Wall Street Journal* (7/24).

Ong, Walter. 1982. *Orality and Literacy: The Technologizing of the Word*. London and New York: Methuen.

Orona-Córdova, Roberta. 1983. "*Zoot Suit* and the Pachuco Phenomenon. An Interview with Luis Valdez." *Kanellos* 1983:95–111.

Ortega, Luis. 1984. "Introduction." In *Carpas de México Leyendas, anécdotas e historia del teatro popular*, edited by Pedro Granados, pp. 3–18. Mexico City: Editorial Universo.

Otten, Ted. 1979. "*Zoot Suit* Stands on Its Own." *P.S.* (3/28).
El país de las tandas: teatro de revista 1900–1940. 1987. Mexico City: Museo Nacional de Culturas Populares.
Paredes, Américo. 1958. *"With His Pistol in His Hand": A Border Ballad and Its Hero.* Austin: University of Texas Press.
————. 1966. "The Anglo-American in Mexican Folklore." In *New Voices in American Studies*, edited by Ray Browne, pp. 113–128. Lafayette, Ind.: Purdue University Studies.
————. 1970. "Proverbs and Ethnic Stereotypes." *Proverbium* 15:511–513.
————. 1978. "On Ethnographic Work among Minority Groups: A Folklorist's Perspective." In *New Directions in Chicano Scholarship*, edited by R. Romo and R. Paredes, pp. 1–32. La Jolla: Chicano Studies Center, University of California, San Diego.
————. 1982. "Folklore, lo Mexicano, and Proverbs." *Aztlán* 13:1–11.
Peña, Manuel. 1980. "Ritual Structure in a Chicano Dance." *Latin American Music Review* 1:47–73.
————. 1985. *The Texas-Mexican Conjunto: History of a Working-Class Music.* Austin: University of Texas Press.
Pérez, Pedro. 1981. "Zoot Suit Review." *La Voz* (10/10) (California State University Fresno), p. 8.
Portilla, Jorge. 1966. *Fenomenología del relajo, y otros ensayos.* Mexico City: Ediciones Era.
Portillo, Rose. 1992. "Frida and Diego: A Personal Stirring." *Los Angeles Times* (8/17).
"Positioning *Zoot Suit*." 1981. Universal Studios marketing report.
Rabkin, Gerald. 1979. "Breaking the Barrios." *Soho Weekly News* (4/5–11), p. 60.
Rael, Juan B. 1965. *The Sources and Diffusion of the Mexican Shepherds' Plays.* Guadalajara: Librería la Joyita.
Ramírez, Elizabeth Cantú. 1990. *Footlights across the Border: A History of Spanish-Language Professional Theater in Texas, 1873–1935.* New York: Peter Lang.
Reyna, José R. 1980. *Raza Humor: Chicano Joke Tradition in Texas.* San Antonio: Penca.
Riley, Clayton. 1979. "*Zoot Suit* on the Great White Way." *Los Angeles Times* (6/3), Calendar, p. 3.
Robles Segura, Margarita. 1983. "Corridos: Perpetuating El Rancho." *Tecolote Literary Magazine* 4:8.
Rodríguez, Alberto, ed. N.d. *Teatro chicano: cuadernos del Pueblo 6.* Mexico City: Cuernavaca.
Rojas Garciadueñas, José. 1935. *El teatro de Nueva España en el siglo XVI.* Mexico City: n.p.
Ross, Fred. 1989. *Conquering Goliath: César Chávez at the Beginning.* Keene, Calif.: United Farm Workers; distributed by El Taller Gráfico.
Sahagún, Bernardino de. 1982. *Florentine Codex (General History of the Things of New Spain).* Vol. I, pt. 1: *Introductions and Indices.* Translated by Charles E. Dibble. Santa Fe: School of American Research and University of Utah.
Said, Edward. 1983. *The World, the Text, and the Critic.* Cambridge: Harvard University Press.
Sánchez, Rosaura. 1985. "Corridos: A New Folk Musical." *Crítica* 1, no. 2. (Spring): 131–133.
Sandi, Luis. 1938. "The Story Retold: Chronicle of the Theatre in Mexico." *Theatre Arts Monthly* 22, no. 8:611–617.
Segura, Andrés. 1973. "Continuidad de la tradición filosófica náhuatl en las danzas de Concheros." *El Cuaderno* 3, no. 1:16–33.

Shank, Theodore. 1974. "A Return to Mayan and Aztec Roots." *Drama Review* 18, no. 4:56–70.

Sharp, Christopher. 1979. N.t. *Women's Wear Daily* (3/27).

Shibley, George. 1979. "Sleepy Lagoon: The True Story." *Westword* (1/15), p. 88.

Simon, John. 1979. "West Coast Story." *New York Magazine* (4/9), p. 93.

Stone, Judy. 1982. "Bandido." *San Francisco Chronicle* (1/1).

Sullivan, Dan. 1977. "'Rose' by El Teatro Campesino." *Los Angeles Times* (7/8), part IV, p. 1.

———. 1978. *"Zoot Suit* at the Taper Forum." *Los Angeles Times* (4/24), part IV, pp. 1, 11.

"The Talk of the Town: Actos." 1967. *The New Yorker* (8/19).

El Teatro Campesino. 1989. *Teatro Campesino Newsletter* (5/15). San Juan Bautista.

El Teatro Campesino and Luis Valdez. 1971. *Actos*. San Juan Bautista: Menyah Productions. [Reprinted in Valdez (1990).]

Thompson, Thomas. 1979. "A Dynamo Named Gordon Davison." *The New York Times Magazine* (3/11).

Tía Cleta. 1974. Nos. 4–9.

Tobar, Hector. 1993. "Mexican Actor Cantinflas of 'Around the World' Dies." *Los Angeles Times* (4/21), section A, p. 8.

Trombetta, Jim. 1981. *"Zoot Suit* and Its Real Defendants." *Los Angeles Times* (10/11), Calendar, p. 4.

Valdez, Luis. 1966. "Theatre: El Teatro Campesino." *Ramparts* (July):55–56.

———. 1971a. "The Actos." In *Actos*, edited by El Teatro Campesino and Luis Valdez, pp. 5–6. [Reprinted in Valdez (1990).]

———. 1971b. "Notes on Chicano Theater." In *Actos*, edited by El Teatro Campesino and Luis Valdez, pp. 1–4. [Reprinted in Valdez (1990).]

———. 1972a. "La plebe." In *Aztlán: An Anthology of Mexican American Literature*, edited by L. Valdez and S. Steiner, pp. xiii–xxxiv.

———. 1972b. "El Teatro Campesino." In *Aztlán: An Anthology of Mexican American Literature*, edited by L. Valdez and S. Steiner, pp. 359–361.

———. 1973. *Pensamiento serpentino*. San Juan Bautista: Cucaracha Publications. [Reprinted in Valdez (1990).]

———. 1978a. "From a Pamphlet to a Play." *Zoot Suit* program. Mark Taper Forum.

———. 1978b. "Once Again, Meet the Zoot Suiters." *Los Angeles Times* (8/13), part V, p. 3.

———. 1989. "Felipe Cantú, Original Teatro Member, Dies April 26, 1989." *El Teatro: El Teatro Campesino Newsletter* (5/15).

———. 1990. *Luis Valdez—Early Works: Actos, Bernabé and Pensamiento Serpentino*. Houston: Arte Publico Press.

———. 1992. *Zoot Suit and Other Plays*. Introduction by Jorge Huerta. Houston: Arte Público Press.

Valdez, L., and S. Steiner, eds. 1972. *Aztlán: An Anthology of Mexican American Literature*. New York: Random House.

Watt, Douglas. 1979. *"Zoot Suit* Slithers in at the Winter Garden." *New York Daily News* (3/26), p. 21.

Waugh, Julia Nott. 1955. *The Silver Cradle*. Austin: University of Texas Press.

Williams, Raymond. 1973. "Base and Superstructure in Marxist Cultural Theory." *New Left Review* 82:3–16.

————. 1977. *Marxism and Literature*. Oxford and New York: Oxford University Press.
Yarbro-Bejarano, Yvonne. 1979. "From *acto* to *mito*: A Critical Appraisal of the Teatro Campesino." In *Modern Chicano Writers*, edited by J. Sommers and Tomás Ybarra-Frausto, pp. 176–185. Englewood Cliffs: Prentice-Hall.
————. 1981. "The Image of the Chicana in Teatro." *El Tecolote* 2, nos. 3–4:8, 10.
————. 1983. "Teatropoesia in the Bay Area: Tongues of Fire." Kanellos 1983:78–94.
————. 1985. "Chicanas' Experience in Collective Theatre: Ideology and Form." *Women & Performance* 2, no. 2:45–48.
————. 1986. "The Female Subject in Chicano Theatre: Sexuality, 'Race,' and Class." *Theatre Journal* 38, no. 4:389–407.
Yarbro-Bejarano, Yvonne, and Tomás Ybarra-Frausto. 1980. "*Zoot Suit* y el movimiento chicano." *Plural* (April) IX–VII, no. 103:49–56.
Ybarra-Frausto, Tomás. 1983. "La chata noloesca: *figura del donaire*." Kanellos 1983:41–51.
————. 1984. "I Can Still Hear the Applause. La Farándula Chicana: Carpas y Tandas de Variedad." In *Hispanic Theatre in the United States*, edited by Nicolás Kanellos, pp. 45–60. Houston: Arte Público Press.
————. 1991a. "Rasquachismo: A Chicano Sensibility." In *Chicano Art: Resistance and Affirmation, 1965–1985*, edited by Teresa McKenna and Yvonne Yarbro-Bejarano, pp. 155–162. Los Angeles: Wight Art Gallery, University of California.
————. 1991b. "Exhibiting Cultures." In *The Poetics and Politics of Museum Display*, edited by Ivan Karp and Steven D. Lavine, pp. 128–150. Washington: Smithsonian Institution Press.
"Zoot Suit." 1978. *Variety* (8/18), p. 14.
"Zoot Suit Badly Tailored Truth, Good Dramatic Fit." 1979. *New York Daily News* (3/28).
"Zoot Suit Breaks Mark Taper Mark." 1978. *The Hollywood Reporter* (10/9).

Performances and Films

Los ABCs. 1968. El Teatro Campesino.
El achinique. 1967. El Teatro Campesino.
Acto on Education. 1968. El Teatro Campesino.
Acto on Welfare. 1967. El Teatro Campesino.
Actos y canciones. 1976. El Teatro Campesino.
The American Dream. 1970. El Teatro Campesino.
Baile de los gigantes. 1974. El Teatro Campesino. Fifth Annual Chicano Theater Festival, Teotihuacan, Mexico.
Bandido. 1981. Directed by Luis Valdez. El Teatro Campesino Playhouse, San Juan Bautista.
Bandido! The American Melodrama of Tiburcio Vásquez, Notorious California Bandit. By Luis Valdez. 2d draft. ts. San Juan Bautista.
Bernabé. 1969. By Luis Valdez and El Teatro Campesino.
El botón. 1977. El Teatro Campesino.
La burra. 1967. El Teatro Campesino.
Calavera de Tiburcio Vásquez. 1969. El Teatro Campesino.
La carpa de los Rasquachis. 1972. Performed by El Teatro Campesino. ts. San Juan Bautista.
La carpa de los Rasquachis. 1978. El Teatro Campesino Tour.

Chale con el draft. 1970. El Teatro Campesino.

The Commercial. 1969. El Teatro Campesino.

The Complex. 1968. El Teatro Campesino.

Conference of the Birds. 1973. El Teatro Campesino with Peter Brook.

La conquista de México. 1968. El Teatro Campesino.

La conquista del Perro-Minetti. 1967. El Teatro Campesino.

"El Corrido." 1976. Directed by Luis Valdez. PBS (11/18).

Corridos. 1972. El Teatro Campesino. Los Angeles Inner City Cultural Center.

Los Corridos. 1982. Directed by Luis Valdez. El Teatro Campesino Playhouse, San Juan
     Bautista (9/16–10/31).

"Corridos." 1987. Directed by Luis Valdez. PBS.

Corridos: A New American Musical. 1984. Directed by Luis Valdez. Variety Arts Theatre, Los
     Angeles (12/1–12/30).

Corridos: A New Folk Musical. 1984. Directed by Luis Valdez. Old Globe Theater, San
     Diego (10/4–11/6).

Corridos: A New Music Play. 1983a. By Luis Valdez. Final draft. TS.

Corridos: A New Music Play. 1983b. Directed by Luis Valdez. Marines' Memorial Theater,
     San Francisco (4/20–7/4).

Don Juan. 1983. By James Bierman. Directed by Luis Valdez. El Teatro Campesino
     Playhouse, San Juan Bautista.

Fin del mundo. 1980. By Luis Valdez. TS. San Juan Bautista.

La gran carpa cantinflesca. N.d. Performed by El Teatro Campesino. TS. San Juan Bautista.

I am Joaquin. 1969. Produced by El Teatro Campesino.

I Don't Have to Show You No Stinking Badges. 1985. Directed by Luis Valdez. El Teatro
     Campesino Playhouse, San Juan Bautista.

I Don't Have to Show You No Stinking Badges. 1986. Directed by Luis Valdez. Theatre Center,
     Los Angeles.

I Don't Have to Show You No Stinking Badges. 1987. Directed by Luis Valdez. Lyceum, San
     Diego.

Juanito. 1968. El Teatro Campesino.

La lucha de un pueblo. 1967. El Teatro Campesino.

El machete. 1968. El Teatro Campesino.

Los mafiosos. 1967. El Teatro Campesino.

Máscaras del barrio. 1968. El Teatro Campesino.

El mercante de muerte. 1967. El Teatro Campesino.

El mero Xmas de Juanito Raza. 1970. El Teatro Campesino.

The Militants. 1969. El Teatro Campesino.

No saco nada de la escuela. 1969. El Teatro Campesino.

The Orientation. 1968. El Teatro Campesino.

Pastorela. 1974. El Teatro Campesino.

Pastorela. 1976. Street performance. San Juan Bautista.

La Pastorela. 1991. PBS.

El patrón. 1967. El Teatro Campesino.

El patrón. 1970. El Teatro Campesino.

La pesadilla de cinco pesos. 1972. El Teatro Campesino.

Quinta temporada. 1966. El Teatro Campesino.

Rose of the Rancho. 1936. By David Belasco and Richard Walton Tully. New York: Samuel
     French.

Rose of the Rancho. 1977. By David Belasco and Richard Walton Tully. Adapted by César
    Flores and Luis Valdez.
Rose of the Rancho. 1981. By David Belasco and Richard Walton Tully. Adapted by César
    Flores and Luis Valdez. Directed by Frank Condon.
Schenley Contract. 1966. El Teatro Campesino.
The Shrunken Head of Pancho Villa. 1968. By Luis Valdez.
Soldado razo. 1971. El Teatro Campesino.
Soldier Boy. 1982. By Judith Shiffer Pérez and Severo Pérez. Directed by Luis Valdez. El
    Teatro Campesino Playhouse, San Juan Bautista.
La suegra. 1967. El Teatro Campesino.
Tres uvas. 1966. El Teatro Campesino.
La union de "No hay." 1967. El Teatro Campesino.
Los vatos locos de Vietnam. 1970. El Teatro Campesino.
El velorio. 1972. El Teatro Campesino.
Los vendidos. 1967. El Teatro Campesino.
Los vendidos. 1972. KNBC special filming. El Teatro Campesino.
Viene la muerte cantando. 1975. El Teatro Campesino.
Vietnam campesino. 1970. El Teatro Campesino.
La Virgen de Tepeyac. 1971. El Teatro Campesino.
Zoot Suit. 1978a. Directed by Luis Valdez. Center Theatre Group, Mark Taper Forum,
    Los Angeles (4/20–4/30).
Zoot Suit. 1978b. Directed by Luis Valdez. Mark Taper Forum, Los Angeles (8/17–
    10/1).
Zoot Suit. 1978–1979. Directed by Luis Valdez. Aquarius Theater, Hollywood (12/3–
    9/15).
Zoot Suit. 1979. Directed by Luis Valdez. Winter Garden Theater, New York (3/25–
    4/30).
Zoot Suit. 1981. Directed by Luis Valdez. Universal Films.

Index

Page number in bold face refers to a photograph on that page. The notation (ch) is used to denote fictional characters. When an endnote is cited, the page number that the note refers to follows in parentheses—for example, 254n.2 (163). The distinction observed in the text between Chicano and Chicana/o and other related forms is maintained in this index. Where possible, English translations appear with main entries in Spanish, excluding titles of works.